D1570867

Death Penalty for Juveniles

Death Penalty for Juveniles

VICTOR L. STREIB

Indiana University Press

BLOOMINGTON AND INDIANAPOLIS

345.73
S742d

Library of Congress Cataloging-in-Publication Data

Streib, Victor L.
    Death penalty for juveniles.

    Bibliography: p.
    Includes index.
    1. Capital punishment—United States—History.
2. Juvenile justice, Administration of—United
States—History.   3. Juvenile delinquency—United
States—History.   I. Title.
KF9227.C2S77 1987   345.73'087   86-46237
ISBN 0-253-31615-4   347.30587

CONTENTS

FOREWORD

To appreciate the task that Victor Streib has set himself in the book that lies before us, it may be helpful to think about some larger questions concerning criminal responsibility and retributive justice. Remote as these matters may seem from the death penalty for juveniles, the truth is that we cannot understand and appreciate his signal contribution without at least some understanding of this broader context.

It has long been taken as a mark of civilization that the law should not hold strictly liable for punishment all those who cause even the gravest harms. Harm caused is not enough to establish criminal guilt: *mens rea*, a "guilty mind"—malicious intention, in particular—is also required before harming the innocent is a felonious crime. Consequently, the law recognizes a distinction between murder and manslaughter, and the difference between them turns on the knowledge and intention with which the victim was killed. Since the time of Aristotle, lawyers and judges as well as moralists and philosophers have agreed in principle that it is wrong to punish a person for causing harm if that person was not fully responsible for his criminal act. No one can be fully responsible for his deeds (good or bad) if his action was not intentional, or if he did not know what he was doing, or if he could not have prevented himself from doing it.

A case in point is the law of insanity. Punishing someone who was insane at the time he committed a crime, no matter how grave the crime or dangerous the criminal, has been deemed morally improper because the point of punishing (or threatening to punish) such an offender is undercut by his lack of full responsibility. Accordingly, when the law must deal with a person who was insane at the time he caused another's death, some form of nonpunitive confinement is typically authorized as a substitute. Society of course deserves to be protected from such dangerous offenders, but they do not deserve to be punished for the harm they have caused.

Notice that it is not mercy but retributive justice that leads us to refuse to punish the insane. The same retributive principles are reflected in the Supreme Court's rulings a decade ago that it would be "cruel and unusual punishment" to punish such crimes as rape or kidnapping with the death penalty, because the severity of this punishment is disproportional to the gravity of the crimes, terrible though rape and kidnapping are. Mercy in some cases, as well as equity in others, may properly lead to a reduction of the sentence that a court has imposed on an offender. But refusing to punish the insane at all, and refusing to punish nonhomicidal offenders with the death penalty, should not be seen as mercy or charity. These policies are commended in the name of justice.

Seen against this background, the problem of punishing juveniles—children, minors, anyone not lawfully an adult—poses a complex and perplexing challenge: What does justice dictate as the proper policy, and how much (if at all) should that policy be tempered by consideration of mercy? No doubt juveniles can cause harm rivaling in its extent anything that adults can do. But this by itself settles nothing, because the same is true of the harms caused by the insane. We must not neglect the factor of responsibility and its sources, because it provides the setting in which the actual intentions and intentional conduct of juveniles are formed.

The habits and capacities of the young are the product of a physical and social environment over which they have had no control. In childhood each of us is a hostage to fortune, good or ill, of the immediate family and neighborhood into which nature's lottery has cast us. This commonplace truth is crucially relevant to how juvenile offenders should be treated by the criminal justice system. Our laws, civil as well as criminal, reflect the truth that children are less responsible for their circumstances and hence for their conduct than are adults. Every sensible parent and teacher recognizes that behavior intolerable when exhibited by adults must be patiently borne and thoughtfully reshaped when exhibited by the young. No one disputes this where the behavior of infants and preschoolers is concerned; many are less sure on this point when coping with pubescent or adolescent girls and boys; still fewer believe that reason or justice requires tolerance based on youth when dealing with men and women who have reached twenty-one, or even eighteen, the conventional ages of majority.

What all this shows is that the criminal law needs a line to mark off preadults from adults, and that we are not in agreement about precisely where to draw the line. Such disagreement and uncertainty are especially troubling where the crime is murder and the offender is a teen-aged juvenile. Should the death penalty still be permissible in a few such cases, or in all—or should it be absolutely prohibited? Victor Streib's book answers this question. The issue in controversy is not abstract or speculative: As I write, thirty-eight persons are under death sentence—and less than a year ago a young man was executed—for crimes committed while under age eighteen.

As the pages below point out, the law as it now stands is settled that youth at the time of the crime is a legally mitigating factor that must be weighed in the sentencing of anyone convicted of murder. It is also true that prosecutors are reluctant to indict those under age eighteen for first-degree murder, juries are reluctant to convict and sentence teen-agers to death, and judicial and executive authorities are reluctant to carry out these sentences when they are imposed. Even the general public, which in recent years has overwhelmingly supported the death penalty, is not strongly in favor of it for the young. What is not yet settled is whether there should be a national constitutional prohibition against such executions. Victor Streib is not alone in believing there should be. He writes for many when he says, "My unavoidable conclusion is that . . . the death penalty for juveniles makes no sense legally, criminologically, or morally."

The merit of this conclusion can be fairly and rationally evaluated only against the background of the fullest possible information about recent and current practice, and the history and current status of the relevant law (statutory and constitutional, state and federal). All this information is provided in this book. For the first time we have at our fingertips the answers to myriad questions about juveniles and the death penalty. The book is a model of patient and resourceful investigation and is bound to advance understanding in legislatures, courts, and the general public. Anyone who reads it will find it difficult not to agree that it is high time to recognize the injustice of the death penalty for the young and to regard it as the "cruel and unusual punishment" it really is.

Hugo Adam Bedau
January 1987

PREFACE AND
ACKNOWLEDGMENTS

My interest in the death penalty for juveniles dates from 1976 when I first came across evidence that such a practice had actually been followed in this country. Despite diversions to research and write about other topics, I continued to gather what information I could about this practice as the years went by. In 1981 I turned my attention to this subject in earnest. At each stage I was repeatedly astounded to find that I had only scratched the surface of what I was to learn was a centuries-old practice involving hundreds of children.

The early stages of my research produced sporadic papers and articles reporting what I knew at the time. But I continued to compile information, learning even more about the subject and having to correct some of the assumptions and statements I had made earlier. Now I feel confident to report the results of all of this research. The information reported in this book should be taken as my latest findings and, where it is in conflict with my earlier publications on this topic, it is intended to correct those earlier efforts.

In this research I have tried my best to maintain the posture of the objective seeker of knowledge and to avoid the role of advocate for any one position. I have tried to separate myself from the conventional legal research methodology that typically is conducted to bolster a previously held conviction about what results should obtain. That methodology encourages the researcher to seek knowledge about the issue and then to report only the findings that help prove the researcher's previously held conviction, either greatly discounting or remaining conveniently silent about conflicting evidence. My view of the researcher's role is to report everything discovered that affects the issue in question and then leave to the advocates and political action groups the task of arguing about what is right or wrong.

As hard as I tried to hew to that model of research, my discoveries repeatedly led me to find fault with the practice of the death penalty for juveniles. I nonetheless have attempted to report everything of relevance in this volume, including the good, the bad, and the ugly. Even now, after all of this information has been collected in one place and I have painstakingly edited it one more time from cover to cover, I cannot remain completely neutral and objective. My unavoidable conclusion is that, as horrible as the crimes of juveniles can be, the death penalty for juveniles makes no sense legally, criminologically, or morally.

As do all researchers who conduct such a major inquiry, I owe enormous debts to many people. Almost all my work was done at the university at which I am honored to be allowed to serve, Cleveland State University. I am particularly grateful for the Summer Research Grant from the Cleveland-Marshall Fund and for the research grant from the League of Ohio Law Schools. Most of all, I am indebted to the support and understanding of Robert L. Bogomolny, dean of our law college.

People outside my university community have been equally helpful. I benefited greatly from the early assistance of Dan Hopson, then a law professor at Indiana University. I have relied heavily on the death penalty research of such people as Hugo Bedau, William Bowers, and Michael Radelet. My regular consultations with Henry Swarzschild of the American Civil Liberties Union have been of great assistance. My reliance on the data collection efforts of the NAACP Legal Defense and Educational Fund, Inc., is obvious.

Two individuals deserve special mention. One is a recognized giant in the field of death penalty research, Watt Espy. He generously opened his files to me originally when I sought to identify each juvenile execution and has remained a loyal and priceless contributor to this research ever since. Along with so many other death penalty researchers, I have achieved this level in my research only by standing on the shoulders of Watt Espy.

The other particularly special person is Lynn Sametz, a child developmentalist and juvenile justice researcher. She has been a constant and unparalleled source of support, information, and guidance in this research. Her willingness to serve in this capacity is especially appreciated given her even more important other role in my life, that of being my wife and the mother of our children.

Many others who have helped in this research must go unnamed. Some are law students who served as research assistants, some are secretaries who typed and retyped draft after draft, some are copy editors who transformed my crude language into readable prose, and some are faculty colleagues who patiently listened to my discourses and gently provided suggestions for revisions.

The last persons to be thanked are those who serve as the subject matter of this book. The long list of persons executed for juvenile crime can be found herein. Their stories have revealed to me the full, real-life dimensions of my research. The shorter but no less sobering list of persons awaiting juvenile execution adds even more to my understanding. In contrast to their 281 brothers and sisters who have already given their lives to this practice, perhaps some of the thirty-eight persons waiting their turn will be spared. It is to that goal that I dedicate this book.

INTRODUCTION

Ronald Ward and Paula Cooper were sixteen-year-olds who should have been immersed in the heady experiences of first dates, algebra, the latest fads, and the music of teenagers. Instead, they sat on death row in Arkansas and Indiana, the youngest of America's 1,800 death row inmates. Ward and Cooper were sentenced to death for crimes committed in 1985 when they were only fifteen years old.

Arkansas and Indiana were two of the fifteen states that, at this writing, had persons sentenced to death and awaiting execution for crimes committed while under age eighteen. Oklahoma's Wayne Thompson was also only fifteen when he committed his capital crime, as were Pennsylvania's Joseph Aulisio and North Carolina's Leon Brown. Too young for all other rights and privileges of adults, they nonetheless were afforded our most adult criminal penalty.

Thirty-seven persons awaited execution in late 1986 for crimes committed when they were age fifteen, sixteen, or seventeen. All but two were male; most were black. While the juvenile court age limit varies somewhat from state to state, these thirty-seven death row inmates would be considered juveniles in most states. A major goal of our justice system is to guide and protect juvenile offenders, but these thirty-seven have been chosen for mankind's harshest criminal sanction—death.

A quarter of a century ago the prestigious authors of the Model Penal Code concluded that "civilized societies will not tolerate the spectacle of execution of children." They were wrong. The United States has "tolerated" the execution of at least 281 "children" (those whose crimes were committed while under age eighteen). This practice began as early as 1642 in Plymouth Colony and has continued to our time.

This book explores a variety of perspectives on the American experience with juvenile death sentences and executions. Part I focuses on the fundamental issues involved in this phenomenon. To lay a foundation for understanding the unusualness of the practice of exposing juveniles to the death penalty, chapter one presents an overview of the special treatment afforded juveniles in all legal systems in the United States and in our society in general. The juvenile justice system is described in some detail, including its concern for children as offenders and for children as victims. From this overview stems the conclusion that children generally are not treated the same as adults in our legal systems.

Chapter two turns to the much narrower issue of the constitutionality of the death penalty for juveniles. While no appellate court has yet found this practice to be unconstitutional, the bases of constitutionality rulings on the death penalty for adults point to a substantial lack of constitutional justification for the death penalty for juveniles. Chapter three completes the discussion of the issues by exploring the current state laws on this question. Particular attention is given to the statutes in the thirty-six death penalty jurisdictions and their provisions for imposing this ultimate punishment for crimes committed at various minimum ages. Then the state court opinions interpreting these statutes and precedent rulings are described and categorized.

Part II deals with the actual executions of persons for crimes committed while under age eighteen. Chapter four provides an overview of the 281 executions and the general characteristics of the crimes involved, the offenders, and the victims. For readers interested in more details about these cases, the appendix provides names, dates, and other information.

Chapters five and six provide insights into the nature of the people and the crimes behind the statistics through detailed studies of some of these 281 cases. Chapter five includes eighteen cases from 1642 to 1930, beginning with a sixteen-year-old boy hanged in Plymouth Colony for bestiality. Included are three cases of twelve-year-olds, the youngest persons ever executed in the United States. The case of the youngest at the time of the crime, an Indian boy only ten years old, is also described. The youngest in this century, a Florida boy only thirteen years old at the time of the crime, is the last case in chapter five.

Chapter six picks up these case studies in the 1930s and continues through 1986. The best-known case, that of fourteen-year-old George Stinney in 1944, is given special attention. Also described are the cases of the fifteen-year-old in Louisiana who twice went to the electric chair and the seventeen-year-old in Texas who was the last juvenile to be executed for rape. The chapter ends with detailed descriptions of the three executions in 1985 and 1986, for crimes committed by seventeen-year-olds.

Chapter seven analyzes the experience of a typical state, Ohio. The evolution of the state law is considered, as are the nineteen juvenile executions in Ohio from 1880 to 1956. Ohio recently joined the growing ranks of states that prohibit the death penalty for crimes committed while under age eighteen.

Chapter eight puts another perspective on these 281 juvenile executions, trying in a different way to understand the persons involved. The focus is on the attitudes and concerns of the condemned juveniles as they approached their death by state execution. Rough categories of such attitudes have been formed, ranging from indifference to defiance and from fear to religious conversion.

The last section of the book, part III, looks to the future of the death penalty for juveniles. Chapter nine sets the stage with information about the thirty-eight juveniles on death row in late 1986. The declining sentencing rate in recent years is explored, as well as the characteristics of the crimes, offenders, and victims in these thirty-eight cases. In contrast to Ronald Ward and Paula Cooper, who were the youngest, Larry Jones was almost thirty years old and had been under a juvenile death sentence for almost twelve years. James Morgan had been sentenced to death three times for a crime committed at age sixteen. Another sixteen-year-old, Heath Wilkins, represented himself at his sentencing hearing and expressly asked the judge to sentence him to death. The judge granted his request.

Chapter ten attempts the difficult task of predicting developments. After a brief retrospection, evidence is presented to show that society is rejecting juvenile death penalties and that the trend in law is away from them. Finally, seven criteria are offered as appropriate bases for future decisions about the continued viability of the death penalty for juveniles.

Death Penalty for Juveniles

PART I

The Issues

ONE

Juveniles in Law and Society

Fundamental to our American legal system is the premise that "children have a very special place in life which law should reflect."[1] Children are significantly different from adults and simply cannot be shuttled mindlessly into adult legal processes. Law has reflected the unique nature of childhood in many ways, both for children who are offenders and for children who are victims.

This chapter focuses primarily on the juvenile justice system, which is responsible for protecting children and the general public from harm while observing an intricate network of legal rights and procedures for those involved. The juvenile justice system presents many different appearances to those who come in contact with it. Children arrested for misbehavior and brought before a stern judge may perceive the system to be just like the punitive adult criminal justice system, but on a smaller scale. For parents who bring their errant children to the juvenile court as a last resort, the system may appear to be the superparent who can discipline even the most exasperating teenager. For others who are drawn into it as complainants, witnesses, and consultants, the system may appear to be dominated by law and lawyers to the exclusion of logic and rationality. Each observation is warranted, for the juvenile justice system is all these things and more.

A range of information about this perplexing sociolegal system is presented in this chapter, with the goal of making it more accessible and understandable. Also briefly explored are the processes that result when a child commits a traffic offense or a serious criminal offense for which the child may be shunted to traffic court or criminal court or left in juvenile court. This chapter also documents the accepted premise of the special treatment afforded children and juveniles within Anglo-American legal systems and throughout society in general. Based on this premise, chapter two will provide some basic information about the death penalty in general and then consider the special treatment of juveniles in relation to the death penalty.

HISTORY AND PHILOSOPHY OF JUVENILE JUSTICE

Law and legal systems tend to be defined more from the standpoint of the evolution of social movements than from a purely logical standpoint. To understand the present constitutionalized juvenile justice system, its history and development must be considered. The philosophy of juvenile justice is largely a continuation of a very old premise that children must be protected from themselves and others and that law can provide the necessary protection if children's families cannot or will not.

ADVENT OF THE JUVENILE COURT

The first formal juvenile court was created in Chicago in 1899,[2] but even before then children had received special treatment under the law. Due to their immaturity, children under seven could not be convicted of crimes under English and American criminal law.[3] Children between seven and fourteen could not be convicted unless the government proved they had an adult's ability to have criminal intent.[4]

Even if children were convicted in criminal court, their sentence commonly was less severe than an adult's would have been. Thus, not only did the law make children a special class of criminals but even in the functioning of the criminal justice system children were treated somewhat more compassionately than adults.[5]

Early juvenile institutions were exemplified by the New York House of Refuge, established in 1825, and the Chicago Reform School, established in 1855.[6] These and similar later institutions were founded to avoid harsh criminal penalties for child offenders and to provide conventionally approved moral, ethical, political, and social values and role models for deprived, unfortunate children.

The juvenile court was a product of the social and political movements of the 1890s and early 1900s. Some persons have characterized them as progressive child welfare movements reaching out to rescue children from the harsh criminal justice system.[7] Others have suggested that they simply imposed middle-class values on poor and powerless children.[8]

Whatever the motives, the juvenile court idea took root in Illinois and Colorado in 1899 and spread throughout the country. By 1912 about half the states had juvenile justice legislation; by 1925 all but two states had juvenile courts.[9] The juvenile court concept remains strong today, with 3,455 courts hearing juvenile cases in the United States.[10]

SOCIALIZED ERA OF JUVENILE JUSTICE

From the beginning of the juvenile justice system in 1899 until the United States Supreme Court decision *In re Gault*[11] in 1967, the system operated under a concept of law and justice fundamentally different from other American judicial systems. This period has been labeled the era of the socialized juvenile justice system.[12] Instead of being a legal system that reacted to violations of law or provided a forum for resolution of legal disputes, the system attempted to intervene before serious law violations occurred. It tried to predict the behavior of the child involved rather than deliberating over evidence of past criminal acts. It was designed to offer a child approximately the same care, custody, and discipline that a loving parent would give.

The socialized system was often described as an adaptation of the medical treatment model applied to troubled children. Its job, according to one description, included "early identification, diagnosis, prescription of treatment, implementation of therapy, and cure or rehabilitation under aftercare supervision."[13] The emphasis was not on punishment but on rescue. As a Pennsylvania court stated in 1905, "Whether the child deserves to be saved by the state is no more a question for a jury than whether the father, if able to save it, ought to save it."[14]

It would be correct to consider the socialized system as the supreme foster parent. Acting in the capacity of parent, the state might well expect almost absolute obedience to its parental admonitions. The concept of the child having extensive rights to effectively challenge such parental guidance and care is foreign to our society. Parents have, within very wide guidelines, total, unchallengeable authority to force the child to do what the parents see as best for the child. Thus, since a special legal system was being established to act in behalf of parents, it is not surprising that a similar unchallengeable authority was given to that system.

This socialized system was functionally much like the present constitutionalized system except for the legal procedures required by *In re Gault* and its progeny. All the basic functions were performed in the socialized system that are performed in the constitutionalized system, albeit in a much more informal and perfunctory manner. The socialized system simply left presentation of the child's side of the case to the same police officer or probation officer who was responsible for presenting the state's side of the case.

The socialized juvenile justice system split from the comparatively legalistic criminal justice system in 1899 and spent perhaps the first thirty or forty of its sixty-eight years trying to match its idealistic rhetoric with realistic action. It became more and more socialized in that it tried more new and individualized treatment techniques to react to delinquency. The constitutionalized system that replaced it in 1967 was also more rhetoric than action during the first few years of its life; only recently has it become what could be called truly legalistic, or constitutionalized.

CONSTITUTIONALIZED ERA OF JUVENILE JUSTICE

The beginning of the constitutionalized era of the juvenile justice system came in 1967, the year the Supreme Court decided *In re Gault.*[15] After this time, juvenile courts were required to follow certain constitutional guidelines (though several local juvenile courts had been following similar guidelines before 1967).

The constitutionalization of the system was anticipated in 1966 by the Supreme Court in *Kent v. United States:*

> While there can be no doubt of the original laudable purpose of juvenile courts, studies and critiques in recent years raise serious questions as to whether actual performance measures well enough against theoretical purpose to make tolerable

> the immunity of the process from the reach of constitutional guaranties applicable
> to adults. . . . There is evidence, in fact, that there may be grounds for concern
> that the child receives the worst of both worlds: that he gets neither the protections
> accorded to adults nor the solicitous care and regenerative treatment postulated for
> children.[16]

While *Kent* held that the waiver hearing must respect the essentials of constitutional due process and fair treatment, *Gault* held that such is also the case
for adjudicatory hearings.

Within a few years after *Gault* the Supreme Court had decided two other
major cases dealing with the juvenile justice system. In *In re Winship*[17] the
Court held that proof beyond a reasonable doubt in delinquency cases is among
the essentials of due process and fair treatment required by *Gault*. But in
McKeiver v. Pennsylvania[18] the Court held that trial by jury in the juvenile
justice system's adjudicatory hearing is not a constitutional requirement.

In *Kent, Gault,* and *Winship* the Supreme Court revised fundamental
premises of the juvenile justice system. No longer were juvenile court judges
permitted to ignore procedural niceties in order to do what they thought best
for the child. The Court concluded that the system was largely incapable of
matching action with rhetoric, for two main reasons: a significant gap existed
between social scientists' aspirations and their abilities and there was an apparent lack of funding and personnel to operationalize the social knowledge
that was available.

In *McKeiver*, however, there seems to have been a rekindling of faith in
the ability of the system to achieve its goals. It is now coming back to a middle
ground between the socialized and the constitutionalized phases. The Supreme
Court noted this perspective in a 1984 juvenile justice case: "We have tried,
therefore, to strike a balance—to respect the 'informality' and 'flexibility' that
characterize juvenile proceedings, and yet to ensure that such proceedings
comport with the 'fundamental fairness' demanded by the Due Process
Clause."[19]

These procedural requirements had a profound effect on the operant philosophy and ambience of the juvenile court process. Ensuring that most juveniles were represented by a defense attorney meant that the hearings were
converted from informal conferences into adversarial contests quite similar to
criminal trials. Tightened evidentiary requirements put more attention on the
elements of the offenses charged and less on the child.

PRESENT ERA OF JUVENILE JUSTICE

The philosophical premises of the original juvenile courts have not been
immune to the political and social pressures of the past twenty years. The blind
faith placed in juvenile court judges always to do the best for the child came
under critical appraisal.[20] The notion of coerced treatment came more and more
to be equated with punishment despite official disclaimers to the contrary.[21]
Individualized treatment for each child came to be seen as rife with abuse of

discretion and as resulting in grossly unequal handling of similar children and similar offenses.[22]

The juvenile justice system of the mid-1980s retains the essence of these philosophical roots, but in the context of a court of law. The system's procedures have been brought into line with criminal court procedures, and the focus is somewhat more on punishment and prevention than on the treatment of errant children. More serious juvenile offenders are being shunted from juvenile court to criminal court, and very minor offenders are being handled informally outside juvenile court. The juvenile court continues, however, to process the broad midsection of juvenile offenders and to view them in a parental or clinical manner.

CHILDREN AS OFFENDERS

The concept of children as offenders encompasses the instances in which persons under the juvenile court age limit (usually eighteen) commit acts that harm or threaten to harm the person or property of others or, in some cases, of themselves. If the offender were over the age limit, such an act would be considered a crime; it is treated differently solely because the actor is still legally a child.[23]

Children as offenders are to be distinguished from children who are victims either of the acts of others or of circumstances in general. Children as victims are discussed later in this chapter.

SUBSTANTIVE LAW CONCEPTS

Substantive law, as contrasted with procedural law, defines the conduct and activities that are prohibited and authorizes state-imposed sanctions if such conduct or activities are proved. These offense definitions inherently include some defense issues, such as the defense of lack of intent to steal where the definition of the offense requires such an intent. For the juvenile justice system, that covers the definitions of acts of delinquency and status offenses and the defenses inherent therein. Other categories of substantive law offenses by children are traffic offenses and serious criminal offenses.

Traffic Offenses. Original juvenile court laws in many states treated traffic offenses no differently from other offenses, including all offenses within the jurisdiction of the juvenile courts.[24] The inclusion of traffic offenses within juvenile court jurisdiction has come under considerable pressure in recent years.[25] One basis for this pressure is the widely held view that committing a routine traffic offense does not call for major court intervention in a young driver's life to effect rehabilitative treatment. A second basis is the heavy volume of traffic cases involving sixteen- and seventeen-year-old drivers, which prevents juvenile courts from providing each child with individual attention.

The trend is to relegate less serious traffic offenses to traffic court.[26] There the teenage driver is treated just as an adult driver is treated. More serious traffic offenses, such as reckless homicide, tend to remain in juvenile court and are processed as regular delinquency cases. Some jurisdictions allow the trial proceedings to be held in either juvenile court or traffic court, but the Supreme Court has made it clear that trials in both courts for the same offense would be unconstitutional.[27]

Status Offenses. This category of juvenile offenses is labeled differently from state to state but tends to include the same kind of acts and statuses. Labels often used are persons in need of supervision (PINS), children in need of supervision (CINS or ChINS), wayward children, undisciplined children, and unruly children. All these labels cover a range of noncriminal behaviors by children and may account for up to half the workload of juvenile courts.[28]

Behaviors typically included as status offenses are those by any child "who does not subject himself to the reasonable control of his parents, teachers, guardian, or custodian, by reason of being wayward or habitually disobedient; who is an habitual truant from home or school; or who so deports himself as to injure or endanger the health or morals of himself or others."[29] Status offenses are comparatively vague, broad, all-encompassing behaviors that could easily be interpreted to include the behavior at some time of every child.[30] Most children have been habitually disobedient at least for short periods, and most have deported themselves at some time so as to injure themselves or someone else.

The result of this definition is that juvenile courts exercise essentially unchecked power to find almost any child to be a status offender. As described later in this chapter, the juvenile courts also have power to order almost the same dispositions for status offenders as for delinquents. Status offender jurisdiction thus remains broad and sweeping when compared with the narrower delinquency jurisdiction.[31]

Delinquency Offenses. An act of delinquency is defined generally as a violation of a state or local criminal law. It is an act that would be a crime if committed by an adult.[32] The elements of the offense are proven in the same manner as they would be for an adult in criminal court, with the only significant difference being the young age of the defendant/respondent.

Some states have limited this broad definition of delinquency by excluding the most serious criminal offenses, or the most minor ones, or both.[33] Such jurisdictions may exclude, for example, any criminal offense punishable by death or life imprisonment—that is, only the most serious felonies.[34] At the other end of the scale, some jurisdictions exclude such minor crimes as traffic offenses and fish and game law violations.[35] Children violating such laws are handled directly by the misdemeanor court that has jurisdiction over these offenses.

Several states include as acts of delinquency the violation of a federal law or of another state's law even though such acts may not be violations of the subject state's law.[36] A few states continue the now largely outmoded policy of including under delinquency such conduct as truancy, disobedience, and running away, which today most commonly comprise the separate category of status offenses.[37]

Some acts of delinquency are law violations that apply only to children.

Violations of curfew laws by minors is the most common example; others include possession of air guns or drinking alcohol while under age. Although these acts of delinquency are violations of state law, they are acts that would not be crimes if committed by adults.

Serious Criminal Offenses. Some states, such as Louisiana, expressly exclude certain offenses from juvenile court jurisdiction and place them within criminal court jurisdiction regardless of the age of the offender.[38] Such offenses include murder, manslaughter, rape, robbery, burglary, and kidnapping. Other states, such as North Carolina, place all cases in criminal court if the offender could receive the death penalty, at least if the offender is age fourteen or older.[39]

If the child is prosecuted in criminal court for a serious criminal offense, the case proceeds essentially as it would for any adult. The child receives all the rights and protections of adult criminal defendants but also faces all the adult criminal sentences. Except for the special substantive law defenses described in the next section of this chapter, the child's youthful age is ignored.

Exclusion of serious criminal offenses from juvenile court jurisdiction appears to be, for these offenses, a rejection of rehabilitation and an embracement of retribution and deterrence. The retribution premise underlying harsh criminal penalties is that the community is always outraged by serious offenses, regardless of the age of the offender, and feels the need to express its social and moral condemnation through severe punishment of the offender.[40] The deterrence premise assumes that authorization of such severe punishments will deter everyone, including children, from committing serious offenses.[41] Infliction of severe punishment on a particular child will convince that child never to repeat the offenses. Retribution and deterrence are the primary foundations of criminal sanctions for adults and, in some cases, are also imposed on persons under the juvenile court age limit.

Jurisdictional and Substantive Law Defenses. Many state statutes and several model statutes have included the child's need for treatment as a requirement for the juvenile court's finding of either an act of delinquency or a status offense.[42] This requirement is not the same as the one concerning the right to treatment, which is a part of the juvenile court disposition, but a much earlier consideration of the child's need for treatment even before the court takes control of the matter. It stems from the treatment orientation of the juvenile court, the premise being that the juvenile court should not concern itself with children who do not need treatment. Thus a need for treatment must be found before the juvenile court may begin to act. This preliminary finding of a need for treatment has been more of a rhetorical ideal than a practical bar to juvenile court action.

Closely related to the need for treatment consideration is the defense of insanity as it has been developed in adult criminal court. It is generally accepted as a defense to conviction of an adult crime if the defendant was legally insane at the time of the crime.[43] The result is that the adult criminal court must find the person not guilty and turn the case over to a civil commitment process for the dangerously mentally ill. The same reasoning seems applicable in juvenile court if the issue is whether the juvenile knew what he or she was doing at the time of the delinquent acts. Use of the insanity defense in juvenile court has been sporadic and nonuniform across the states, however, and in several cases it has been rejected in order to permit the juvenile court to attempt to help the child.[44]

Minimum and maximum age limitations are also critical to juvenile court jurisdiction and authority. Since juvenile courts handle children and not adults, an age line must be drawn between childhood and adulthood. For more than two-thirds of the states, the maximum age is established as eighteen years.[45] Juvenile court has jurisdiction only over those persons under age eighteen at the time their offense was committed.

The minimum age limit is not so clearly established. Under early English common law and modern American criminal law, children under age seven always were excluded from criminal court jurisdiction and children under fourteen were excluded unless the prosecution could prove they were mature enough to have adult criminal intent.[46] Some states, such as California, have imposed this principle upon juvenile courts.[47] Most states have not addressed the minimum age question; they simply do not, as a matter of practice, process cases involving very young children. A recent study has verified, however, that some very young children, even those age seven to nine, are being handled to some extent by juvenile courts.[48]

JUVENILE JUSTICE JURISDICTIONS AND PROCEDURES

When children within the age limits of juvenile court jurisdiction commit acts of delinquency or status offenses, the juvenile justice system typically has the authority to intervene and to process them accordingly. Nevertheless, most such juvenile offenses never come to the attention of the system and thus no legal procedures ensue.[49]

It is the rare adult who never committed any offenses as a child—minor shoplifting, disobedience to parents, jaywalking, skipping classes at school, or drinking beer while under age—but very few were reported to the police or the juvenile court for these common adolescent behaviors. Thus, the beginning premise is that most delinquent and status offenses never come to the attention of the system.[50] For those that do, a fairly detailed and complex process is followed.

Precourt and Extracourt Procedures. It is not unusual for juveniles and their parents voluntarily to contact the police juvenile officer or the juvenile probation officer without having been arrested or asked to come in.[51] In these cases they are seeking help which they believe these agencies can provide. Most often the family is referred to other social service agencies for the assistance they request.

In some cases official court action is deemed necessary. If so, the process will continue in juvenile court, and the juveniles will have waived any right to object to the means by which they came to the court's attention.

Before considering the procedures—including the use of force, if necessary—by which juveniles are taken into custody, it should be noted that in a majority of cases in which the police could make such an arrest they instead divert the would-be cases to handling by informal means. That is, they have sufficient legal grounds (probable cause) to arrest the juveniles but nevertheless decide that such an arrest would not be the best way to handle the misbehavior. In lieu of an arrest, the police may give the juveniles oral reprimands, send them home, issue them warning notices of some sort, or just tell them to get help from various community agencies.[52] This informal adjustment of juvenile cases has always been common in most jurisdictions.

In the more serious cases and those involving children who have committed past offenses or who are particularly uncooperative with police, the offense may well result in the child's being taken into police custody. The primary legal requirement that must be met before the child can be taken into custody is probable cause that an offense has been committed and that this particular child committed the offense. Probable cause is a level of evidence or certainty that would lead a reasonable person to believe that the child committed the offense.[53]

The arrest of a child is not significantly different from the arrest of an adult. Considerable physical force can be used to effect the arrest—up to and including deadly force if absolutely necessary, although that is rare. According to the seriousness of the offense, it is not unusual for the child to be handcuffed and taken to the police station by armed police officers. Such a show of force and secure custody would not be used for status offenders accused of committing noncriminal offenses.

Contemporaneous with the arrest are a wide variety of police investigative activities that may be necessary to gather evidence for use in the case being prepared against the juvenile. These activities may involve, for example, search of the child's person, home, car, or school locker. These searches usually require probable cause to believe that seizable items exist in these places, with the probable cause being at a level of certainty similar to that for arrest.

Some searches and seizures do not require independent probable cause. If the child is arrested, the police have the authority automatically to search the child at the time of the arrest.[54] Searches of the child's room in the parents' home can be effected by gaining the parents' consent, even if it is over the child's objection. Searches of school lockers can be conducted by school officials, who have master keys and thus access to all school property.

Police questioning of a juvenile is controlled generally by the U.S. Constitution. While the matter is not perfectly clear, it would seem that prior to custodial questioning the police must give juveniles the required warnings, which include the right to remain silent and to have an attorney present during questioning.[55] Some states prohibit questioning of children when their parents are not present. Others require that the child consult with an attorney before being allowed to make any statement.[56]

Juvenile courts have been quite reluctant to allow police to photograph or fingerprint juvenile detainees, but these taboos have been relaxed somewhat recently.[57] The juvenile has a right to have counsel present at a lineup identification procedure only if it occurs after the juvenile has been formally charged with an offense.[58] The right to counsel does not apply to situations in which the juvenile and the victim/witness are brought together in an early confrontation for identification purposes.[59]

After a juvenile is arrested, the issue arises as to what to do with him until further hearings and activities take place. Is he to remain in jail or in a juvenile detention center, or is he to be released to his parents? Local laws most frequently require the police to contact the child's parents and a juvenile probation officer promptly after the child has been taken into custody. In the majority of cases, the parents come to the police station or the juvenile center and pick up their child after promising to bring the child to subsequent meetings and hearings with juvenile court personnel. Juveniles usually do not have the adult right to post bail, but the juvenile's release to parents is thought to be a superior alternative.[60]

If there are no parents to take the child, if the child's parents refuse to take the child, or if the situation is so serious that release seems inappropriate, the child may be detained pending further proceedings. The initial decision to do so is made on the spot by a juvenile probation officer, but soon thereafter a detention hearing is held before a juvenile court judge.[61]

The decision to detain the child usually stems from a belief that the child would not appear for subsequent hearings or might commit more offenses while released. The belief that defendants would not appear for subsequent proceedings is a historically accepted reason for denying pretrial release to juveniles or bail to adults. In addition, the policy of denying pretrial release to juveniles to prevent interim offenses has been approved as constitutionally acceptable by the Supreme Court.[62] Such pretrial detention of juveniles is permitted in almost all states today.

Initiation of Juvenile Court Jurisdiction. The foregoing description of police procedures presumes that the subject was under the juvenile court age but that a juvenile court case had not yet been formally initiated. If the police do not decide to just ignore the case, it is referred to the juvenile court for further proceedings. Usually the next step is an intake hearing, conducted by the juvenile probation officer on behalf of the juvenile court judge.

At this intake hearing, which is the first stage of the juvenile court process, potential cases are screened for appropriateness for further, more formal action. Typically, the juvenile probation officer meets with the child and parents to discuss the police charges. The child is asked to give his or her side of the story, and all try to determine whether or not formal court action will be necessary to resolve the matter.[63]

Many if not most cases are diverted from formal court action at this juncture and the children are sent to various community agencies for informal counseling and treatment. Court officials nevertheless retain the right and power to reactivate the case and send it on to juvenile court should the informal diversion prove ineffective or should the child refuse to cooperate.

An informal juvenile justice system exists parallel to and often in competition with the formal one. This informal system is a collage of social service agencies that serve the young people of a community but that are not necessarily a regular part of the formal system.[64] Such agencies, the recipients of referrals from formal system agencies, include youth service bureaus, drug abuse counselors, community mental health clinics, and regular probation officers acting in an unofficial capacity in supervising a child under "informal probation."

The informal system performs the same functions and tasks that the formal system performs but does so in a much less restricted, legalistic, and procedurally defined fashion.[65] For example, the decision regarding the truth of an allegation is made not by a judge in a courtroom after a hearing but by a probation officer or other counselor in a closed conference after a brief discussion. The choice of the most appropriate disposition for the child is made in a similar fashion. Often the formal system serves as a backup for the informal one, allowing system agents to threaten the child with processing in the formal system if he does not cooperate with the informal one.

If the case is not diverted at the intake hearing, the probation officer initiates a formal juvenile court petition under the authority of the juvenile court judge. This juvenile petition establishes a formal prosecution of the juvenile in a court of law.[66]

In delinquency cases, the juvenile petition alleges that the child violated certain specific laws on a certain date in a certain place in a certain manner. Status offender petitions are somewhat less specific but also allege the violation that is the basis of the case. It is these allegations that become the focus of the subsequent adjudication hearing in juvenile court, so accuracy and provability are crucial to the progress of the case.

Trying Juveniles in Adult Criminal Court. Even though the persons committing the offenses are within the age limit for juvenile court, several means exist by which their cases could be processed in adult criminal court rather than in juvenile court. The consequences of this change of court are enormous. While juvenile court is limited to ordering probation or perhaps institutionalization until the child is age twenty-one, the criminal court typically has the full range of criminal sentences available even for young teenage offenders, including long terms in prison and even the death penalty.[67]

Some states have always excluded some very serious law violations from juvenile court, leaving them in adult criminal court as described earlier in this chapter. In these instances the case against the child always is filed directly in adult court and never goes through the juvenile court procedures.[68]

Another alternative method by which the case could be filed directly in adult criminal court is illustrated by those few states that give the prosecuting attorney the discretion to file cases either in juvenile court or in adult criminal court.[69] When, for example, a child commits a very serious criminal act, such as murder or rape, it is left solely to the local prosecuting attorney whether to prepare a juvenile petition alleging an act of delinquency or a criminal charge alleging a crime.

The first alternative for direct filing means that the state legislature in enacting the statute decided that certain cases should always be handled by adult criminal court regardless of the characteristics of the child offender. The second alternative for direct filing leaves this decision to the prosecutor to make on a case-by-case basis. Neither leaves much leverage in the hands of the child or the attorney or gives the juvenile court the ability to receive a case it thinks is appropriate for juvenile jurisdiction.

The other means by which a person of juvenile court age could end up in adult criminal court is for the juvenile court to waive its original jurisdiction over the case and transfer the case to the other court.[70] This process begins with the filing of a juvenile court petition as previously described. For cases involving very serious offenses by juveniles who are near the maximum juvenile court age and have a record of past offenses, the prosecutor may file a motion in juvenile court to transfer the case to adult criminal court.

The very first case in which the Supreme Court directly considered juvenile justice issues, *Kent v. United States*,[71] involved this waiver and transfer process. The *Kent* ruling required juvenile courts considering transfer of juvenile cases to criminal court to hold a hearing, determine the facts of the case, give reasons for any decision to transfer, and allow the juvenile's attorney free access to reports and other evidence being considered. This procedure ensures that a fairly thorough consideration will be made before any juvenile case is waived to criminal court.

Juvenile Court Adjudication Procedures. In juvenile court the trial is referred to as the adjudication hearing. A full hearing is actually held in few cases, since the prosecutor and the defense attorney commonly plea bargain into a consent agreement in which the child admits the offenses in return for a more desirable disposition.[72] While plea bargaining is not as pervasive in juvenile justice as it is in criminal justice, it still is an important means by which a large number of juvenile cases are handled.

If the adjudication hearing is held, it is quite similar in procedure to the criminal court trial. The prosecutor presents the evidence for the state tending to prove that the juvenile committed the offenses alleged in the petition, and the defense counters with evidence tending to cast doubt on the state's evidence.

Before the late 1960s, this hearing was quite informal and seldom involved legal evidence or lawyers. However, the Supreme Court changed that in 1967. In *In re Gault*,[73] the Court imposed the requirements of constitutional due process upon the juvenile court's adjudication hearing. These constitutional requirements include the right to counsel for the juvenile, the right to notice of the charges and hearings, the right to confront and cross-examine opposing witnesses, and the right to remain silent and not testify against one's self.

These basic procedural rights were bolstered in 1970 when the Supreme Court decided that delinquency cases must be proved beyond a reasonable doubt by the state, which is the same very difficult level of proof required in adult criminal cases.[74] Since the general rules of evidence from criminal court are also followed in juvenile court, these juvenile adjudication hearings are now almost indistinguishable from criminal trials.

The one key difference for juvenile cases is that the Constitution does not require that they be decided by juries.[75] Thus, in almost all states the adjudication hearing is presented to the juvenile court judge alone, who returns the verdict and decides on the proper sentence or disposition. Also juvenile hearings are almost always closed to the public.[76]

Evidence is presented at adjudication hearings much as it is at any trial. The prosecutor will normally call witnesses and present physical evidence and the defense attorney will cross-examine the witnesses and challenge the evidence. The roles then switch, with defense attorneys presenting their case and prosecutors doing the challenging.[77]

At the conclusion of the adjudicatory hearing the juvenile court judge decides whether the state has proved its case. If the case has been proved, the court finds the child to be a delinquent or a status offender, according to what the petition alleged and the evidence proved. If the case has not been proved, then the judge so finds and releases the child from any custody or futher proceedings. While the terminology is different from the criminal court's "guilty" and "not guilty," the functional results are the same.

Juvenile Court Disposition Procedures. If the child has been adjudicated to be a delinquent or a status offender, then the juvenile justice process moves into the sentencing or dispositional stage. During the period between the adjudication hearing and the disposition hearing, the probation officers prepare a social history or presentence report. This report documents the child's family environment, school record, past offenses or problems known to the court, and similar information. If community or state resources permit, the child may undergo various psychological tests and evaluations to determine amenability to various modes of treatment. All this information is put into the social history report, which then serves as the most important item of evidence relied upon by the judge at the disposition hearing.[78]

The disposition hearing is typically scheduled a few days or weeks after the adjudication hearing in order to give all concerned ample time to gather evidence concerning the most appropriate disposition for the child. In addition to the probation officer's social history report and disposition recommendation, the juvenile court considers evidence and disposition recommendations presented by the juvenile's attorney, the parents, and anyone else knowledgeable about the child.[79]

The juvenile court is not permitted to choose a juvenile disposition designed to punish the child for wrongdoing. True to the principles on which it was founded, the juvenile court may only treat and rehabilitate children, not punish them. Therefore, in choosing the best disposition for a particular child, the court must shun pressure from some sources to "get tough" with juveniles and punish them for what often are very serious offenses against people and their property. This treatment-not-punishment limitation continues to make juvenile court actions misunderstood by the general public and many social critics.[80]

The dispositional alternatives available to the juvenile court judge in delinquency and status offender cases are some form of probation and some form of institutionalization. Generally, younger juveniles with minimal previous offenses who have not committed very serious offenses tend to be placed on probation, while institutions are reserved for older juveniles with several past offenses who have committed more serious offenses this time.[81]

JUVENILE CORRECTIONS

The primary reason for existence of the juvenile justice system is to treat and rehabilitate young offenders before they mature into an adult life of crime. Given this premise, the correctional stage of the system is the key to its success. Unfortunately, correction of juvenile misbehavior is a complex and difficult task, success in which is all too rare.[82]

Probation and Community Placements. If placed on probation, the juvenile remains under the general supervision of the juvenile court through its probation officers.[83] Beyond this universal condition of probation, the other conditions of various forms of probation are tailored to fit each case.

The most common form of juvenile probation requires the juvenile to report to the probation officer regularly for counseling sessions and to live at home as before the court proceedings. The juvenile continues to attend the same school, hold the same job, and so forth. The other conditions of probation, such as not leaving town without court permission or being at home even earlier than the curfew laws require, are only a minor nuisance for the child. Moreover, given the heavy caseloads of most probation officers, the supervision the juvenile receives while on probation may be minimal.

A common variation is to require the child to live somewhere in the community other than at the parental home. This new location may be the home of a relative or family friend or an independent group foster home or shelter care facility. This provision works to break up the juvenile's living pattern that led to the difficulties. The common theme of probation nonetheless is maintained, since the child remains in the community and is essentially free to carry on life without severe disruptions.

If the child does well under the conditions of probation, he or she is released from probation after a period of time, and juvenile court authority ends. Should the child violate one or more of the conditions of probation, however, probation may be modified or even revoked by the juvenile court judge at a subsequent hearing. Revocation of probation means that the child is committed to an institution.

Institutionalization. The other primary choice open to the judge at the disposition hearing and at the probation revocation hearing is to commit the child to the care and custody of a juvenile institution. This choice requires the juvenile court to terminate its authority over the child and transfer the child to the authority of juvenile corrections personnel who operate the state institutions.[84]

Since most states have only one juvenile institution, juvenile courts have only one option. While there may be one institution for boys and one for girls or one for delinquents and one for status offenders, the choice is still limited to one institution for a particular child. In such populous states as California and Texas, juvenile courts may commit the child to the control of a central juvenile correctional authority, which in turn determines which institution is best for the child.[85]

Juveniles typically are committed to institutions until they reach age twenty-one (unless they are released sooner by the institution).[86] That means several years of potential confinement for the fourteen- to sixteen-year-old. In practice, however, very few children are kept in institutions for more than a year or two. Like adult prisoners, children are often released early; that is done under the status of juvenile parole, often called juvenile aftercare.[87]

The conditions of juvenile aftercare are similar to those of juvenile probation. The children return to live in their communities, often with parents or with relatives, and attend their former schools. They are supervised generally by parole/aftercare officers. If they do well on this status, it is terminated after a year or so. If they violate the conditions of aftercare, they can be brought back to the institution to resume serving the time of the original commitment there. This aftercare revocation procedure is controlled by institution personnel, not by the juvenile court judge, but the personnel still must provide a fair process for the child in making this decision to revoke.

CHILDREN AS VICTIMS

These descriptions of substantive offenses and the legal procedures that follow such offenses focus on acts committed by children that are seen as harmful to the children themselves or to others. This section shifts the focus to children as victims of acts by others or of circumstances in general.

SUBSTANTIVE LAW CONCEPTS

The substantive law of child victimization includes definitions of the three primary categories of children as victims. While the labels and categories vary from state to state, they are commonly referred to as dependent children, neglected children, and abused children.[88]

The classic dependent child is the hapless orphan, left vulnerable and parentless, clearly needing intervention by the state to provide surrogate parental custody. Other dependent children may not be orphans but nevertheless are clearly without sufficient parental care—the parent or guardian suffers debilitating physical illness, for example, or is mentally retarded or psychotic. Such cases commonly result in long-term hospitalization of the parent or guardian, leaving the child without proper parental custody for what could be months or years.

Neglected children are those without proper parental care and custody whose parents are typically quite capable of providing proper care but refuse to do so.[89] The child's needs and situation are the same as those of the dependent child; the parents' culpability is the significant difference between neglect and dependency. Neglect cases include families in which the parents have sufficient income but choose to spend it on possessions and entertainment rather than on the needs of their children.

Child abuse includes the worst offenses against children and may involve severe injury, rape, and even death of the child. While child abuse may be seen as simply an aggravated form of child neglect, it typically involves willfully injuring a child, not just ignoring the child's needs. The essence of the definition of child abuse is a physical injury by other than accidental means that causes a substantial risk of death or serious injury.[90]

LEGAL PROCESSES IN DEPENDENCY,
NEGLECT, AND ABUSE CASES

Almost always these cases are handled by the local welfare department, often in cooperation with the local juvenile or family court.[91] If the welfare department cannot intervene successfully and correct the problem informally, the next step is to involve the juvenile court by seeking a dependency, neglect, or abuse petition. The most serious child abuse cases, such as murder, may be referred to criminal court.

Dependency cases usually come to the attention of the welfare department or the court as the result of a family's request for assistance. Since no culpability is being alleged concerning the child or any member of the family, only the possible embarrassment of being dependent on public support would deter such self-reporting. In some cases a child is found by the police under circumstances suggesting a status offense, such as a curfew violation, but the case is reported as a dependent child case because this sort of assistance is what is really needed.

Child neglect and abuse are seen as quite serious by legal authorities, and all states require reporting of known or suspected child abuse.[92] Persons who routinely become aware of such cases because of their occupations—physicians, nurses, teachers—are required to report them or suffer civil or criminal penalties for failure to do so. Other persons are permitted to make such reports; some states require everyone to report cases.

Reports are usually made to child welfare or protection agencies or to law enforcement agencies.[93] Persons making such reports, whether voluntarily or as required by law, are protected from subsequent lawsuits by embarrassed and angry parents. Conditions required to be reported include physical or mental injury, sexual abuse or exploitation, and neglect by persons responsible for the child's welfare. Such persons include parents and guardians as well as private and public institutional personnel who abuse children in their care. All reports are to be investigated promptly.

Procedural rights in neglect and abuse cases have lagged behind those in delinquency and status offender cases, but the trend is toward requiring more formality in proceedings and more rights for the children and adults involved in the cases.[94] The right to attorneys, paid for by the state if necessary, to represent all parties is becoming fairly common. Similarly accorded is the right to notice of the precise allegations made and the time, place, and topic of hearings to be held concerning the case.

Neglect and abuse hearings have become more adversarial than they were in the past and have taken on most of the characteristics of a delinquency hearing or a criminal trial.[95] The legal rules of evidence apply, and the accused parents or guardians have full rights to present their case to the court. The party alleging the neglect or abuse, usually the state, has the burden of proving the case by a least a preponderance of the evidence in ordinary cases.

Most cases result in a somewhat informal court-ordered agreement protecting the children from harm while requiring the parents to accept assistance with their problems. The most severe action the court may take is to terminate the parental rights of the mistreated child's parents, leaving the child available for adoption and custody by others. Such cases involving termination of parental rights must be proved by clear and convincing evidence, and the parents must be given even more procedural rights.[96] The Surpeme Court has not required that an attorney be appointed to represent poor parents in all termination proceedings but has left that to be determined on a case-by-case basis.[97]

Child abuse and neglect cases can also end up in adult criminal court. Intentionally injuring a child is the crime of assault and battery, and premeditatedly killing a child is no less murder simply because the victim is so young. Thus, many states permit criminal charges to be brought in these cases, and neglectful and abusive parents face criminal punishment.[98]

FUTURE TRENDS IN JUVENILE LAW

The ebb and flow of political and social currents that in part gave birth to the field of juvenile law have continued to work changes in this field. The only certainty for the future of juvenile law is that changes will continue, and some of the directions for these changes are becoming apparent.

The pressure on the juvenile justice system to become more punitive seems destined to continue and perhaps to increase in intensity.[99] This pressure directly counters the fundamental premise of the juvenile justice system that expressly limits the system to treatment and rehabilitation of juvenile offenders. Indeed, the sociopolitical climate is reversing itself, since the original impetus for starting the system in the early 1900s was to remove children from the harsh, punitive criminal justice system.[100]

The trend is to become more punitive with juvenile offenders regardless of the means necessary to accomplish this end. One means that is gaining popularity is to increase the number of cases transferred from juvenile to criminal court and to increase the discretion given to prosecutors to file cases directly in criminal court. That taps the punitive function of the criminal court without compromising the treatment premise of the juvenile court. This alternative is being used most frequently for the older, violent juvenile offender.

The other trend that seems destined to continue to be signficant is the effort to remove status offenders from the formal juvenile court process and to handle these cases through some form of informal community mediation or arbitration forum.[101] That frees the juvenile court to follow its comparatively strict and formal legal process with delinquency offenders while permitting the less legalistic, family-support mechanism to assist in correcting the problems of the disobedient or truant child.

Finally, it seems clear that the juvenile court and the rest of the juvenile justice system will continue to exist much as it has in the eighteen years since *Gault*. It will continue as a highly innovative social experiment for handling children's misbehavior and will undoubtedly register at least as many failures as successes. It most certainly has its shortcomings, but it seems clearly better than any alternative now available.

CONCLUSIONS

The foregoing description of the treatment of child offenders and victims within American legal systems can be distilled into a few recurring and pervasive themes. First, even for the worst offenses by children, legal processes have been followed for more than a century that are markedly less harsh and punitive than those for similar offenses by adults. Attempts are made to protect children during the legal processes and to impose nonpunitive, treatment-oriented sanctions on them for their offenses. Retribution and deterrence, the age-old justifications for adult criminal sanctions, have only recently made minor inroads into the practice of juvenile corrections.

Second, children or juveniles are treated as a special class, usually separate from the processes and programs for adults. Even though juveniles, just like adults, sometimes commit horrible offenses and sometimes suffer horrible abuses, juvenile offenders and victims are legally, socially, and politically different.

Third, at some age a child becomes an adult. Psychologically, physiologically, and socially, this change occurs over a range of years and not just on a certain birthday. Nevertheless, American legal systems, of which the juvenile justice system is typical, have tended to opt for age requirements or restrictions. Thus we have fixed ages for voting, marrying, leaving school, and driving, regardless of the child's advanced or retarded developmental stage. While waiver and concurrent jurisdiction provisions have blurred this age-certain line somewhat in the juvenile justice system, age eighteen remains the common dividing line between the protected status of juvenile and the punishable status of adult.

TWO

Constitutional Law
and the Juvenile Death Penalty

Although the issue of the constitutionality of the death penalty for juveniles has never been decided by the United States Supreme Court,[1] various facets of the legality of this practice have been considered by that court and by many other courts and legislatures. This chapter explores the question of the existence of a constitutionally mandated minimum age below which the states may not venture in carrying out this practice. If such a nationwide minimum age exists or should exist, its justifications can be found in recent interpretations of the eighth amendment to the United States Constitution. First let us consider precisely what the Supreme Court has said about this issue.

SUPREME COURT RULINGS

The Supreme Court's holding in *Gregg v. Georgia*[2] launched the present era. In *Gregg* a majority of the Court held that the death penalty does not violate per se the eighth amendment.[3] While the age issue was not specifically before the Court in *Gregg*, the concern for the age of the offender emerged even in this case. The Court approved of the Georgia statute's guided discretion for consideration of aggravating and mitigating factors by the jury in the sentencing hearing.[4] In passing, the Court endorsed the requirement that the jury consider the characteristics of the offender, including such hypothetical questions as the following: "Are there any special facts about this defendant that mitigate against imposing capital punishment (*e.g.*, his youth, . . . ?)."[5] In a companion case to *Gregg*, the Court approved of a Texas statute that provided that the sentencing jury "could further look to the age of the defendant"[6] in deciding between life imprisonment and the death sentence.

In subsequent cases the Court continued to favor guided discretion statutes, such as those approved in *Gregg*, and to reject mandatory death penalty statutes. A major holding was *Roberts v. Louisiana*,[7] in which the Court found unconstitutional a statute that provided for a mandatory death penalty for the killing of a police officer. Stressing the need for consideration of mitigating circumstances in all death penalty cases, the Court once again expressly mentioned the youthfulness of the offender as an appropriate mitigating factor and noted that it is expressly relevant in many jurisdictions.[8]

In 1978 the Supreme Court decided two cases from Ohio that made clear the requirement that sentencing juries and judges must consider all relevant mitigating factors proffered by the defendant, including the youthfulness of the offender. The lead decision of *Lockett v. Ohio*[9] held that such unlimited consideration of mitigating factors was constitutionally required, in part because without such a requirement under the Ohio statute "consideration of defendant's comparatively minor role in the offense, or age, would generally not be permitted, as such, to affect the sentencing decision."[10]

The companion case to *Lockett* was *Bell v. Ohio*.[11] In this case the appellant was only sixteen years old at the time of the murder for which he was subsequently convicted and sentenced to death.[12] At the sentencing hearing Bell's attorney had expressly argued that Bell's youth should be considered as a mitigating factor, but the Ohio statute prohibited introduction of any mitigating factors beyond those few expressly permitted. The Supreme Court reversed Bell's death sentence, relying on the reasoning and requirements expressed in *Lockett*.[13] The Court did not address Bell's contention that the death penalty was disproportionate as applied in his case (an argument that presumably would have stressed Bell's youth), since the case had already been resolved under the *Lockett* rationale.[14]

A few years later the Supreme Court agreed to decide the specific issue of the constitutionality of the death penalty for an offense committed when the defendant was only sixteen years old.[15] In its final holding, however, the Court in *Eddings v. Oklahoma* avoided the constitutionality issue and instead sent the case back for resentencing after full consideration of all mitigating factors in line with the *Lockett* holding.[16] On the issue of the offender's youth the Court observed:

> The trial judge recognized that youth must be considered a relevant mitigating factor. But youth is more than a chronological fact. It is a time and condition of life when a person may be most susceptible to influence and to psychological damage. Our history is replete with laws and judicial recognition that minors, especially in their earlier years, generally are less mature and responsible than adults. Particularly "during the formative years of childhood and adolescence, minors often lack the experience, perspective, and judgment" expected of adults.[17]

In the five-to-four decision in *Eddings* the majority avoided deciding the constitutionality issue.[18] In contrast and rebuke, Chief Justice Burger dissented and found no constitutional bar to the death penalty for this sixteen-year-old's crime.[19] Burger's dissent was joined by Justices Blackmun, Rehnquist, and White, making at least four members of the Court who would have decided the issue then and there—to the detriment of Eddings.

Since *Eddings*, the Supreme Court has been asked repeatedly to consider the constitutionality issue but thus far has regularly rejected those requests.[20] The determination of the legality of the death penalty for juveniles is thus left to each individual jurisdiction. The only constitutional mandate is that each jurisdiction must permit consideration of the youth of the offender as a mitigating factor by the sentencing jury and judge.

UNIQUE CONSTITUTIONAL RIGHTS FOR JUVENILES

The Supreme Court has made clear its view that the death penalty is uniquely harsh and that such a severe and irrevocable penalty for crime must be subjected to the most stringent safeguards.[21] One category of such stringent safeguards has been the appropriateness of the death penalty given the individual characteristics of the defendant.[22] Among the individual characteristics singled out for particular constitutional scrutiny in death penalty cases has been the youthful age of the defendant.[23]

The Supreme Court has been quite willing to "assume juvenile offenders constitutionally may be treated differently from adults."[24] Manifestations of this different treatment are limitations on youths' right to vote, make a contract, purchase liquor, sue or be sued, dispose of property by will, serve as jurors, enlist in the armed services, drive vehicles, marry, or accept employment.[25] As Justice Frankfurter aptly noted, "Children have a very special place in life which law should reflect."[26] That juveniles are less mature and responsible than adults is a premise often recognized by the Supreme Court.[27] Given the great instability of the behavior of adolescents, it has stated, they "cannot be judged by the more exacting standards of maturity."[28]

Because of this inherent immaturity and the need for tailored governmental response to children's misbehavior, the unique and independent juvenile justice system, discussed in chapter one, was established in part to liberate these children from the harsh punishments of the criminal justice system. This separate legal system for juveniles has been constitutionally domesticated but nonetheless has been permitted to function in a unique manner where justified by the special needs of the children it serves.[29]

The major goal of the juvenile justice system is to treat and rehabilitate the adolescents it serves.[30] But some persons who come before the juvenile court or who are within the age group focused on by the juvenile court are deemed inappropriate candidates for the treatment and rehabilitative services that the state has to offer.[31] On these persons—chronologically juveniles or children but situationally labeled adults—the adult criminal justice system is imposed.[32] This denial of the benefits and protections of the juvenile justice system may result not only from particular characteristics of the juvenile but also from the lack of a broad range of juvenile services available to the juvenile court.[33]

Prosecution in the adult criminal courts subjects the juvenile to the harshest of criminal sanctions, including the death penalty in many jurisdictions.[34] But it cannot be assumed that these children are now adults for all purposes under law simply because they find themselves in adult criminal court. They still cannot vote, contract, marry, or drive commercial vehicles. Ironically, these juveniles are even prohibited from serving on juries such as the ones deciding their fate. Their adultlike acts that have placed them in criminal court are not justification for treating them as adults for purposes of their constitutional and other legal rights. Their youth continues to relegate them to a special category under law; case-specific exclusion or expulsion from juvenile court cannot and does not change that.[35]

EXCESSIVE AND DISPROPORTIONATE

The eighth amendment forbids the imposition of cruel and unusual punishments. This category of impermissible punishments, according to the Supreme Court, is not a static concept but is to be reexamined "in light of contemporary human knowledge."[36] The eighth amendment "must draw its meaning from the evolving standards of decency that mark the progress of a maturing society,"[37] the Court has decreed, and any criminal sanction "must accord with 'the dignity of man,' which is the 'basic concept underlying the Eighth Amendment.'"[38] Consideration of eighth amendment challenges to specific punishments is to be informed by objective factors to the maximum possible extent: "[A]ttention must be given to the public attitudes concerning a particular sentence—history and precedent, legislative attitudes, and the response of juries reflected in their sentencing decisions are to be consulted."[39]

To address these issues independently, each of the following subsections focuses on a single issue. Nevertheless, these factors must not be weighed in isolation but should be combined in a final evaluation of the acceptability of the death penalty for juveniles.

HISTORY AND PRECEDENT

The formal characterization of the juvenile justice system as a system of law was a clear rejection of harsh adult punishment for the unlawful acts of children.[40] The perceived inappropriateness of such harsh punishments for youths was not a new concept. It has been an informal premise of Anglo-American criminal justice systems since well before the beginning of the juvenile justice system. While younger offenders may not have had de jure benefit of less harsh punishments, research has indicated that they did receive de facto benefits, including shorter sentences, special incarceration facilities, community-based sanctions, or outright commutation of criminal sentences.[41]

The death penalty for such youths has always been most rare.[42] Research at England's Old Bailey revealed that although more than one hundred youths had been sentenced to death from 1801 to 1836, none had been executed.[43] The death penalty for juveniles was commonly avoided, either by bringing only a minor charge or by not prosecuting them at all.[44] While some cases do exist, it appears settled that execution of youths was never at any time common in England.[45] Since 1908 the death penalty has been prohibited for crimes committed while under age sixteen in England.[46]

The death penalty for juveniles has been similarly rare in the United States.[47] And though many have been sentenced to death by a jury, the commutation rate for teenagers on death row has been very high.[48] From the 1890s through the 1920s, the number of executions for crimes committed while under age eighteen ranged from twenty to twenty-seven per decade, comprising from

1.6 percent to 2.3 percent of all executions (table 2–1). As the number of all executions rose dramatically during the 1930s to 1,670 for the decade, the number of juvenile executions also rose, reaching a total of forty-one; but that was still only 2.5 percent of the total.

The peak for juvenile executions came in the 1940s. The total number reached fifty-three, and the percentage of all executions reached 4.1. The United States was executing an average of 129 persons a year, five of whom had been under age eighteen at the time of their crimes. After the 1940s the total number of executions per decade dropped precipitously, and juvenile executions dropped even more dramatically. Only sixteen juveniles were executed in the 1950s (2.2 percent of all executions) and only three in the 1960s (1.6 percent). Juvenile executions ended temporarily in 1964 after Texas executed James Echols, who was age seventeen at the time of his crime of rape.[49]

All executions ended temporarily in 1967 with the execution of Luis Monge in Colorado, then resumed on January 17, 1977, with the execution of Gary Gilmore in Utah.[50] Of the sixty-six persons executed from then until November 1, 1986, only three were juveniles: Charles Rumbaugh in Texas on September 11, 1985, James Terry Roach in South Carolina on January 10, 1986, and Jay Kelly Pinkerton in Texas on May 15, 1986.[51]

LEGISLATIVE ATTITUDES

It is settled in American law that young persons do not have the same statutory rights, responsibilities, and liabilities as do adults. These special statu-

TABLE 2–1. Total Executions and Juvenile Executions by Decade

Decade	Total Executions[a]	Juvenile Executions[b]	
1890s	1,215	20	(1.6)
1900s	1,192	23	(1.9)
1910s	1,039	24	(2.3)
1920s	1,169	27	(2.3)
1930s	1,670	41	(2.5)
1940s	1,288	53	(4.1)
1950s	716	16	(2.2)
1960s	191	3	(1.6)
1970s	3	0	(0.0)
1980s[c]	63	3	(4.8)
Total	8,546	210	(2.5)

Note: Figures in parentheses are percentages.
[a]Sources of data: W. BOWERS, LEGAL HOMICIDE 54 (1984), and NAACP LEGAL DEFENSE AND EDUCATIONAL FUND, INC., DEATH ROW, U.S.A. 4–5 (Oct. 1, 1986).
[b]See chapters four, five, six, and seven and the appendix for detailed information about juvenile executions. Seventy-one juvenile executions occurred before 1890, making a total of 281.
[c]To November 1, 1986.

tory categories for youths include rights to vote, contract, purchase liquor, sue or be sued, dispose of property by will, serve as jurors, enlist in the armed services, drive vehicles, marry and accept employment, and many others.[52]

The special legislative attitudes toward youths are reflected most vividly in the establishment of juvenile justice systems within each state. Youths within these systems receive special treatment not available to adults and are not punished for their misdeeds as adults would be for the same acts. Thirty-eight states set age eighteen as the age limit for juvenile court jurisdiction.[53]

Youths who do not obtain or who are cast out of the sanctity of juvenile court may face adult criminal punishment for their misdeeds.[54] For thirty-six states this spectrum of adult criminal punishment includes the death penalty.[55] But youths are usually given special protection even under death penalty statutes.

Protections for juveniles under death penalty statutes have shown a dramatic increase in the past quarter century. A much harsher legal environment existed in the early 1960s, as a 1962 Associated Press survey of the legal possibilities in criminal proceedings involving children reveals.[56] Of forty-one death penalty states at that time, the minimum age for the death penalty was age seven in sixteen states, age eight in three states, age ten in three states, and ages twelve to eighteen in nineteen states.[57]

The situation today is quite different. Fourteen states[58] expressly exclude youths under age sixteen, seventeen, or eighteen from their death penalty statutes. Some of these states have maintained the death penalty as part of their criminal sanctions for many years but have never included juveniles. Texas, in which the juvenile court age is seventeen, has excluded its juveniles (under seventeen) from the death penalty at least since 1897.[59] Texas is a charter member of the core of death penalty states, but in this century it has never executed juveniles under seventeen for their misdeeds.

Other states have more recently come to exclude juveniles from their death penalty statutes. Ohio saw two of its death penalty statutes struck down as unconstitutional in the 1970s.[60] The Ohio legislature then enacted a new, fully developed, and apparently valid statute.[61] For the first time in its history, Ohio decided to prohibit the death penalty for crimes committed while under age eighteen.[62]

Nebraska joined this legislative trend against the death penalty for juveniles by amending its statute in 1982. The new Nebraska statute also prohibits the death penalty for crimes committed while under age eighteen.[63] In 1985, Colorado also changed its death penalty statute to remove the possibility of execution for crimes committed while under age eighteen.[64]

Two other recent converts are Oregon and New Jersey. Oregon's 1985 capital punishment statute sets a minimum age of eighteen at the time of the crime before it can be applied.[65] New Jersey changed its capital punishment statute in January 1986 to establish a minimum age of eighteen.[66]

In 1980, the Kentucky legislature completely revised the state's juvenile code and included a provision prohibiting the death penalty for crimes committed while under age eighteen.[67] But because of funding difficulties, the new code was never implemented and was repealed in 1984. While the repeal took with it the prohibition against the death penalty for juveniles, it cannot be interpreted as a rejection of this statutory protection for juveniles but only as an inability to fund a new and expensive juvenile court system. The statute came in part as the result of a public outcry in the case of Todd Ice, a black child sentenced to death for a crime committed at age fifteen.[68]

Twelve other states have established a minimum age limit through either their juvenile court waiver statutes or their statutes giving concurrent or exclusive jurisdiction to criminal court for capital murders committed by offenders of a certain age or older.[69] While these statutes do not specifically address the issue of minimum age for the death penalty, they do provide a clear indication of legislative intent to protect youthful offenders from the harshness of criminal sanctions in general.

The death penalty statutes in an additional seven states expressly require the sentencing body to consider, as a mitigating factor, the youth of the offender.[70] While this requirement does not amount to a complete prohibition of the death penalty for juveniles, its special treatment of youths makes legislative attitudes clear. Another fifteen jurisdictions prohibit the death penalty for all offenders.[71]

In sum, over 94 percent of the jurisdictions (48 of 51) either prohibit the death penalty for all offenders (including juveniles), prohibit the death penalty for juveniles at some minimum age, prohibit any criminal court jurisdiction over juveniles under a certain minimum age, or statutorily require sentencing judges and juries to consider youth as a mitigating factor in the death penalty decision. Only three states[72] have no legislative provisions for either establishing a minimum age for the death penalty or requiring that youthful age be considered a mitigating factor in the death sentencing decision. Only one of these three states, Oklahoma, has prisoners under a juvenile death sentence.[73] This overwhelming legislative rejection of or disenchantment with the death penalty for juveniles is increasing and cannot be ignored.

JURY SENTENCING PATTERNS

As mandated by recent decisions of the Supreme Court and by almost all state death penalty statutes, juries and judges deliberating on the choice between the death penalty and life imprisonment for a convicted murderer must expressly consider, as a mitigating factor, the youthfulness of the offender. The result has been an extreme reluctance to impose juvenile death sentences. Executions of persons for crimes committed while under age eighteen has always been fairly rare, about 2.5 percent of all executions, as table 2–1 shows. From this one might well conclude that juries always have been reluctant to sentence youths to death.

This reluctance is apparently increasing, since the number of juvenile death sentences imposed has decreased significantly since 1982 (table 2–2). Eleven such sentences were imposed in 1982, nine in 1983, six in 1984, four in 1985, and seven during the first ten months of 1986.

While the number of juvenile death sentences has been declining signifi-

TABLE 2–2. Juvenile Offenders Sentenced to Death, 1982 to November 1, 1986

Year	Offender[a]	Age at Offense	Race	State	Status 11–1–86
1982	Barrow, Lee Roy	17	W	Tex.	Reversed in 1985
	Cannon, Joseph J.	17	W	Tex.	On death row
	Carter, Robert A.	17	B	Tex.	On death row
	Garrett, Johnny F.	17	W	Tex.	On death row
	Johnson, Lawrence	17	B	Md.	Reversed twice but resentenced to death in 1983 and 1984
	Lashley, Frederick	17	B	Mo.	On death row
	Legare, Andrew	17	W	Ga.	Reversed in 1983; resentenced to death in 1984; reversed in 1986
	Stanford, Kevin	17	B	Ky.	On death row
	Stokes, Freddie	17	B	N.C.	Reversed in 1982 but resentenced to death in 1983
	Thompson, Jay	17	W	Ind.	Reversed in 1986
	Trimble, James	17	W	Md.	On death row
1983	Bey, Marko	17	B	N.J.	On death row
	Cannaday, Attina	16	W	Miss.	Reversed in 1984
	Harris, Curtis P.	17	B	Tex.	On death row
	Harvey, Frederick	16	B	Nev.	Reversed in 1984
	Hughes, Kevin	16	B	Pa.	On death row
	Johnson, Lawrence	17	B	Md.	Reversed in 1983 but resentenced to death in 1984
	Lynn, Frederick	16	B	Ala.	Reversed in 1985 but resentenced to death in 1986
	Mhoon, James	16	B	Miss.	Reversed in 1985
	Stokes, Freddie	17	B	N.C.	On death row
1984	Aulisio, Joseph	15	W	Pa.	On death row
	Brown, Leon	15	B	N.C.	On death row
	Johnson, Lawrence	17	B	Md.	On death row
	Legare, Andrew	17	W	Ga.	On death row
	Patton, Keith	17	B	Ind.	On death row
	Thompson, Wayne	15	W	Okla.	On death row

TABLE 2–2. (Cont'd.)

Year	Offender[a]	Age at Offense	Race	State	Status 11-1-86
1985	Livingston, Jesse	17	B	Fla.	On death row
	Morgan, James	16	W	Fla.	On death row
	Ward, Ronald	15	B	Ark.	On death row
	Williams, Raymond	17	B	Pa.	On death row
1986[b]	Comeaux, Adam	17	B	La.	On death row
	Cooper, Paula R.	15	B	Ind.	On death row
	LeCroy, Cleo D.	17	W	Fla.	On death row
	Lynn, Frederick	16	B	Ala.	On death row
	Sellers, Sean R.	16	W	Okla.	On death row
	Wilkins, Heath	16	W	Mo.	On death row
	Williams, Alexander	17	B	Ga.	On death row

[a]See chapter nine notes 2–38 for sources of information about these offenders.
[b]First ten months only.

cantly each year, the number of adult death sentences has remained fairly constant at a rate of 250 to 300 a year.[74] Thus the decline in juvenile death sentences is particularly indicative of a different attitude by juries in capital cases if the offender is under age eighteen at the time of his crime rather than older.

The result of this decline in juvenile death sentences is revealed by the changing populations on death row. In December 1983, thirty-eight (2.9 percent) of the 1,289 persons on death row were under juvenile death sentences (table 2–3). This total of thirty-eight is apparently an all-time high for juvenile death sentences.

During the following two and three-quarter years the total death row population increased by 548 persons but the number of juveniles remained constant. On November 1, 1986, only thirty-eight (2.1 percent) of the 1,800 persons on death row had committed their crimes while under age eighteen (table 2–4). That represents a constant number of juveniles on death row during a period in which there was a 44 percent increase in the adult death row population.

Approximately 9.2 percent of criminal homicides from 1973 through 1983 were committed by persons under age eighteen, at least if the arrests for those crimes are indicative of the persons who actually commit them (table 2–5).[75] While only a small percentage of these criminal homicides were capital murders, it seems reasonable to assume that juveniles commit roughly the same proportion (9 percent) of capital murders as of all criminal homicides. In striking contrast to this 9 percent commission rate, juveniles have received a maximum of 2 percent to 3 percent of all capital sentences imposed over this period.

Other factors may be partly responsible for this gross difference in arrests and sentencing. Many juveniles arrested for murder and nonnegligent homicide are retained within the juvenile court that typically has exclusive original jurisdiction. Of those transferred to or directly charged in adult criminal court, at least some are not charged with capital offenses. These and other factors are compounded by the reluctance of criminal court juries to impose harsh criminal sanctions, including the death penalty, on juveniles.

Justice Brennan's view of the message from such reluctance is persuasive:

> When an unusually severe punishment is authorized for wide-scale application but not, because of society's refusal, inflicted save in a few instances, the inference is compelling that there is a deep-seated reluctance to inflict it.[76]

Such a deep-seated reluctance to sentence youths to death is reflected dramatically in the declining rate of juvenile death sentences, the declining juvenile death row population, and the minuscule proportion of juvenile murderers actually sentenced to death.

CONTEMPORARY STANDARDS OF DECENCY

Criminal punishments that run contrary to popular sentiment can and ought to be banned.[77] The death penalty for juveniles is such a punishment because it is in conflict with contemporary theory and practice.[78] An example of the reaction that may be precipitated is the public outcry that resulted from death sentences for a sixteen- and a seventeen-year-old imposed in the late 1960s.[79]

Leaders in the legal, criminological, and social policy fields almost universally oppose the death penalty for juveniles. The prestigious American Law Institute excluded the death penalty for crimes committed while under age eighteen from its influential Model Penal Code, concluding that "civilized societies will not tolerate the spectacle of execution of children."[80] This position was also adopted by the National Commission on Reform of Criminal Law.[81]

In August 1983 the American Bar Association adopted as its formal policy a resolution stating that the association "opposes, in principle, the imposition of capital punishment upon any person for any offense committed while under the age of eighteen. . . ."[82] That was the first time in the history of the organization that it took a formal position on any aspect of capital punishment. The *Washington Post* endorsed the ABA's policy and urged it as a minimum requirement for jurisdictions having capital punishment.[83]

All European countries forbid the death penalty for crimes committed while under age eighteen.[84] More than three-fourths of the nations of the world (seventy-three of the ninety-three reporting countries) have set eighteen as the minimum age for the death penalty.[85] The United Nations endorsed this position in 1976.[86] Another indication of the present global attitude is the condemnation of the death penalty by Pope John Paul II, the first such position by any pope in history.[87] Even in time of war, the Geneva Convention prohibits execution of civilians under age eighteen at time of offense.[88]

Recent public opinion polls in the United States suggest that support is strong for the death penalty in general, with 70 percent in favor in 1986—about the highest since 1936.[89] A different result has occurred, however, in the few

TABLE 2–3. Persons on Death Row in December 1983 for
Crimes Committed while under Age 18[a]

State	Prisoner	Age at Offense	Sex	Race
Alabama	Davis, Timothy	17	M	W
	Jackson, Carnel	16	M	B
	Lynn, Frederick	16	M	B
Florida	Magill, Paul	17	M	W
	Morgan, James	16	M	W
	Peavy, Robert	17	M	B
Georgia	Burger, Christopher	17	M	W
	Buttrum, Janice	17	F	W
	High, Jose	16	M	B
	Legare, Andrew	17	M	W
Indiana	Thompson, Jay	17	M	W
Kentucky	Ice, Todd	15	M	B
	Stanford, Kevin	17	M	B
Louisiana	Prejean, Dalton	17	M	B
Maryland	Johnson, Lawrence	17	M	B
	Trimble, James	17	M	W
Mississippi	Cannaday, Attina	16	F	W
	Jones, Larry	17	M	B
	Mhoon, James	16	M	B
	Tokman, George	17	M	W
Missouri	Lashley, Frederick	17	M	B
Nevada	Harvey, Frederick	16	M	B
New Jersey	Bey, Marko	17	M	B
North Carolina	Oliver, John	14	M	B
	Stokes, Freddie Lee	17	M	B
Oklahoma	Eddings, Monty	16	M	W
Pennsylvania	Hughes, Kevin	16	M	B
South Carolina	Roach, James Terry	17	M	W
Texas	Barrow, Lee Roy	17	M	W
	Battie, Billy	17	M	B
	Burns, Victor Renay	17	M	B
	Cannon, Joseph John	17	M	W
	Carter, Robert A.	17	M	B
	Garrett, Johnny F.	17	M	W
	Graham, Gary L.	17	M	B
	Harris, Curtis Paul	17	M	B
	Pinkerton, Jay K.	17	M	W
	Rumbaugh, Charles	17	M	W

[a]Sources of data: NAACP LEGAL DEFENSE AND EDUCATIONAL FUND, INC., DEATH
ROW, U.S.A. (Dec. 20, 1983); Brief for Petitioner at 19a app. E, Eddings v. Oklahoma,
455 U.S. 104 (1982); and communications with defense attorneys and state officials.

TABLE 2–4. Persons on Death Row on November 1, 1986, for Crimes Committed while under Age 18[a]

State	Prisoner	Age at Offense	Sex	Race
Alabama	Davis, Timothy	17	M	W
	Jackson, Carnel	16	M	B
	Lynn, Frederick	16	M	B
Arkansas	Ward, Ronald	15	M	B
Florida	LeCroy, Cleo	17	M	W
	Livingston, Jesse	17	M	B
	Magill, Paul	17	M	W
	Morgan, James A.	16	M	W
Georgia	Burger, Christopher	17	M	W
	Buttrum, Janice	17	F	W
	High, Jose	16	M	B
	Legare, Andrew	17	M	W
	Williams, Alexander	17	M	B
Indiana	Cooper, Paula R.	15	F	B
	Patton, Keith	17	M	B
	Thompson, Jay	17	M	W
Kentucky	Stanford, Kevin	17	M	B
Louisiana	Comeaux, Adam	17	M	B
	Prejean, Dalton	17	M	B
Maryland	Johnson, Lawrence	17	M	B
	Trimble, James	17	M	W
Mississippi	Jones, Larry	17	M	B
	Tokman, George	17	M	W
Missouri	Lashley, Frederick	17	M	B
	Wilkins, Heath	16	M	W
New Jersey	Bey, Marko	17	M	B
North Carolina	Brown, Leon	15	M	B
	Stokes, Freddie Lee	17	M	B
Olkahoma	Sellers, Sean R.	16	M	W
	Thompson, Wayne	15	M	W
Pennsylvania	Aulisio, Joseph	15	M	W
	Hughes, Kevin	16	M	B
	Williams, Raymond	17	M	B
Texas	Cannon, Joseph John	17	M	W
	Carter, Robert A.	17	M	B
	Garrett, Johnny	17	M	W
	Graham, Gary	17	M	B
	Harris, Curtis Paul	17	M	B

[a]Sources of data: NAACP LEGAL DEFENSE AND EDUCATIONAL FUND, INC., DEATH ROW, U.S.A. (OCT. 1, 1986); and sources cited for table 2–3. See table 9–4 for more information about these cases.

TABLE 2–5. Murder and Nonnegligent Manslaughter Arrests by Age Group, 1973–1983

Year	Total Arrests	Under Age 18		Age 18 and Over	
1973	14,399	1,497	(10.4)	12,902	(89.6)
1974	13,818	1,399	(10.1)	12,419	(89.9)
1975	16,485	1,573	(9.5)	14,912	(90.5)
1976	14,113	1,302	(9.2)	12,811	(90.8)
1977	17,163	1,670	(9.7)	15,493	(90.3)
1978	18,755	1,735	(9.3)	17,020	(90.7)
1979	18,264	1,707	(9.3)	16,557	(90.7)
1980	18,745	1,742	(9.3)	17,003	(90.7)
1981	20,432	1,858	(9.1)	18,574	(90.9)
1982	18,511	1,579	(8.5)	16,932	(91.5)
1983	18,064	1,345	(7.4)	16,719	(92.6)
Total	188,749	17,407	(9.2)	171,342	(90.8)

Note: Figures in parentheses are percentages.

polls of the general public that have asked specifically about the death penalty for young offenders. The earliest that could be found was conducted in November 1936.[90] On the general issue of capital punishment, 61 percent favored it, but where the offender was under age twenty-one, only 46 percent favored it.[91] The last nationwide indication from the general public on this narrower issue was a February 1965 Gallup survey, which reported that while 45 percent supported the death penalty in general, only 23 percent favored it for persons under twenty-one years of age.[92] These two polls, conducted at the peak and the valley of general public support of capital punishment, suggest that at no time has there been majority support of capital punishment for crimes committed by persons under twenty-one. It seems reasonable to assume that even a smaller percentage would have favored the death penalty for persons under eighteen.

A recent poll of lawyers confirms these findings and inferences. An American Bar Association poll conducted in September 1984 revealed that 68 percent of the lawyers polled favored the death penalty in general, down slightly from 69 percent in favor in 1983.[93] But 53 percent were opposed to the death penalty for crimes committed while under age eighteen.[94] While 41 percent of male lawyers supported the death penalty for juveniles, only 25 percent of women lawyers supported it. A January 1985 poll of law students revealed that while 61 percent favored the death penalty in general, a majority opposed "the execution of murderers younger than 18."[95] One could reasonably assume that these opinions of lawyers and law students are not much different from the opinions of the general public.

More recent polls have been conducted in Nashville, Tennessee; Macon,

Georgia; and the state of Connecticut. Even in such bedrock capital punishment locales as Nashville and Macon, the 400 persons polled in each city in December 1985 responded over two to one against the death penalty for crimes committed while under age eighteen.[96] A telephone survey of 509 respondents conducted in Connecticut in May 1986 had similar results.[97] While 68 percent favored capital punishment in general, only 31 percent favored it for crimes committed while under age eighteen.[98]

The issue in essence is not whether the death penalty is officially authorized but whether it is acceptable to society. Every reasonably reliable public opinion poll ever conducted on the question of the death penalty for juveniles has found that a majority of the respondents oppose it. Justice Brennan stated the issue succinctly:

> The question under this principle, then, is whether there are objective indicators from which a court can conclude that contemporary society considers a severe punishment unacceptable. Accordingly, the judicial task is to review the history of a challenged punishment and to examine society's present practice with respect to its use. Legislative authorization, of course, does not establish acceptance. The acceptability of a severe punishment is measured, not by its availability, for it might become so offensive to society as never to be inflicted, but by its use.[99]

While still legislatively authorized by many U.S. jurisdictions, the death penalty for juveniles is fast disappearing throughout the world and is increasingly condemned by leaders of American criminal jurisprudence. As society matures, it develops new standards of decency to replace earlier, less informed standards. Our society's and the world's contemporary standards of decency reject the death penalty for juveniles and demand that we relegate the practice to our less civilized past. As Attorney David Bruck wrote in the *New York Times:*

> A decent society places certain absolute limits on the punishments that it inflicts— no matter how terrible the crime or how great the desire for retribution. And one of those limits is that it does not execute people for crimes committed while they were children.[100]

MEASURABLE CONTRIBUTION TO GOALS OF PUNISHMENT

Regardless of any controversy surrounding the death penalty in general, this criminal sanction has been characterized by the Supreme Court in its major death penalty opinions as achieving, to varying degrees, the goals of retribution, general deterrence, and specific deterrence or incapacitation while obviously rejecting the goals of reformation, rehabilitation, and treatment of the offender.[101] The death penalty cannot be justified, however, unless it makes a measurable contribution to the goals of retribution and deterrence, since it is otherwise too harsh compared with long-term imprisonment. A careful analysis of the death penalty for juveniles reveals that it makes no such measurable contribution to these goals for these offenders. It is not reasonably capable of advancing a legitimate state interest and thus cannot be justified under the United States Constitution.

RETRIBUTION

In an earlier time (1949) the Supreme Court made clear its dissatisfaction with retribution as a justification for criminal sanctions: "Retribution is no longer the dominant objective of the criminal law."[102] The goal of societal retribution or legal revenge achieved through execution of an offender more recently was referred to favorably by both Chief Justice Burger and Justice Stewart.[103] In contrast Justice Marshall's view is that the eighth amendment precludes retribution for its own sake.[104] All these observations were made in cases involving adults sentenced to death.

Retribution as a justification for criminal punishment, including the death penalty, has been a concept with many interpretations.[105] These many interpretations have been limited to only two having legal import according to the Supreme Court: the institutional revenge model and the just deserts model.[106]

The Supreme Court gave specific attention to the retribution issue in *Enmund v. Florida*.[107] Justice White, writing for the majority, expressed the retribution issue in this manner:

> As for retribution as a justification for executing Enmund, we think this very much depends on the degree of Enmund's culpability—what Enmund's intentions, expectations, and actions were. American criminal law has long considered a defendant's intention—and therefore his moral guilt—to be critical to "the degree of [his] criminal culpability." . . . .
>
> For purposes of imposing the death penalty, Enmund's criminal culpability must be limited to his participation in the robbery, and his punishment must be tailored to his personal responsibility and moral guilt.[108]

Even if the execution of an adult for revenge or retribution is constitutionally permissible, this justification for the death penalty loses its appeal when the object of righteous vengeance is a child. Juveniles do not "deserve" harsh punishments in the same way that mature, responsible adults might. Society does not feel the same satisfying, cleansing reaction when a child is executed. Nonresponsible actors, whether children, retarded adults, or insane persons, by their very nature deserve and usually receive pity and treatment rather than the revenge of an outraged society anxious to "kill them back."[109] Experts in sentencing youthful offenders have concluded as much:

> [A]dolescents, particularly in the early and middle teen years, are more vulnerable, more impulsive, and less self-disciplined than adults. Crimes committed by youths may be just as harmful to victims as those committed by older persons, but they deserve less punishment because adolescents may have less capacity to control their conduct and to think in long-range terms than adults. Moreover, youth crime as

such is not exclusively the offender's fault; offenses by the young also represent a failure of family, school, and the social system, which share responsibility for development of America's youth.[110]

Execution of persons whose crimes were committed while under age eighteen is not necessary to serve the ends of retribution. More than sufficient retribution is achieved by sentencing such persons to long prison terms.

GENERAL DETERRENCE

General deterrence from the death penalty has been the subject of heated debate among criminology scholars.[111] Various members of the Supreme Court have disagreed about the general deterrent effects of the death penalty. Justices Brennan and Marshall have concluded that no verifiable general deterrent effect exists.[112] Justice Stewart acknowledged the lack of clarity in the empirical evidence but observed:

> We may nevertheless assume safely that there are murderers, such as those who act in passion, for whom the threat of death has little or no deterrent effect. But for many others, the death penalty undoubtedly is a significant deterrent. There are carefully contemplated murders, such as murder for hire, where the possible penalty of death may well enter into the cold calculus that precedes the decision to act.[113]

Justice Stewart's observations provide an excellent model for analysis of any general deterrent effect from the death penalty for juveniles. Given these observations and premises, it would seem that two important considerations are juveniles' perception of death and whether juveniles tend to act out of passion and impulse or from cold, calculated decisions.

The Supreme Court has observed that young persons are inexperienced and unable to avoid detrimental choices in general.[114] They are going through "the period of great instability which the crisis of adolescence produces."[115] Juveniles "generally are less mature and responsible than adults."[116] The *Eddings* majority noted favorably the generally accepted conclusions about the impulsiveness and irresponsibility of juveniles.[117]

Most social scientists would agree that juveniles live primarily for today with little thought of the future consequences of their actions.[118] Adolescents are in a developmental stage of defiance of danger and death and are attracted to flirtations with death from a feeling of omnipotence.[119] Such well-known adolescent behavior was noted long ago for juveniles sentenced to death: "On one occasion a boy showed delight at being placed in the condemned cell, apparently because it gave him status in the eyes of his fellow prisoners."[120]

Child development research reveals that the ability to engage in mature moral judgments develops significantly during middle and late adolescence, reaching a plateau only after an individual leaves school or reaches early adulthood.[121] Most adolescents have insufficient social experience for making sound value judgments and understanding the long-range consequences of their decisions.[122] Supreme Court opinions have recognized this universally under-stood principle: "[D]uring the formative years of childhood and adolescence, minors often lack the experience, perspective, and judgment to recognize and avoid choices that could be detrimental to them."[123] All of this generally ac-cepted information about typical adolescent behavior leads to the conclusion that juveniles do not commonly engage in any "cold calculus that precedes the decision to act."[124] Thus the Supreme Court's premises behind its assumed general deterrence of the death penalty simply do not apply in any reasonable manner to juveniles.

Even if a few juveniles might engage in a cold, premeditated calculus before committing the act, they would know that even though the death penalty might be authorized for juveniles the probability of their ever being executed for their acts is almost nil.[125] Without some reasonable degree of certainty, any possible general deterrent effect disappears.[126]

SPECIFIC DETERRENCE AND INCAPACITATION

Proponents of the death penalty, whether for juveniles or for all offenders, point out that at least execution of an offender specifically deters and incapa-citates that individual offender. An executed prisoner will never commit another murder. This justification for the death penalty for juveniles is not of course incorrect; it simply sanctions too much punishment for too little additional result.

Long-term imprisonment of young offenders affords society comparable protection against their future crimes. We know, as Justice Marshall has pointed out, that murderers generally are "extremely unlikely to commit other crimes either in prison or upon their release."[127] More specifically, we know that juvenile murderers tend to be model prisoners and have a very low rate of recidivism when released.[128] If the goal is prevention of future murders by these juveniles, long-term imprisonment is of comparable specific deterrent impact and negates any need for the death penalty for juveniles.

REFORMATION, REHABILITATION, AND TREATMENT

The inescapable conclusion is that the death penalty for juveniles makes no measurable contribution to the constitutionally accepted goals of the death penalty. This ultimate punishment does, however, totally reject the one sen-tencing alternative normally thought most appropriate for young offenders—rehabilitation.[129] Execution irreversibly abandons all hope of reforming a teen-ager and thus is squarely in opposition to the fundamental premises of juvenile justice and comparable sociolegal systems. A Kentucky court stated that "in-corrigibility is inconsistent with youth; . . . it is impossible to make a judgment that a fourteen-year-old youth, no matter how bad, will remain incorrigible for the rest of his life."[130]

Capital punishment of our children inherently rejects humanity's future, which begins with the habilitation and rehabilitation of today's youth.[131] Such costly rejection should not be made if it makes no measurable contribution to the goals of criminal justice in general or to the death penalty in particular.

ARBITRARY, CAPRICIOUS,
AND FREAKISH MANNER

To paraphrase Justice Stewart, death sentences for juveniles are cruel and unusual in the same way that a juvenile being struck by lightning is cruel and unusual.[132] The few juveniles selected for the death penalty are a very small proportion of all juveniles who commit criminal homicides, and actual execution of such juveniles is so rare as to be freakish. As Justice Marshall noted, "[W]here life itself is what hangs in the balance, a fine precision in the process must be insisted upon."[133] Such a fine precision in the death penalty for juveniles has not been and probably can never be achieved.[134]

Just how arbitrary, capricious, and freakish juvenile executions have been was demonstrated in table 2–1. In the past century juvenile executions accounted for only 2.5 percent of all executions. Since the 1940s they have dropped precipitously and only three have occurred in the past twenty-two years. While execution of adults in the mid-1980s is no longer front-page news, execution of a juvenile is so rare as to be most newsworthy.[135]

One might argue that the rarity of the death penalty for juveniles stems solely from the rarity of criminal homicides by juveniles. But that is not a sufficient explanation. Since 1973, when the death penalty entered its modern era, juveniles have accounted for about 9.2 percent of the arrests for murder and nonnegligent manslaughter, as table 2–5 showed. This proportion has been steadily declining, from 10.4 percent in 1973 to 7.4 percent in 1983.

A 1986 report from the U.S. Department of Justice[136] stated that 198,000 arrests were made for murder or nonnegligent manslaughter during the ten-year period from 1975 through 1984.[137] Assuming that approximately 9 percent of the arrestees were under age eighteen, some 17,820 such juveniles were arrested. During this period, 2,384 persons entered prison under a sentence of death.[138] Of these condemned prisoners, it seems reasonable to estimate that approximately eighty (3 percent) were under juvenile death sentences.

In sum, during this ten-year period juveniles accounted for 9 percent of the criminal homicides, 3 percent of the death sentences, and none of the executions. Only 1.3 percent of adults arrested for criminal homicide (2,304 of 180,180) received the death sentence, an incredibly small proportion. A microscopically small proportion—only 0.4 percent—of juveniles arrested for criminal homicide (80 of 17,820) received the death penalty. These figures are for the entire nation. If the inquiry were confined to any one state, the numbers would be so minuscule as to be even more freakish. Moreover, as already noted, the number of juveniles on death row is not increasing despite substantial increases in the adult population on death row.[139]

If the number of juveniles selected for death sentencing and possible execution is only a tiny portion of the number of juveniles who commit capital crimes, how are they selected? In an analysis of the cases of the eleven adults selected for execution from 1977 through 1983, the conclusion was that they were not unique and no rational basis could be discerned for their resulting in execution.[140] Justice Brennan concluded that these adult executions were not "selected on a basis that is neither arbitrary nor capricious, under any meaningful definition of those terms."[141] Extrapolating from these conclusions about adult executions, the inference seems much stronger in the matter of juvenile death sentences and executions. Their even rarer and more random pattern of occurrence leaves no alternative to the conclusion that they are most freakishly imposed. No rational selection process can be determined, and one is left to conclude that the basis of selection is arbitrary and capricious.

AGE EIGHTEEN IS MOST APPROPRIATE

If a constitutional line is to be drawn below which the death penalty will not be permitted, what is the most appropriate age at which such a line should be drawn? At what age do children become adults in our society for purposes of legal duties and responsibilities? For the vast majority of situations that age is eighteen.

Thirty-eight states now set eighteen as the jurisdictional age limit for their juvenile courts.[142] These states exemplify the common premise that adult responsibility for criminal acts normally should begin at eighteen. Exceptions can and are made with waiver and concurrent jurisdiction provisions but the de jure age is eighteen.

Ten of the fourteen states that expressly prohibit the death penalty for youthful offenders have set the age at eighteen.[143] The Model Penal Code minimum age for the death penalty remains at eighteen, after age fourteen was considered and rejected by the American Law Institute.[144] Age eighteen is also the most common age of majority established in American law for noncriminal purposes. For example, the twenty-sixth amendment establishes the right to vote at age eighteen.

Internationally, age eighteen is the age chosen by the many countries that prohibit the death penalty for juveniles.[145] International treaties, joined by the United States, also use age eighteen as the cutoff point.[146] And the Geneva Convention on the wartime death penalty for civilians uses eighteen as the minimum age.[147]

A second-level, less satisfactory choice would be to set the minimum age for the death penalty at the juvenile court age for the particular jurisdiction. That would give constitutional imprimatur for the present practice in Georgia, Nevada, New Hampshire, and Texas, all of which use age sixteen or seventeen because that is their juvenile court age. However, this choice would allow nonuniformity to continue throughout the various jurisdictions. The states presumably would be free to lower their juvenile court age to an extremely low age without constitutional ramifications on the death penalty issue. Furthermore, the present range of minimum age from eighteen to ten[148] would continue, leaving vastly different death penalty liabilities from state to state.

For these reasons one minimum age limit for the death penalty should be established. Because eighteen is the age commonly used for similar purposes, it is the only reasonable choice for a minimum age for the death penalty.

CONCLUSIONS

Does the eighth amendment prohibit the death penalty for crimes committed while under age eighteen? The Supreme Court has avoided giving a direct answer to this question but has provided a general analytical framework from which answers may be derived. The foregoing analysis suggests that the most persuasive answer, given this general analytical framework, is yes—the death penalty for juveniles is cruel and unusual under the eighth amendment. This answer follows from a step-by-step consideration of the supporting arguments for the death penalty as they apply to adolescents. In this application, the force of these supporting arguments either disappears or in some cases suggests that the threat of the death penalty may become an attraction to death-defying adolescents.

Presently the thirty-six death penalty jurisdictions are doing whatever they wish. All must give the age of the offender great weight in mitigation of the death penalty, and most expressly prohibit application of their death penalties to their juveniles, at least at some age minimum. While some state courts have tried to resolve the constitutional question themselves, most simply have left the issue to the state legislatures, which are increasingly considering amending their statutes to join the trend against the death penalty for juveniles.

A uniform, nationwide policy is needed, and such a policy flows most reasonably from the eighth amendment. It is beyond argument that American law would not permit the death penalty for a very young child—the three-year-old toddler, say, who shoots Mommy to death with Daddy's handgun. It is also settled that American law may permit the death penalty for adults—the thirty-year-old, say, who shoots his mother to death with his father's handgun. The only issue, then, is at what age the line will be drawn between these two polar positions. At present no universally accepted line exists, except the line at age seven for criminal responsibility of any kind.[149]

The line should be drawn at age eighteen, since that is by far the most common age for similar restrictions and limitations. This line should emanate from the eighth amendment and should be imposed by the Supreme Court.

THREE

State Laws and
the Juvenile Death Penalty

The previous chapters outline the evolution of the law on the death penalty for juveniles and present several persuasive justifications for concluding that the practice is unconstitutional. Because the United States Supreme Court has not decided this constitutional issue, the various U.S. jurisdictions have broad discretion to resolve the matter however they wish.[1] The only clear, nationwide mandate they must honor is to afford the youthfulness of the offender great weight as a mitigating factor.[2]

This chapter explains the means by which the jurisdictions have exercised their discretion. These jurisdictions include the fifty states and the District of Columbia. Brief consideration is also given to federal law in this area. This analysis was made in late 1986, at a time when several states were considering changes in their death penalty statutes; any changes enacted since that time are not reflected in this analysis.

THE STATUTES

Federal death penalty statutes have been under a considerable cloud since the *Furman*[3] and *Gregg*[4] cases were decided because many of the provisions in these statutes conflict with the principles established in the two cases.[5] Although the United States Code authorizes the death penalty for at least fifteen offenses, it seems generally agreed that "the death penalty cannot constitutionally be imposed under [these] provisions. . . ."[6] Procedures being followed in federal criminal trials thus are constitutionally inadequate and render the statutory provisions meaningless.

Each year a new federal bill is introduced to put in place an apparently valid federal death penalty statute. Yet another such bill, a proposed federal capital punishment statute requiring a minimum age of eighteen at the time of the crime, was pending before the Senate in 1986, but similar bills have stalled in previous years in the House of Representatives.[7] Although President Reagan expressed support for this legislation in his state of the union address on February 6, 1985,[8] no comprehensive new federal death penalty statute seems likely to be adopted in the near future.

In the fifty states and the District of Columbia the statutory laws divide into four major categories. In the first group are states that have no death penalty statutes, thus excluding the death penalty not only for juveniles but also for adults. States in the second group have statutes authorizing the death penalty but specifically excluding juveniles. A third group authorizes the death penalty for anyone convicted of certain crimes in adult criminal court but sets a minimum age for being tried in that court. The last group has statutes that authorize the death penalty but have no express provisions for sparing youthful offenders.

No Valid Death Penalty Statutes

Fifteen of the fifty-one jurisdictions have no legally valid death penalty statutes.[9] They do not execute anyone. Several of these jurisdictions have been without a death penalty for many years (table 3–1).

During the past half-century an additional seven states had periods during which they abolished the death penalty, but all subsequently reestablished it.[10] These states—Arizona, Colorado, Delaware, Missouri, South Dakota, Tennessee, and Washington—are now among the thirty-six states with valid death penalty statutes.

The fifteen jurisdictions without valid death penalty statutes typically still provide for adult criminal court jurisdiction over the most serious juvenile law violations. The offending juveniles are either prosecuted directly in criminal

TABLE 3–1. Jurisdictions without Valid Death Penalty Statutes

Jurisdiction	Year of Last Valid Statute
Alaska	1957
District of Columbia	1973
Hawaii	1957
Iowa	1965
Kansas	1973
Maine	1887
Massachusetts	1984
Michigan	1963
Minnesota	1911
New York	1985
North Dakota	1975
Rhode Island	1979
Vermont	1972[a]
West Virginia	1965
Wisconsin	1853

[a]Vermont's statute, not amended since Furman v. Georgia (1972,) is clearly invalid.

court or are transferred from juvenile court to criminal court. But even if these juveniles are convicted in criminal court they cannot receive the death penalty, since the court has no legal power to sentence anyone to death, regardless of age. This means of excluding juveniles from the death penalty should be kept in mind and compared with the means outlined in the next two sections.

MINIMUM DEATH PENALTY AGE

Fourteen states have death penalty statutes that include language unequivocally prohibiting the death penalty for juveniles (table 3–2).[11] Ten states set the minimum age at eighteen, three at seventeen, and one at sixteen.

Typical of the language used in these statutes are these two examples:

Notwithstanding any other provision of law, the death penalty shall not be imposed upon any person who is under the age of 18 at the time of the commission of the crime.[12]

When it is shown that a person convicted of a capital offense without a recommendation for mercy had not reached his seventeenth birthday at the time of the commission of the offense, the punishment of such person shall not be death but shall be imprisonment for life.[13]

Such statutes provide for procedures that are almost identical to those for adults accused of capital crimes, but they exclude juveniles when the final sentencing decision is reached. Since the typical statute provides for a choice between the death penalty and life imprisonment, the sole option for juveniles convicted of a capital offense in these states is life imprisonment.

MINIMUM CRIMINAL COURT AGE

In addition to the fourteen states that set a minimum age in their capital punishment statutes, twelve states establish a minimum age limit through two other statutory means. These twelve have a range of minimum ages from ten to fifteen (table 3–3).

TABLE 3–2. Jurisdictions with Death Penalty Statutes Excluding Juveniles[a]

Jurisdictions	Minumum Age in Statute
California, Colorado, Connecticut, Illinois, Nebraska, New Jersey, New Mexico, Ohio, Oregon, Tennessee	18
Georgia, New Hampshire, Texas	17
Nevada	16

[a]See chapter two note 58 for citations to statutes.

TABLE 3–3. Death Penalty Jurisdictions with Minimum Criminal Court Age[a]

Jurisdiction	Minimum Criminal Court Age
Louisiana, Virginia	15
Alabama, Arkansas, Idaho, Kentucky, Missouri, North Carolina, Utah	14
Mississippi	13
Montana	12
Indiana	10

[a]See chapter three notes 14 and 18 for citations to statutes.

One of the means of establishing a minimum age for the death penalty is to give exclusive original jurisdiction over all juvenile crime to the juvenile courts and then establish a minimum age for waiver of juvenile court jurisdiction and transfer to adult criminal court. Only if a juvenile meets or exceeds this minimum age can he or she be transferred to and prosecuted in criminal court and thus be in jeopardy of receiving criminal punishment, including the death penalty. Eight states follow this means.[14] Four of them use age fourteen.[15] Virginia uses age fifteen, Mississippi age thirteen, Montana age twelve, and Indiana age ten.[16]

In these eight states the case begins in juvenile court. Usually the prosecuting attorney must petition the juvenile court if consideration is to be given to transferring the case to adult criminal court. While the decision to seek transfer is almost always the prosecutor's, the final decision to transfer rests with the juvenile court judge.[17] That places the decision in the judicial branch of the government, which is accustomed to hearing pro and con arguments from attorney-advocates and coming to a reasoned decision appropriate under the circumstances.

The juvenile court judge will be aware that in criminal court the juvenile may face the death penalty. Given the tendency of juvenile court judges to be somewhat merciful and understanding toward juvenile misbehavior, at least as compared with prosecutors, this process for choosing between keeping the case in juvenile court or transferring it to criminal court seems to favor the juvenile to some degree, at least where capital cases are involved.

The other statutory means for establishing a minimum age for the death penalty is to give concurrent or exclusive original jurisdiction to adult criminal court if the crime is capital murder and the defendant is of a certain age or older. Four states follow this procedure.[18] Arkansas, Idaho, and North Carolina use age fourteen, while Louisiana uses age fifteen.

Under this second mechanism, the juvenile court judge is taken out of the decision-making process. If the statutes provide for concurrent jurisdiction between the criminal and the juvenile court, the decision about which court to file the case in is left to the prosecuting attorney. Since either court could hear the case, total discretion rests with the prosecutor.

If the statutes provide for exclusive jurisdiction in criminal court for certain kinds of crimes, then the legislature that enacted the statute has predetermined the court and the juvenile's possible eligibility for the death penalty. No discretion exists for either the juvenile court judge or the prosecuting attorney to choose which court is most appropriate for a certain child and a certain case: All juveniles who have committed certain crimes must be prosecuted in criminal court.[19]

Either of these two processes may place the juvenile in criminal court. If the charge includes a capital crime, the juvenile may face the death penalty. The common theme is that the jurisdictional statutes, not the death penalty statutes, have established a minimum age for persons in the criminal courts.

AGE AS AN EXPRESS MITIGATING FACTOR

Seven states have no minimum age limits in either their death penalty statutes or their jurisdictional statutes but do specifically list the age of the offender as a mitigating factor in their death penalty statutes (table 3-4).[20] In compliance with major Supreme Court holdings, all states must allow evidence proffered by the defendant on any mitigating circumstance, including youthfulness of the offender.[21] Going even further, these seven states have statutorily specified the age of the offender as one mitigating factor to be considered. That suggests that these jurisdictions have a particular concern about capital crimes by juveniles.

Mitigating factors are introduced by defense attorneys near the end of the sentencing phase of a capital trial. Any point can be raised as a mitigating factor as long as it is reasonably relevant and material to the case at hand. Youthfulness of the offender would be raised to gain the sympathy of the sentencing jury and judge, nudging them toward a life imprisonment sentence rather than a death sentence. Mitigating factors are balanced against the aggravating factors introduced by the prosecuting attorney, and the sentencing jury and judge then render their decision.

NO MINIMUM AGE PROVISIONS

The remaining three jurisdictions have apparently valid death penalty statutes and permit mitigating factors to be considered but have not specifically listed the offender's age as a mitigating factor in their statutes.[22] In these states— Delaware, Oklahoma, and South Dakota—the defendant may offer his or her youthfulness as a mitigating factor, but this factor is not mentioned in the death penalty statute and no minimum age is set forth in any other statute.

A reasonable assumption is that these states either did not consider capital crimes by juveniles when drafting their statutes or did not believe that youthful age was a particularly important mitigating factor. That is an especially interesting question in the case of Oklahoma, because this state was the focus of

TABLE 3–4. Death Penalty Jurisdictions with Age of Offender as Mitigating Factor[a]

Arizona, Florida, Maryland, Pennsylvania, South Carolina, Washington, Wyoming

[a]See chapter two note 70 for citations to statutes.

attention in the leading case on this issue, *Eddings v. Oklahoma*.[23] Since the *Eddings* decision, Oklahoma has sentenced a juvenile even younger than Eddings to death: Wayne Thompson, who was only fifteen years old at the time of his capital crime.[24]

MINIMUM AGES ACROSS ALL STATUTORY CATEGORIES

Twenty-six of the thirty-six death penalty states thus have established, by whatever means, a minimum age of the offender for determining eligibility for the death penalty, while no minimum age whatsoever is established in ten of these states (table 3–5).

Of the states that do establish a minimum age, ten use age eighteen directly in their death penalty statutes. Seven states have established age fourteen as the minimum as a result of their juvenile court waiver statutes or through their exclusive or concurrent jurisdiction provisions. While that operates to establish a minimum age for the death penalty, it is more precisely a minimum age for criminal court jurisdiction in general; it would appear that these seven states

TABLE 3–5. Minimum Offender Age for Death Penalty (36 Jurisdictions)

Age at Offense	Jurisdiction
10	Indiana
12	Montana
13	Mississippi
14	Alabama, Arkansas, Idaho, Kentucky, Missouri, North Carolina, Utah
15	Louisiana, Virginia
16	Nevada
17	Georgia, New Hampshire, Texas
18	California, Colorado, Connecticut, Illinois, Nebraska, New Jersey, New Mexico, Ohio, Oregon, Tennessee
No minimum	Arizona, Delaware, Florida, Maryland, Oklahoma, Pennsylvania, South Carolina, South Dakota, Washington, Wyoming

gave no specific consideration to the narrower issue of a minimum age for the death penalty. The rest of these twenty-six states have minimum ages ranging from ten to seventeen. Of course, all states that have death penalty statutes must allow youthfulness of the offender to be considered as a mitigating factor.[25]

THE CASES

Case law in these fifty-one jurisdictions has developed in a fairly inconsistent fashion. In this analysis these jurisdictions are arrayed according to the date of their decision on the death penalty for juveniles—before or after the 1982 *Eddings* case. If their decision came after *Eddings*, they are listed according to their interpretation of and reliance on *Eddings*—and here in particular the wide variation in the cases is quite surprising.

CASES BEFORE *EDDINGS*

Before the Supreme Court handed down its decision in *Eddings,* several state supreme courts addressed the issue of severe criminal punishments for juveniles. A case often cited is *Workman v. Commonwealth,*[26] in which a fourteen-year-old boy was sentenced to life in prison without possibility of parole for the crime of rape. The Kentucky Supreme Court found such severe punishment to be cruel and unusual under the Kentucky constitution when applied to a juvenile.[27]

Other state cases have dealt directly with the death penalty for juveniles. *State v. Stewart*[28] was a Nebraska case decided under the then-new Nebraska statute that made the age of the offender one of several mitigating factors to be considered. The court interpreted the statutory provision to apply to a sixteen-year-old offender and, in combination with the absence of any significant criminal record, to "mitigate strongly against the imposition of the death penalty."[29] The Nebraska Supreme Court reduced the juvenile's sentence from death to life imprisonment.

Lewis v. State[30] dealt with a sixteen-year-old Georgia offender sentenced to death for murdering a police officer in the course of a robbery. This case arose before Georgia amended its statute to prohibit the death penalty for crimes committed while under age seventeen.[31] The case was reversed on a juror-selection issue but is important in this analysis for the comments found in a concurring opinion. Noting that only one sixteen-year-old had been sentenced to death under Georgia's 1973 statute (in a case that had been reversed for jury instruction errors), the concurring justice opined that "the death penalty has been so rarely imposed upon persons under seventeen as to make the death sentence in this case excessive and disproportionate and hence unconstitutional."[32] Soon thereafter the Georgia legislature amended the death penalty statute.

The final pre-*Eddings* case that should be mentioned is *People v. Davis.*[33] Like *Workman*, the *Davis* case concluded that life imprisonment without possibility of parole should not be imposed for crimes committed while under age eighteen. The California court in *Davis* had to read this exclusion for juveniles into a fairly vague statute and opted, as did the Kentucky court in *Workman*, to prohibit such a harsh criminal sanction for juveniles. These four pre-*Eddings* cases are only selected examples of many cases decided along similar lines.[34]

IMPACT OF *EDDINGS*

Eddings v. Oklahoma[35] was decided by the United States Supreme Court on January 19, 1982, and has been relied on by many lower courts since then. As discussed earlier, the Court reaffirmed that the youthfulness of the offender is a mitigating factor of great weight that must be considered, but it avoided any direct holding on the constitutionality of the death penalty for juveniles.[36] Several lower courts have nonetheless read more into the *Eddings* holding than seems reasonable.

Eddings *Interpreted as Holding No Constitutional Bar*. Cases such as *High v. Zant*[37] and *State v. Battle*[38] have cited *Eddings* as having held that the death penalty for juveniles is not per se cruel and unusual punishment in violation of the eighth amendment. This proposition, however, is precisely the one that was presented to and avoided by the Supreme Court in *Eddings,* much to the dissatisfaction of Chief Justice Burger in writing his dissent.[39] The state courts in such cases as *High* and *Battle* may have been assuming that a holding that the youthfulness of the offender is a mitigating factor of great weight carries with it an inherent premise that the death penalty for such youthful offenders is not per se a violation of the eighth amendment. But no reasonably objective reading of *Eddings* can permit such an assumption, particularly in light of Justice O'Connor's observation in her concurring opinion: "I, however, do not read the Court's opinion . . . as deciding the issue of whether the Constitution permits imposition of the death penalty on an individual who committed a murder at age 16."[40]

Lower Court Cases Holding No Constitutional Bar. Most lower courts have agreed that *Eddings* did not settle the constitutionality issue, but some then have gone on to decide the issue themselves. Two illustrative cases are *Prejean v. Blackburn*[41] and *Trimble v. State*.[42] The *Prejean* court interpreted the eighth amendment to focus on the kind of punishment and not the characteristics of the offender so long as the punishment is not the result of bias or prejudice. Thus the constitutionality claim of Dalton Prejean, age seventeen at the time of his crime, was found to be "without merit."[43]

In *Trimble* the offender was seventeen years and eight months old at the time he brutally kidnapped, raped, and killed the victim.[44] He appealed his death sentence to the Maryland Supreme Court, claiming among other issues that the U.S. Constitution prohibited the death penalty for crimes committed while under age eighteen.[45] The Maryland court noted that *Eddings* left this question open but that the issue could be resolved by reference to other U.S. Supreme Court cases on the constitutionality of the death penalty in general.[46]

The *Trimble* court's analysis of other lower court cases led it to observe that no other court had found a constitutional bar to the death penalty for juveniles.[47] The *Trimble* court concluded that indicators of society's evolving standards of decency did not reject this punishment for Trimble because it was authorized by the Maryland legislature as one of "29 states [that] permit the execution of juveniles in some circumstances."[48] This strong legislative endorsement outweighed the apparent jury reluctance to sentence juveniles to death, the prohibition of this punishment by most countries of the world, and the significant body of scholarly thought that rejects the death penalty for juveniles.[49]

The *Trimble* court also concluded that the penological goals of retribution and deterrence would be served by execution of juveniles and that this sentence therefore was not excessive or disproportionate. It held that the eighth amendment did not prohibit execution of Trimble but said it would take a case-by-case approach to future cases challenging the death penalty for juveniles.[50]

Lower Court Cases Leaving the Constitutional Issue Undecided. A third approach to *Eddings* is exemplified by such cases as *Cannaday v. State.*[51] In *Cannaday*, the Mississippi Supreme Court, noting that the U.S. Supreme Court had not found the death penalty for juveniles to be unconstitutional, left the matter there without attempting its own eighth amendment analysis. The court reversed Attina Cannaday's death sentence on other grounds but expressly excluded the eighth amendment as a basis for that reversal.[52] The *Cannaday* approach is supported by such cases as *Ice v. Commonwealth*[53] and *Tokman v. State.*[54]

The *Tokman* opinions are particularly revealing in that they suggest considerable reluctance by the Mississippi Supreme Court to allow the death penalty for juveniles. The majority opinion found no constitutional grounds for prohibiting the death penalty for this seventeen-year-old, but a dissenting judge observed: "I find it deeply disturbing that the life of a youth should be taken in punishment for his crime, the justification for it being that it is the law of this state which dictates the result if due process is afforded."[55] The dissenting judge would have gone further, believing that the defendant's youth and background provided the basis for reversing the death sentence and imposing a sentence of life imprisonment.[56]

Youth as a Compelling Mitigating Factor. A final group of state court cases placed strong emphasis on the great mitigating weight to be given the defendant's youth, as required by the *Eddings* case, and then found it to be so compelling that the death sentence had to be reversed. *State v. Valencia*[57] is a leading example of this group of cases. The offender was only sixteen when the murder was committed but was sentenced to death by the trial court three times in succession despite intervening sentence reversals by the appellate courts.[58] The Arizona Supreme Court finally set aside the death penalty and ordered that Valencia be sentenced to life imprisonment.[59]

The *Valencia* court did not rule out capital punishment for all juveniles but concluded that the age of the offender was "a substantial and relevant factor which must be given great weight."[60] The clear impression from the case is that only the most extraordinary facts would justify the death penalty for a juvenile.

This concept is further exemplified by the dissent in *Magill v. State.*[61] In this case, Florida, the state with the largest death row population in the nation,[62] decided to uphold the death sentence for seventeen-year-old Magill, the only juvenile on the state's death row. The rarity and the disconcerting effect of this decision were evident in the dissent:

> Appellant's age should have been given greater weight in mitigation. . . . This court has thus far vacated the death sentence of every defendant who has been under the age of eighteen. . . . That is not to suggest that the death penalty should never be imposed on a minor. However, because of society's great concern for its juveniles, great significance should be attached to the fact that a person accused of a capital felony is a minor, especially a minor who is unemancipated.[63]

Another case in line with the *Valencia* decision and the *Magill* dissent is *Harvey v. State*.[64] The *Harvey* court also gave great weight to the offender's youthful age and, on the basis of this and other mitigating factors, found the death sentence disproportionate in this case. Still other courts have given great weight to the youth of the offender.[65]

The lower court decisions, then, have gone in at least four directions. Some have erroneously assumed that *Eddings* decided the constitutional issue of the death penalty for juveniles. Others have agreed that *Eddings* left this question undecided and then went on to decide the issue themselves, to the detriment of the young offenders before them. Still others have relegated the matter totally to their legislatures, finding no restrictions from *Eddings* or any other source. And some have focused on the *Eddings* observation that youthfulness of the offender is to be given great weight as a mitigating factor and then have usually gone on to find this great weight to be a compelling reason in the case before them to reduce the juvenile's sentence from death to a lesser penalty.

CONCLUSIONS

From this variety of approaches taken by the thirty-six death penalty jurisdictions, it is difficult to get a clear understanding of the state laws on the death penalty for juveniles. Some general conclusions nevertheless can be outlined that may be of some assistance.

Few states have statutes permitting the death penalty regardless of age. Of the fifty-two jurisdictions considered (fifty states, the District of Columbia, and the federal government), forty-two (81 percent) prohibit the death penalty either for all persons or for juveniles under a certain age. Sixteen do it by excluding all death penalties; fourteen by fixing a minimum age in their death penalty statutes; and twelve by setting up minimum ages for criminal court jurisdiction. Of the ten jurisdictions that do not flatly prohibit the death penalty for juveniles under a certain age, seven nonetheless have expressly designated the age of the offender as an important factor to be considered in mitigation of the death penalty. The three remaining jurisdictions that have neither prohibited the death penalty for juveniles nor expressly noted the significance of age in their death penalty proceedings are still required by major Supreme Court holdings to consider youthful age as a mitigating factor of great weight.[66]

State court interpretations of these statutory schemes have varied, but some pervasive themes have emerged. First, throughout Anglo-American legal history the youthfulness of an offender has always been considered in mitigation of the punishments authorized for law violations. Second, while a few state courts have erroneously inferred that *Eddings* held no constitutional bar to juvenile death penalties, most have concluded that the Supreme Court did not decide this issue but simply noted that youthfulness must be included as a mitigating factor of great weight. The courts have then gone on to see if the trial courts have indeed given such weight to the age of the offender. Finally, no court that has addressed the issue squarely has found a state or federal constitutional bar to the death penalty for juveniles. Many have struck down juvenile death penalties in specific cases as unwarranted but have limited their action to those individual cases. An extraordinary number of trial and appellate judges have expressed a personal repugnance to juvenile death penalties but most have not been willing to substitute their personal philosophies for that of the sentencing judge and jury.

Indications of a trend seem to be appearing. More and more state legislatures, trial courts, and appellate courts are excluding juveniles from the death penalty. Specific provisions are appearing in statutes recently amended by legislatures. Trial courts, even when they are authorized to sentence juveniles to death, are very rarely doing so. Appellate courts are finding a variety of reasons to reduce the death penalties of juveniles without imposing a blanket prohibition on all such sentences. State law seems to be moving, however gradually, away from the death penalty for juveniles.

PART II

The Executions

Juvenile Executions, 1642 to 1986

At least 15,000 legal, nonmilitary executions have occurred in the United States since colonial times.[1] Executions for crimes committed while under age eighteen have accounted for only 281, or 2 percent of the total. These 281 executions occurred from 1642 through 1986 for a variety of crimes and in a variety of jurisdictions. The appendix gives a complete inventory of the 281 cases.

This chapter presents a broad overview and explores the known factual information concerning these 281 executions. Chapters five and six provide detailed case studies of several noteworthy cases, and chapter seven gives an in-depth analysis of a typical state's experience with executions of juveniles.

GENERAL CHARACTERISTICS

The first satisfactorily documented juvenile execution occurred in 1642, when Thomas Graunger was executed in Roxbury, Massachusetts, for bestiality.[2] Graunger apparently was sixteen years old at the time of his crime and execution. His capital crime was that he had sodomized a horse and a cow. The most recent execution (as of November 1, 1986) for a crime committed while under age eighteen occurred on May 15, 1986,[3] when Texas executed Jay Kelly Pinkerton for a murder he committed at age seventeen.[4] In the 344 years between the Graunger and Pinkerton executions 279 other persons were executed for crimes committed while under age eighteen. These executions have been categorized by the period in which they occurred (table 4–1).

The low figures for juvenile executions in the seventeenth and eighteenth centuries are suspect. While general population and total capital crime levels were much lower then than now, the strikingly lower number of known lawful executions is probably a result of poor record keeping, difficulty in documenting such old cases today, and the fact that many death penalties before 1900 were illegal executions by lynching.[5] During the nineteenth century the number of juvenile executions per decade increased steadily and totaled eighty-four for the century.

Executions of both juveniles and adults reached maximum frequency in the twentieth century. The number of juvenile executions per decade increased steadily to an all-time high of fifty-three in the 1940s but then dropped off dramatically. Juvenile executions ended temporarily in 1964 and did not resume until 1985.[6]

TABLE 4–1. Total Executions and Juvenile Executions by Period

Period	Total Executions[a]	Juvenile Executions	
1642–1699	Unknown	2	
1700–1799	Unknown	5	
1800–1809	Unknown	0	
1810–1819	Unknown	2	
1820–1829	Unknown	2	
1830–1839	Unknown	3	
1840–1849	Unknown	4	
1850–1859	Unknown	6	
1860–1869	Unknown	12	
1870–1879	Unknown	15	
1880–1889	Unknown	20	
1890–1899	1,215	20	(1.65)
1900–1909	1,192	23	(1.93)
1910–1919	1,039	24	(2.31)
1920–1929	1,169	27	(2.31)
1930–1939	1,670	41	(2.46)
1940–1949	1,288	53	(4.11)
1950–1959	716	16	(2.23)
1960–1969	191	3	(1.57)
1970–1979	3	0	(0.00)
1980–11–1–86	63	3	(4.76)
Total	8,546	281	

Note: Figures in parentheses are percentages.
[a]Source of data: W. BOWERS, LEGAL HOMICIDE 54 (1984) and NAACP LEGAL DE-
FENSE AND EDUCATIONAL FUND, INC., DEATH ROW, U.S.A. 4–5 (Oct. 1, 1986).

Table 4–1 also includes data for all executions regardless of the age of the offender, beginning with the 1890s. The number per decade remained fairly constant until the 1930s, when executions reached their peak. They then declined rapidly, particularly after the 1940s, and ended temporarily in 1967. They resumed in 1977 with Utah's execution of Gary Gilmore and in the mid-1980s averaged about twenty per year.

The percentage of total executions constituted by juvenile executions, also shown in table 4–1, rose steadily from the 1890s. It more than doubled by the 1940s, to a peak of 4.11 percent. It then fell rapidly to zero in the 1970s. The percentage of 4.76 for the 1980s (as of November 1, 1986) is probably a temporary aberration.

It appears that as Americans became more and more willing to execute persons for their crimes they became even more willing to execute juveniles. These data also suggest that American willingness to execute juveniles for their crimes has fallen off markedly since the 1940s to a very low level.[7]

AGE OF OFFENDERS

All 281 of these executions were of offenders who were under age eighteen at the time of their crimes. The range of ages is somewhat surprising, from a few days before the eighteenth birthday down to age ten (table 4–2).

Two cases have been identified of executions for crimes committed at age ten. One is a poorly documented Louisiana execution in September 1855 of a ten-year-old child. The other is a relatively well-documented case of the 1885 execution of James Arcene by federal authorities in Arkansas. Although Arcene was only ten years old when he robbed and murdered his victim, he escaped and avoided arrest for many years, reaching age twenty-three before being executed.[8]

As table 4–2 shows, well over half these 281 offenders were age seventeen at the time of their crimes. Eighty-two percent were ages sixteen or seventeen. Executions of persons under age fourteen at the time of their crimes have been quite rare, with only twelve cases documented out of 15,000 executions in American history. Only one such case occurred in this century.[9] In fact, during this century 90 percent of all juvenile executions were for crimes committed at age sixteen or seventeen. Executions of younger juveniles were much more common before 1900.

Delving beneath this overview of the general age range of executed offenders might promise to reveal distinct patterns according to the race of the offender and the offense involved. But a breakdown of the age data into these two categories seems not to fulfill this promise (table 4–3).

When age of offender is considered within major categories of race of offender, no distinct pattern emerges. The average age at the time of the crime

TABLE 4–2. Juvenile Executions by Age of Offender

Age at Offense	1642–1899		1900—11-1–86		Total	
10	2	(2)	0	(0)	2	(1)
11	1	(1)	0	(0)	1	(0)
12	5	(6)	0	(0)	5	(2)
13	3	(3)	1	(1)	4	(1)
14	6	(7)	5	(3)	11	(4)
15	13	(15)	15	(8)	28	(10)
16	25	(28)	50	(26)	75	(27)
17	34	(38)	119	(63)	153	(55)
Total	89	(100)	190	(100)	279	(100)
Age unknown	2		0		2	
Grand total	91		190		281	

Note: Figures in parentheses are percentages.

TABLE 4–3. Juvenile Executions by Age, Race, and Offense

Age at Offense	Race of Offender				Offense			
	Black	White	Other/ Unknown	Total	Murder	Rape	Other/ Unknown	Total
10	0	0	2	2	1	0	1	2
11	1	0	0	1	1	0	0	1
12	3	0	2	5	5	0	0	5
13	3	1	0	4	1	2	1	4
14	9	2	0	11	9	2	0	11
15	19	5	4	28	24	3	1	28
16	48	21	8	75	60	13	2	75
17	100	39	14	153	123	23	7	153
Total	183	68	28	279	224	43	12	279
Age Unknown	2	0	0	2	2	0	0	2
Grand total	185	68	28	281	226	43	12	281
Average age	16.2	16.4	15.7	16.2	16.2	16.2	15.8	16.2

for black offenders was 16.2 years and for white offenders was 16.4 years. (The third category, other race or unknown race, can be ignored.) For age of offender within the major crime categories of murder and rape, again no distinct age pattern emerges. The average age is essentially the same, 16.2 years.

Under English and American law, age fourteen has traditionally been an important line for presuming criminal capabilities. While persons under seven are conclusively presumed to be incapable of entertaining criminal intent, this presumption of incapacity is rebuttable for children seven to fourteen.[10] For offenders fourteen or older, the law presumes they have adult capabilities for entertaining criminal intent. Thus the infancy defense applies only to offenders under fourteen.

Table 4–3 also provides data for the twelve offenders executed for crimes committed while under age fourteen. Only one was white. Seven were black, two were American Indian, and the race of two is unknown. Thus only 10 percent of offenders under age fourteen were white, while (as the data in table 4–5 will show) about 25 percent of offenders age fourteen to eighteen were white. The youngest white juvenile ever executed was thirteen, whereas the age range falls to eleven for blacks and ten for American Indians. This apparent racial pattern is explored in more detail in the next section of this chapter.

Of the 281 executed juveniles, only nine were female (table 4–4). The earliest such case that could be documented occurred in 1786 and the latest in 1912. Two juvenile females are under a sentence of death at this writing and are appealing their cases.[11]

While the number of cases is too small for sophisticated analysis, the average age for the executed female juveniles was 15.1 years, compared with 16.2 for the male juveniles. Eight states have executed female juveniles, ranging geographically from South Carolina (two executions) to Connecticut and from Missouri to New Jersey. All executed females were black except one American Indian; no white female has ever been executed for a crime committed while under age eighteen. Eight of the nine crimes were murders of white victims; three-fourths of the victims were children. One crime was theft in which the victim was a white man.

RACE OF OFFENDER

An overview of these 281 executions arrayed according to the race of the offender shows a heavy racial imbalance (table 4–5). Executed white juveniles comprise only one-fourth of executed juveniles whose race is known.

Blacks constitute the overwhelming majority of these offenders, 69 percent. And the proportion is not attributable to an eighteenth and nineteenth

TABLE 4–4. Female Juvenile Executions

Name	Date	State	Age	Race	Offense	Victim
Ocuish, Hannah	12–10–1786	Conn.	12	Amer. Indian	Murder	WF6
Mary	9–30–1838	Mo.	16	B	Murder	W child
Keen, Rosan	4–26–1844	N.J.	16	B	Murder	WM adult
Spain, Amy	3–10–1865	S.C.	17	B	Theft	WM adult
Eliza	2–7–1868	Ky.	12	B	Murder	W girl
Wallis, Mary	2–10–1871	Md.	16	B	Murder	W child
Shipp, Caroline	1–22–1892	N.C.	17/18	B	Murder	B child
Brown, Milbry	10–7–1892	S.C.	14	B	Murder	W child 1
Christian, Virginia	8–16–1912	Va.	16	B	Murder	WF60
		Average age 15.1				

TABLE 4–5. Juvenile Executions by Race of Offender

Race	1642–1899		1900—11–1–86		Total	
Black	47	(54)	138	(75)	185	(69)
White	31	(36)	37	(20)	68	(25)
Other						
Chinese	0	(0)	3	(2)	3	(1)
American Indian	7	(8)	1	(1)	8	(3)
Mexican-American	2	(2)	4	(2)	6	(2)
Total	87	(100)	183	(100)	270	(100)
Unknown	4		7		11	
Grand Total	91		190		281	

Note: Figures in parentheses are percentages.

century practice of executing slaves and poor blacks. The percentage of blacks rose dramatically from 54 before 1900 to 75 after 1900, while the percentage of whites fell from 36 to 20. The other races involved seem insignificant in number and unremarkable. For example, seven of the eight American Indians were executed before 1900, when members of this race generally had fewer legal rights and suffered more injustices than they have in this century. Suggestions that there have been comparable improvements in social and legal justice for blacks are called into question by the rapidly rising percentages for blacks.

In analyzing the race of offender factor according to the type of offense committed, murder and rape—which together comprise 95 percent of the offenses—are the only crimes considered separately (table 4–6). This analysis shows race to be quite important within these two categories.

Most obvious is that all forty-three rape cases resulting in executions of juveniles involved black offenders. No juvenile offender of any race other than black has ever been executed for rape. (Table 4–8 provides further information about executions for rapes by juveniles.)

Black juveniles were executed for murder in 74 percent of their cases and for rape in 23 percent. Almost all white juveniles executed had committed murder (93 percent). The only known exceptions were two arsonists and two sodomists in early Massachusetts and a Confederate spy in Arkansas.[12]

Research concerning all executions of offenders of all ages has found that 96.5 percent of the white executed offenders had committed murder and 2.2 percent had committed rape.[13] Of the nonwhites, 80.7 percent had committed murder and 17.9 percent had committed rape. Thus these data show that the race of the executed offender has a similar impact for juvenile offenders and for all offenders.

While the race of the offender is of major interest, the race of the victim, too, has always had an impact in death penalty cases and is an issue of importance in death penalty law at present.[14] A breakdown in terms of the race of the victim in the 220 juvenile cases in which this factor could be determined reveals that in striking contrast to the fact that 69 percent of the executed offenders were

TABLE 4–6. Juvenile Executions by Race of Offender and Offense

Race	Offense						Total	
	Murder		Rape		Other/Unknown			
Black	136	(74)	43	(23)	6	(3)	185	(100)
White	63	(93)	0	(0)	5	(7)	68	(100)
Other	17	(100)	0	(0)	0	(0)	17	(100)
Unknown	10	(91)	0	(0)	1	(9)	11	(100)
Total	226	(80)	43	(15)	12	(5)	281	(100)

Note: Figures in parentheses are percentages.

black, only 9 percent of the victims were black (table 4–7). And since 1900 only 4 percent of the victims have been black. Overwhelmingly, the victims have been white—89 percent overall and 93 percent since 1900. In ninety instances the race of the victims could not be determined with satisfactory reliability, but it seemed reasonable to assume that most of them were also white. Thus the 89 percent figure for white victims is somewhat conservative.

An analysis of executions for rape by state shows that twelve states, all in the South, have executed juveniles for this crime (table 4–8). These states form a block, beginning with Maryland, sweeping down the East Coast and a bit inland, and continuing along the Gulf westward to Texas, leaving out only Mississippi.

Of the forty-three rape cases ending in juvenile executions, all but one involved black offenders who raped white victims. Georgia is by far the leader in this practice, having executed eleven such rapists. Nevertheless, only 27 percent (eleven of forty-one) of Georgia's juvenile executions have been for rape. Kentucky has executed only eleven juveniles, but five (45 percent) have

TABLE 4–7. Juvenile Executions by Race of Victim[a]

Race		1642–1899		1900—11–1–86		Total	
Black		13	(17)	6	(4)	19	(9)
White		64	(82)	132	(93)	196	(89)
Other							
Chinese		0	(0)	4	(3)	4	(2)
American Indian		1	(1)	0	(0)	1	(0)
		78	(100)	142	(100)	220	(100)
	Unknown	20		70		90	
		98		212		310	

Note: Figures in parentheses are percentages.
[a]Excluding five juvenile executions for crimes without human victims (arson, bestiality, and spying).

TABLE 4–8. Juvenile Executions for Rape by State

State	Executions	State	Executions
Georgia	11	Virginia	4
Kentucky	5	South Carolina	2
North Carolina	5	Arkansas	1
Alabama	4	Louisiana	1
Florida	4	Maryland	1
Texas	4	Tennessee	1
		Total	43

been for rape. At the other end of the scale, Tennessee also has executed eleven juveniles, but only one (9 percent) for rape.

Data in the appendix reveal that a high proportion of the rape victims were children. About one-third were girls under age eighteen; three were age eight, one seven, two six, and one four.

OFFENSE LEADING TO EXECUTION

As shown in table 4–6, 80 percent of these juvenile executions were for murder and 15 percent for rape. An analysis of these data along with data for all other juvenile capital crimes according to the period in which the executions occurred shows that the rape cases tend to be a modern phenomenon, with about 84 percent (thirty-six of forty-three) occurring since 1900 (table 4–9).

While murder cases constitute 81 percent of the cases in which the offense is known, the data categorization technique used in table 4–9 obscures other important information. Of the 226 murder cases, nineteen were instances of rape or attempted rape in which the offender also killed his victim. Thus cases involving sexual assault actually total sixty-four, or 23 percent of the 280 cases for which the crime is known (forty-three rapes, two attempted rapes, and nineteen rape/murders). Thirty-five percent of the murder cases (eighty of 226) involved a robbery or burglary that resulted in a murder.

The other crimes are few in number but surprising. Perhaps one's view is clouded by a 1980s perspective that sanctions the death penalty only for the worst forms of murder. At any rate, it seems odd that juveniles have been executed for such crimes as arson, assault and battery, attempted rape, bestiality, and robbery—none of which resulted in the taking of a human life or, in some of the cases, even any injury to any human being.

Considering all crimes and all 275 victims for whom the sex is known, 43 percent were female and 57 percent were male (table 4–10). All the victims of

TABLE 4–9. Juvenile Executions by Offense

Offense	1642–1899		1900—11–1–86		Total	
Arson	2	(2)	0	(0)	2	(1)
Assault & Battery	1	(1)	0	(0)	1	(0)
Attempted Rape	0	(0)	2	(1)	2	(1)
Bestiality	2	(2)	0	(0)	2	(1)
Murder	76	(84)	150	(79)	226	(81)
Rape	7	(8)	36	(19)	43	(15)
Robbery/Theft	1	(1)	2	(1)	3	(1)
Spying	1	(1)	0	(0)	1	(0)
Total	90	(100)	190	(100)	280	(100)
Unknown	1		0		1	
Grand total	91		190		281	

Note: Figures in parentheses are percentages.

the forty-three rape cases were female. The proportion of female victims overall has increased from 36 percent before 1900 to 46 percent since then.

EXECUTIONS BY STATE AND REGION

Thirty-six jurisdictions have executed persons for crimes committed while under age eighteen, including thirty-five states and the federal government (table 4–11).

TABLE 4–10. Juvenile Executions by Sex of Victim[a]

Sex	1642–1899		1900—11–1–86		Total	
Male	56	(64)	102	(54)	158	(57)
Female	31	(36)	86	(46)	117	(43)
Total	87	(100)	188	(100)	275	(100)
Unknown	11		24		35	
Grand total	98		212		310	

Note: Figures in Parentheses are percentages.
[a]Excluding five juvenile executions for crimes without human victims (arson, bestiality, and spying).

TABLE 4–11. Number of Total Juvenile Executions by Jurisdiction

Jurisdiction	Executions	Jurisdiction	Executions
Georgia	41	Missouri	6
North Carolina	19	New Jersey	5
Ohio	19	Pennsylvania	5
New York	18	Connecticut	3
Texas	18	Indiana	3
Virginia	18	Nevada	3
Florida	12	Washington	3
Alabama	11	Arizona	2
Kentucky	11	Delaware	2
South Carolina	11	Minnesota	2
Tenneseee	11	Illinois	1
Louisiana	9	Iowa	1
Federal	8	Montana	1
Massachusetts	8	New Mexico	1
Maryland	7	Oregon	1
Arkansas	6	Utah	1
California	6	Vermont	1
Mississippi	6	West Virginia	1
		Total	281

Georgia is by far the leader with forty-one juvenile executions—more than double the number executed by its nearest competitors. The second tier of states with a considerable number of juvenile executions includes not only the southern states of North Carolina, Texas, and Virginia but also the northeastern industrial states of New York and Ohio. Florida and Texas, the leaders in executions overall in the 1980s, are not among the leaders in juvenile executions throughout American history.

The heaviest concentrations are obviously in the more populous and older states east of the Mississippi River and particularly along the Eastern Seaboard. The Deep South states, except for Louisana, are consistently heavy, but so are such northeastern states as Massachusetts, New York, and Ohio. Many central and western states, from North Dakota down to Oklahoma and back up to Idaho, have never executed any juveniles. The only western state with many such executions is California, and its six are still only 1 percent of its total of 500 executions in the past 100 years.[15]

Of the four national census regions, the South accounts for 65 percent of the total juvenile executions, or 183 of 281 (table 4–12). Almost two-thirds of these executions were in the South Atlantic division of the Southern region. The Western region accounts for only 6 percent (18), and the two Northern regions fill in the remainder, with 14 percent in the Northeast and 11 percent in the North Central states. Federal jurisdictions account for 3 percent (8) but have not executed any juveniles for more than a century.

Table 4–12 also provides a regional analysis according to race of offender and offense. More than half the offenders in the Northeast, North Central, and West regions were white, but only 7 percent in the South. Juveniles executed in the South were black in 91 percent of the cases.

As already mentioned, all forty-three rape cases were in the South. The North Central and the West regions have executed juveniles only for murder, while the Northeast has a few old executions for arson and bestiality.

A state-by-state breakdown of the Northeast region by race of offender and offense shows that Massachusetts, most of whose cases are quite old, is the leader. It has the two arson and the two bestiality cases. The Mid-Atlantic division has only three states, but they tend to be heavy on the death penalty: New Jersey, New York, and Pennsylvania. New Jersey stands out; 80 percent of its executed offenders (four of five) were black. In Pennsylvania, on the other hand, all executed juveniles were white, not counting one for whom the race is unknown. All the offenses in all the Northeast states were murder, except for the old Massachusetts cases. The six states in the New England division have had few juvenile executions; three had none at all.

In the North Central region Ohio is clearly the leader, having over three times as many juvenile executions as its nearest competitor (table 4–14).[16] One-third of the Ohio executions were of black offenders—the general pattern throughout the region. Missouri is somewhat of an anomaly, in that 75 percent of its executions (three of four) were of black offenders. Exactly half (six of twelve) of the states in this region have never executed any juveniles.

TABLE 4-12. Juvenile Executions by Region, Race of Offender, and Offense

Region and Division	Race				Offense				Total
	Black	White	Other	Unknown	Murder	Rape	Other	Unknown	
Northeast									
New England	1	9	2	0	8	0	4	0	12 (4)
Mid-Atlantic	9	16	2	1	28	0	0	0	28 (10)
Total	10 (26)	25 (64)	4 (10)	1 (0)	36 (90)	0 (0)	4 (10)	0 (0)	40 (100) (14)
North Central									
East North Central	8	14	1	0	23	0	0	0	23 (8)
West North Central	3	4	0	2	9	0	0	0	9 (3)
Total	11 (37)	18 (60)	1 (3)	2 (0)	32 (100)	0 (0)	0 (0)	0 (0)	32 (100) (11)
South									
South Atlantic	104	5	0	2	79	27	5	0	111 (40)
East South Central	34	4	0	1	29	10	0	0	39 (14)
West South Central	24	4	3	2	25	6	1	1	33 (12)
Total	162 (91)	13 (7)	3 (2)	5 (0)	133 (73)	43 (24)	6 (3)	1 (0)	183 (100) (65)
West									
Mountain	0	4	3	1	8	0	0	0	8 (3)
Pacific	0	5	3	2	10	0	0	1	10 (4)
Total	0 (0)	9 (60)	6 (40)	3 (0)	18 (100)	0 (0)	0 (0)	0 (0)	18 (100) (6)
Federal (all jurisdictions)									
Total	0 (0)	5 (68)	3 (32)	0 (0)	7 (88)	0 (0)	1 (12)	0 (0)	8 (100) (3)
Nationwide									
Total	183 (68)	70 (26)	17 (6)	11 (0)	226 (81)	43 (15)	11 (4)	1 (0)	281 (100) (100)

Note: Figures parentheses are percentages.

TABLE 4-13. Northeastern Region Juvenile Executions by Race of Offender and Offense

Division and State	Race				Offense				Totals
	Black	White	Other	Unknown	Murder	Rape	Other	Unknown	
New England									
Connecticut	0	2	1	0	3	0	0	0	3
Maine	0	0	0	0	0	0	0	0	0
Massachusetts	1	6	1	0	4	0	4	0	8
New Hampshire	0	0	0	0	0	0	0	0	0
Rhode Island	0	0	0	0	0	0	0	0	0
Vermont	0	1	0	0	1	0	0	0	1
Total	1	9	2	0	8	0	4	0	12
Mid-Atlantic									
New Jersey	4	1	0	0	5	0	0	0	5
New York	5	11	2	0	18	0	0	0	18
Pennsylvania	0	4	0	1	5	0	0	0	5
Total	9	16	2	1	28	0	0	0	28
Region Total	10	25	4	1	36	0	4	0	40

TABLE 4-14. North Central Region Juvenile Executions by Race of Offender and Offense

Division and State	Race				Offense				Totals
	Black	White	Other	Unknown	Murder	Rape	Other	Unknown	
East North Central									
Illinois	0	1	0	0	1	0	0	0	1
Indiana	2	1	0	0	3	0	0	0	3
Michigan	0	0	0	0	0	0	0	0	0
Ohio	6	12	1	0	19	0	0	0	19
Wisconsin	0	0	0	0	0	0	0	0	0
Total	8	14	1	0	23	0	0	0	23
West North Central									
Iowa	0	1	0	0	1	0	0	0	1
Kansas	0	0	0	0	0	0	0	0	0
Minnesota	0	2	0	0	2	0	0	0	2
Missouri	3	1	0	2	6	0	0	0	6
Nebraska	0	0	0	0	0	0	0	0	0
North Dakota	0	0	0	0	0	0	0	0	0
South Dakota	0	0	0	0	0	0	0	0	0
Total	3	4	0	2	9	0	0	0	9
Region									
Total	11	18	1	2	32	0	0	0	32

The picture is quite the opposite in the Southern region (table 4–15), which accounts for almost two-thirds of American executions. All jurisdictions in this region except the District of Columbia and Oklahoma have executed juveniles. The South Atlantic division, far ahead of the other two divisions, includes the three leading states: Georgia, North Carolina, and Virginia. Georgia, the clear leader with forty-one juvenile executions, has more than any other entire region. The South Atlantic division also contains Florida and South Carolina, which have twelve and eleven executions respectively.

The East South Central division is fairly well balanced. Alabama, Kentucky, and Tennessee each have eleven executions, almost twice as many as Mississippi. In the West South Central division Texas leads with eighteen executions, despite the fact that since the nineteenth century Texas law has prohibited the death penalty for crimes committed while under age seventeen.[17] Thus almost all these Texas executions were of persons age seventeen at the time of their crimes. In striking contrast, Texas's neighbor Oklahoma has never executed a juvenile.

For race of offender for the Southern region, the data are unequivocal. Ninety-one percent of the offenders (162 of the 178 whose race is known) were black. For the South Atlantic division, 95 percent (104 of 109) were black. Three states in this division—Delaware, Maryland, and Virginia—have never executed any juvenile who was not black. Of Georgia's forty-one, all but two (95 percent) were black. This racial pattern is borne out also in other divisions; in the East South Central division, for example, all of Alabama's juvenile executions were of blacks. In the whole Southern region, only 7 percent of the executed juveniles (thirteen of 178) were white.

The Southern region has executed juveniles for a variety of crimes, but by far the most common are murder (73 percent) and rape (23 percent). The Virginia data are unusual. This state has executed juveniles not only for murder and rape but also for assault and battery, attempted rape, and robbery.[18] These unusual capital crimes constitute 22 percent (four of eighteen) of Virginia's juvenile executions. South Carolina and Texas have also executed juveniles for robbery.

The Western region has had a minimal number of executions of juveniles (table 4–16). Five of the thirteen states in this region have never executed any juveniles, and four have executed only one. California has the most, but even so it has only six, a small sum given the large number of executions of offenders of all ages in this large and populous state.

No black juvenile has ever been executed in any of the thirteen states of the Western region. Of the fifteen cases in which the race of the offender is known, 60 percent (nine of fifteen) were white. Reflecting the ethnic makeup of the Western states, 20 percent (three) were American Indian and 20 percent (three) were Mexican-American. All the executions in these states were for murder.

TABLE 4–15. Southern Region Juvenile Executions by Race of Offender and Offense

Division and State	Race				Offense				Totals
	Black	White	Other	Unknown	Murder	Rape	Other	Unknown	
South Atlantic									
Delaware	2	0	0	0	2	0	0	0	2
District of Columbia	0	0	0	0	0	0	0	0	0
Florida	11	1	0	0	8	4	0	0	12
Georgia	39	2	0	0	30	11	0	0	41
Maryland	7	0	0	0	6	1	0	0	7
North Carolina	17	1	0	1	14	5	0	0	19
South Carolina	10	1	0	0	8	2	1	0	11
Virginia	18	0	0	0	10	4	4	0	18
West Virginia	0	0	0	1	1	0	0	0	1
Total	104	5	0	2	79	27	5	0	111
East South Central									
Alabama	11	0	0	0	7	4	0	0	11
Kentucky	9	2	0	0	6	5	0	0	11
Mississippi	5	0	0	1	6	0	0	0	6
Tennessee	9	2	0	0	10	1	0	0	11
Total	34	4	0	1	29	10	0	0	39
West South Central									
Arkansas	4	1	0	1	5	1	0	0	6
Louisiana	8	0	0	1	7	1	0	1	9
Oklahoma	0	0	0	0	0	0	0	0	0
Texas	12	3	3	0	13	4	1	0	18
Total	24	4	3	2	25	6	1	1	33
Region Total	162	13	3	5	133	43	6	1	183

TABLE 4–16. Western Region Juvenile Executions by Race of Offender and Offense

Division and State	Race				Offense				Total
	Black	White	Other	Unknown	Murder	Rape	Other	Unknown	
Mountain									
Arizona	0	0	2	0	2	0	0	0	2
Colorado	0	0	0	0	0	0	0	0	0
Idaho	0	0	0	0	0	0	0	0	0
Montana	0	1	0	0	1	0	0	0	1
Nevada	0	2	0	1	3	0	0	0	3
New Mexico	0	0	1	0	1	0	0	0	1
Utah	0	1	0	0	1	0	0	0	1
Wyoming	0	0	0	0	0	0	0	0	0
Total	0	4	3	1	8	0	0	0	8
Pacific									
Alaska	0	0	0	0	0	0	0	0	0
California	0	2	2	2	6	0	0	0	6
Hawaii	0	0	0	0	0	0	0	0	0
Oregon	0	1	0	0	1	0	0	0	1
Washington	0	2	1	0	3	0	0	0	3
Total	0	5	3	2	10	0	0	0	10
Region									
Total	0	9	6	3	18	0	0	0	18

CONCLUSIONS

This nation and its colonial antecedents have executed 281 juveniles over the past three and one-half centuries. The practice of juvenile executions, like that of criminal executions in general, peaked in the 1930s and 1940s. Executions of juvenile offenders ended temporarily in 1964 but began again in 1985.

While some persons have been executed for crimes committed as young as age ten, most of the juvenile offenders were age sixteen or seventeen when they committed their crimes; the average age was just over sixteen years. The younger offenders, particularly those under age fourteen, were executed in the greatest numbers before 1900. That is also true of the nine female juveniles executed. The last female juvenile execution was in 1912.

Whites constitute only one-quarter of the executed juveniles and only 20 percent of those executed since 1900. In striking contrast, the victims of these capital crimes were overwhelmingly whites, 89 percent overall and 93 percent since 1900. Eighty-one percent of these executions were for murder and 15 percent for rape. All forty-three rape offenders were black, all but one of their victims were white, and all the states that executed them were southern.

In line with the historical pattern for all executions in this country, the southern states predominate in juvenile executions, with 65 percent of the total. Georgia is the leader, with forty-one juvenile executions. Other leading states are North Carolina, Ohio, New York, Texas, and Virginia. Thirty-five states and the federal government have executed juveniles for their crimes.

This summary of the characteristics of these executed children and their crimes raises more questions than it answers. But perhaps it will at least serve to refute the commonly held belief that the death penalty has always been reserved for our most hardened criminals, the middle-aged three-time losers. While they are often the ones executed, offenders of more tender years, down even to prepubescence, also have been killed lawfully, hanging from our gallows, restrained in our gas chambers, sitting in our electric chairs, and lying on our hospital gurneys.

FIVE

Early Case Studies, 1642 to 1930

The previous chapter provides an overview of the characteristics of all 281 juveniles executed in American history. While the data allow informed presumptions to be made about the kinds of offenders, victims, crimes, and executions involved, they do not reveal intimate details of the offenders' lives, their trials, and their final days. This chapter and the next put a few of the cases under the microscope for closer analysis.

Cases were selected for more detailed analysis because of their uniqueness or their representativeness in regard to such factors as the age of the offender, the kind of crime, the jurisdiction, and the period in which the crime occurred. Included are the first juvenile execution in American history and the last juvenile execution as of this writing. The jurisdictions include federal, state, territorial, and colonial. The locations range from California to New York, Washington to Florida, and Texas to Connecticut. Both boys and girls and blacks, whites, Hispanics, and American Indians are represented. The range of ages is ten to seventeen at time of crime and twelve to twenty-eight at time of execution.

This chapter presents illustrative cases for the early years of American history, from colonial times to the early part of the twentieth century. Chapter six carries on this presentation, beginning in the 1930s and continuing through 1986. The characteristics of the two sets of cases seem determined primarily by the times in which they occurred, but the similarities are striking, particularly the legal principles involved.

An overriding factor in choosing cases for analysis was the availability of sufficient reliable information about the case to provide an adequate basis for the study. For a majority of the 281 juvenile executions only minimal information is available, barely enough to confirm that the subjects were actually executed for crimes committed while under age eighteen. The cases chosen for analysis provided much more detailed information, many including several appellate court opinions and regular press coverage of significant events. Predictably, more detailed information was readily available for the more recent cases in chapter six. The older cases in this chapter presented much more difficult research obstacles.

The information for each case study comes from a variety of sources, differing with each case. The reliability of this information depends on the reliability of the various sources, whether newspaper or magazine articles or appellate court opinions. In most cases it was possible to cross-check key data on ages, dates, and names so that errors and inconsistencies could be found and corrected. Of course, such research and analysis techniques are not fool-proof, and such sources are not error-free. The following case analyses thus are as accurate as these inherent limitations will permit.

THOMAS GRAUNGER; EXECUTED 1642; PLYMOUTH COLONY, MASSACHUSETTS[1]

The hanging of Thomas Graunger was the first known execution on Ameri-can soil for a crime committed while under age eighteen. Graunger was a servant boy in Plymouth Colony, presumably white and of European heritage, and apparently age sixteen. His crime was bestiality—genital copulation with a mare and a cow. His trial centered on Leviticus 20.15: "And if a man lie with a beast, he shall surely be put to death: and ye shall slay the beast."

Graunger's execution was described as a sad spectacle. Before executing the boy the authorities first killed the mare, then the cow, and finally all the young calves. Then, to provide the final and complete compliance with the Bible, Graunger was hanged until he died, still only sixteen years old.

WILLIAM BATTIN; EXECUTED AUGUST 15, 1722; COLONIAL PENNSYLVANIA[2]

The life of William Battin, a white male, began in Wiltshire, England, where he was reasonably well educated and cared for by his parents. Young William fell into a pattern of lying, pickpocketing, and other thieving, causing his parents much concern for his future. He started running away from home in his early teenage years, sometimes staying away for weeks. Then, in the boy's own words: "My father, feeling that there was not any good like to come of me, ordered me to be brought over a servant into this Province of Penn-sylvania."[3]

This dull, ignorant, and socially irresponsible teenager landed in Phila-delphia and became an indentured servant to John Herman, a Chester County farmer. After a few months with Herman, Battin returned to his habits of stealing and running away. Within the year Herman sold Battin to Joseph Pyle of Bethel, Pennsylvania. Battin went to live in the home of Mr. and Mrs. Pyle and their three children, ages six, four, and one. He became a trusted servant and a caretaker for the Pyle children. By this time he had reached age sev-enteen.

One Saturday evening when his master and mistress were visiting neigh-bors, Battin, after putting the three children to bed, took a candle upstairs to the attic to get an apple. Then, perhaps "enslaved by the Devil" as Battin later saw it, he decided to set fire to the house and escape from his indentured servitude. He assumed everyone would believe that he and the three children had died in the fire and no one would come looking for him. But shortly after setting fire to the attic he changed his mind and quenched it with water.

He went back downstairs to sleep by the fireplace but later awoke to find that the attic fire had reignited and was raging through the roof. It was beyond his ability to quench it this time. He quietly calmed the sleepy complaints of the children and left the house with the children secure in their beds. He ran to the neighbor's house to get the Pyles but falsely assured them that their children were safely out of the house. When they and others arrived to fight the fire it was completely out of control. No one was able to save the children and the house was destroyed.

At first Battin concealed the true origin of the fire and his failure to save the children. Finally he confessed his acts and was subsequently convicted of arson and murder, both capital offenses. He was sentenced to die.

As was the custom then and now, persons awaiting execution are counseled to accept religious beliefs. Battin did so shortly before his execution, although there is no indication of any significant religious belief before then. He signed with his mark a written statement transcribed and read for him at the gallows. The statement in part included a message to other children: "I greatly desire all youth may take example by me, and have a care how they disobey their parents, which if I had not done, I should not have been here this day, and brought to this untimely end."[4] He also offered his final prayer to his newfound God: "I yield my body to this shameful and ignominious death this 15th day of August, 1722, being about seventeen years of age, hoping that God will have mercy upon my poor soul. Lord Jesus, receive my spirit."[5]

HANNAH OCUISH;
EXECUTED DECEMBER 20, 1786; CONNECTICUT[6]

The unhappy and brutal life of Hannah Ocuish ended when she was only twelve years and nine months old. She was born in March 1774 in Groton, Connecticut, to a Pequot Indian mother and an unknown white father. The mother's alcoholism and other problems caused her to abandon Ocuish and two older brothers in their early childhood. The Ocuish children became notorious for robbing and harassing local citizens. Ocuish was placed with a New London family by the local selectmen but her mother was unsatisfied with that arrangement, took Ocuish away when she was only six years old, and placed her with a widow who lived just outside New London. Apparently retarded, the pre-pubescent Ocuish was widely known as a "fierce young savage."[7]

On Friday, July 21, 1786, at about 9:00 A.M., Ocuish saw six-year-old Eunice Bolles, who was on her way to school. Bolles, the daughter of a prominent New London family, had complained a few weeks earlier that Ocuish had taken strawberries from her, and Ocuish still bore a grudge. Ocuish lured the young girl into a wooded area by the offer of a piece of calico. There Ocuish pummeled the child with a stone and then strangled her to death. An amateurish attempt to cover the body with stones from a fence to make the death appear accidental was easily seen though later by investigators.

Ocuish was arrested the next day and taken to look at the dead child's body. She burst into tears and confessed, quickly changing her earlier story about seeing four boys in the area of the crime. Her uneasiness soon subsided, and she seemed reasonably content and happy as she awaited her trial the following October.

After pleading not guilty on the advice of counsel, Ocuish seemed unconcerned at her trial. In stark contrast, the presiding judge could barely speak and the spectators could not refrain from tears. The evidence led the judge to conclude: "You have killed, and that in a barbarous and cruel manner, an innocent, helpless and harmless child."[8] Judge Law carefully sifted through the facts of the crime and balanced them against the legal presumption of mental incapacity of a twelve-year-old. His findings were not in the defendant's favor, stating that "all of these circumstances have supplied the want of age, and clearly evinced that you must have been conscious of guilt at the time of doing the facts, and renders you a proper subject of punishment."[9] He delivered his sentence of death on October 12, 1786.

The sentencing judge was keenly aware of the tender age and low mentality of the prisoner. Later observers noted that "The only alleviating circumstances in this case were the extreme ignorance and youth of the criminal. These were forcible arguments but not at that day sufficient weight to reprieve from execution."[10] The judge seemed determined to send a message to other children inclined to echo Ocuish's crimes. His words on this point seemed to presume that children might be deterred by the fate of Ocuish, for he stated that "the sparing of you on account of your age, would, as the law says, be of dangerous consequences to the public, by holding up an idea, that children might commit such atrocious acts with impunity."[11] After advising Ocuish to turn to Jesus Christ for mercy, the judge closed with flowery phraseology:

> Nothing now remains but to pass the painful sentence of this court—which is, That you be returned from hence to the gaol from whence you came, and from thence be carried to the place of execution—and there be hanged with a rope by the neck, between the Heaven and earth, until you are dead, dead, dead and may the Lord, of his infinite goodness and sovereign grace, have mercy on your Soul.[12]

Ocuish spent the next ten weeks in jail awaiting her execution date. She seemed unconcerned about her fate until a visitor to her cell explained what it meant. Suddenly aware, she cried for most of the day. Some serenity reappeared, but she again became distraught a few days before the execution.

Workmen erected a scaffold in the rear of New London's meetinghouse. As seems understandable for a twelve-year-old retarded girl, "At the place of execution she said very little—appeared greatly afraid, and seemed to want somebody to help her."[13] A lengthy sermon was preached by the Reverend Henry Channing of Yale College, who made much of "the tremendous sentence which puts a period to the life of one, who had never learned to live."[14] After the sermon and prayers, Ocuish thanked the sheriff for his kindnesses to her and stepped forward to be hanged until she was "dead, dead, dead."

CLEM; EXECUTED MAY 11, 1787; VIRGINIA[15]

Clem was the second of the three twelve-year-olds executed in American history. He was a black slave owned by Hartwell Seat of Sussex County, Vir-

ginia. Clem's crimes were the murders of his master's two sons, Henry and
Miles Seat. Although a comparatively formal and elaborate criminal process
was followed in Clem's case, it took less than a month to get from crime to
execution.

Early in the day of April 13, 1787, Clem argued with Henry, and Henry
hit Clem with a tobacco stick. Clem nursed his wounds and a grudge against
the white boy throughout the day. At about 4:00 P.M., Henry and Miles began
walking to a neighbor's plantation. Clem followed them on the pretense of
getting some rice seed but with the apparent motive of renewing his row with
Henry.

Clem caught up with the Seat boys and began beating them with a stick.
He knocked Miles unconscious and chased down Henry. After killing Henry
with four blows with the stick, he carried Henry's body to a swamp. Miles
recovered and began accosting Clem, who then killed Miles with the same
stick and dumped both bodies into the swamp. Both victims died of the head
wounds inflicted by Clem's stick.

The bodies of the victims were soon discovered, and the coroner was
notified. The next day the coroner assembled twelve local men and held an
inquest at Hartwell Seat's plantation. The report of this inquest, as well as a
deposition taken of Clem by the coroner, were instrumental in condemning
the twelve-year-old.

Clem was tried, convicted, and sentenced to hang by the Court of Oyer
and Terminer at the Sussex County courthouse. With no chance of appellate
review or other delay, Clem was hanged outside the courthouse. Allowing for
the era's typical lack of specificity of slaves' ages, Clem was apparently only
twelve years old at the time of his crime and execution.

JAMES GUILD; EXECUTED NOVEMBER 28, 1828; NEW JERSEY[16]

James Guild was only twelve years and five and one-half months old at
the time of his crime but lived another fourteen months before being hanged.
Known as Little Jim, he was a black servant of Joshua Bunn in Hopewell,
Hunterdon County, New Jersey. He was variously described as mischievous
or vicious, but observers seemed to agree that "He was a precocious boy, well
developed, illiterate, profane, shrewd in worldly matters, but never had attended Sunday school, and was absolutely lacking in education of his moral or
religious qualities."[17]

Guild's crime was the brutal murder of Mrs. Beaks, a white, sixty-year-
old grandmother. During the day of September 24, 1827, Guild was cutting
corn in Bunn's field directly across from Beaks's home. Sometime in mid-
afternoon, Guild went over to Beaks's to ask her to return a gun her son had
borrowed from Guild's master. She refused his request and verbally abused
him for his presumptuousness in making such a request. Immediately angered,
he grabbed a nearby horse yoke and struck her. He turned to leave but became
concerned that she would report the assault to his master. He then beat her
on the head until she was unconscious and dying.

At about 5:00 P.M., two or three hours after the crime, the victim's grandson returned home and discovered her still alive but bleeding profusely. Despite attempts to help by neighbors and passersby, Beaks died early that evening from her wounds and loss of blood. A coroner's inquest held that evening questioned Guild but he denied any knowledge of the crime.

The next morning Guild was again working in the cornfield across from the crime scene. Strongly suspected by many persons, he was brought over to the Beaks house and questioned aggressively. He refused to touch the dead body, and this reaction was later used as evidence of his guilt. After one of his inquisitors, a justice of the peace, suggested to him that "it would be a pity to hang so fine a boy,"[18] Guild began to incriminate himself by telling a variety of stories. He was taken to jail at about 1:00 P.M. and questioned so intensively that his resulting written confession was held inadmissible at his trial. However, he repeated his confession the next day and several times thereafter and these statements were used against him at his trial.

The trial began on Friday, May 9, 1828, in Flemington, the Hunterdon County seat. Three or four attorneys who had been appointed to represent Guild raised a variety of defenses. Apparently the only evidence produced by the state was that the crime had occurred and that Guild had confessed to it several times.

Guild was only two days away from his thirteenth birthday when his trial began. Thus, since he was under age fourteen, the common-law rule was followed to presume his mental incapacity to have criminal intent. The state had to overcome this presumption of incapacity and did so at the trial by presenting evidence that Guild was "smarter than common black boys of his age."[19] Other evidence and findings cast doubt on the prudence of this conclusion: "He had intelligence enough to know when he did wrong, but was wanting in discretion, and could not fully appreciate the consequences of crime. . . . He is passionate, mischievous, insolent, but he does not bear malice."[20]

The trial took only two days. At the close of evidence the judge told the jurors that, in light of Guild's age, they should resolve all doubts in his favor as to the reliability of the confessions and his criminal intent. The jury deliberated less than three hours and returned a verdict of guilty of murder, which carried an automatic sentence of death. The trial judge delayed formal entrance of judgment and sentencing to allow Guild's attorneys to appeal the case.

The New Jersey Supreme Court affirmed Guild's conviction in October 1828. The court's opinion is thorough and meticulous for this period and affirms all actions of the trial court. The higher court found that the details provided in Guild's admissible confessions could not have been known by anyone other than the perpetrator. Noting the trial judge's sincere cautioning of the jury about Guild's youthfulness, the court concluded that he was old enough to have his confessions considered and old enough to be convicted. It returned the case to the trial court for sentencing, the only lawful option being the death penalty.

While awaiting execution, Guild conducted a mock trial with mice he had captured in his cell. The trial, complete with twelve mice jurors, resulted in the ceremonial hanging of the mouse defendant. The press reported that Guild's attitude toward this mock trial seemed the same as it had been all during his fourteen months of imprisonment, that of not really comprehending his situation.

On execution day several thousand persons came to Flemington to witness Guild's hanging. To accommodate the crowds, the gallows was erected in a large field just outside town. The procedure followed its solemn course, complete with black hood and noose around the neck. But Guild shook off the hood as the trapdoor was sprung, and true to the end to his reputation for ingenuity, he balanced precariously on his toes at the edge of the drop. The sheriff rushed back up the steps and pushed Little Jim's toes off the edge and into thin air. Guild was thirteen years seven and one-half months old.

GODFREY; EXECUTED JULY 16, 1858; ALABAMA[21]

Godfrey was the third of the three persons executed at age twelve years. A slave known alternately as Godfrey and Alfred, he had been sold in 1856 to Mrs. Margaret Stuart of Mobile, the grandmother of his murder victim, four-year-old Lawrence Gomez. Godfrey seemed bright enough and served as a baby-sitter for the young white boy.

Godfrey's exact age was unclear. Mrs. Stuart thought he was about twelve at the time of his crime, but his original owner set his age at ten or eleven. The best estimate seems to be that of his original owner, and so this case study assumes that Godfrey was just barely eleven years old on April 30, 1857, the date of his crime.

The day before, Godfrey had fought with the Gomez child over a kite. Late the next morning, Mrs. Gomez left her son in Godfrey's care while she visited neighbors across the street. When she returned she found her son lying in the yard, alive but fatally injured by deep hatchet wounds. Godfrey first claimed that marauding Indians had committed the acts, but no Indians were found in the vicinity. Meanwhile, Godfrey had difficulty explaining the blood on his clothing and the hatchet found nearby. Later that evening, Godfrey admitted to a neighbhood playmate that he had killed the victim for breaking his kite.

Godfrey was tried in July 1857 in the City Court of Mobile. The jury returned a verdict of guilty of murder. The judge reserved sentencing until a decision could be reached by an appellate court.

The Alabama Supreme Court affirmed Godfrey's conviction in spring 1858, finding the state's evidence sufficient to overcome the presumption that so young a child could not have had malicious criminal intent for murder. The court relied on reports of several old cases of convictions of children, including that of James Guild, although it mistakenly said Guild was less than twelve years old at the time of his crime.

Godfrey was hanged at 12:10 P.M. in Mobile. He had prepared no formal last words but said he hoped he would meet everyone in a better world. It seems reasonable to calculate his age at execution as less than twelve and one-half years, apparently making him the youngest person executed in American history.

DAVID OWEN DODD; EXECUTED JANUARY 8, 1864; FEDERAL[22]

David Dodd was a white farm boy in Arkansas when the Union Army moved in and took over. He later earned the distinction of being the only juvenile executed for spying against the United States government. When he was hanged at Little Rock, he was "a mere child, only seventeen years old and small for his age."[23]

Dodd was born in Texas on November 10, 1846. His family moved to Saline County, Arkansas, a few years later. He was a cadet at St. John's College in Little Rock before the Civil War began. When the Union Army captured Little Rock, Dodd moved with his family back to Texas. They left hurriedly and could not transport many of their belongings, including the cattle on their Arkansas farm.

In October 1863, Dodd's father sent him back to the farm to tend to the cattle. When he left on this family mission, he was only sixteen. His first step was to obtain a pass from the Confederate Army. A family friend, General Fagan, gave Dodd the pass and asked him to visit Little Rock and check on the Union forces there. Dodd promised to do what he could.

Dodd then went to the family farm near Benton, Arkansas, and took care of the cattle. Next he went on to Little Rock, where he stayed for about three weeks, obstensibly to visit old schoolmates. Since he was a young boy just turned seventeen, he was ignored by the Union forces and allowed informal access to the headquarters area. Dodd apparently collaborated with more mature and sophisticated Confederate spies who provided him with papers detailing the strength and status of the Union forces. He hid these papers in the sole of his shoe and started back to his family in Texas.

With a pass from Union headquarters, he made it through two checkpoints on his way home. Just as he was almost beyond the reach of Union forces, he was picked up by a squad of Union cavalry. Several searches finally uncovered the papers in his shoe. He was taken back to Little Rock to be tried as a spy.

His trial in mid-December, 1863, was brief. It was presided over by General Steele, commander of the Union forces in Little Rock, who found him guilty and signed his death warrant. The general was understandably reluctant to impose this sentence and offered to release Dodd if he would name the accomplices who prepared the papers for him. Dodd thanked the general but refused to betray his friends.

While awaiting his fate in the army jail, Dodd was visited daily by a Methodist minister from Little Rock. When his execution date arrived, his last words identified himself with past patriots: ". . . and like Nathan Hale, my only regret is that I have but one life to give to my country."[24] His death came in a manner dictated by his youth and stature: "The drop fell. The child-like form dangled writhing in the air, and so slender and light was the body that the soldiers present had to pull and jerk it in order to break his neck."[25]

Dodd has the distinction of being the only executed juvenile remembered as a hero. His remains were buried in a local cemetery by an organization of prominent women of Little Rock and his grave is still marked with a dignified white monument. He was also honored by a Little Rock veterans organization, which named itself the David O. Dodd Camp, Union of Confederate Veterans.

ELIZA; EXECUTED FEBRUARY 7, 1868; KENTUCKY[26]

Eliza, also referred to as Susan, was a black girl about twelve years old at the time of her crime. She had lived with the William Graves family as a servant near New Castle in Henry County, Kentucky, for about four weeks before her crime. She had also served as a nurse and baby-sitter for the two-year-old son, Walter.

Eliza was very affectionate toward Walter, seemingly tolerant of the problems typically encountered in caring for a two-year-old. At about two o'clock in the afternoon on August 15, 1867, Eliza, Walter, and some other children were playing around the Graves farm and went to the barn for some straw. When they returned Walter was not with them. A search for him by his mother and others was unsuccessful, so they sent for Mr. Graves and some neighbors.

Walter was found in a thicket behind the barn about two hours later, his head bashed in with a large stone. He died later that evening. Eliza was questioned immediately but at first denied any knowledge of the crime. When threatened with lynching by the neighbors, she finally confessed and took them to the stone she had used to kill Walter. She was arrested, and a probable cause hearing was conducted the next day. After several witnesses testified, Eliza was ordered held for trial. On September 4 she was indicted by the grand jury for murder. Her arraignment followed the next morning and her trial began immediately.

The trial judge excluded Eliza's confession from evidence because it was not given voluntarily. Nevertheless, the stream of witnesses against her, including the mother and father of the victim, proved the case adequately. No witnesses testified for Eliza. The prosecutor was thus able to overcome the presumption against criminal liability for a defendant so young. On September 6, the jury returned a verdict of guilty. The defendant's motion for a new trial was denied and her execution date was set.

Near the scaffold erected behind the courthouse in New Castle,, several hundred men, both blacks and whites, impatiently awaited the hanging. Women and children were relegated to doorways and windows of surrounding buildings. At precisely 2:00 P.M., thirteen-year-old Eliza appeared in a plain black gown and cap. As she ascended the steps her body trembled, perhaps from the cold of the day but more likely from mortal fear.

A short prayer was said by Reverend Cox, the white preacher Eliza had asked for when she could not understand the black preachers who had been attending her. The silent reverence of the gathering was disturbed once by a drunken fight but the hanging proceeded. The trapdoor was sprung and "she writhed and twisted and jerked many times, but at last was still—in death."[27]

Three stout black men cut her body down and carried it off for burial in the black cemetery. Meanwhile, other members of the crowd asked for and received short pieces of the rope as souvenirs.

JOSEPH NUANA; EXECUTED MARCH 6, 1874; WASHINGTON TERRITORY[28]

In the mid-nineteenth century, the Hudson Bay Colony established sheep on San Juan Island off what is now the state of Washington. To tend these sheep they imported Hawaiians. Joseph Nuana's father was one of these sheepherders. He settled near Kanaka Bay on the island, married an Indian woman, and had several children, including the son who came to be known as Kanaka Joe.

Kanaka Joe Nuana grew up in the shack town on the island and attended school for only a short time. His crime, committed at age sixteen, was to be so shocking and brutal as to label him a "foul fiend," but for some observers that seemed misleading: "A reporter, set to glimpse a 'ruffianly demon,' noted with a shock that the prisoner seemed nothing more or less than a 'mere boy' to him."[29] Although Nuana had inherited his mother's Indian appearance, he identified with his father's Hawaiian background and looked down on his Indian acquaintances.

At the other end of the island's social and economic spectrum was Captain James Dwyer. This "strapping man of the sea"[30] had led an adventurous life that had included a long-term relationship with an Indian woman who had borne several of his children. He had made regular commercial sailing trips between Victoria, British Columbia, and the offshore islands before changes were effected in sailing lines and customs requirements when the United States took control of the islands. These new requirements convinced him to settle down. He sold his sloop and moved to a run-down farm on San Juan Island, which had become a U.S. territory after the Pig War. Dwyer took a new bride, Salina, sixteen years his junior, and moved to the farm in September 1872. She became pregnant soon after the wedding.

Captain and Mrs. Dwyer were on their farm at about midday on Thursday, May 15, 1873, the captain plowing a field with his team of horses while Salina, eight and one-half months pregnant, sat on the front porch of their home. Kanaka Joe Nuana approached Dwyer in the field, and the two men began arguing over Nuana's claim of a property interest in Dwyer's farm. As Dwyer turned to continue his plowing, Nuana shot him in the back of the head with a borrowed shotgun. The terrified Salina ran into her house and locked the door. Nuana shot through a window and wounded her and then climbed in and shot her again, this time fatally. He quickly ransacked a trunk, took two watches and fourteen dollars, and ran away.

Almost twenty-four hours later a neighbor who came to return Dwyer's strayed calf found the bodies. Captain Dwyer was lying dead in the newly plowed field, his team of horses still standing beside him, unable to free themselves. His young wife's body was found in the house. A coroner's inquest was held over the bodies that same day and then they were released to friends in Victoria for burial.

The funeral for the Dwyers was held in Victoria the next day. Nuana and some friends were in Victoria enjoying themselves that day, unaware that they were prime suspects in the crime or that substantial rewards were being offered both in Victoria and in Washington Territory. Since the Dwyers were British nationals killed in U.S. territory, the investigation included dual efforts by authorities in Victoria and in Washington Territory. Victoria police were joined by a Washington lawyer, Thomas Murphy, in their search for Nuana. Nuana and his friends were arrested a few days later as they casually strolled down a main street in Victoria.

The Victoria police questioned Nuana and his friends but could find sufficient evidence against only Nuana. Nuana's story kept changing each time he related it, but he consistently avoided accepting any blame for the murders. A prolonged extradition hearing in Victoria in early June considered Nuana's fate. His court-appointed barrister aggressively attacked the evidence and caused several continuances in the proceedings. Finally, on July 18, Nuana admitted the Dwyer murders and a similar murder of another San Juan settler the year before.

Nuana was extradited in late October after the Victoria courts accepted an extradition order signed by President Grant. Stanchioned and chained, Nuana was taken by steamer from Victoria to Port Townsend in Washington Territory. He seemed to enjoy being the center of attention and was reportedly behaving as if he was off to a celebration rather than a murder trial. He remained cheerful during his three-week trial in the District Court of Port Townsend, unaware that his conviction for murder would make him the first and last person ever hanged in that city.

A scaffold was erected on the beach in Port Townsend and a crowd of 200 persons began the celebrations early. The stores and saloons had a thriving trade and a nearby brewery reported a record day's business. Nuana had made clear his views of his future: "I would sooner be dead than live in jail here."[31] He walked briskly up the steps and addressed the crowd: "I am very sorry for what I have done. All hands, goodbye."[32]

Arriving at the scaffold at 9:40 A.M., Nuana was hanged at 10:05. As the drop fell, the knot slipped and Nuana began slowly strangling. Seeing the problem, the sheriff jerked and swung on the rope to close the knot. It took twenty minutes for Nuana to die. He was seventeen years old.

JAMES ARCENE; EXECUTED JUNE 26, 1885;
FEDERAL/ARKANSAS[33]

James Arcene was the youngest executed juvenile at time of crime in American history but one of the oldest at time of execution. Arcene was a full-blooded Cherokee living in Indian Territory near what is now Tahlequah, Oklahoma. He killed a white man there when he was only ten years old, a crime for which he was hanged almost thirteen years later.

Arcene and an adult Cherokee, William Parchmeal, were in a store in Tahlequah on November 25, 1872. They noticed Henry Fiegel, an older Swede, make a small cash purchase. Parchmeal and Arcene decided to rob Fiegel and followed him out of town to a wooded area. They bludgeoned him with a large stone and, on Parchmeal's orders, young Arcene shot him four times. They took some of his clothing and all his money—twenty-five cents.

Circling buzzards brought passersby to the body the next day. Parchmeal and Arcene were suspected immediately, but no substantial investigation was launched and no effort was made to arrest them. Many years later a new deputy marshal became interested in the case. He began to compile evidence and finally obtained arrest warrants for Parchmeal and Arcene. On March 30, 1884, Arcene, then about twenty-two years old, was arrested for selling whiskey on the reservation. Parchmeal was arrested four months later.

Arcene and Parchmeal were later charged with Fiegel's robbery and murder and were tried in the federal district court at Fort Smith, Arkansas, in November or December 1884. The result was a hung jury. The U.S. attorney brought them to trial again on March 18, 1885. At their joint trial each had an appointed attorney to represent him and each tried to put the blame for the crime on the other. The jury took forty-eight hours to find them both guilty of murder on March 28, 1885. Both were sentenced to hang.

Since no court appeals were permitted from that unique territorial court, Arcene and Parchmeal sought intervention from the U.S. president. He declined to intervene, leaving them no other avenue to challenge their convictions and sentences. As their execution date neared, Parchmeal corroborated Arcene's story that Parchmeal had given Arcene the pistol and had told the ten-year-old boy to shoot Fiegel. They agreed that Arcene was so young then that he could not fully understand what he was doing.

Arcene and Parchmeal were both hanged at Fort Smith on the same day. They sang Cherokee spirituals before their executions. By that time the spectacle was not that of the hanging of a prepubescent boy for murder but of an adult man who had a long criminal record. Nevertheless, the sole reason Arcene was hanged was that he committed a crime when he was only ten years old.

EDWARD ALONZO DEACONS;
EXECUTED JULY 10, 1888; NEW YORK[34]

Edward Deacons was one month beyond his sixteenth birthday when he committed his capital crime. An itinerant tramp who went door to door asking for handouts, Deacons was the youngest son and the self-described "pet" of a white family about whom little is known. It is known that he had a difficult childhood and that his time as a tramp gave him an appearance and speech suggesting maturity beyond his years. Reporters noted that he also came to enjoy excursions beyond the truth as a sort of private game.

At just before 3:00 P.M. on August 16, 1887, Deacons knocked on the door of Mrs. Ada Stone on Hayward Avenue in East Rochester, New York. Her husband was away at work, but her young son was at home. When Stone refused

Deacons's request for food, an argument ensued. The prosecutor later said that Deacons attempted to rape Stone, but no physical evidence substantiated this notion and Deacons denied it. It is known that Stone slapped and insulted Deacons, sending him into a rage. His response was to hit her several times with his walking stick. He carried her unconscious body down to the cellar, where she recovered and renewed the struggle. He then tied a flour sack tightly around her neck and she became still.

Deacons said that Stone was alive when he left her in the cellar. She was dead, however, when her husband found her that evening after work. By that time Deacons had jumped a freight train to Canandaigua, New York, where he spent the night sleeping in a boxcar. The police investigated the crime immediately and thoroughly, first questioning and then arresting the victim's husband. Further questioning and investigation resulted in his release two days later.

Deacons was arrested for being a tramp as he slept in the boxcar in Canandaigua on the night following the murder. Given the nature of the crime in East Rochester, Deacons was taken back there for questioning. He finally confessed on September 6 and gave many other confessions at later dates. He even composed his confessions in simple verses for his own amusement and to the astonishment of police, prosecutor, and newspaper reporters.

Deacons was indicted for murder by a grand jury on October 25 and arraigned on October 27. The judge appointed lawyers to represent Deacons and his trial began on January 30, 1888. Many witnesses testified to having seen him in East Rochester on the day of the crime, and his confessions seemed to seal his guilt. Undaunted, he testified that he was innocent, denying his many previous confessions and calling all the state's witnesses liars. He was convicted of murder and his sentence of death was imposed on February 10.

The New York Court of Appeals affirmed his conviction and sentence on May 4. It found his confessions to be admissible and the evidence to be sufficient to prove his guilt. On June 4, the trial court set his execution date. Governor Hill refused to intervene with clemency, evoking a bravado laugh from Deacons.

The evening before his execution, Deacons was visited by his sister, Mrs. Van Schouten. That night he ate fruit and lemonade and played "Home Sweet Home" on his harmonica. The fruit gave him severe indigestion and he refused breakfast the next morning.

He was led to the scaffold at 10:00 A.M., accompanied by the sheriff and two Catholic priests. He had joined the Catholic Church while awaiting execution. He was defiant to the end: "Friends, the law is about to take the life of an innocent man. That is all I have to say."[35] His arms were pinioned to his sides and the drop fell at 10:24. He was pronounced dead fifteen minutes later. He had not reached his seventeenth birthday. His sister took custody of the body and attended to his burial.

BRAD BEARD; EXECUTED DECEMBER 17, 1897; ALABAMA[36]

Brad Beard, known as Bud to his friends, was a black boy barely fourteen years old living on his family's farm near Reform in northwestern Alabama. In

March 1897, his older brother Andy eloped with a white girl. The group of white men who caught up with the couple shot and killed Andy and brought the girl back to be convicted and imprisoned for miscegenation. A few months later Brad met a fate similar to his brother's, although Brad's came legally.

Brad Beard was large and muscular for his age and looked several years older. On November 2, 1897, he was working for a white neighbor and was told to chop wood. The farmer's seven-year-old daughter, Ella May Crockett, was told to gather chips and take them to the house. The farmer then left to attend to other matters.

Instead of chopping wood, Beard attacked and raped the girl and then ran into the woods. The girl told her father what had happened and a physician confirmed the rape. Seriously injured, the girl almost died but was able to attend the grand jury hearing and trial.

A posse similar to the one that had killed his brother pursued Beard and quickly captured him. He was not shot, however, but was arrested and brought back for trial. The sheriff moved Beard around from jail to jail to avoid a lynching.

Beard was indicted on the testimony of the victim and the medical evidence. His trial followed almost immediately in Carrollton, and he was convicted and sentenced to die. The governor sent special state forces to prevent a lynching during the trial. The local newspapers reported that Beard cried almost constantly from the time of his sentence.

Although Beard was hanged only six weeks after his crime, the waiting period gave rise to a considerable fear of lynching. Beard was incarcerated in the Jefferson County Jail in Birmingham until the execution date arrived. A week before his execution the sheriff sneaked him back into the Pickens County jail in Carrollton. Beard was terrified at the prospect of being hanged for a crime he continued to deny having committed.

Beard was hanged just after 11:00 A.M. on the scaffold outside the courthouse in Carrollton. The ceremony was peaceful, with few persons caring enough to come to witness the spectacle. Beard's last wish was to meet everyone in heaven. The trapdoor sprung and he died quickly, the first person to be hanged in Pickens County since Civil War days.

MONK GIBSON; EXECUTED JUNE 28, 1908; TEXAS[37]

The controversy over Monk Gibson's age was more than simply confusion concerning his birth date. If he was seventeen at the time of his crimes, he was eligible for the Texas death penalty. But if he was only sixteen, he could not be executed for the crimes. It appears that he was born in September 1888, making him just past his seventeenth birthday at the time of his crimes. At any rate, the jury must have believed he was seventeen, because this black male was hanged for mass murder.

Gibson lived in the black section near Edna, Texas, with his family. As a bizarre harbinger of his fate, Gibson as a child had played at hanging a young girl and she was severely injured before the game could be stopped.

About September 14, 1905, the family of J. F. Conditt moved onto a small farm in this black section. They were the first white family in the area; that, along with their ending of the communal use of a water supply on the farm, caused some tension among the black residents. Gibson began working at the Conditt farm and taking some meals there within a few days after the Conditt's arrival.

On September 28, at about 10:00 A.M., Gibson and a friend, Felix Powell, were working on the Conditt farm. Mr. Conditt had left home six hours earlier to harvest rice in a distant field. His wife, Lora, remained at home with their five children: Mildred, age twelve; Herschell, ten; Jesse, six; Joseph, three; and Lloyd, ten months old. Powell had earlier been rebuffed by Mildred in his sexual propositions to her and decided to have his way regardless. As part of a plan to rape Mildred, Gibson and Powell descended upon the family with an adz and a knife. During or after the rape, they brutally killed Lora and her four oldest children, leaving the baby unscathed.

At noon Gibson ran to nearby black neighbors to report the bloody scene and to accuse two unknown black men he claimed to have seen chasing Mrs. Conditt. The black neighbors sent Gibson on to report the crimes to the nearest white persons, who promptly returned with him to the Conditt farm to discover the five bodies and the crying baby. The neighbors then sent Gibson to get Mr. Conditt. He did so, returning with him to the farm.

Questioning of Gibson and examination of the crime scene made it apparent that the victims had not given any alarm and must have known the murderer. Gibson changed his story several times and had difficulty explaining the blood on his clothes and hands. He was arrested and subjected to "questioning and persuasion, which was not always the gentlest variety."[38] Crowds of angry armed men converged on the town jail and a lynching seemed probable.

That night, as the sheriff was hurriedly taking Gibson from the jail to transport him to the next county for safekeeping, Gibson escaped. Huge posses were formed to scour the countryside. The sheriff asked for assistance from the Texas Rangers, and three days after the escape the governor ordered the national guard in to help. None of these searchers, or their bloodhounds, could find Gibson. Like any frightened teenage boy, he had run for home, and he hid in his father's barn while the posses looked everywhere for him. He finally gave himself up on October 5, simply because he got hungry.

Four days later Gibson was indicted by the Jackson County grand jury for being an accessory to Powell's murder of Mrs. Conditt. Powell was also indicted but the two were given separate trials. Like Gibson, Powell was convicted; he was hanged on April 2, 1907, for his part in the crimes. Gibson was granted a change of venue on October 17, 1905, to San Antonio in Bexar County because an impartial trial jury could not be impaneled in Jackson County. The trial in Bexar County resulted in a hung jury, apparently because the jury had insufficient information on the identity and role of others in Gibson's crimes.

Venue was changed again, this time to DeWitt County. At the start of this trial the attorneys went through 190 men before agreeing on a jury of twelve. The questions to the prospective jurors centered on their ability to give the defendant as fair a trial as they would a white man. This theme arose again during the district attorney's opening argument: "Do not let it be said, gentlemen of the jury, that a jury of DeWitt County citizens can only hang a white man."[39] That was a reference to the fact that up to that time only whites had been executed in the county. The jurors did not disappoint the district attorney; they convicted Gibson and he was sentenced to death.

The Texas Court of Criminal Appeals affirmed the conviction and sentence on April 22, 1908. Gibson's attorney raised many grounds in the appeal but was unsuccessful on all of them. Among other issues, the court approved of the impaneling of an all-white jury to try a black defendant. It also rejected Gibson's claim that he was only sixteen at the time of his crime, noting that the jury had heard his argument on that issue and must have concluded that he was seventeen or they could not have sentenced him to death under Texas law.

Gibson was hanged in Cuero in DeWitt County. His execution was the cause of much excitement there and elsewhere. A chartered train arrived in Cuero with over 500 persons aboard from Wharton and Edna, where the crime had been committed. The hanging was witnessed by 2,500 persons. Gibson, then nineteen, maintained his innocence to the end.

IRVING HANCHETT; EXECUTED MAY 6, 1910; FLORIDA[40]

Irving Hanchett was born in the spring of 1895 into a poor white family in New Haven, Connecticut. He had an older sister and two younger sisters. He was raised in New Haven under difficult circumstances, and his truancy put him in the state reform school at age ten. During his four years there, his mother visited him only three times. In the third year, his father committed suicide and Hanchett was not notified until after the funeral.

What seems to have been Hanchett's one lucky break came in the person of a Mr. Wooley. Wooley and his wife lived in Connecticut in the summer and Florida in the winter. As they prepared to return to Deland, Florida, in the fall of 1909, they decided to find a boy to help them in their orange groves. Hanchett was released to them from the state reform school on October 12, and they all went south a few weeks later.

Hanchett's short residence in Florida did not go well. He worked for the Wooleys, earning fifty cents a week plus room, board, and clothing. But Mr. Wooley had just about decided to return him to the reform school in the spring because, in Wooley's view, Hanchett "wouldn't tell the truth, he wouldn't only work when he was a mind to, and he was a thief besides."[41] Socially, Hanchett was also unsuccessful, a "practically friendless boy."[42]

Cleavy Tedder was the fifteen-year-old daughter of Perry and Emma Tedder, prominent orange growers in the Deland area. At 4:00 P.M. on Saturday, February 12, 1910, Tedder and her girl friend left Tedder's home to go to the store and post office in the village. The two girls passed Hanchett on the main street and nodded but didn't speak. Hanchett had admired Tedder from a distance for some time but had never spoken to her. She was a year older than the fourteen-year-old boy and in another social circle.

Hanchett decided to wait for Tedder to return along the road from her errand. Tedder's girl friend left her at the store and went home. Tedder completed her business and began riding her bicycle home. Hanchett confronted Tedder and became angry when she dismissed him in a fresh manner. He jerked her off her bicycle, leaving it and the mail she was carrying at the edge of the road. He dragged Tedder into the adjoining field and attacked her with his knife. She pleaded for him to stop, promising not to tell anyone what had happened. Hanchett ignored her pleas, inflicting seventy stab wounds from her neck to her hips. Hanchett later denied any rape motive and the girl's body was found fully clothed and apparently not sexually violated. He ran across the field and went the back way to the Wooley house. After washing his bloody hands in the basin on the back porch, he ate dinner and went to bed early, about 7:00 P.M.

Tedder's toppled bicycle on the edge of the road led passersby to investigate and find her body in the tall grass of the field at about 6:30 P.M. Many local people, including Tedder's father and a woman physician, came to the scene. Several began to follow footprints leading away from the body but early darkness prevented a careful search. The physician examined the body, noting the cause of death and that she had not been raped.

The sheriff first suspected a local black man but changed his mind after a brief questioning. He then went to Tedder's friend's house and learned of the encounter with Hanchett. The sheriff went to the Wooley house, arriving at 7:30 P.M. to find private citizens already there and questioning Hanchett, who apparently was a natural suspect in the minds of many. The sheriff arrested Hanchett and seized his knife and clothing. Taking Hanchett to Tedder's body, which was still lying in the field, the sheriff forced him to look at the body with the hope of stimulating a confession. Hanchett seemed only a little nervous and denied any knowledge of the crime.

Evidence gathered the next morning sealed Hanchett's fate. The footprints leading away from the body were tracked directly to the Wooley house and matched Hanchett's shoes. Examination of Hanchett's knife and clothing revealed bloodstains. The washbasin on the back porch still contained bloody, soapy water, and bloody paper towels lay nearby. Faced with this evidence and after further questioning from the sheriff, Hanchett admitted killing Tedder but said he didn't know why he did it. Talk of lynching caused the sheriff to take Hanchett out of the local jail and transport him to Daytona for safekeeping.

On April 6, Hanchett was indicted by the grand jury of Volusia County for the premeditated murder of Cleavy Tedder. His court-appointed attorneys had only two days to prepare his defense. He was arraigned on Friday, April 8, and pleaded not guilty. The trial began immediately. The jury was selected that morning and testimony began that afternoon. The trial went through the next day and the jury received the case at 7:30 P.M. The jury announced its verdict on Monday morning at 9:00—guilty of first-degree murder and without recommendation of mercy. That same morning the judge sentenced Hanchett with the standard language: "you shall be hanged by the neck until you are dead, and may the Lord have mercy on your soul."[43]

While awaiting execution, Hanchett was baptized by Father Curley into the Catholic faith and seemed buoyed by the hope of a happy eternity. Saying he had no fear and was ready to die, "he always ate heartily and showed no concern over his approaching execution."[44]

On Friday morning at 10:30 a crowd of 200 men and women was gathered in the county jail yard in Deland for the hanging. Hanchett, accompanied by the sheriff, three deputies, and Father Curley, walked with a firm step, appearing slightly pale but not nervous. Just barely fifteen years old, he mounted the scaffold and said: "Mercy, my Jesus; my Jesus, mercy. Goodbye everyone."[45] The fall broke his neck and he was pronounced dead fourteen minutes later. His hanging came less than four weeks after he was found guilty and less than three months after Tedder's murder.

VIRGINIA CHRISTIAN;
EXECUTED AUGUST 16, 1912; VIRGINIA[46]

Of the 281 persons executed for crimes committed while under age eighteen, only nine have been female offenders. The first, Hannah Ocuish, was discussed earlier in this chapter. The last was Virginia Christian.

Virginia Christian was born on August 15, 1895, to poor black parents in Hampton, Virginia. Her mother, who had a reputation for dishonesty, became paralyzed when Christian was thirteen years old. Her father was a hardworking laborer, but his wages of $1.25 a day fell short in supporting his invalid wife and eight children. Therefore the older children, including Christian, had to quit school and work to support the family. It was generally agreed that their home and family life was squalid and miserable and that Christian had adopted her mother's habits of immorality, dishonesty, and thievery. Added to these factors was Christian's "dubious mental responsibility."[47]

For several years Christian served as a laundress for Mrs. Ida Virginia Belote, a fifty-one-year-old member of a prominent white family in the area. Belote accused Christian of stealing a skirt from her laundry on March 18, 1912. An argument ensued, with Belote hitting Christian first with a cuspidor and then with broken pieces of the cuspidor. Christian went into a blind rage, grabbed a broomstick from a window, and struck Belote on the forehead. To stifle Belote's screams, Christian stuffed a towel down Belote's throat, finally killing her by suffocation. Still angry, Christian left with Belote's purse containing several dollars and a ring.

Several hours later the victim's body was discovered. Officers went to Christian's house soon thereafter and arrested her. In response to questioning, Christian admitted her acts against Belote but expressed surprise that she was dead and claimed no intent to kill her.

A lynching of Christian was narrowly avoided. At her trial, which was conducted only two weeks after the crime, she was represented by two black lawyers. The social position and popularity of the victim stood in stark contrast to the Christian family background and to Christian's unkempt appearance and rude manner in describing the crime. Because her previous admissions made her defense problematic, her lawyers decided not to put her on the witness stand. She was convicted and sentenced to death in April 1912 in the Elizabeth City County Court.

In the face of unfriendly press coverage and Christian's confessions to reporters, her black lawyers persisted in seeking clemency from the governor. Although they got two temporary reprieves, they gave up by August 5. With no other lawyers willing to take up her case, the National Association for the Advancement of Colored People (NAACP) launched an aggressive if ill-fated public campaign on her behalf. The organization stimulated the sending of many letters to the governor seeking permanent clemency, and it petitioned him on the grounds of Christian's ignorance and youth (sixteen at time of crime), her wretched family environment, and the lack of evidence of any premeditation on her part.

The NAACP's efforts did not move the governor. Christian celebrated her seventeenth birthday on August 15 and was electrocuted the next day. She gained the unfortunate distinction of being the first female to die in Virginia's electric chair. Her death left unanswered the fundamental question raised by her supporters: "Why has it (Virginia) not a law forbidding the execution of children of sixteen?"[48] Three-quarters of a century later, Virginia still had no such law.[49]

LEON CARDENAS MARTINEZ, JR.;
EXECUTED MAY 11, 1914; TEXAS[50]

Leon Martinez was born in Gallega, State of Durango, Mexico, apparently on June 10, 1896; his parents followed the common practice of not getting a birth certificate or establishing other official records of his birth. By his fifteenth birthday, Martinez was boasting to friends that he was eighteen. This typical adolescent exaggeration was to cost him his life.

Martinez's parents lived in Mexico with their nine children until April 3, 1906, when they moved to El Paso, Texas. In 1908 they moved to Reeves County, Texas, near the small town of Saragosa. The whole family remained Mexican nationals. In 1911 Martinez was living with his father in Saragosa while his mother was living with the other children in nearby Toyah, Texas. On February 8 that year, Martinez began working at Crenshaw's general store in Saragosa. Regarded as a bright boy, he got along well there.

On Saturday morning, July 22, 1911, Miss Emma Brown, a local white woman in her late twenties, was shopping in the store and conversed with Martinez. According to Martinez, Brown "promised him some personal favors to be consummated at a later meeting."[51] More candidly, the fifteen-year-old Martinez believed that Miss Brown had agreed to have sexual intercourse with him and he decided to pursue the agreement.

At 4:00 P.M. Martinez, riding his horse, confronted Brown in her buggy on a road outside town. He asked her to comply with her earlier promise. When she rebuffed him, an argument erupted. Brown was a "stout, strong, vigorous woman,"[52] but Martinez was armed with a .25-caliber pistol and a knife. He shot at her four times, hitting her at least once. She jumped out of her buggy and ran. When Martinez caught up to her, she hit him with her hands and a stick. Martinez then stabbed her six times in the back and chest. He later said she was still standing when he retreated and went on his way. Martinez returned to Saragosa, ate dinner, and then worked a few more hours at Crenshaw's store.

Brown was found dead near her buggy that evening. The medical examination of her body the next morning established the stab wounds as the cause of death. Horse tracks at the crime scene revealed a hoof defect identical to that of Martinez's horse. This and other circumstantial evidence led to the arrest of Martinez that afternoon, Sunday, July 23. He confessed orally to the sheriff and in writing to the district attorney that evening. Because of the presence of an unruly mob, he was transferred to the Midland jail for safekeeping. Texas Rangers were called in to protect him pending trial.

The grand jury of Reeves County indicted Martinez on July 25 for first-degree murder. The trial was scheduled to begin three days later in Pecos, the county seat. The court appointed a Pecos attorney to represent Martinez but, unsatisfied with this option, Martinez's father also hired an El Paso lawyer. The two lawyers, both former judges, represented Martinez together, scrambling to prepare a defense in a day or two. They were not permitted to talk with their client until the morning of his trial.

The trial began on Friday morning, July 28. The key items of evidence against Martinez were his confession and the tracks of his horse at the crime scene. There was no evidence to prove who was riding his horse at the time, and his confession was made before he had a lawyer. The defendant's case centered on the inadequacies of the prosecution's evidence and Martinez's age. His parents both testified that he was born on June 10, 1896, making him only fifteen years old at the time of the crime. But state witnesses testified that Martinez himself had said he was seventeen or eighteen, and this testimony convinced the jury.

On the second day of the trial, the jury convicted him of murder and recommended a sentence of death. Even before Martinez was sentenced by the judge two hours later, the defense attorney from El Paso had left town in response to a threatening crowd. At 4:00 P.M., exactly one week to the hour after the murder of Miss Brown, the judge sentenced Martinez to be hanged for his crime, ignoring the boy's claim that "I am not old enough to be hanged."[53]

The local Pecos defense attorney had tried earlier to be excused from representing Martinez but to no avail. He reluctantly stayed with Martinez through the sentencing but withdrew his earlier announced notice of intention to appeal the verdict and sentence. This attorney had also been the object of threats from the angry crowd; he had also received a strong personal request to withdraw from one of his major clients, the local banker and hotel owner. He complied but was subsequently fired as the bank's lawyer.

The swift judgment in Martinez's case was followed by almost three years of legal maneuvering to obtain a lighter sentence. These efforts were greatly hampered by the lack of an official notice of appeal by the trial lawyers. Several politically active groups, including the Socialist Party and the Industrial Workers of the World (IWW), contributed about $50,000 to the legal expenses of the appeals and collateral challenges. Governor Colquitt granted a short reprieve for the case to be considered by the Texas Court of Criminal Appeals, which heard Martinez's habeas corpus arguments on November 3, 1911. The court's two-to-one decision was handed down on March 12, 1912, and took sixty-four pages to explain. The dissenting judge, extremely concerned about aspects of the case, including Martinez's age, said that "there is grave doubt as to whether or not the accused is above 16 years of age, and under our laws no one under 17 years of age can be lawfully given the death penalty."[54] A rehearing was denied on April 10. The governor was unsympathetic to Martinez's claims, responding instead to a petition from many county residents to let the boy hang. The governor did permit additional short reprieves and the case was taken to the United States Supreme Court, which denied relief on January 12, 1914. After one final reprieve, Martinez was sentenced to die on May 11, 1914.

Meanwhile, Martinez had been moved from the Midland jail to the Abilene jail and then to the Waco jail to frustrate the desires of various lynching parties. Still one month shy of his eighteenth birthday, Martinez became the only person ever hanged at Pecos. He remained unrepentant to the end, stating that he had killed Brown in self-defense. He refused any religious counseling or rites at his execution.

His father claimed the boy's body and took it back to the new family home in Waco for funeral services. Martinez's body was viewed by a reported 7,000 visitors in the two days before the funeral. Representatives of the Socialist Party and the IWW delivered stirring eulogies at his funeral, but his family buried him privately in the Waco cemetery.

CHARLES E.T. OXNAM;
EXECUTED MARCH 3, 1916; CALIFORNIA[55]

Charles Oxnam, white, was age seventeen chronologically when he shot and killed his burglary victim but his mental age was that of an eight-year-old. He had suffered serious illnesses as a child and was considered "so mentally defective that he could not learn."[56] He was also morose and timid and had a violent temper. Orphaned at age sixteen, he began to get into difficulties with the law.

Almost unemployable, Oxnam went to a Los Angeles employment agency on December 21, 1914. There he was engaged in conversation by Charles Witt, six years his senior in age and several levels his superior in intellect. Witt persuaded Oxnam to accompany him on a burglary that night of the home of a wealthy retiree, William M. Alexander. They went to the victim's house at

2:00 A.M. Oxnam was so frightened that Witt had to threaten him before he would enter the house.

Finally agreed, they opened a window and crawled through. Oxnam carried a pistol and Witt was armed with a chisel. Mr. and Mrs. Alexander were awakened as the burglars entered their bedroom and had to be restrained at gunpoint by Oxnam while Witt searched for valuables. During an ensuing struggle between Mr. Williams and Oxnam, the pistol discharged. Williams was killed and Oxnam was wounded in the leg. The burglars fled and escaped to hide in a rented room in the Los Angeles area. Both were arrested shortly afterward and readily confessed their crime.

One month later Oxnam was prosecuted in adult Superior Court in Los Angeles County. The California law required a previous petition and hearing in juvenile court before transferring such a case to adult court but that was never done in Oxnam's case. And, since his trial attorney never objected at Oxnam's adult trial, the California Supreme Court ruled that this right to juvenile court consideration was forever lost to Oxnam.

Oxnam was tried separately from Witt. Oxnam's sole defense was that he was "an imbecile, feeble-minded, mentally deficient, and without sufficient reasoning power to understand the nature of his acts."[57] The defense called many lay and expert witnesses to testify about Oxnam's first seventeen years of life. The psychiatrists and psychologists characterized Oxnam as a low-grade moron with the mental age of eight. This defense of insanity and diminished responsibility was to no avail. Oxnam was convicted of first-degree murder and sentenced to death.

The California Supreme Court affirmed his conviction and sentence on May 20, 1915, just about the time Oxnam was turning eighteen. The high court found adequate basis for the trial court's ruling that Oxnam was sane and approved of the procedures followed there. Appeals were made to the governor for clemency, still raising the issue of Oxnam's sanity and mental responsibility. During the summer of 1915, a select committee of the American Psychological Association examined Oxnam at San Quentin and found him to be so mentally defective as to be unresponsible for his acts. Still the governor was unconvinced and more tests and evaluations were conducted.

The last such tests found Oxnam to be sane on March 2, 1916, and on that day the governor made his final statement in the case, denying any reprieve or clemency. At 10:00 the next morning, Oxnam was hanged. Still only eighteen years old, Oxnam "went to the scaffold at San Quentin penitentiary quivering and weeping. He sobbed until the drop fell."[58]

FORTUNE FERGUSON, JR.;
EXECUTED APRIL 27, 1927; FLORIDA[59]

The case of Fortune Ferguson, Jr., must be considered despite the dearth of attention given to the case at the time. Ferguson was one of the many black boys executed for raping white girls, but he had a unique distinction. He was apparently only thirteen years old at the time of his crime, making him the youngest offender executed in this century. George Stinney, discussed in the next chapter, was younger at execution but Ferguson was the youngest at time of crime.

On June 4, 1924, apparently just before Ferguson's fourteenth birthday, he raped an eight-year-old white girl in Alachua County, Florida. Nothing is known about the circumstances of the crime or the investigation but it is known that justice came swiftly. Ferguson was indicted for rape on June 9 and pleaded not guilty at his arraignment two days later.

The criminal justice trial and sentencing process took just one day, June 16. That morning, Ferguson was found to be indigent and an attorney, Robert W. Davis, was appointed to represent him (for a fee of fifty dollars). The trial began immediately. Evidence was presented, arguments were made, a jury verdict was rendered, and final judgment and sentencing were imposed before the close of business that day. Although the jury did not recommend mercy in the case, the judge had the discretion to chose between life imprisonment and death. He chose death.

A new appellate attorney for Ferguson took the case to the Florida Supreme Court and the U.S. Supreme Court. The Florida court affirmed Ferguson's conviction and sentence on June 27, 1925, and denied a rehearing on September 25. Ferguson's attorney argued the case before the U.S. Supreme Court on February 28, 1927, but the Court dismissed the case that same day for want of a federal question.

Ferguson lived only two months longer. No record could be found of any attempts to gain executive clemency but it is certain that, if made, they were unsuccessful. He was executed at 2:30 P.M. on Wednesday, April 27, 1927, at the Florida State Farm in Raiford. Almost three years after his crime, he was still only sixteen years old.

SIX

Recent Case Studies, 1930 to 1986

The federal government began reporting detailed data and analyses for the death penalty in 1930, and thus that year serves naturally as a dividing line between early and recent executions. The number of juvenile executions rose dramatically about this time, peaking in the 1940s. And the amount and probably the accuracy of information about juvenile executions becomes much greater with the advent of the 1930s.

It is not clear, however, that the more recent cases are different in character from the earlier cases. Aside from such obvious changes over the years as the abolition of slavery and a slowing down of the legal process, the cases seem similar in kind of crime, section of the country where prosecuted, and other such considerations. Nonetheless, these recent cases are more relevant than the earlier ones to the late 1980s since they are examples of the imposition of the death penalty on juveniles by the modern American criminal justice process.

MANUEL HERNANDEZ; EXECUTED JULY 6, 1934; ARIZONA[1]

On a cool Saturday morning, January 21, 1933, Manuel Hernandez, age seventeen, and his brother Fernando, age eighteen, went hunting rabbits. They lived with their mother in a rural area just east of Casa Grande in Pima County, Arizona, and understood very little English. Manuel carried their shotgun and the two brothers consumed two pints of whiskey as they walked along.

Near the highway they saw an old man sitting by his campfire. He was Charles P. Washburn, a sixty-five-year-old prospector from Needles, California. The Hernandez brothers concocted a plan to rob Washburn. As Manuel engaged him in conversation from the front, Fernando sneaked around from the rear, picking up an abandoned car wheel spindle as he went. Fernando struck Washburn on the head, knocking him unconscious. The Hernandez brothers dragged Washburn about 170 yards back into the brush, where Manuel shot and killed the old man.

They took thirty-five dollars from him and dumped his body into an abandoned well, covering it with dirt and brush. They drove off in his Model T Ford truck but abandoned it a short distance away when it mired down. Manuel tossed the murder weapon in a mesquite bush. They walked back home, told their mother good-bye, and left for Chandler, Arizona, a few miles north of their home.

Washburn's body was found the next day. Police who found the shotgun under the bush two or three days later identified it as belonging to the Hernandez family. Fernando had returned home again by then and was arrested for the murder. His detailed confession implicated Manuel, who was arrested in Chandler. Manuel provided a complete written confession, which later was instrumental at his trial. Manuel and Fernando were held in the Pinal County jail in Florence.

The county prosecutor filed an information charging both Manuel and Fernando with first-degree murder. They waived a preliminary hearing on February 8 and were held without bail. Still without counsel or interpreter, they were unsuccessful at a hearing on April 8 in having the information set aside. Their cases were severed and set for trial.

Manuel was represented by appointed counsel at his trial in mid-April. The state's evidence was compelling, including Manuel's written confession, and his testimony at the trial did not contradict the confession. Under Arizona law at the time, the jury had the sole discretion concerning sentences of life imprisonment or death. The defendant's age was deemed relevant only in regard to intent to murder and not necessarily for purposes of choosing the sentence. The judge instructed the jury that persons over age fourteen were presumed capable of having a murderous intent and that

> the age of this defendant is to be considered by you only for the purposes of determining whether or not he had, at the time of the alleged crime, sufficient mental capacity to entertain a criminal intent; that is, to distinguish between right and wrong, and sufficient mental capacity to intend to do the wrongful act charged in this information.[2]

On May 16 the jury convicted Manuel of murder and set the penalty at death. The trial judge sentenced him to hang according to the current Arizona law. The same fate was announced for Fernando at the end of his trial.

On October 23 a new amendment to the Arizona constitution changed the method of execution to the gas chamber and did away with hanging. When the Arizona Supreme Court considered the appeal, it found that this change could legally be imposed on Manuel. The defendant challenged the trial court's instruction concerning the limited use of age by the jury, but the Arizona Supreme Court concluded that "There is no other ground upon which age may be admitted and considered."[3]

Both Manuel and Fernando were scheduled to die in Arizona's new gas chamber. The night before the execution Manuel tried to save his older brother's life by claiming that Fernando had nothing to do with the murder. It was to no avail. At 5:00 the next morning they entered the gas chamber and sat in specially fitted adjoining chairs. Strapped in the new death chairs, they held hands as the cyanide pellets were dropped. Manuel died at 5:11 A.M., one minute earlier than his older brother.

MONROE HASTY; EXECUTED SEPTEMBER 16, 1935; FLORIDA[4]

Monroe Hasty's parents lived in Orlando but Monroe, a sixteen-year-old black boy, roomed and boarded in Eldridge, Florida, to be nearer his job. The job was doing yard work, and among his clients were George and Helena Loucakis, white owners and operators of a gasoline station and general store near Eldridge. Hasty was very well thought of by everyone who knew him. He was able to read and write and had never been in any trouble with the law. George Loucakis was later to testify that Hasty had been an excellent boy— that is, before he shot and killed George's wife.

Mr. and Mrs. Loucakis lived in the back part of their home and had their store in the front room. Behind their home they had a chicken coop, some stacked firewood, and other typical homestead staples. They had owned and operated the store for four years and were popular in the community. And, as was to become significant later on, Helena Loucakis's brother was a deputy sheriff for their county.

Around the first of June, 1934, Hasty visited his parents in Orlando. While there, he spent $8.50 for a pawn shop pistol, his first. He was fascinated by guns, despite a childhood accident in which he shot his brother while playing with a gun. When he returned to Eldridge he carried his new gun with him.

On Friday, June 7, Hasty did his customary yard work around the Loucakis place. He decided to return that night to steal some chickens. Just after midnight he was hiding behind the woodpile, smoking a cigarette and trying to get the nerve to grab some chickens and run. George had gone to bed and Helena was sitting at her desk by the screened window, finishing the bookkeeping and counting the cash from the day's business. Hasty sneaked up to the window, with his gun in the waistband of his trousers.

Apparently thinking he could rob her, Hasty placed the pistol against the screen and shot Mrs. Loucakis in the abdomen as she rose to close up for the night. Hasty panicked and ran away, forgetting the cigarettes and lighter he had left behind the woodpile as well as any plan of robbery. Mrs. Loucakis called out to her husband but had difficulty arousing him. He finally stumbled sleepily out of bed to find his wife mortally wounded. After helping her into bed he ran to the front of the store, blowing a whistle and firing his gun to alert the neighborhood.

A neighbor ran to get the victim's brother, the deputy sheriff, while George telephoned a doctor, an ambulance, and the sheriff's office. By 1:30 A.M. Saturday the scene was swarming with law-enforcement officers, ambulance attendants, a doctor, and many neighbors and passersby. They found the bullet hole in the screen with powder burns around it, indicating a point-blank shot. Hasty's cigarettes and lighter were found by the woodpile, and his footprints were traced from there to the window and back. Meanwhile, emergency surgery was performed on Mrs. Loucakis, but she died on Sunday.

Hasty was arrested before dawn the morning of the shooting and taken to the crime scene. Interrogated intensively for the next several days, he gave a variety of explanations for what had happened. He was transported first to the Deland jail, then to the Orlando jail, and finally to the Tampa jail 145 miles away. His written confession provided on June 14 stated that he had been stealing chickens and the pistol had accidentally discharged as he was closing the chicken-pen gate, a considerable distance behind the house. The powder burns on the screen and the empty cartridge found next to the window rendered Hasty's version unlikely at best.

Hasty was indicted by the Volusia County grand jury on July 18, and an attorney was appointed to represent him. Since Hasty was only sixteen years old, the court ordered that his parents be notified, and his father was with him at his trial. At 9:00 A.M. on July 26 he was arraigned and the one-day trial began immediately. After hearing all the state's witnesses, the jurors went out to inspect the crime scene. They returned to the courtroom to hear the defense evidence, which consisted only of Hasty's testimony.

That evening the jury returned a verdict of guilty of first-degree murder and made no recommendation of mercy. At 9:00 A.M. the next day, the trial judge sentenced Hasty to be electrocuted for his crime. The defense attorney moved for a new trial but his motion was denied on July 30.

Hasty's case was appealed to the Florida Supreme Court. That delayed his execution but was ultimately unsuccessful. The court affirmed his conviction and sentence on May 6, 1935, and denied a rehearing on August 29. Less than two weeks later the governor signed Hasty's death warrant, giving him one more week to live. Hasty, at age seventeen, was electrocuted in the Raiford prison.

WILLIE JAMES WHITFIELD;
EXECUTED AUGUST 19, 1938; ALABAMA[5]

Willie "Bo" Whitfield was a sixteen-year-old black boy living on the outskirts of Montgomery, Alabama, in the fall of 1937, the depth of the Great Depression. Whitfield occasionally slept in boxcars at the nearby railyard, had a reputation as a thief, and was wanted on a charge of robbery of forty-three dollars from a vending machine. Still legally a child and childish in appearance, Whitfield had little more than a year to live.

Nearby was the Carter Hill Road general store, owned and operated by fifty-nine-year-old Fred Heins. A member of a well-liked local white family, Heins had lived in the Montgomery area for thirty years and had run the store for the past five years. At about 5:00 A.M. on Friday, September 17, 1937, Heins was reading his morning newspaper in a lawn chair outside his store. Whitfield, having slept in a boxcar the night before and needing money badly, came to the store that early morning to rob it. He brought with him an ax that he had stolen recently from a nearby garage.

Whitfield smashed the ax into Heins's head, crushing his skull, and dragged the dying man into the store. Whitfield ran away after grabbing a shotgun and a few dollars from the till. Stashing the shotgun in some weeds and the ax in a railroad culvert, he went home to wash the blood off and change his bloody shirt. By 6:00 A.M. a passerby had discovered the pool of blood by the lawn chair and a trail of blood into the store. The police were alerted and they found the victim's body on the floor of the store. The coroner arrived and concluded that Heins had been murdered. Using bloodhounds to track the killer, the police found the ax fifty yards away, covered with Heins's hair and blood.

The first suspect was a black man who was arrested but soon released after preliminary questioning. The police then arrested and questioned a white hitchhiker but he was also released. Suspicion then focused on a known thief and robber from the local area, Willie Whitfield. At 6:00 that evening the police arrested Whitfield near his home. They found his bloody shirt in the house and easily gained a confession from Whitfield, who then led them to the shotgun. Whitfield first tried to put the blame for the crime on an older black man but subsequent police questioning of that man revealed a satisfactory alibi.

Early the next morning Whitfield was incarcerated in the relatively secure Kilby Prison as a precaution against escape or lynching. On Sunday he made a complete confession, admitting sole responsibility for the crime. This confession was to become instrumental at his trial.

Whitfield was indicted for first-degree murder, and proceedings began in the adult criminal court in Montgomery County. Whitfield's attorney moved to transfer him to juvenile court since he was still only sixteen years old. The adult court decided to retain jurisdiction. Next the defense moved to delay proceedings long enough to determine Whitfield's mental competence to stand trial. When that motion was also denied, Whitfield pleaded not guilty and went to trial. He was convicted and sentenced to death.

Whitfield's conviction and sentence were upheld by the Alabama Supreme Court on June 16, 1938. Since his original execution date had passed while the appeal was pending, a new date was set. Still at Kilby Prison, Whitfield became rebellious. He fashioned a small knife and expressed his intent "to take somebody with him."[6] He was prevented from doing so and settled down to consult with the prison minister.

At 12:01 A.M. on the appointed day, Whitfield became the youngest person to die in Alabama's electric chair. His final words were part prayer, part confession, and part complaint: "I'm goin' on home. . . . tell 'em all I'm going on home to rest with Jesus. Preacher, all you all, goodbye. I'm ready to go. I've made up with the Good Master. If I hadn't did what I did I wouldn't be ready to go. . . . don't pull those straps so tight."[7]

DOMINICK GUARIGLIA;
EXECUTED JANUARY 26, 1939; NEW YORK[8]

Dominick Guariglia was an Italian boy growing up in a rough neighborhood on the East Side of Manhattan. At age fifteen he had been arrested for burglary but the charges had been dismissed. At age seventeen he was involved with a gang of hoodlums several years older than he was and bearing a variety of ethnic surnames (Chaleff, Ertel, Friedman, O'Loughlin, and Zimmerman). Probably after perpetrating a series of robberies, their last robbery went wrong and cost four lives.

The late-night restaurant at 144 Second Avenue had been the target of a robbery two weeks earlier and had been given special police protection. At 3:15 A.M. Friday, April 10, 1937, two plainclothes detectives, Foley and Gallagher, were sitting with the restaurant owner at a table near the entrance. Four males, including Guariglia, entered the restaurant with guns drawn. Foley reached for his weapon and was shot to death by O'Loughlin. Gallagher then wounded O'Loughlin and a gun battle ensued.

Guariglia was arrested along with Friedman at the scene. O'Loughlin escaped from the restaurant but was arrested at a hospital a short time later. Chaleff and Zimmerman were arrested soon thereafter and over a year later a sixth man, Ertel, was arrested. Guariglia was held without bail and soon was indicted along with the others on a felony-murder charge. They confessed and came to trial in the Court of General Sessions of New York County. Their prosecutor was a politically ambitious district attorney named Thomas E. Dewey, later governor of New York and Republican candidate for the presidency.

Guariglia, only seventeen at the time of the crime and the youngest member of the gang by several years, relied on the defenses of duress and mental incapacity at his trial. He was convicted and sentenced to death, as were the other members of the gang. On December 9, 1938, the New York Court of Appeals affirmed their convictions and death sentences. The executions were scheduled for six weeks later at the Sing Sing prison.

Strong efforts were made with the governor for clemency, led by an ad hoc group known as the Joint Committee to Aid the Five East Side Boys. Their mothers sat in the front row in hearings before the governor and a petition was presented with 35,000 signatures. Their efforts were 40 percent successful. Chaleff and Zimmerman had their sentences commuted to life but Guariglia, Friedman, and O'Loughlin were not spared.

At 11:06 P.M. Guariglia was executed at age eighteen, in between the executions of Friedman and O'Loughlin. Guariglia prayed with the prison's Catholic chaplain on the evening of his execution. As he was being strapped into the electric chair, he smiled but said nothing.

WILLIE B. CLAY, EDWARD POWELL, AND NATHANIEL WALKER; EXECUTED DECEMBER 29, 1941; FLORIDA[9]

These three black boys lived near each other in Jacksonville, Florida, in the late 1930s. At the time of their crime, Clay and Powell were fifteen years old and Walker was fourteen. Each came from somewhat disrupted families but had supportive relatives in Jacksonville. While they were not particularly accomplished students, they had completed several grades successfully in the public school system. They were friends and enjoyed doing things together. They were to die in the same electric chair, within a few minutes of each other.

One Saturday evening in the hottest time of summer, August 6, 1938, they rode their bicycles to the neighborhood store with a plan to rob it. Mrs. Mary Louise Curtis, age fifty-nine and nearly blind, ran the small store out of her modest home. She became so concerned about the three black boys loitering around her store that she asked neighbors to watch them for her.

At 8:30 P.M. the three boys entered the store to carry out their robbery plan. Either Mrs. Curtis fought with them or they panicked for other reasons, but the robbery went awry. One of the boys (it never became clear which one) struck her on the head with an iron bar and she fell to the floor fatally injured. The boys abandoned their robbery intent and ran from the store, temporarily escaping capture.

Neighbors who heard the scuffle and saw the boys run out went into the store and found the gravely wounded proprietress. She died in the early morning hours on Sunday. The murder spurred a month-long investigation and search for her killers. The police found a set of fingerprints at the scene and began to look for the person who left them there.

Walker and Powell were arrested on September 10 as they were attempting an armed robbery of a Jacksonville restaurant. Police investigation revealed that Walker's fingerprints matched those found at the scene of the murder of Mrs. Curtis. They questioned Walker and Powell about that crime, and on September 11 the two boys made a full confession. They even accompanied police to the crime scene and explained how it had happened. Their confessions implicated Clay in the crime. Clay was then arrested, and his confession corroborated the statements of Walker and Powell. All three boys were later to claim that the police obtained these confessions by kicking and beating them with blackjacks and rubber hoses, but they were never able to substantiate their claims.

On October 18 the Duval County grand jury indicted Clay, Powell, and Walker for murder, robbery, and various other crimes associated with the events of August 6. Each pleaded not guilty at the joint arraignment on November 8, and one attorney was appointed to represent the three defendants. He had only twenty days to prepare their defenses, as their joint trial began on November 28. Ample evidence was presented against the three defendants, including their written confessions.

At 10:00 A.M. on December 8 the jury returned a verdict of guilty of first-degree murder for all three defendants and did not recommend mercy for any of them. The defense attorney's motion for a new trial was denied on that date and Clay, Powell, and Walker were sentenced to death by the judge. By this time Clay had turned sixteen, but Powell and Walker were still only fifteen.

The case was appealed to the Florida Supreme Court, which ultimately affirmed all three convictions and death sentences on May 24, 1940. Within the technical provisions of the Florida law, persons could be sentenced to death for crimes committed while age fourteen or fifteen, but the feelings of the court on this issue seemed to suggest a desire for a different outcome: "The ages of the defendants here present a very serious question. We feel that this question, under the laws of Florida, is addressed to the discretion of the Board of Pardons."[10] The court's feelings were apparently not shared by the Board of Pardons. Despite extensive consideration of their cases by the board and the governor, their death sentences were not commuted.

The three childhood friends and fellow murderers were electrocuted at Raiford prison. Walker, the youngest, only eighteen years and four months old, died first, at 9:08 A.M.. Powell died thirteen minutes later; he was eighteen years and eight months old. Clay, four days past his nineteenth birthday, died eighteen minutes after Powell.

EUGENE BURNAM; EXECUTED MARCH 27, 1942; KENTUCKY[11]

Eugene Burnam was a fifteen-year-old black boy living with his mother and older brother in Lexington, Kentucky. In 1938 Burnam had been arrested and prosecuted in juvenile court for a relatively minor trespass and burglary. A year later he was doing janitorial work after school in a local hardware store and was well thought of by his teacher and his employer. Unlike most of the juvenile death penalty defendants, Burnam had the family and community backing to be certain of a strong resistance to his fate.

On Saturday night, April 1, 1939, he attempted to rape a twenty-four-year-old white woman but was frightened off. On Wednesday night, April 5, he tried the same thing with a twenty-two-year-old white woman but was similarly unsuccessful. Shortly after 10:00 P.M. the next evening he achieved his goal.

Mrs. Hazel Perkins, age twenty-two and also white, was walking toward a bus stop after visiting her brother and his family. She had lived with her mother since being separated from her husband. Burnam confronted Mrs. Perkins, described as a "comely brunette,"[12] as she was walking near an alley. He forced her into the alley and raped her. Burnam threatened to kill Perkins with his knife if she didn't cooperate and refused her offer of money to leave her alone. During the fifteen to twenty minutes of the rape, Perkins saw Burnam plainly in the illumination of the streetlight.

After Burnam left, Perkins ran to a nearby restaurant to call the police. Officers examined the crime scene and picked up a trail that led them to Burnam's house. They found Burnam in bed, his knife still in his trousers pocket. They arrested him at 11:30 P.M., little more than an hour after the rape. Other officers took Perkins to the police station and she identified Burnam when he was brought in. They then took her to the hospital, where a medical examination confirmed recent sexual intercourse.

Burnam was questioned throughout the night and finally confessed. He later was to claim that his confession was beaten out of him but the courts ultimately decided that was not the case. He was moved to the county jail soon after signing his written confession. His earlier attempted rape victims also identified him as the perpetrator.

It took four trials and almost three years to move from crime to execution. The day after the crime, April 7, a preliminary hearing was held in juvenile court. A subsequent indictment for forcible rape caused the juvenile court to transfer his case to adult court on Monday, April 10. He was arraigned on that day and directed to plead not guilty. The court appointed counsel to represent Burnam and scheduled his trial to begin on April 13.

Burnam's attorneys moved for an assessment of his mental competence to stand trial, but the three physicians who examined him found him sane. That caused a week's delay, and the trial began on April 20, still only two weeks after the rape of Perkins.

This first trial was brief. Concern about possible disruption caused the bailiffs to search the spectators as they entered the courtroom. The case was called at 2:25 P.M. and the jury was impaneled forty-five minutes later. The state's evidence relied on Perkins's testimony and that of the examining physician, the investigating police officer, and the juvenile court judge. The defense called Burnam's mother, teacher, and employer, but Burnam did not testify in his own behalf. Defense counsel "asked that the jurors be more lenient because of the youth's age."[13] The jury received the case at 10:14 that evening and returned their verdict thirty-eight minutes later, finding Burnam guilty of forcible rape.

Burnam's court-appointed attorneys moved for a new trial two days later. Such motions are typically denied immediately and routinely, but this trial judge took several months before finally deciding to grant the motion. In the interim, friends of Burnam's family hired three black lawyers from Louisville to represent him, and his court-appointed attorney withdrew from the case. The new lawyers filed additional briefs on the motion for a new trial, claiming improper and inflammatory prosecutive evidence at trial, and that apparently tipped the balance in Burnam's favor.

At Burnam's second trial, which began on November 22, 1939, he was represented by the three Louisville lawyers. This trial took two days for the jury selection and evidence, with the jury receiving the case at 10:00 P.M. on November 24. By noon on November 25, the jury had not decided on its verdict and met again with the trial judge in open court. The judge encouraged them to continue deliberating, implying that he might keep them for several days to get a verdict. The jury returned a verdict of guilty two hours later. Burnam was sentenced to death by the judge.

The judge's implied threat to the jury resulted in reversal of the case by the Kentucky Court of Appeals on May 31, 1940. Burnam's third trial was held six months later but resulted in a hung jury. Nevertheless, the prosecutor, who had pursued the Burnam case from the beginning, would not give up. Within days Burnam's fourth trial began.

This trial was Burnam's longest and was to be his last. It began in late November 1940 and took a long time to select a jury, with the defense making a determined but unsuccessful effort to place blacks on the jury. A guilty verdict was not returned until January 26, 1941. The trial judge denied Burnam's motion for a fifth trial. Two days later he gave the death sentence to Burnam, by then only two weeks away from his seventeenth birthday.

Burnam's attorneys continued to fight for his life. They again took his case to the Kentucky Court of Appeals but this court ruled against him on October 31, 1941, and refused to rehear his appeal on February 20, 1942. Burnam's attorneys continued to seek additional appellate court review and clemency from Governor Keen Johnson. They talked with the governor for an hour on the telephone on the evening before Burnam's execution.

Burnam was electrocuted at 1:10 A.M. at the state prison in Eddyville. Apparently "smiling as he entered the death chamber,"[14] he was just over age eighteen.

PAUL GIACOMAZZA; EXECUTED JUNE 30, 1942; MASSACHUSETTS[15]

Only seventeen at the time of his crime, Paul Giacomazza was the last juvenile executed in Massachusetts. He lived with his father, mother, and sister and had a typical working-class Catholic family life. He had a good record in high school and in various jobs. His mother was loyal to the end, visiting him the afternoon before he was executed.

Two of Giacomazza's friends, William Lenehan and James Nickerson, were driving around in Lenehan's car on the evening of September 9, 1940. They stopped by a pool hall in Malden, Massachusetts, and picked up Giacomazza. Their aimless cruising eventually took on a purpose—to rob a gasoline station. At 11:30 P.M. Lenehan parked some distance away from a Shell station in Melrose. Giacomazza and Nickerson walked to the station, each armed with a handgun.

The station's night manager was Oscar E. Thomas, whose large size and rugged appearance belied his age of seventy-four. Thomas had been a robbery victim in the past. He had been shot in the elbow several years earlier and now kept his own handgun hidden in a desk drawer. Only a month previously he had used it to shoot at two thieves. He was not an easy mark.

Nickerson entered the station first and walked into the restroom behind where Thomas was sitting. Giacomazza then entered the front door with his handgun pointed at Thomas. Thomas reached for his gun and the would-be robbers panicked. Nickerson shot Thomas in the back and Giacomazza shot Thomas in the wrist. They ran from the station, jumped in Lenehan's car, and sped away.

Thomas calmly called the police to report the robbery attempt and to describe the robbers. He then sat waiting patiently for them to arrive. They responded immediately and took Thomas to the hospital, where he was to linger for fifty-one days before dying of complications from the back wound and heart problems. Meanwhile, Giacomazza and Nickerson were dropped off by Lenehan, who drove away only to run out of gas a short distance away. A passing motorist who stopped to give Lenehan a lift was a key witness at the later trial.

The police immediately cordoned off the area but the assailants had already escaped. A month later they threw the murder weapons into the Charles River, later to be found by a police diver. Nickerson joined the U.S. Army in November and was feted by local citizens' organizations for being such a loyal American. Giacomazza continued to commit robberies and was arrested in April 1941 for one in Belmont, Massachusetts. Continued police investigation resulted in Lenehan's arrest. He made a complete written confession on May 13, 1941. Nickerson was arrested at an Army training camp soon thereafter.

Lenehan decided to cooperate with the prosecutor and to testify at the trial of Giacomazza and Nickerson. He pleaded guilty and was convicted of being an accessory to murder, receiving a sentence to the Concord Reformatory. Giacomazza and Nickerson were indicted for first-degree murder, and their trial began in late November. They had separate attorneys who worked in concert during the joint trial. The defendants were convicted and the judge sentenced them to death in mid-December. After the trial judge denied their motion for a new trial, the Supreme Judicial Court of Massachusetts affirmed their convictions and sentences on May 25, 1942.

Their lawyers continued to seek relief from the governor. One petition, from the Massachusetts Council for the Abolition of the Death Penalty, had 1,000 signatures. The parole board voted against them after a hearing on June 12, 1942, and afterward both Giacomazza and Nickerson signed full confessions. The most bizarre twist occurred when the prison warden received a telephone call threatening a dynamite explosion at the prison if the execution took place as scheduled.

All of it was to no avail. Giacomazza's mother visited her only son for the last time on the afternoon of June 29, 1942. A Catholic priest spent the evening with Giacomazza, preparing him for what was to come. The execution took place shortly after midnight the next day. Nickerson died at 12:17 A.M., and Giacomazza, by then barely nineteen years old, died eight minutes later.

EDWARD HAIGHT; EXECUTED JULY 8, 1943; NEW YORK[16]

Edward Haight was a troubled high school dropout. He was only sixteen years old at the time of his crime but appeared older, being six feet tall and muscular. A dark-complexioned Caucasian, he had a history of stealing cars and trying to escape from pursuing police. He bragged of an exploit two years earlier, in which he and a friend tied a girl to the front bumper of a car and drove her around for an hour. He also told of filling a fountain pen with his own blood. At age fourteen he had been examined by psychiatrists, who advised close supervision for several years.

Haight's family life in Stamford, Connecticut, had been chaotic. His uncle had been in Sing Sing prison for ten years and his father had spent long terms in various prisons. When Haight was thirteen, a fire destroyed his house and killed his mother. He and the two other Haight children began living with a series of foster parents, but he "found neither stability, security nor parental love in any of these substitute homes."[17] All of that contributed to Haight's early stage of psychosis and total lack of moral values.

Late on Sunday evening, September 13, 1942, Haight stole a station wagon in Stamford and began to search for a woman. He pulled over a woman who was driving on the Merritt Parkway and announced his intentions but was frightened off by her dog in the back seat. He later tried to pick up a woman who was walking home from work but she too rebuffed him. By Monday evening he apparently was getting desperate.

At about 6:30 P.M. he saw two white girls walking along the street near Bedford Village, New York. The girls, eight-year-old Helen Lynch and her seven-year-old sister, Margaret, had been playing that afternoon at a friend's house near their home. The Lynch girls and their two sisters lived with their father in Bedford Village, their mother being confined to a hospital for tuberculosis. Haight enticed the girls into his car and they were never seen alive again.

Haight apparently tried to rape the girls, at least the eight-year-old. Unsuccessful, he beat them and tied them up. Sometime during the night he threw Margaret into the Beaver Dam Brook and Helen into the Kensica Reservoir. Both girls died by drowning. Their father had called the police but a search, joined by the New York and Connecticut police, the Federal Bureau of Investigation, and hundreds of townspeople, produced no immediate results. Haight went home, abandoning the stolen car on the way.

The car, found the next day, provided several clues to the thief's identity. That afternoon three children wading in the Beaver Dam Brook found Margaret's body. Evidence from the car and her body led the police to arrest Haight at his Stamford home at 7:00 P.M. He still had the gas ration book with him from the stolen car he had abandoned. Two hours later he confessed to the crimes and led police to Helen's body.

Haight waived extradiction and was taken from Connecticut to White Plains, New York, for criminal proceedings. He was indicted immediately on two counts of kidnapping and two counts of murder. Examination by two state psychiatrists found him competent to stand trial. He was arraigned on September 24, and his appointed defense counsel was given one month to prepare for trial.

The trial began on October 26 in White Plains. A jury of six men and six women was selected, and the state began presenting its considerable evidence against Haight. The sole defense was insanity, resting on the testimony of one psychiatrist called by Haight's attorney. This expert was the only defense witness, since Haight's attorney changed his mind about putting Haight on the witness stand. In his closing statement to the jury, Haight's attorney summarized his position: "I do not ask you to turn this unfortunate boy out. I ask you to return a verdict of not guilty by reason of insanity, so he can be placed in an institution where he belongs."[18]

The jury received the case just before 5:00 P.M. on November 5 and decided it by 6:30. The verdict was guilty as charged, carrying with it a mandatory death penalty. On November 17 the judge imposed the automatic sentence. Haight was reported to have worn a "half-wistful, other-world smile."[19] The case was not over yet, as review by an appellate court was also automatic in death penalty cases.

This appeal was argued on April 15, 1943, before the New York Court of Appeals, which affirmed Haight's conviction and sentence six weeks later without opinion, apparently finding nothing of significance to discuss. Following that came seven months of continued but vain attempts to gain a judicial review or clemency from Governor Thomas E. Dewey.

Haight passed the time on Sing Sing's death row by eating, gaining thirty pounds in the eight months between trial and execution. On July 7, 1943, he seemed anxious and lonely: "I guess this is my last day and I am only seventeen. I wish somebody would come and visit me. I'd like some company."[20] Haight was executed at Sing Sing the next day.

GEORGE JUNIUS STINNEY, JR.; EXECUTED JUNE 16, 1944; SOUTH CAROLINA[21]

George Stinney's case is the most famous of all juvenile executions for a variety of reasons. He was a black boy accused of trying to rape and then killing two white girls in the South. His judgment was particularly swift and unencumbered. And, at age fourteen years and eight months, he was the youngest person executed in this century.

Stinney lived with his family in the small lumber-mill town of Alcolu, South Carolina. He had been born on October 21, 1929, in Pinewood, moving the fifteen miles to Alcolu at age twelve. His parents, George, Sr., and Amie, were sharecroppers and his father also worked in the lumber mill. They were a fairly typical, hardworking couple who regularly attended the local black Baptist church. They lived in a shack owned by the mill with their five young children, of whom George, Jr., was the oldest. Stinney was able to read and write and was just finishing the seventh grade when he committed his crimes.

On Friday afternoon, March 24, 1944, Stinney was tending to a grazing cow in a field near the railroad tracks just outside Alcolu. Riding along the tracks on a bicycle were two white girls, daughters of co-workers of Stinney's father at the mill. The owner of the bicycle was Betty June Binnicker, an eleven-year-old girl in the sixth grade, whom Stinney found attractive. Riding in tandem with her was Mary Emma Thames, only eight years old and in the first grade. They asked Stinney where they might find some wildflowers to pick and he suggested a spot in a wooded area.

He led the two girls to the flowers. They proceeded to clip some with their scissors and accumulated a small bouquet. Stinney left to walk back to the railroad tracks but turned, picked up a railroad spike, and walked back to the girls. He made sexual advances to the Binnicker girl. Refused, he lashed out at both girls. He bashed in the Thames girl's skull with the spike and chased after the Binnicker girl. He tried to rape her but apparently was not successful. He hit her with the spike and she died instantly, as had the Thames girl. Stinney dumped the girls' bodies and their bicycle into a water-filled ditch, where the bodies remained partially submerged through the night. He then ran home to eat his supper and sleep one last night in his own bed.

The families of the victims became alarmed when they did not return at nightfall. A search party of 200 persons spent the night looking for them but darkness prevented any reasonable chance of success. Shortly after dawn the next morning, searchers found the girls' footprints leading from the railroad and into the woods. They followed them, finding first the scissors, then a crumpled bouquet of flowers, and finally the water-filled ditch with the two bodies.

After a brief investigation an arrest warrant was issued that day for Stinney. He was arrested by the local constable and questioned aggressively. Forty minutes after his arrest, Stinney signed a written confession. Strong feelings and talk of a lynching swept the rural community, so that evening Stinney was moved out of the county jail to an undisclosed location. The strong community feelings apparently carried over to the entire Stinney family. As soon as Stinney was arrested, the mill owner told Stinney's father to leave Alcolu. The entire family left, never to return.

On March 29 a coroner's inquest concluded that Stinney had murdered the two victims and recommended action by a grand jury. The grand jury responded, indicting Stinney for both murders. Council was appointed to represent Stinney since his family had no money to hire counsel. His appointed counsel was C. N. Plowden, a thirty-one-year-old fledgling politician anxious to avoid unfavorable publicity. His subsequent representation of Stinney was uninspired and probably legally inadequate.

The next regular court session was to begin in late June, but several influential politicians thought that was too long to wait. The state solicitor convened a special session of the court in Manning, Clarendon County, for the sole purpose of holding Stinney's trial. The defense neglected to ask for a change of venue to a less emotionally charged community.

The trial was conducted on April 24, exactly one month after the crime. An estimated 1,500 persons crowded the tiny courtroom and spilled over onto the surrounding courthouse lawn. Stinney wore a faded blue work shirt and blue denim pants. During the morning twenty-four prospective jurors were examined before the jury of twelve local white men was impaneled at 12:30 P.M. The trial proceeded with evidence of the murder of Binnicker and, given the result of that charge, Stinney was never tried for the Thames murder. The prosecution's evidence took only thirty minutes to present. No evidence and no witnesses were presented by the defense, but Stinney's attorney did raise the issue of Stinney's extreme youthfulness. The jury received the case at 4:55 P.M. and returned its verdict ten minutes later. Stinney was found guilty of murder with no recommendation of mercy and was sentenced to die.

The defendant's version of the facts was either poorly presented or omitted altogether. Stinney's first statement to the police claimed that the girls had attacked him and that he had fought them off in self-defense. However, his later confession changed the facts to those presented by the prosecution at trial. Stinney's family later expressed the belief that the little girls had been killed elsewhere by a white murderer and that the bodies had been taken to the black neighborhood to divert suspicion. The Stinney family never accepted the court's conclusion that Stinney committed the crimes, believing that his confession had been forced from him by his interrogators.

After the trial ended, defense attorney Plowden never saw Stinney or any member of his family again and never advised them of any right to appeal or challenge the sentence. If the attorney had filed a one-sentence notice of appeal and taken the case to the South Carolina Supreme Court, Stinney's execution would have been stayed for at least a year.[22] On May 28 Stinney was taken from the county jail to the South Carolina Penitentiary in Columbia. While there the fourteen-year-old boy wrote to his mother, claiming innocence and begging her to help him, but "All she knew how to do was pray."[23]

Despite the total lack of legal representation after trial, Stinney's case was pursued by a variety of community, ministerial, and union organizations. The governor received fifty letters and telegrams urging clemency. The state Board of Pardons considered the case but recommended no clemency. The NAACP sent a special protest to the governor on June 12 but did not achieve the desired end.

The attitude of the community was actually quite mixed. Some agreed with those seeking clemency. An ensign in training at Charleston said that "No adult human—humane—being could believe that a boy so young, hardly in his adolescence, should be held morally and legally responsible for his acts to the extent that his life should be taken for his misdeeds."[24] Others were much less sympathetic: "As for myself, I feel sorry for the parents of the boy, but if he was old enough to commit the crime, he is old enough to pay the penalty. At this enlightened age, this boy was old enough to know the penalty for such a deed."[25]

To resolve the dilemma, Governor Johnston visited Stinney on death row on June 14. Afterward he announced that the brutality of the crime outweighed Stinney's youthfulness. Some have noted that the governor was challenging the incumbent U.S. senator in a July primary and may have thought it was too costly politically to commute Stinney's sentence.

As his execution date drew near, Stinney alternately studied the Bible and made additional confessions of guilt. On Sunday, June 11, he was visited by his family for the last time. His execution was set for Friday. Just before his execution he told the sheriff that he was sorry he had committed the crime and hoped God and his parents would forgive him. He slept well the night before he died and appeared calm when he arose the next morning.

Just after 7:00 A.M. Stinney was led from his deathhouse cell to the adjoining room with the electric chair. Fifty witnesses were assembled there. Forty of them came from the rural area where the crime occurred, including both fathers of the little girls Stinney had killed. As Stinney entered the death chamber carrying his Bible with him, he "appeared far more at ease than some of those who came to watch him die."[26]

The electric chair in which Stinney was seated was designed for adults. He was only five feet one and weighed only ninety-five pounds, about typical for a boy age fourteen years and eight months. According to a newspaper report, "He is calm, a relief to the guards, who fumble with the straps designed for larger victims. As the current surges through his body, Stinney's wide-eyed face emerges from under the loose-fitting mask on his head. Tears are flowing from his eyes."[27] Three jolts of electricity hit Stinney, beginning at 7:30 A.M. He survived only three minutes.

Stinney's body was taken to a funeral home in Sumter, South Carolina, for a private family funeral. Soon after the funeral the Stinney family moved north, settling outside New York City. A foster brother living in Brooklyn in the 1980s remembered the incident vividly and angrily: "They sat in judgment and they killed an innocent kid like they was God Almighty. They took him, they tried him, and they fried him."[28] Stinney's sister, only nine years old in 1944, later said: "They railroaded that child. What was the purpose of executing him so fast?"[29]

FRANK LOVELESS; EXECUTED SEPTEMBER 29, 1944; NEVADA[30]

Frank Loveless had problems as a boy growing up in Indiana. One of them, a penchant for burglaries, landed him in the Indiana reformatory. Still only fifteen years old, he and a friend, Dale Cline, escaped from the reformatory on August 15, 1942. The typical juvenile escapee might run to hide near home but Loveless and Cline decided to head west. They used their carefully honed skills at car theft and burglary to facilitate the trip.

They arrived in Elko, Nevada, on Wednesday evening, August 19, having covered some 2,000 miles in four days. The trip had frayed their nerves and strained their friendship. They quarreled sometime that night and decided to split up the next morning. Cline kept the stolen car they had been driving and Loveless walked around looking for another car to steal. At 9:15 A.M. on August 20 Loveless found one with the keys in the ignition and drove it out of town, heading west on the main highway. Cline followed in the other car.

The owner of the Elko car discovered it missing almost immediately and authorities in surrounding areas were notified. The law-enforcement agent in Carlin, the next town west of Elko, was A. H. Berning, a fifty-six-year-old grandfather who had been constable there for twenty-six years. Berning took up his post on the eastern side of Carlin, watching for the stolen car to arrive. He saw it approaching, flagged it over, and walked up to speak to the driver. Seeing a mere boy at the wheel, he chose not to draw his weapon but to talk the boy into surrendering. Speaking with a reluctant but determined voice, Berning said, "I have got to take you in, Buddy."[31]

Loveless seemed to agree, so Berning walked around and got in the car, sitting in the right front passenger's seat. A struggle ensued over Berning's revolver and he was shot twice by Loveless. The first shot just grazed Berning but the second hit him in the neck and instantly paralyzed him. Loveless began driving west again with the mortally wounded Berning still in the front seat. Loveless, followed by Cline, parked the car by the side of the road near a highway construction site about twenty miles from his encounter with Berning. He hopped into Cline's car and they drove on, leaving Berning slumped in the abandoned car.

Other patrol cars soon found the abandoned car and Berning. Workers at the construction site described Loveless and Cline and their car. Meanwhile, Loveless admitted to Cline that he had shot Berning, resulting in another quarrel. Cline made Loveless get out and drove away. Loveless, now hitch-hiking, was picked up within minutes by the police. Cline led the police on a

200-mile chase, stopping only when his car was blasted by a police shotgun at a roadblock. Both suspects were taken back to Elko for questioning. They were interrogated at length and by the next day the crying teenagers had made full written confessions.

Berning died soon thereafter and was buried on Monday, August 24. The funeral for the popular constable was attended by many local persons as well as by his wife, two daughters, and four grandchildren. The local newspaper expressed the outrage of the community on the day of the funeral:

> There should be some means of bringing this youth to trial so that he may be incarcerated in the Nevada state prison. The supreme penalty can hardly be expected, but he should be jailed for the rest of his life. . . . The people of this state will wish to see justice done in this case and they will have no sympathy for a youth, regardless of the fact that he is only 15, who killed an officer of the law in such cold blood.[32]

That same afternoon the coroner's jury in Elko found Berning's death to be murder and accused Loveless of being the murderer. The Elko prosecutor agreed, filing an information charging Loveless with murder. Since Loveless was only fifteen his case began in juvenile court. But because of the seriousness of the crime charged and Loveless's prior juvenile record, his case was quickly transferred to the adult criminal court in Elko. In that court Loveless faced not another term in a juvenile reformatory but a long prison sentence or the death penalty.

His first trial resulted in a nonspecific jury verdict. The state's evidence was strong, including the signed confession by Loveless and testimony by Cline about what Loveless had done. The jury announced its finding that Loveless was guilty as charged, but the informational charge had not specified first-degree or second-degree murder. Nonetheless the trial judge sentenced Loveless to death based on the jury verdict.

Although Loveless's attorney did not object to the verdict or move for a new trial, the verdict and sentence were considered on appeal by the Nevada Supreme Court. It found no merit in the appellate claims raised by Loveless's attorney but became interested on its own motion in the strange jury verdict. After ordering the case reargued on that issue, the court reversed the conviction and death sentence on April 21, 1943.

The Elko prosecutor tried Loveless again and this time avoided the mistakes of the first trial. He used the same facts and evidence that were presented at the first trial, including the signed confession. Testimony of witnesses from the first trial was read into the record. The defendant admitted the killing but argued that the crime was no more than second-degree murder. This time the jury's verdict was guilty of first-degree murder, leaving to the trial judge the choice of penalty between life imprisonment and death. The judge chose death. When the motion for a new trial was denied, the case went again to the Nevada Supreme Court on appeal.

The appellate court refused to reconsider issues it had decided against Loveless on the first appeal and found the second jury verdict to be reasonable and legally valid. It affirmed the conviction and sentence on August 16, 1944. That was two years after Loveless had escaped from the reformatory. He was now seventeen.

Loveless awaited his execution with considerable anxiety. He converted to the Catholic faith in July and spent the day before his death crying. On the day of his execution he wrote letters to his father, grandmother, and brother back in Indiana. His last request to the prison warden was to "send some roses to my grandmother."[33] At 6:24 P.M., accompanied by a Catholic priest, Loveless was taken into the gas chamber. Gathered to watch the execution was the smallest number of witnesses in the history of gas executions in Nevada. Loveless died at 6:30 P.M., the youngest person ever executed in that state.

WILLIE FRANCIS; EXECUTED JUNE 7, 1947; LOUISIANA[34]

This case seems ordinary in most ways. Willie Francis was a black fifteen-year-old who killed a prominent white man in the South. He was arrested, tried, convicted, and sentenced to death, with little to distinguish the case. The problem came in implementing the death sentence. Francis was subjected to the electric chair twice, with over a year separating the two trips.

Francis worked part time at a local drugstore in his hometown of St. Martinsville, Louisiana. The drugstore was a popular hangout for white teenagers. The owner was Andrew Thomas, a fifty-four-year-old white pharmacist whose brother was the chief of police. Thomas had once reprimanded Francis and Francis harbored a desire for revenge. Late in the evening of November 7, 1944, just shortly before his sixteenth birthday, Francis set out to satisfy that desire.

Francis hid behind Thomas's home in St. Martinsville, waiting for Thomas to return after closing the store. Just after midnight Thomas drove his car into the garage behind his home. As he walked to the rear steps, Francis confronted him at gunpoint. A violent struggle followed and Francis shot four times. One shot missed but the others hit Thomas once in the chest and twice in the back. Francis grabbed the victim's wallet and watch and escaped.

The crime scene provided few clues. Despite an aggressive investigation of this murder of the police chief's brother and a $500 reward for information about the perpetrator, the case remained unsolved for nine months. Francis was a key suspect in the case and finally was arrested in Port Arthur, Texas, and returned to St. Martinsville on August 6, 1945. Francis still had Thomas's wallet on him when he was arrested. He admitted the crime and signed a complete confession. He took police to where he had hidden the murder weapon and it was still there. He had pawned the watch for five dollars and it too was recovered.

Because Francis was too poor to afford a lawyer, the court appointed two lawyers to represent him. His trial began on Wednesday, September 12, on an indictment for first-degree murder. It ended the next day with a conviction of first-degree murder. Francis was sentenced to death on September 14. At his trial and sentencing, Francis seemed uninterested and showed little emotion. His execution was scheduled for May 3, 1946. Efforts at appellate relief from the courts and clemency from the governor were unsuccessful. The death warrant was signed on March 29, and Louisiana's portable electric chair was brought to the the the St. Martinsville jail.

Just after noon on the scheduled date, Francis was placed in the chair and strapped down and the hood was placed over his face. The switch was thrown and, as Francis reportedly described it, the brief current "tickled him a bit, but did not hurt much."[35] A wire had burned out in the chair. To the complete surprise of his executioners, Francis withstood the presumably deadly current and then called out to have his hood taken off because he was smothering. It was quickly removed. A newspaper report said that "Following this the switch was released, the youth unstrapped, and the witnesses sat spellbound as he straightened up and walked unaided from the jail accompanied by police."[36] Francis later recalled that as he awaited execution he was thinking about heaven and wondering what hell was like. He also said: "The Lord was with me."[37]

The chair would have to be repaired and tested before it could be used again. The warden called the governor with the strange news and a six-day reprieve was granted to repair the chair. Francis's lawyers, on the other hand, thought that their client had been punished enough. They asked for and received a month-long reprieve in order to take their case to the Louisiana Supreme Court.

The attorneys argued that a second attempt to execute Francis would violate the constitutional prohibitions against double jeopardy and cruel and unusual punishment. The Louisiana court refused to bar a second electrocution on this theory but the U.S. Supreme Court granted certiorari on June 9, agreeing to consider the case on this issue. Ecstatic, an attorney for Francis suggested yet another basis for his appeal: "I still say that Francis' delivery from the electric chair was an act of God."[38]

In their appeals the attorneys claimed no irregularities in the indictment, trial, conviction, or sentence. Their sole issue was whether a second attempt at execution was barred by the constitutional prohibitions against double jeopardy and cruel and unusual punishment. This argument, the first of its type heard by the Supreme Court, received the attention of the national news media but was not persuasive to the Court. On January 12, 1947, in a five-to-four vote, the Court ruled that Louisiana could make a second attempt to electrocute Francis.

Francis and his lawyers continued to fight the electrocution in the Louisiana courts and executive offices. Having twice turned down Francis's requests for clemency, the Board of Pardons considered his arguments again on April 18, 1947. Four days later, the board again refused clemency. Francis had his last chance before the Louisiana Supreme Court but lost on May 15. His lawyers had exhausted all avenues for relief and Francis sat in the St. Martinsville jail awaiting his fate.

The portable electric chair was brought back to the jail, repaired and presumably working just fine. On June 7 Francis was once again led to the chair. The straps were placed around his arms and legs and the smothering hood was placed over his face. This time the execution device worked without a flaw. Francis was nineteen when he died, after what a St. Martinsville newspaper called "one of the longest delays of justice in the Parish's history."[39]

JAMES LEWIS, JR., AND CHARLES TRUDELL; EXECUTED JULY 23, 1947; MISSISSIPPI[40]

James Lewis and Charles Trudell were fourteen-year-old black boys living in Natchez, Mississippi. In mid-February 1946 they began working in a nearby sawmill operated by Harry McKey. McKey was a white businessman with a wife and seven children. From all reports he was kind to Lewis and Trudell and they had no reason, save the desire for money, to do what they did to him.

On February 23, 1946, the two boys robbed McKey of sixty-four dollars. During the robbery Trudell shot McKey to death with a pistol. They left his body in the sawmill's woodlot and escaped. The body was not found until a week later. Few persons were sympathetic to the perpetrators: "It was a deliberately planned and heartlessly executed assassination for the sole purpose of robbery. . . . "[41]

Lewis and Trudell were arrested soon after the body was found. With threats of lynching running through the community, the prosecutor moved aggressively. Before seeking an indictment against them, the prosecutor obtained permission from the local juvenile court judge to prosecute them for murder in the Wilkinson County Circuit Court. With that step out of the way, their cases moved swiftly.

The grand jury indicted Lewis and Trudell jointly for murder but they were granted separate trials. Their confessions were the primary evidence against them but that was more than sufficient: ". . . the proof was so conclusive that there was nothing for the jury to debate except whether the death sentence should be imposed, and nothing but the youth of the assassin was left to bear upon that question."[42] Trudell was indicted, tried, convicted, and sentenced to death, all on March 18, less than a month after the crime. Lewis's case followed and moved with equal rapidity.

Both cases were taken on appeal to the Mississippi Supreme Court. It refused on November 11 to interpret the Mississippi constitution "to confer upon the juvenile court the right to offer refuge to a juvenile capital offender for reform."[43] The attorneys for Lewis and Trudell then took the case to the governor for clemency. After talking with the two boys in their jail cells, the governor denied clemency on January 4, 1947.

The case had received national media attention, and concerned citizens from as far away as Oakland, California, traveled to Mississippi to plead with the governor for mercy. The governor refused to give in but did allow several stays of execution so that the case could be taken to various appellate courts. The Mississippi Supreme Court also allowed stays of execution as the defendants' lawyers prepared to take the case to the U.S. Supreme Court. They were joined in the petition for certiorari by Thurgood Marshall, a young lawyer gaining a national reputation for advocacy in such cases who was later to become solicitor general of the United States and still later the first black justice of the U.S. Supreme Court. Even Marshall's considerable talents were not enough to convince the Supreme Court, which denied certiorari on May 5 and again on June 1.

Lewis and Trudell's execution, after four reschedulings (it had originally been set for April 26, 1946, by the trial court and was subsequently rescheduled for December 13, 1946, then for January 17, 1947, then for March 18, 1947, and then for April 18, 1947), was now again rescheduled, for July 23, 1947. Both boys continued to reaffirm their guilt and seemed unconcerned about their fate. They read comic books and plunked guitars to pass the time in the Woodville jail. But as the final, unchangeable execution date approached their mood grew more serious. Their families came to visit them every Sunday and they were received into the Catholic Church by two local priests. Trudell was now sixteen years old but Lewis had not yet celebrated his sixteenth birthday.

The night before their execution the boys were in constant prayer with the two priests and seemed ready to accept the inevitable. Trudell said, "I don't fear a thing. I feel alright and I'm praying."[44] Lewis seemed more resigned: "I know we're going to die and we're prepared."[45]

One of the boys' attorneys had suggested the appropriate procedures to be used in their execution:

> It occurs to my mind that neither of the children is sufficiently large to fit into the various attachments of the electric chair. Therefore, I should like to respectfully suggest that we seat them as we do our children at the dinner table, that we place books underneath them in order that their heads shall be at the proper height to receive the death current; and I further urge that the books used for this purpose be the "Age of Reason," "The Rise of Democracy in America," a copy of the "Constitution of the United States," and an appropriately bound edition of the Holy Bible. Then, with one current of electricity the State of Mississippi can destroy all simultaneously.[46]

His suggestion was not followed and the execution proceeded as it would have for adults. The portable electric chair was brought to the Woodville jail and adjusted to fit the prospective occupants. Lewis died at 1:19 A.M. Trudell lived only twelve minutes longer.

WILLIE MARVIN JACKSON, JR., AND HERMAN LEE MILLER; EXECUTED JUNE 15, 1954; GEORGIA[47]

Willie Jackson was a native of Athens, Georgia, where he ran afoul of the juvenile authorities. He was placed in the Georgia Training School for Boys at Milledgeville. There he met and became friends with Herman Miller, a native of Savannah, Georgia, who had had similar juvenile problems. Both were black and both were born in 1936, but Jackson was five months younger than Miller. They did well at the training school and had been granted trusty status.

On June 28, 1953, Miller was almost four months beyond his seventeenth birthday but Jackson was still only sixteen. They were helping to search a local wooded area for a boy who was missing from the training school. Nearby was Georgia College. A white, eighteen-year-old female student came riding her horse through the wooded area next to the training school. Jackson and Miller stopped her horse, overpowered the young woman, and raped her. Aside from the trauma of the rape, the victim was not otherwise injured and continued to attend her college classes.

She reported the rape to the authorities and an investigation ensued. Jackson and Miller were indicted on July 21 and were taken directly to the Baldwin County Superior Court in Milledgeville, an adult criminal court, even though they were clearly within the juvenile court age limit. On August 28 the adult criminal court tried, convicted, and sentenced them to death.

For some unknown reason a routine appeal of their death sentences was never pursued. Their attorneys first petitioned the state Board of Pardons and Paroles for commutation of their death sentences to life imprisonment. The board denied their petition on September 23. The attorneys then sought a writ of habeas corpus from the Georgia Supreme Court. The major thrust of this collateral attack on Jackson and Miller's convictions was that original jurisdiction lay in the juvenile court and not the adult court. The court disagreed, holding that the Georgia constitution gave the adult court jurisdiction over all capital cases and that the more recent juvenile court statutes had not displaced the constitutional provision. The court handed down its decision on February 9, 1954, and it denied a rehearing on February 24.

The trial court had originally set the execution date for Jackson and Miller for October 14, 1953. Stays were granted to allow for clemency petitions and court reviews. The boy rapists were executed just two weeks short of one year after their crime. Jackson was seventeen when he died and Miller was eighteen.

WILLIAM SNYDER BYERS;
EXECUTED JANUARY 12, 1956; NEW YORK[48]

William Byers was a seventeen-year-old New York City white boy who had been expelled from a public high school and a private academy for truancy. He was living with his mother. He had become quite upset on learning that he was an illegitimate child, but otherwise he seemed to be passive and somewhat aimless but also attractive and a good dancer. It was this last attribute that caught the attention of Theresa Gresch, a fifteen-year-old white girl living nearby. Byers and Gresch began a long love affair, "not quite children playing with adulthood."[49]

Theresa Gresch lived with her mother in a third-floor cold-water flat in a slum area of Manhattan. Her father was dead and her mother worked two jobs to support them. Mrs. Gresch, age forty-three, worked in a shoe factory during the day and did cleaning most evenings. Her young daughter had the apartment to herself after school and through the evening. Fantasizing a life as a single woman in New York, Gresch liked to invite Byers over each evening and entertain him as she saw fit.

On the evening of February 25, 1954, the young couple lost track of the time. Mrs. Gresch came home from her cleaning job and caught them together in bed. She threw the embarrassed Byers out and lectured her chagrined daughter about her behavior. But since Mrs. Gresch continued to work day and night, she was unable to exercise any meaningful control over her daughter's behavior.

The nightly assignations of the young couple continued, apparently with Mrs. Gresch's knowledge and hopes for the best. She began a pattern of noisily entering the apartment when she arrived home and this unspoken agreement to warn them worked for a few days. On the evening of March 4, however, she neglected to warn them and again caught them in bed together.

Byers was outraged. He argued with Mrs. Gresch in her small kitchen and knocked her unconscious with a hammer. Then he stabbed her twenty-one times in the chest and abdomen with a kitchen knife. Later asked why he killed her, Byers said: "She embarrassed us."[50]

Byers and the victim's daughter then devised a bizarre means of hiding their crime. They recruited a teenage boy who lived in the next apartment to help them put the body into the kitchen washtub and encase it in plaster of paris, believing that would hide the body and prevent it from decaying. Satisfied with their solution, they locked the door to the kitchen and used Mrs. Gresch's hard-earned wages to go on a shopping spree the next day. They held raucous parties in the apartment for the next four nights. When their guests asked why they were locked out of the kitchen, Byers and Gresch joked about her mother's body being in there.

After the four days and nights of partying, Byers left for the Marine Corps on March 8. Gresch continued to live in the apartment, rearranging the furniture to her liking and playing out her fantasy of the single woman in New York. With Byers away and unavailable for partying, she recruited the previously helpful neighbor boy to take Byers's place. After two weeks the stench from the victim's body could no longer be ignored by the neighbors. They alerted the police, who discovered the bizarre scene in the kitchen.

Gresch was arrested immediately as an obvious suspect. An assistant district attorney questioned the fifteen-year-old girl for twenty-four hours and finally got her to make a statement. She blamed Byers. Arrested soon thereafter at Parris Island, Byers was interrogated and confessed after twenty minutes. He was brought back to New York for further criminal proceedings.

Byers and Gresch were indicted on April 7 for first-degree murder. Their trial was delayed by a variety of pretrial maneuvers by their individual lawyers. Both defendants received psychiatric examinations at Bellevue Hospital and were found mentally competent to stand trial. Byers tried at first to renew his relationship with Gresch and joked about his fate in a letter to her while awaiting trial: "If I do get the electric chair, I hope that they do not burn me too badly.

Maybe medium rare, or well done, but not to a crisp."[51] But he was not able to regain his former place in his codefendant's eyes. During their trial, which finally began in late January, they seldom even glanced at each other. Each seemed determined to put the blame on the other.

Gresch stuck by her original statement that Byers had killed her mother and that her only involvement was in helping to clean up the mess. Byers repudiated his original confession and testified that Gresch was the murderer and that he only helped clean up. When asked why he originally had admitted he killed the victim, he responded: "Well, I tried to protect Terry when I told the first story. But I can't die for her."[52] Defense counsel attempted to prove that their clients were insane at the time of the crime but had little evidence on which to base such a claim. On February 10 the all-male jury convicted Byers of first-degree and Gresch of second-degree murder.

Gresch was sentenced to serve twenty years to life in prison. Her former boyfriend was sentenced to death. Attempts at appellate relief delayed his execution but only for a short time. On December 1 the New York Court of Appeals affirmed his conviction and sentence, scheduling the execution for five weeks later.

Byers was electrocuted at Sing Sing prison at 11:04 P.M. at age nineteen. Accompanied by a Catholic priest, "he went to his death at a slow, indifferent trot, chewing bubble gum."[53]

LEONARD MELVIN SHOCKLEY;
EXECUTED APRIL 10, 1959; MARYLAND[54]

Leonard Shockley lived with his parents in a rural area near Boxiron, Maryland, and accompanied them when they moved across the state line to Omar, Delaware. They were a fairly typical rural black couple with several children. Leonard, who was sixteen, was particularly close to his brother Harold, who was seven years older. Leonard was no longer attending school and had been unemployed for a few weeks.

On the cold and cloudy morning of January 16, 1958, Leonard, Harold, and a sister drove back to their old neighborhood in Worcester County, Maryland. Leonard drank a pint of wine on the way. They dropped the sister off at a friend's house and drove to a rural store owned and operated by Mrs. Sarah Hearne, a thirty-nine-year-old white mother of three.

Around 1:00 P.M. the brothers drove past the Hearne store twice to be certain Mrs. Hearne was alone. They parked outside and Leonard went in. He took his knife from the sheath on his belt and confronted the storekeeper. He hit her in the face with his fist and then stabbed her several times in the chest and back and cut her throat with his knife. Either during or after this attack, he ripped off Hearne's pants in an apparent attempt to rape her. Harold entered the store as Leonard was attacking Hearne and tried to open the cash register but it jammed. They ran from the store and drove away, taking only the blood on their hands and clothes to show for their attempted robbery.

A witness saw the Shockley car outside the store and heard a scuffle inside but left without entering the store. Mrs. Hearne was fatally injured but managed to stumble out of the store to watch her assailants drive away. She stumbled on to her house behind the store, leaving a trail of blood, and died inside her home. The witness alerted the police but it was too late to save Hearne's life.

Leonard and Harold were arrested at 9:15 that evening at their home in Omar. Investigators found blood on their clothing and car. After questioning at the police barracks in Georgetown, Delaware, they both confessed to their involvement in the crime. They were transferred to Maryland for trial.

The Shockley brothers were jointly indicted by a grand jury in Worcester County for robbery and murder under a felony-murder formulation. A change of venue was granted and the cases were moved to Cambridge in Dorcester County. Mental examinations of Leonard and Harold, which indicated that they were competent to stand trial, were later introduced as evidence at their trials.

The defendants were granted a severance and were tried separately. The trials were held before a three-judge panel since the defendants had waived their right to a jury trial. Key evidence against them included their confessions and the testimony of the eyewitness who saw their car outside the store. Leonard was tried and convicted on April 7, 1958, and received a sentence of death. Harold was tried and convicted the next day for having aided and abetted Leonard's robbery and murder of Mrs. Hearne. His sentence was life in prison.

On January 19, 1959, just over a year after their crimes, the Maryland Court of Appeals upheld the convictions and sentences of both brothers. The court found the evidence quite sufficient against Leonard. The evidence against Harold was less clear-cut but a majority of the court also affirmed his conviction and sentence. Further attempts at appeal and petitions for clemency were equally unsuccessful.

As his big brother began serving a life sentence in the Maryland prison, Leonard Shockley prepared to die in the Maryland gas chamber. He entered the chamber at 10:00 P.M. on April 10. The chamber was sealed and the cyanide pill dropped into the pail of sulfuric acid three minutes later. The electrocardiograph equipment noted his death one minute later. He was still only seventeen years old when he died, the youngest person executed in Maryland in this century.

JAMES ANDREW ECHOLS; EXECUTED MAY 7, 1964; TEXAS[55]

Very little about the case of James Echols makes it unusual. He was a black male executed for raping a white female in the South. The importance of the case is that he was the last person executed for a crime committed while under age eighteen prior to the present decade of executions. Echols was seventeen years old at the time of his crime, not legally a juvenile under Texas law but nonetheless under the juvenile court age of the vast majority of U.S. jurisdictions.

Echols had committed juvenile offenses when he was fourteen and fifteen. He had been incarcerated but his lawless tendencies had not been changed. At age seventeen he graduated to more serious problems.

On the afternoon of April 16, 1962, Echols was drinking heavily with four other black males. They committed a robbery to get some cash and then decided they needed to find a different car. At about 9:00 P.M. they saw a white couple sitting in a parked car. In the car was an eighteen-year-old woman, already the mother of two children, and her boyfriend.

Two of Echols's accomplices forced the couple into the back seat and drove them away in their own car, with Echols and the others following in the other car. They parked behind a schoolhouse and began to beat the male victim. Echols's threatening words, remembered at his trial, were "I'm going to kill you, you white son of a bitch."[56] After a struggle, the intended murder victim escaped and ran away to notify the police.

The woman was blindfolded and forced to lie on the floor of the car. Both cars were driven some distance away before the victim's car was abandoned. The woman was transferred to the other car and driven to a secluded area. There, at knifepoint, she was raped by all or most of the five men—Echols was later to claim that he was asleep in the car when the rapes occurred but the court did not believe his story. The men tied up the victim and left her to wriggle free sometime later.

Early the next morning the woman identified all five men as her rapists. A medical examination confirmed her recent sexual intercourse. Articles of her clothing were found at the rape scene. The police went to Echols's home to find him but he was not home yet. When he returned he was arrested and taken in for questioning.

After aggressive police questioning, which Echols said included threats and force, he gave a written confession of his involvement in the crimes. The other four rapists were also quickly arrested and accused of the crimes. One of the perpetrators was under age seventeen and thus a juvenile under Texas law. He was sent to a juvenile training school. The other four, including Echols, were jointly indicted for rape. They were tried separately in the Harris County District Court in Houston.

Two of the rape and kidnapping defendants were convicted and received combined sentences of life imprisonment plus sixty-two years. The other two, James Echols and Lawrence O'Connor, were convicted and sentenced to death. Echols appealed his case to the Texas Court of Criminal Appeals, claiming among other things that the district attorney and the police had suppressed evidence that may have been valuable to the defense. The court was not convinced, affirming Echols's conviction and sentence on June 19, 1963, and denying a rehearing four months later.

Echols's execution date was stayed several times as his attorney sought appellate and clemency relief. On April 26, 1964, O'Connor was executed for his part in the crimes. Echols lived only a short time longer. He maintained that he was innocent and was wrongly convicted but came to accept his fate. He was baptized into the Catholic faith by the prison chaplain.

On the day before he died Echols said he had believed that his innocence had been proved at his trial but then laughed loudly and said: "I guess I was wrong."[57] Echols also reflected upon his newly embraced religion: "No one wants to die, but I would rather die knowing God than not knowing him."[58] As he entered the execution chamber and to sit in the electric chair at 12:02 A.M. he expressed his thoughts: "I have no hard feelings against anyone and I want to thank everyone for what they have done for me."[59] He was dead at age nineteen.

CHARLES F. RUMBAUGH;
EXECUTED SEPTEMBER 11, 1985; TEXAS[60]

Charles Rumbaugh was born on June 23, 1957, one of several children in the west Texas white Catholic family of Harvey and Rebecca Rumbaugh. Raised in a constantly moving family with a violent, alcoholic father, Rumbaugh committed his first serious offense (breaking into a schoolhouse) at age six. At seven he was wild and uncontrollable: "I was a little devil; always getting into trouble with the police; running away from home, burglary, car theft, vandalism, arson, truancy, sniffing glue, etc. I committed hundreds of crimes during the 6 years before I was sent to reform school."[61]

Rumbaugh was placed in the reform school by the juvenile court when he was thirteen. He spent the next four years there, fulfilling his ambition to learn how to commit more and better crimes. In Rumbaugh's own words, the Texas juvenile justice system "took a 13 year old troubled boy and turned out a hardened criminal."[62] Already blinded in one eye by a childhood accident, Rumbaugh began during this series of juvenile incarcerations a lifelong practice of self-mutilation. By the time he reached manhood his body was covered with scars from suicide attempts and crude tattoos.

Soon after turning seventeen Rumbaugh was released from the reform school. Quite predictably, he now began his life of crime in earnest. He resumed the armed robberies that he had begun at age twelve: "I would run in and stick a gun in someone's face and say give me your money and they'd give me their money."[63] He stayed near his west Texas origins but moved around relentlessly. Soon he was in a mental hospital for treatment of manic depression. He escaped from the hospital early in 1975 and continued his life of crime.

A few days after committing a robbery in San Angelo on March 28, 1975, Rumbaugh went to stay with two sisters and a brother who were living in a cheap apartment in downtown Amarillo. Near the apartment was the tiny, one-room jewelry store of Michael Fiorillo, a fifty-four-year-old white bachelor who lived in an apartment above the store. Fiorillo worked long hours, having few other interests in life, and was a popular member of the Amarillo community.

Soon after arriving in town Rumbaugh had noticed the tiny store and decided to commit his next robbery there. Early on Friday morning, April 4, he left the apartment, taking his gun with him, and went to wait for Fiorillo to open his store. At around 8:30 Fiorillo arrived, unlocked the front door, and entered the store to prepare for another day's business.

Rumbaugh rushed into the store and, pointing his gun at the jeweler, demanded his money. Much to Rumbaugh's surprise, Fiorillo resisted and reached for his own gun in a drawer. They struggled and Rumbaugh got the better of him. Rumbaugh shot once at Fiorillo's head but missed. The next shot was on target, hitting Fiorillo in the chest and passing through his lung to lodge in his spine. Fatally injured, Fiorillo pleaded for help from his assailant. Rumbaugh ignored him, took the gun Fiorillo had used to protect himself, and grabbed money from Fiorillo's wallet and cash register.

Rumbaugh returned to the apartment and had his sister dump his bloody clothes in an alley trash barrel. About 9:00 A.M. the barber next to Fiorillo's jewelry store arrived to open his shop. Entering the jewelry store to greet his business neighbor and friend, the barber found Fiorillo lying dead on the floor. The police were called and a thorough investigation revealed little solid evidence to identify the robber and murderer. An autopsy that afternoon recovered the bullet from Fiorillo's spine.

Meanwhile, the San Angelo police had notified the Amarillo police of Rumbaugh's robbery on March 28 and provided a possible address for Rumbaugh in Amarillo—the apartment rented by Rumbaugh's sister. When Amarillo police officers arrived there on April 4 to arrest Rumbaugh for the San Angelo robbery, they saw him coming down the stairs. After a gunfight in which Rumbaugh was shot in the hand, they arrested him and seized his gun, the one he had just stolen from the Fiorillo jewelry store. As Rumbaugh was hospitalized under police guard, other officers searched the apartment and found the gun Rumbaugh had used to murder Fiorillo. They also found his bloody clothes in the trash barrel.

On April 6 the police took Rumbaugh from the hospital to jail and questioned him about the Fiorillo robbery and murder. Rumbaugh provided a detailed written confession and was held for further proceedings in the case. On April 7 the investigating officers filed a capital murder complaint against Rumbaugh. He was denied release on bond and an attorney was appointed to represent him. Rumbaugh was indicted on April 10 by the Potter County grand jury. Then began a long preparation for his capital murder trial. He celebrated his eighteenth birthday in the Amarillo jail.

Rumbaugh sought to delay his trial permanently by his actions on December 8. Early that morning Rumbaugh and other jail inmates escaped. Their freedom lasted only until 4:00 P.M., when their stolen van was stopped by a police officer. In the attempt to get the escapees into the police station, the officer's gun was seized. He was struck and stabbed but managed with help to complete the arrests. Rumbaugh blamed their capture on the unwillingness of a fellow escapee to use the officer's gun: "You should have handed me that pistol. How come you didn't hand it to me, man, I would have blowed his head off."[64] Turning to the injured officer, Rumbaugh said: "If I had a gun I sure as hell would have shot you, man."[65] These statements, typical of Rumbaugh, were later interpreted by the appellate court as Rumbaugh's being "engaged in boasting and in making himself out to be a fearsome desperado in the eyes of his companions and in the face of peace officers."[66] Rumbaugh and the others were returned to the Amarillo jail.

Finally, on March 29, 1976, Rumbaugh's trial for the robbery and murder of Fiorillo began. After a week the jury of nine men and three women was impaneled. Testimony began on April 5 and Rumbaugh was convicted the next day. One key item of evidence was an oral confession he had made. The punishment phase of the proceedings, which began on April 7, resulted in a death sentence.

Rumbaugh's attorney moved for a new trial and was granted a hearing. As the hearing began on August 13, Rumbaugh was searched entering the courtroom. Officers found a six-inch knife taped to his leg. The new trial was denied and the appellate process on the murder conviction and death sentence began. Next, Rumbaugh was tried for kidnapping and assault on a police officer in connection with the escape from jail. On March 3, 1977, he was convicted and received a ten-year sentence.

Rumbaugh seemed resigned to his death sentence, writing in a letter that "if they were to come to my cell and tell me I was going to be executed tomorrow, I would feel relieved, in a way. The waiting would be over. I would know what to expect. To me, the dying part is easy; its the waiting and not knowing that's hard."[67] He had many more years to wait. On June 20, 1979, just before Rumbaugh's twenty-second birthday, the Texas Court of Criminal Appeals reversed his murder conviction and death sentence because of the admission into evidence at trial of his oral confession. The court denied the state of Texas a rehearing on November 28, and the case was set for retrial.

The new trial before the same trial judge began in mid-April, 1980. Rumbaugh's insanity defense, relying on the testimony of a psychiatrist, a psychologist, and two social workers, was unsuccessful. The result was the same and Rumbaugh once again was under a sentence of death. His prosecutor seemed ambivalent about the outcome: "It kind of bothered me a little. He was awfully young and he had some tough breaks in life. But Chuckie is very violent, a really hardened killer, and society has to protect itself."[68]

The appellate process began again. On June 30 Rumbaugh's younger sister was killed in a traffic accident, adding more grief to his already difficult situation. Almost two years later, on March 3, 1982, the Texas Court of Appeals affirmed his conviction and sentence and denied a rehearing on April 7. His execution date, rescheduled many times in the preceding six years, was set for July 23, 1982. Rumbaugh, exhausted from the long process, instructed his attorneys to take no further action to delay his execution.

Rumbaugh's parents, whom he never saw during all his years in jail, agreed to file a next-friend petition for state habeas corpus relief on July 16. It was quickly denied by the Texas trial and appellate courts but the federal district court granted a stay of execution to allow time to consider it. Following a mental examination of Rumbaugh to determine his competence to waive legal efforts on his behalf, the federal hearings here held on February 4 and 24, 1983.

The court heard evidence that although Rumbaugh was profoundly depressed he was rational. This evidence was dramatically challenged by Rumbaugh as he testified on February 24. He pulled out yet another hidden knife, pointed it at the marshal, and said "Shoot!"[69] The marshal shot him in the heart and lungs. Rumbaugh eventually recovered. Despite this episode, the federal court found Rumbaugh to be mentally competent and dismissed his parents' petition.

The parents, on the urgings of Rumbaugh's attorneys, appealed this dismissal to the Fifth Circuit Court of Appeals. It also found their son to be rational, affirmed the dismissal of their appeal on February 20, 1985, and denied a rehearing on March 21. Meanwhile, Rumbaugh sank deeper into depression, as excerpts from a letter he wrote reveal:

> I feel like I have been traveling down a long, dark and winding tunnel for the past nine years—the length of time I have been on death row—and now I can see no end to the tunnel, no light at the end of it, just more long years of the same. I have reached the point where I no longer really care. . . . I'm so damn tired and disgusted with sitting here and watching my friends take that final trip to the execution chamber, one after the other, while I continue to wait and speculate about when my time will come. They're killing me a little bit each day.[70]

His wait was almost over. On July 1 the U.S. Supreme Court refused to grant certiorari in his case. By now he was twenty-eight years old, facing execution for something he did at age seventeen. The final, not-to-be-changed execution date was September 11, 1985. Amnesty International and many other organizations protested his impending execution. The *New York Times* ran a major story on the case and on juvenile executions in general the day before he died.[71] Rumbaugh waived them all away: "Look where it's at now. I have no more appeals. You've got to accept this some time."[72]

The day before his execution Rumbaugh was visited by friends he had corresponded with over the years and by three sisters and a brother-in-law. His mother went to the prison the day before he died but at the last minute decided not to see him. Rumbaugh clung to an optimistic outlook concerning his parents: "I suppose they still care about me in a distant way, as I do about them, but I really don't know what they think or feel since I haven't heard from them."[73]

Shortly after midnight Rumbaugh faced his execution calmly. Ten years earlier, when he was arrested, he had boasted to the police that "I ain't going nowhere but the electric chair."[74] But while awaiting death, he had outlived the Texas electric chair. The state had instituted death by lethal injection.

Rumbaugh, who had been raised a Catholic, refused communion and requested that no religious persons be with him at his death. He did, however, remember his religious teachings in his last statement to the witnesses at his execution: "About all I can say is goodbye. For the rest of you, even though you don't forgive me my transgressions, I forgive you for yours against me. That's all I wish to say. I'm ready to begin my journey."[75] He was strapped into the customized hospital gurney and intravenous tubes were inserted into each arm. A harmless saline solution was started, soon replaced by the lethal drugs. He died at 12:27 A.M. at age twenty-eight after ten and one-half years on death row. He was the first person to die for a crime committed while under age eighteen in the post-*Furman* era of capital punishment. Was he deterred by the death penalty? "I was 17 years old when I committed the offense for which I was sentenced to die," Rumbaugh had said, "and I didn't even start thinking and caring about my life until I was at least 20."[76]

JAMES TERRY ROACH; EXECUTED JANUARY 10, 1986; SOUTH CAROLINA[77]

Terry Roach was born into a poor white family in Seneca, South Carolina, that was burdened by the mother's illnesses and the father's absenteeism while driving a truck. Terry was further limited by mental retardation and an I.Q. of around 70. Not surprisingly, he did not do well in school and dropped out as soon as he could; he also was involved with drugs and had a personality disorder—all of which contributed to his placement in a state reform school. In 1977 he escaped from the reform school and embarked on his brief adulthood.

Roach found shelter in a rented house near Fort Jackson, South Carolina. The transient residents of the house were unemployable dropouts involved in a variety of antisocial activities, including extensive abuse of drugs. Some were considerably older and cleverer than Roach and he easily fell under their domination. One was a twenty-two-year-old soldier named Shaw.

On Saturday, October 29, 1977, Roach, age seventeen, and Mahaffey, age sixteen, were spending the morning riding around with Shaw in Shaw's car, consuming beer, marijuana, THC, and PCP. Shortly after noon, the threesome decided to look for a girl to rape. They drove by a baseball park just northeast of Columbia, South Carolina.

Parked by the baseball field were Thomas Taylor, a seventeen-year-old white male, and Carlotta Hartness, his fourteen-year-old white girl friend. They were schoolmates at a local private academy and both were from prominent families in the area. Shaw drove his car up beside the parked Taylor car. Roach pointed a rifle at Taylor and they demanded Taylor's wallet. On a signal from Shaw, Roach shot Taylor three times, killing him instantly. The murderers then drove off with the Hartness girl to a secluded area. After repeatedly raping her, first Roach and then Shaw shot the girl and killed her. They left quickly but Shaw returned later to mutilate the dead girl's body.

Given the horribleness of the crimes and the prominence of the victims' families, community outrage was high. On November 3, after five days of intensive investigation, Mahaffey, Roach, and Shaw were arrested. All three were indicted on two counts of murder, two counts of conspiracy, and rape, kidnapping, and armed robbery counts. Mahaffey agreed to testify against the other two to get a lighter sentence. The prosecutor sought the death sentence for Roach and Shaw.

On December 12 the two waived their right to a jury trial and pleaded guilty. The three-day sentencing hearing followed. The judge considered mitigating factors for Roach, including his youthful age, his lack of previous violent crimes, his emotional and mental condition, and his having acted under Shaw's domination. These factors were outweighed by the heinousness and multiplicity of the crimes, resulting in a death sentence for both defendants on December 16.

Roach's court-appointed attorney, Walter Brooks, had his own problems with the law. Almost a year before his representation of Roach, Brooks had been charged in bar disciplinary proceedings with various irregularities in his law practice and with involvement in illegal drug trafficking. These charges were still pending while he represented Roach. Over two years later, he was disbarred from practicing law in South Carolina based upon these charges. However, his representation of Roach was found to be constitutionally adequate.

The South Carolina Supreme Court unanimously affirmed the convictions and sentences of Roach and Shaw on May 28, 1979. Certiorari was denied by the U.S. Supreme Court on January 7, 1980. The standard defense efforts at collateral attack through state and federal courts followed, resulting in at least four postponements of Roach's execution date. The state trial court denied his habeas corpus petition on July 9, and the state supreme court affirmed the denial a year later, on July 17, 1981. Interim orders and stays were obtained from federal courts in the next few years but no permanent relief was granted to either Roach or Shaw.

South Carolina executed Shaw on January 11, 1985, for his part in the crimes, but attorneys for Roach continued their losing battle to avoid a similar fate for their client. The federal district court had denied Roach's habeas corpus petition and, on January 7, 1985, the Fourth Circuit Court of Appeals heard arguments on appeal of that decision. The appeals court affirmed the denial of habeas corpus on March 20. Roach's execution date was reset again, and this time it was not to be changed.

As Roach's case received more and more statewide attention, South Carolina legislators introduced a bill to set the minimum age for the death penalty at eighteen at the time of the crime. This bill was still pending when Roach was executed and its chances for passage died with him. As the execution date approached, the governor received numerous pleas to grant clemency to Roach. In addition to the predictable sources of such pleas, they also came from Mother Theresa in India, former President Carter in Georgia, and the secretary-general of the United Nations. Roach's attorneys even filed a claim with the Inter-American Commission on Human Rights, an agency of the Organization of American States. All were ignored by the governor.

As Roach matured from age seventeen to age twenty-five on death row, his inherited prognosis for Huntington's chorea became manifest and his mental condition deteriorated even further. That was seen as a new issue by his attorneys, since the U.S. Supreme Court had agreed to decide whether a presently insane person could be executed. When the Supreme Court was asked on January 9, 1986, to consider Roach's case in this light and to consider the constitutionality of the death penalty for juveniles, it refused to do so. This rejection of Roach's appeal came despite the fact that his mental condition "raises substantial doubts as to whether Roach has any understanding that he is scheduled to die tomorrow."[78] When the Court finally did hold five months later that the presently insane could not be executed, it was too late for Roach.

On the night of January 9 and into the early morning hours of January 10, Roach tried to gain the approval of those around him and to understand what was about to happen to him. Having lived a third of his life under a death sentence, he appeared to be "a terrified, cornered human being. He personified fear, not evil."[79] The slack-jawed, slow-speaking man spoke with "simple words that a child would use."[80] He paid rapt attention to letters read to him by his attorney, much like a young child listening to a bedtime story.

Others did not see Roach in this light. Characterizing him as "the meanest person I have ever met,"[81] his prosecutor stated: "When people are this mean, this cruel, there's no other way to deal with them. This is an appropriate punishment for this terrible crime."[82] And as the hour of Roach's execution neared, a cheering crowd of two hundred persons gathered outside the prison walls to await the early-morning execution.

Roach spent the night visiting with his family and girl friend, who helped him write his last statement. He practiced reading it over and over but had difficulty pronouncing the big words. He seemed quite interested in the prayers suggested by the prison chaplain, asking which ones were most likely to get him into heaven. After the warden appeared at his cell door and read the death warrant shortly before 5:00 A.M., Roach seemed "calm and resigned as he shuffled into the death chamber."[83]

He was strapped into the electric chair and began his shaky reading of his last statement. Included were the hope that his fate might be a message to other juveniles and a last thought about his crimes: "To the families of the victims, my heart is still with you in your sorrow. May you forgive me just as I know that my Lord has done."[84] Two one-minute surges of electricity hit him and he was pronounced dead at 5:16.

Roach had reached the chronological age of twenty-five when he died for a crime committed at seventeen, but his mental age was fixed at twelve. Is someone like Roach deterred from crime by the threat of the death penalty? His attorney, David Bruck, who was with him when he died, said that "Terry lacked the capacity to think more than a few hours ahead, let alone to the possibility of arrest and execution."[85]

JAY KELLY PINKERTON; EXECUTED MAY 15, 1986; TEXAS[86]

The last person executed for a crime committed while under age eighteen (as of late 1986) was Jay Kelly Pinkerton. He was seventeen when he committed murder in Texas and thus he was not legally a juvenile in that state. He lived almost seven more years before being executed.

Pinkerton, who was white, lived with his parents, Gene and Margie Pinkerton, in Amarillo. He had a criminal record that included burglary, but he was working as an apprentice meat cutter in the fall of 1979.

Mr. and Mrs. Laurence had been married two years and lived with her three children, ages four, five, and nine, in Amarillo a few blocks away from the Pinkertons. The wife and mother, Sarah Donn Laurence, was an attractive white woman age thirty. On the evening of October 26, 1979, Mrs. Laurence took the children to a school across the street to enjoy a Halloween carnival. Returning home about 9:00 P.M., she put the children to bed and watched television while waiting for her husband to return home from working the late shift at a factory. She spoke with him on the telephone and assured him everything was fine at home.

At about 9:30 P.M. Pinkerton entered her home through an open window in the master bedroom. He quietly made his way to the living room and confronted her. Grabbing a ten-inch bowie knife from its rack on the wall, he attacked her viciously, stabbing her thirty times and cutting her throat. During the attack he also abused her sexually, including cutting a small incision in her abdomen to engage in bizarre sexual intercourse. He also cut her vagina and severed her breasts, laying them on the television set.

Pinkerton ran from the house, leaving Laurence dead but her three children unharmed and still asleep. He took with him the murder weapon and the victim's purse. He returned home, showered and changed clothes, and went out again. Laurence's husband got off work at 11:00 P.M. and arrived home thirty minutes later. After finding his wife's body he checked on the children and then looked for the murderer.

The police were called and patrolling officers were notified to search the neighborhood for suspects. Some officers went to Pinkerton's home but his parents refused entry, saying their son had been home all evening. At about 2:30 A.M. other officers saw, chased, and caught Pinkerton in a nearby parking lot. After questioning they released him for lack of evidence. Investigators were left with a witness's general description of a man seen leaving the house at about 10:00 P.M., footprints leading from the crime scene to just across the street from Pinkerton's house, and a handprint in the Laurences' living room. The investigation continued but seemed to be going nowhere.

Pinkerton apparently repeated his crime a few months later. On April 9, 1980, Mrs. Sherry Lynn Welch, a blonde twenty-five-year-old white woman and former beauty queen, was raped and stabbed to death at a furniture store where she worked. Although this crime was never solved, it later seemed probable that the rapist-murderer was the same one who had attacked Mrs. Laurence.

On September 26, 1980, the handprint from the Laurence crime scene was finally identified as Pinkerton's. A warrant was issued for his arrest, exactly eleven months after the crime. Pinkerton was arrested at the Amarillo restaurant where he was then working. His parents immediately hired an attorney.

Pinkerton was indicted by a Randall County grand jury for murder in the course of burglary with the intent to rape the victim. He was kept in the Amarillo jail awaiting trial. While there he became friendly with another jail inmate who was later to testify that "Jay's a hard man to follow. Sometimes he seems nice,

but when he would start telling about the killing, he seemed kind of crazy."[87]
Pinkerton repeatedly bragged about the Laurence crime to his jail audience,
telling of the bizarre means he had used to engage in sexual intercourse with
the victim.

His attorney's motion for a change of venue was uncontested, and the trial,
although still presided over by a judge from Amarillo, was moved to Corpus
Christi. The trial began on May 18, 1981, with jury selection continuing until
May 26 before impaneling of a jury of seven men and five women. As evidence
was introduced, enlarged color photographs of the nude and mutilated victim
remained displayed prominently in the courtroom. The case went to the jury
shortly after noon on May 30.

After deliberating for almost three and one-half hours, the jury found
Pinkerton guilty as charged. The sentencing hearing before the same jury began
immediately. It heard eight to ten witnesses and received other evidence of
aggravating and mitigating factors. Shortly before midnight, the jury returned
a verdict of death after discussing it for an hour. The trial court refused to grant
a new trial on June 27 and a five-year appellate process began.

On July 13, 1983, the Texas Court of Criminal Appeals affirmed the conviction and sentence. It denied a rehearing of the appeal on September 28.
Collateral attacks on the conviction and sentence and requests for clemency
from the governor followed. All were to no avail.

On August 14, 1985, Pinkerton was only a day away from his scheduled
execution. He visited with his brothers and parents and seemed to be calm
and in a good mood. The next day he was taken to the death chamber and
strapped into the special hospital gurney. Tubes were inserted into his arms
and all was ready for the lethal injection. Then the telephone rang; he had
received a stay of execution. The tubes were removed, and he was unstrapped
and taken back to death row to continue his wait.

This stay was subsequently lifted and a new execution date of November
26, 1985, was scheduled. Pinkerton came within ten hours of death this time
before he received another stay. This stay was linked to a death penalty jury
case under consideration by the U.S. Supreme Court which, if decided in the
petitioner's favor, would probably have required reversal of Pinkerton's case.
The Court finally rejected the petitioner's claim, leaving Pinkerton with no
remaining grounds for a continued stay of execution.

His final execution date was set for May 15, 1986. Courts continued to
refuse him relief, and a federal judge rejected a petition carried personally by
Pinkerton's mother. Shortly after midnight Pinkerton was led into the death
chamber and once again strapped into the gurney. Six and one-half years had
passed since his capital crime and Pinkerton had reached age twenty-four. To
the witnesses at his execution he said, "Be strong for me. I want you to know
that I'm at peace with myself and with my God."[88] Pinkerton's father was in
the death chamber with his condemned son and said, "Bye, Jay."[89] The son's
response was overheard by those who came to see him die: "I love you, Dad."[90]

SEVEN

One State's Experience

Ohio, a fairly typical Midwestern industrial state, has had the death penalty in its penal code since soon after it attained statehood in 1803. It has accounted for 344 (4 percent) of the 8,542 state-imposed executions in the nation[1] and 19 (almost 7 percent) of the 281 juvenile executions in American history.[2]

This chapter describes in detail these nineteen Ohio cases and the juveniles who were executed. What attitudes in the various Ohio communities affected by the crimes caused the state to demand the death penalty for killers who were actually just boys? And why has Ohio completely rejected this practice today? These and other questions are addressed in this attempt to understand why Ohio, once a leader in the use of the death penalty for punishment of juveniles, is now among the growing number of states moving away from this practice.

EVOLUTION OF OHIO'S
LEGAL ENVIRONMENT

In 1805, two years after Ohio attained statehood, its newly formed legislature enacted a criminal code that prescribed the sentence of death for such crimes as murder, treason, and rape.[3] This first statute included no express or implied provisions for considering the age of the offender in prescribing the sentence. In 1815 Ohio recategorized its homicide statutes and retained the death sentence for first-degree murder.[4] Although the death sentence for treason was abolished in 1824, Ohio's first-degree murder statute remained basically unchanged until 1898. The 1898 statute gave juries the option of recommending mercy after first-degree murder convictions and of substituting life imprisonment for the death sentence.[5]

During this entire period Ohio statutes did not address the issue of the age of the offender. Ohio courts apparently were deciding these cases under the common-law presumption of maturity at age fourteen. In 1843, in *Clark v. State*,[6] the Ohio Supreme Court implicitly approved a trial judge's jury instructions that a person fourteen or older is presumed to have sufficient capacity to possess the criminal intent required for first-degree murder. A trial court similarly assumed in 1902 that a fifteen-year-old boy accused of first-degree murder "is presumed in law to be accountable for his acts in the absence of proof to the contrary."[7] This presumption of legal maturity at age fourteen comports with the basic premises of Anglo-American law.

In the wake of the national movement at the turn of the century, Ohio enacted statutes to establish a juvenile court with jurisdiction comparable to that of other states' juvenile courts.[8] These statutes provided express language requiring transfer of all cases involving a person under age eighteen to juvenile court if such cases were originally filed in adult courts. It appears, however, that the Ohio juvenile code did not preclude concurrent jurisdiction over felony cases by the Ohio Court of Common Pleas.[9] Therefore, while the intent of Ohio's juvenile code was to protect persons under age eighteen from the harshness and inappropriateness of the adult criminal justice system, some nevertheless were subjected to adult court and received the maximum penalty.

In 1972 the Ohio legislature completely rewrote the parts of the criminal code dealing with the death penalty.[10] The new statute provided for several aggravating and mitigating factors that were to finally determine whether or not the death sentence would be imposed. But in 1978, in *Lockett v. Ohio*,[11] the United States Supreme Court found the Ohio statute to be unconstitutional because it permitted only three mitigating factors.

A companion case to *Lockett* was *Bell v. Ohio*,[12] which involved a boy convicted of a murder committed when he was age sixteen and sentenced to death under the existing Ohio statute. Before this case reached the U.S. Supreme Court, the Ohio Supreme Court had affirmed the conviction and sentence and found implicitly that the death penalty could be imposed on such a young murderer under the existing statute.[13]

The Ohio legislature once again reacted to the U.S. Supreme Court's holdings, and in 1979–1980 it produced its present death penalty statute.[14] This statute expressly prohibits the death penalty for crimes committed while under age eighteen.[15] Such a provision was never included in any previous Ohio statute. Some observers have surmised that this post-*Lockett* age limitation was prompted by the circumstances in *Bell*.[16] State Senator Richard Finan, principal architect and senate sponsor of the bill that became this new statute, recalls that the reasons why this age limitation was instituted included a general sense of fairness and concern for children and "strong reservations about the constitutionality of capital punishment for crimes under the age of eighteen."[17] Thus, after 180 years of a statutorily authorized death penalty for crimes committed while under age eighteen, Ohio has expressly prohibited it.

OHIO JUVENILE EXECUTIONS, 1880–1956

Ohio had sixty-seven adults but no juveniles on death row in 1986.[18] But, although it has discontinued the practice of sentencing juveniles to death, from 1880 through 1956 the state executed nineteen persons for crimes committed while under age eighteen. The following case studies of these nineteen executed juveniles reveal a variety of crimes and criminals. While some similarities of these juvenile murderers and their crimes are notable, each case had unique variations.

GEORGE E. MANN; EXECUTED JUNE 25, 1880[19]

Early records of lawful, official executions are difficult to verify, but it appears that Ohio began the execution of juveniles with a triple hanging of teenage boys. One of them was George Mann, who, like the other two, continued to protest that he was innocent even as he walked to the gallows.

Mann's mother died when he was very young and he lived with his grandmother for several years. After his father remarried, Mann moved in with his father and new stepmother. Mann apparently did not adapt well to this environment and ran away from home several times.

Mann's capital crime occurred during one of these instances of running away from home, this time at age sixteen. Mann became a railroad tramp and began to travel with fifteen-year-old Gustave Ohr and an older man, John Watmough. The three tramps spent Thursday night, June 27, 1879, camped near Alliance, Ohio. As Watmough was napping peacefully after breakfast the next morning, Ohr and Mann devised a plan to rob him. Ohr struck Watmough on the head with a railcar coupling pin and severely injured him. The pair then took Watmough's watch, money, and clothes and ran away. Watmough recovered consciousness just long enough to crawl to a nearby house and utter a few words before he died. The people who heard Watmough's last words alerted the marshal and other townspeople. Ohr and Mann were seen walking along the railroad tracks, apparently trying to find a train to ride out of town. They were arrested only minutes after their crimes and taken to the county jail.

After arrest, a brief investigation was conducted and a trial was scheduled to be held many months in the future at the Stark County Common Pleas Court at the county seat. The trial finally took place in early December and, needing only thirty-five minutes of deliberation, the jury convicted Mann of first-degree murder on December 6. After a separate trial, Ohr was convicted on December 13. On New Year's Eve the trial judge sentenced both Mann and Ohr to be hanged.

Their original execution date was May 7, 1880, but on May 2 Governor Foster granted a temporary reprieve. Since several people petitioned the governor for a reduced sentence, Mann apparently was still hopeful that his sentence would be commuted as late as June 23. The petitions for commutation expressed sympathy with the youth of the condemned.

Mann's hopes for commutation were not realized, and he was hanged in Canton at 11:35 A.M. on June 25. The public hanging of Mann and Ohr, along with John Sammett, was the occasion for a community-wide extravaganza. People came to the small town of Canton in northeastern Ohio by excursion train from as far away as Chicago and Pittsburgh to witness the event. A circus was part of the extravaganza, and the night before the hangings there was music, cannon-firing, speech-making, and similar merriment. The next morning Mann and the two others were hanged in the city square of Canton before an estimated crowd of 10,000 persons. Afterward, sheriff's deputies placed the three bodies in the jail corridor and permitted the crowd to file through and view them. The public viewing lasted almost four hours.

Gustave A. Ohr; Executed June 25, 1880[20]

Gustave Ohr was one of the star attractions in this triple hanging. He was executed for a crime he committed when he was only fifteen years old.

Ohr, born in Bavaria, was an infant when his parents emigrated with him to the United States. His father died when Gustave was still a child, and he lived in Chicago with his mother, who remarried. Ohr left Chicago in the late spring of 1879 and joined up with Mann and Watmough in Fort Wayne, Indiana, while riding the rails. The three proceeded to Alliance, where Watmough was killed.

Mann claimed until his death that it was Ohr who actually struck and killed Watmough, but Ohr steadfastly refused to exonerate Mann. The two were tried before the same judge and in the same courtroom, but their trials were separate and sequential. Following Mann's conviction on December 6, 1879, Ohr's trial was conducted. Ohr was convicted on December 13, and Judge Mayers sentenced them together at a hearing on December 31.

Appeals and petitions for commutation were unsuccessful. Sixteen-year-old Gustave Ohr was hanged on the city square of Canton along with seventeen-year-old George Mann and eighteen-year-old John Sammett.

John Sammett; Executed June 25, 1880[21]

John Sammett's adult life was remarkably brief. He celebrated his eighteenth birthday on June 24, 1880, and was hanged before noon the next day. Sammett was the third of the star attractions at this triple hanging, but his crime was different from the crimes committed by Mann and Ohr.

Sammett was born in 1862 in Massillon, Ohio. His family was of German extraction. Sammett's mother died when he was very young and his father remarried and moved to Columbus, Ohio. The family returned to live in Massillon in 1877, and Sammett became involved in criminal activities.

In August 1879, seventeen-year-old Sammett joined with sixteen-year-old Christopher Spahler and broke into a saloon. After they were arrested, Spahler agreed to testify for the prosecution against Sammett. On November 25, the day before the trial was to begin, Sammett went to see Spahler to try to convince him not to testify for the prosecution. Unsuccessful, Sammett shot Spahler in the chest. Several persons who heard the shot came to the scene to find Spahler dying. He died without speaking a word about what had happened. The police found the murder weapon in a cabinet and Sammett still on the scene. He was arrested immediately for criminal homicide.

A preliminary hearing before the mayor of Massillon produced strong circumstantial evidence against Sammett and he was remanded to jail without bail. While the murder charge was being prepared, Sammett was tried, con-

victed, and imprisoned for the burglary over which he and Spahler had quarreled.

Sammett was indicted on the murder charge by the grand jury of Stark
County, Ohio, and his trial began on February 18, 1880. On March 2 the jury
returned a verdict of first-degree murder. The trial judge sentenced Sammett
to be hanged on June 25, the execution date already set for the two other
teenage residents of Stark County's death row, George Mann and Gustave Ohr.

Appeals and pleas for mercy were unsuccessful. Sammett's more pragmatic
effort, an attempt to dash out of the jail when the fire alarm sounded on the
eve of the executions, was similarly unsuccessful. In the late morning of the
scheduled day, the three boys were led out of the jail and to the scaffold.
Sammett went out first and led the procession. All three were hanged at 11:35
A.M. and were dead before noon.

OTTO LEUTH; EXECUTED AUGUST 29, 1890[22]

Ohio's next execution of a child occurred more than ten years after the
triple hanging. Known as the Cleveland boy murderer, Otto Leuth was labeled
a born criminal by prominent phrenologists of the time. Born in Berlin, Ger-
many, on February 3, 1873, Leuth was only sixteen at the time of his crimes.

Leuth emigrated to the United States with his parents in 1883. Living in
Cleveland, Ohio, the Leuths were known as "honest, respectable people"
whose two-story frame home displayed "unmistakable marks of thrift." But the
family bore the heavy burden of congenital epilepsy, which had strongly affected
them through three generations. Leuth's maternal grandmother suffered convulsions from the age of five, his mother's sister was apoplectic and somnam-
bulistic, and his mother's brother had "attacks of madness." This medical history
was inherited by Leuth's mother and passed on to her son. The mother had
suffered convulsions regularly since age ten. Her nervous disorder resulted in
headaches, spasms, convulsions, and occasionally unconsciousness, and may
have contributed to her suicidal tendencies. She reportedly had homicidal
tendencies toward Otto and had beaten him savagely over several years. These
beatings added to Leuth's other medical problems by leaving him blind in one
eye and with a soft, sensitive depression in the side of his skull, caused by a
poker wielded by his mother during a beating.

As a result of Leuth's inherited epilepsy and considerable injuries from
beatings, he was characterized as a "neglected, undersized boy with his head
which is described as being too ill shapen to exist."[23] Although he was an apt
scholar adept at languages and mathematics and a welcome fiddler at local
dances, he nevertheless was described as not only having a "bad reputation for
general cussedness" but even as "the most depraved creature ever confined
behind the walls of the Penitentiary."[24]

At around 11:30 A.M. on Thursday, May 9, 1889, seven-year-old Maggie
Thompson passed by Leuth's house. With his father working out of town and
his mother in the hospital because of various medical problems, Leuth was

alone. Maggie saw him in front of his house and asked him for some buttons for her collection. Leuth invited her inside and she followed.

Leuth lured Maggie into the bedroom, where he raped her and bashed in her skull with a tinsmith's sledgehammer. He left the girl's body on the bed for six days before he decided something must be done. He hid her body in a shallow cellar under his house and covered it with chloride of lime.

Leuth's attempt to cover up the evidence of his crime was successful for a month. Maggie was missed almost immediately by her parents, who lived just seven houses away from Leuth, and the ensuing search extended for miles around their neighborhood. Since Leuth was one of the most conscientious and untiring searchers, at first no one suspected his involvement in the crime.

Leuth was undone by the stench that began to emanate from underneath his house. A patrolman walking by the house was alerted by a neighbor and a crowd formed that included Maggie's parents. Otto's father was home at the time and he found the body. He crawled under the house and dragged out the decomposed remains.

The police immediately arrested everyone living in the house, not only the Leuths but also the Shreves, who rented rooms in the rear of the house. Soon thereafter, Otto made a full confession at the police station and the others were released.

After his confession on June 9, a month after the crime, Leuth had his preliminary hearing the next day. The preliminary charge was murder, and he was bound over without bail to await action by the grand jury. Even at this early stage of the criminal process, news media were speculating on the possibility that capital punishment was not available for a murderer as young as Leuth.

The grand jury returned a four-count murder indictment against Leuth on June 14, and he entered a not-guilty plea at his arraignment the next day. The trial was scheduled for the fall term to give the defense time to prepare its case and to let the public outcry subside somewhat.

Jury selection started on December 2. Testimony began one week later and was covered in great detail each day by local newspapers. The trial lasted almost four weeks. The major point made by the defense was Leuth's mental disabilities, but the legal insanity defense was never specifically argued by Leuth's attorney. Apparently the attorney was presenting a diminished capacity defense, even though that legal doctrine probably was not extant in Ohio at the time. In his closing argument the attorney reasoned that Leuth should not be convicted but should be confined in a mental hospital because of his admitted dangerousness.

The jury returned its verdict on December 27 after four and one-half hours of deliberation. Leuth was convicted on just one of the four counts, the felony-murder crime of killing the victim with a hammer while attempting to rape her. He was sentenced to death.

Leuth's original execution date was April 20, 1890, but appeals resulted in several stays. His appeal to the Circuit Court of Appeals was unsuccessful

and the Ohio Supreme Court refused to grant certiorari. The governor delayed
the execution for a short period for the Board of Pardons to consider the case,
but the governor ultimately denied relief. Despite some pressure from citizens'
groups, the general public seemed to support the execution.

Leuth was hanged at the Ohio Penitentiary Annex in Columbus at 12:05
A.M. He was seventeen and one-half years old.

WILLIAM TAYLOR; EXECUTED JULY 26, 1895[25]

William Taylor was born in 1877 in a ghetto in Columbus, Ohio, the
illegitimate son of a black woman who had been born in slavery. He was raised
in Columbus, went to school there, and worked there for some time as a
bootblack. Limited by "a very low order of mind," Taylor began to perform
menial labor for a prosperous farmer who lived a few miles north of Columbus
near Worthington.

Taylor and a co-worker were hired to cut firewood by farmer Isaac Yoakum
and were furnished living quarters in a log cabin on the Yoakum farm. The
pair capped a day of heavy drinking with a plan to rob Yoakum, who was known
to carry large sums of money. At about 7:00 P.M. on December 20, 1894, they
hid in a shed on the farm and struck Yoakum a hard blow to the head with a
hickory club when he passed by. Yoakum was severely injured and died a few
days later. Taylor later claimed that his co-felon struck the blow and that he
had only shared in the money robbed from Yoakum, but this argument was to
be unpersuasive to the jury.

Taylor escaped temporarily to Caperton, West Virginia, but was captured
there nine days later at the home of his stepfather. He was arraigned in Worthington and stood trial in Columbus. At trial he testified in his own behalf
but hurt his defense badly by telling several versions of the events. He was
convicted of murder under a felony-murder theory and sentenced to death.

No record could be found of appeals to higher courts or to the governor.
If pursued they were unsuccessful. Taylor was executed by hanging at the Ohio
Penitentiary Annex in Columbus at 12:06 A.M., having been on death row about
six months. With the modernization of executions in Ohio, Taylor was the last
of Ohio's juveniles to be executed by hanging.

WILLIAM HAAS; EXECUTED APRIL 21, 1897[26]

William Haas, an illiterate and orphaned farm boy, had the dubious honor
of being the first Ohio prisoner of any age executed in the electric chair. Haas,
only sixteen years old at the time of his crime, was labeled the boy murderer.[27]

Haas never knew his parents or any other family members. He grew up
in group homes and working on farms in the Cincinnati area. After running
away for a time he returned to the area. He was taken in by a young married
couple, the William Braders, who lived on a suburban truck farm near Clov-
erdale. Haas worked at the Brader farm for room and board and a little money,
sleeping in a bedroom just off Mr. and Mrs. Brader's master bedroom.

Mr. Brader, who regularly sold his produce at urban markets, left for market very early on the morning of July 2, 1896. Later, but still before dawn, Mrs. Brader entered Haas's bedroom and awakened him. According to Haas's subsequent confession, Haas grabbed Mrs. Brader and began choking her, apparently also raping her. When she became unconscious he cut her throat with Mr. Brader's razor. He then placed her body on her bed and set the bed on fire.

Neighbors who discovered the house in flames were able to save most of the house from destruction. Haas fled, walked to Cumminsville, and boarded a freight train to Hamilton. He was captured in the railroad yards there on the night of July 3, less than forty-eight hours after the crime. The next morning he gave a complete confession, saying he wanted to admit all of his crimes.

Haas pleaded guilty and waived his right to a trial by jury. Two judges who jointly heard his case in Cincinnati found him guilty of murder in the first degree. Despite his youth and deprived background, they sentenced him to death. Appeals to higher courts are not reported, but a petition for commutation of the death sentence was presented to the governor. Despite sympathy prompted by Haas's "very weak mind and extreme youthfulness," commutation was denied on April 20.

The next day Haas became the "farm boy [who] was the first victim of Ohio's electric chair."[28] He was electrocuted at the Ohio Penitentiary Annex in Columbus. The execution received major coverage in the press and was described as a "complete success." Nevertheless, the execution apparently was delayed by a malfunctioning dynamo in the electrical plant that operated the electric chair.

HARLEY BEARD; EXECUTED DECEMBER 24, 1914[29]

Harley Beard was a teenage farm worker of "low mentality" who attributed his problems to "bad company, cigarettes and intoxicating stimulants." His well-publicized last words were "I think it is awful to send me to my Father this way."[30]

Apparently an orphan, Beard was age sixteen when he got a job on the Massie farm near Ironton, Ohio, in September 1913. On May 11, 1914, Beard found himself in a heated quarrel with Robert Massie, age forty-five, Robert's sister, Mary, age forty-six, and their mother, Mrs. Dennis Massie, age eighty. Robert Massie struck Beard during the quarrel, and Beard responded by first beating all three members of the Massie family with a club and then ensuring their death with a razor. Beard later claimed that his mistreatment by the Massie family had "brought him to a pitch of frenzy."

Beard immediately boarded a train in Ironton but was arrested as he left the train in Chicago four days later. While awaiting the arrival of Ohio police officers, he made a full confession to the Chicago police. Tried during the summer of 1914, he was convicted and sentenced to death. His appeals were fruitless, and Governor Cox could not find "any element that justified extension of mercy."

As the execution date approached, W. E. Massie, brother and son of the victims, aggressively petitioned the governor for permission to be present at Beard's execution. Permission was denied and the execution was carried out as scheduled.

IGNATIUS (SAM) PUPERA; EXECUTED MAY 9, 1922[31]

Sam Pupera was the first juvenile to be executed in Ohio in the 1920s, a decade in which Ohio executed five juveniles. True to the popular conception of the roaring twenties, Pupera's crime was a New Year's Eve payroll robbery shoot-out, complete with a car chase.

Pupera was born in Pittsburgh on February 21, 1904, of parents who had immigrated from Sicily only a few years earlier. Raised in the poorest parts of Pittsburgh and Cleveland, Pupera left school at age fifteen and began to study barbering. He was arrested for car theft in early December 1920 but escaped from the detention home on December 13. Arrested almost immediately in Pittsburgh on an alcohol charge, he jumped bail. The sixteen-year-old next became involved in the crimes that led to his execution.

Pupera associated with a gang of young men who frequented a pool hall in Cleveland and boasted of various past robberies. Five of them, along with Pupera, developed an elaborate plan to rob the cash payroll from the president and the superintendent of the W. W. Sly Company. At around noon on December 31 these two men were transporting a $4,200 payroll from the bank to the company in their private automobile. The would-be robbers were in a stolen automobile, with Pupera driving and his four accomplices as passengers.

At a predetermined time and place, Pupera drove in front of the payroll automobile and forced it off the road. The company president and the superintendent were shot and killed immediately. Stories conflicted as to which of the robbers actually fired the fatal shots, but at the subsequent trial two witnesses said it was Pupera. The payroll obtained, the sixth gang member arrived with another automobile, in which some of the gang escaped. Pupera ran away on foot and began an extended flight that included Boston, Chicago, El Paso, and Juarez before ending in Los Angeles. Arrested on March 11, 1921, in Los Angeles on a California automobile theft charge, Pupera was recognized as the person wanted for murder in Cleveland.

Extradited back to Cleveland, Pupera was indicted by a grand jury on two counts of first-degree murder. Several witnesses had identified Pupera and other gang members, but Pupera was the first to be located and arrested. Although Pupera admitted his involvement in the robbery and killings, he maintained that he did not shoot either of the victims and had received none of the stolen payroll money. Having passed his seventeenth birthday while hiding from the Cleveland police, Pupera remained guardedly optimistic, commenting: "They'd never send a boy of seventeen to the chair in Ohio, would they?"[32]

Pupera's first-degree murder trial began on May 16. The prosecution apparently proceeded under a felony-murder theory, the killing of the victims having been an integral part of the armed robbery. Two eyewitnesses identified

Pupera as the person who killed both victims, but Pupera testified that he never fired the handgun he had with him at the robbery. In the closing arguments to the jury, both the prosecuting attorney and defense attorney took particular note of the defendant's youthful age.

The case went to the jurors at midday on May 18, and they returned a verdict of guilty of first-degree murder the next morning. Pupera was immediately sentenced to death by the trial judge, with execution set for August 29.

Through various court appeals and petitions to the governor, Pupera received three stays. His age was reported by the press as an important factor in this consideration: "Pupera, who says he is 17 years old, will be the youngest criminal to be electrocuted in the history of the state. . . ." However, he would not have been younger than seventeen-year-old William Haas, who was electrocuted in 1897. In any event, Pupera was to pass his eighteenth birthday before his execution date finally arrived. He was executed in Ohio's electric chair at the Ohio Penitentiary Annex in Columbus.

EMANUEL ROSS; EXECUTED NOVEMBER 26, 1926[33]

Four and one-half years later, Ohio executed another juvenile for a Cleveland murder. Emanuel Ross was also eighteen by the time he was executed but apparently was only seventeen at the time of his crime. Ross was born on August 22 in either 1907 or 1908; reports conflicted. Since the weight of the evidence seemed to be on 1908, it is assumed that he was seventeen at the time of his crime.

Ross was born in Brookhaven, Mississippi, to a poor black mother whose husband soon left. Ross and his mother moved to Chicago when he was thirteen, and Ross went to Cleveland in October 1925, at age seventeen. He worked as a dishwasher but also became involved in criminal activity.

After several hours of drinking and socializing on the evening of November 5, 1925, Ross and a companion, Slim Young, decided to commit a robbery. The target was a confectionery store owned by Isadore Steck on Central Avenue in Cleveland. During the robbery Steck resisted, so Ross shot and killed him. Young took the money from the cash register and the two youths fled.

Two weeks later, Ross was arrested in Chicago based on information provided by the Cleveland police. Ross confessed to the robbery and the homicide. He also provided information that led to the arrest of Young in Detroit. Ross was returned to Cleveland and indicted for first-degree murder under a robbery-murder theory of felony-murder.

His trial began on January 11, 1926, and on January 14 he was found guilty of first-degree murder. The jury did not recommend mercy and the trial judge imposed the death sentence on January 16. The Ohio Court of Appeals for Cuyahoga County upheld the conviction and sentence on May 19. Ross made several attempts to have the Ohio Supreme Court review his case but to no avail. He was similarly unsuccessful with the Board of Clemency and the governor. However, in the interim he received five temporary stays of his execution date.

One issue raised late in Ross's appeal was the fact that he was under the juvenile court age limit but had been indicted and tried in adult Common Pleas Court without ever appearing in juvenile court. One of the stays of execution was granted so that this question could be litigated in a state habeas corpus proceeding. The state trial court decided that Ross was not entitled to a new trial and this decision was not disturbed by the appellate courts. The courts apparently assumed that the adult court had concurrent jurisdiction with juvenile court over cases such as this one and that the state was not required to go through a juvenile court waiver hearing before proceeding to an adult court trial.

Ross finally exhausted the possibilities of forestalling the execution. He died in the electric chair at the Ohio Penitentiary Annex in Columbus at 1:05 A.M. after spending over ten months on death row. The press reported that Ross was "the youngest person to be electrocuted in Ohio"—the same error it made in Pupera's case. Neither Ross nor Pupera was as young as Haas, either at time of crime or at time of execution.

FLOYD HEWITT; EXECUTED JANUARY 6, 1928[34]

Floyd Hewitt at age sixteen stood six feet three and had the body of a large man. But he was mentally retarded from birth, and his attorneys described him as "a moron with a ten-year-old's intellect." The press called him the boy clubber.

Hewitt lived in a rural area near Conneaut, Ohio, and was a neighbor of the Brown family. On the evening of February 14, 1927, Hewitt visited the Brown home. Fred Brown was at work in Conneaut and would not return home until after midnight. Apparently Hewitt attempted a sexual familiarity with Fred's wife, Celia, age 24. A fight ensued, ending when Hewitt struck Celia on the head with a poker and she fell down the stairs. Hewitt then chased the Browns' five-year-old son down to the cellar and killed him with a baseball bat. Hewitt left and walked home before 9:00 P.M.

Mr. Brown returned from work soon after midnight and found his wife's body. Neighbors and the police soon arrived, and the son's body was found in the cellar. By late morning suspicion had fallen on Hewitt. Arrested as he walked casually past the police station, he confessed a few hours later.

Even though Hewitt was only sixteen years old, the prosecutor announced from the beginning that he would seek a murder conviction and the death sentence. Hewitt was indicted for first-degree murder on February 25, and his trial opened on April 4 in Jefferson. Although he was indicted for two first-degree murders (mother and son), he was tried only for the murder of the boy.

During the three-week trial, the state relied heavily on Hewitt's signed confession, while the defense stressed Hewitt's mental disabilities. On April 26 the jury returned a verdict of guilty without a recommendation of mercy. Within minutes the trial judge imposed the death sentence and set August 10 as the date of execution.

Hewitt's appeals to the Court of Appeals, the Ohio Supreme Court, and the Board of Clemency were unsuccessful. As is almost always the case, these efforts did result in several stays of execution and delays of the execution date. The final consideration was by the Board of Clemency on January 5, 1928; it refused to recommend mercy to the governor.

Hewitt was executed at the Ohio Penitentiary Annex in Columbus. Press headlines stating that Hewitt was the "Youngest Ever Executed in Ohio" were apparently correct, since Hewitt was younger even than Haas had been when he was executed. Hewitt's chronological age at execution was seventeen, but his mental age remained ten.

JOHN COVERSON; EXECUTED JANUARY 9, 1928[35]

Seventy-two hours after Hewitt's execution, John Coverson was executed in the same electric chair. Coverson was a black seventeen-year-old who had lived in Cincinnati's black ghetto for ten months before his crime. Coverson knew most of the people who lived in this neighborhood, including the black police officer he murdered.

On May 14, 1927, someone fired several shots at the windows of Mary Easley's house. She summoned Patrolman Olin Wilson, who was off duty and out of uniform, and told him of the shootings. Coverson was one of the spectators, and Easley pointed him out to Wilson as the person who had shot at her windows. Wilson approached Coverson, stating, "I am the law." Coverson shot the officer three times.

Wilson identified Coverson as his assailant before he died the next day from the effects of the gunshot wounds. Coverson was arrested and indicted for "murder with deliberate and premeditated malice [and] . . . with having murdered a police officer while the latter was in the discharge of his duty."[36] He was tried in the fall of 1927, convicted of both counts, and sentenced to death.

The Ohio Court of Appeals for Hamilton County heard Coverson's appeal but affirmed the convictions and the sentence. The court had no hesitation in finding the evidence sufficient to support the verdict but seemed less confident of the conviction of knowingly killing a police officer. While not finding error in this second conviction, the court thought it prudent to point out that the first conviction was sufficient for the death sentence by itself, rendering superfluous its holding on the second conviction.

Subsequent petitions to the Board of Clemency and the governor were unsuccessful. Coverson was executed in the electric chair at the Ohio Penitentiary Annex in Columbus at 7:37 P.M., having spent only a few months on death row.

JAMES (SLEEPY) COLEMAN; EXECUTED JULY 5, 1928[37]

The age of James Coleman was the subject of some confusion. When he was arrested, he gave his name as Green and his age as thirty. His correct name was soon discovered, and it was generally agreed later that he was age eighteen when executed. Since his execution occurred six months after his crime, it is assumed that he was seventeen at the time of his crime.

Coleman, a black, was born and raised in North Carolina. He moved to Portsmouth, Ohio, in 1927 and apparently became involved in several thefts. On the evening of February 6, 1928, Coleman met with William Wilson, an older man, at a pool hall and they decided to walk to a railroad yard to look for jobs or possibly to commit a robbery. As they walked along the street, they were stopped and questioned by a police officer. Without warning or apparent reason, Coleman shot the officer with a concealed handgun and the officer died almost immediately. Coleman and Wilson ran, but police captured them twenty minutes later. According to the local newspaper report, Coleman resisted and "was a badly battered man when he reached police headquarters." Both Coleman and Wilson admitted involvement in the crime but each claimed the other had fired the fatal shots.

Coleman and Wilson were indicted by a special grand jury for Scioto County on two counts, first-degree murder and killing a police officer while in the discharge of duty. At separate trials, both were convicted without a jury recommendation of mercy. The trial judge sentenced them to die in the electric chair. Evidence at the trials indicated that although Coleman had fired the fatal shots, he did so with a gun furnished to him by Wilson and upon a prearranged signal to shoot given him by Wilson.

Wilson appealed and sought clemency, to no avail. But Coleman admitted guilt and did not appeal or seek clemency. Both were executed on schedule in the electric chair at the Ohio Penitentiary Annex. Coleman died at 9:18 P.M., almost exactly six months after he killed the police officer.

Coleman's execution was the last of Ohio's five executions of juveniles in the 1920s—the highest number by far in any decade in Ohio's history. This decade also produced the highest number of total executions of any decade in Ohio's history: eighty-five.[38]

LEE AKERS; EXECUTED JUNE 13, 1930[39]

Lee Akers was a seventeen-year-old black male who was wanted by the police in St. Louis for robbery and burglary. He went to Cleveland to live with his sister and continued his crimes to get money for "eats, whiskey and craps."[40] One robbery ended in homicide.

On Christmas Day, 1928, Akers watched the activity around a gasoline service station in northeast Cleveland until the manager closed for the evening. When Akers approached the manager and demanded money, the manager resisted and chased Akers out of the station office. Akers shot and killed the manager and then took about $100 from the manager's pockets and the cash register.

During the week after the crime, the police first arrested and questioned three prime suspects and then arrested 295 more suspects a few days later. One week after the crime, the police were still holding the three prime suspects and 150 other suspects. This dragnet approach produced information from some of the detainees about Akers, and he was arrested on January 7, 1929.

Akers confessed to the police. He was indicted for first-degree murder on January 10. Six days later he entered a plea of not guilty and filed a motion to determine his sanity. When the jury determined that Akers was sane, he filed a motion to transfer the case to juvenile court. Akers reasserted this motion on April 1 but was denied the requested transfer.

Akers's trial began on April 1, taking one day to select a jury and two days to hear the evidence. On April 3 the jury "returned a death chair verdict in twenty minutes."[41] Although Akers had asked mercy from the court in his guilty plea, he was forced to stand trial in order to have a chance of avoiding the death penalty. Akers's motion for a new trial was denied and the trial judge entered judgment on the verdict on April 6.

The Ohio Court of Appeals affirmed the conviction and sentence on December 9. Akers had argued that the trial court should have granted his motions to transfer the case to juvenile court but the appeals court did not agree. It held that Ohio's Juvenile Court Act did not give juvenile courts jurisdiction over indictable felonies such as first-degree murder nor did it change the common-law rule concerning the capacity of a minor to commit a felony. In any event, the adult criminal court that tried, convicted, and sentenced Akers had at least concurrent jurisdiction to do so.

Akers obtained five reprieves or stays of execution during his appeals and petitions for clemency but was not successful in overturning his conviction or sentence. He had been held at the Columbus city jail until his execution date because of a fire at the Ohio Penitentiary but was executed in the electric chair at the penitentiary as required by the Ohio statute. He was eighteen years old when he died, having spent over fourteen months on death row.

JOSEPH MURPHY; EXECUTED AUGUST 14, 1933[42]

Relatively little information was found about the crime and resulting criminal process for Joseph Murphy. It is known, however, that just before Joseph and his older brother James were executed for their crimes, they were visited on death row by yet another brother, William, who was serving a life sentence for robbery.

At the time of his crime, Joseph Murphy, a black, was seventeen years old. On October 8, 1932, he and James, six years older than Joseph, attempted to rob a bank in Silverton, Ohio, a suburb of Cincinnati. During this robbery attempt they shot and killed the bank cashier. They were arrested soon thereafter when the Cincinnati police learned that they had been boasting about their crimes.

They were tried and convicted of first-degree murder of the cashier, apparently on a felony-murder theory. The Murphy brothers continued to maintain their innocence even after they were convicted, and an eyewitness to the crime later filed a sworn affidavit that they were not the men she saw leaving the bank. That resulted in a reprieve of thirty days.

They were executed at the Ohio Penitentiary Annex, Joseph Murphy first, at 8:50 P.M., and his brother ten minutes later. Both were highly critical of the criminal justice process that brought them to this end and continued to maintain that they had not committed the crimes.

PANG YOUNG; EXECUTED JULY 12, 1939[43]

Even less information was found about the case of Pang Young. What does seem clear is that he was the first Oriental executed at the Ohio Penitentiary Annex in Columbus and apparently the only Oriental ever executed in Ohio (at least since 1885).

Young came to the United States from Canton, China, in 1922 at the age of two. At age seventeen, on the evening of July 12, 1938, he attempted a holdup in Cincinnati. His victim was a black laundryman, James King. When King did not do as Young instructed, a struggle ensued and King was fatally shot. Young later characterized the killing as accidental, claiming that he did not intend to shoot the victim. Young apparently tried unsuccessfully to poison himself with strychnine later the same night.

Young was tried and convicted of first-degree murder, going to Ohio's electric chair at 8:16 P.M., exactly one year after his crime was committed. He was variously described as "a childlike Oriental" and a "sobbing Chinese." The press seemed distantly curious, noting that no one ever knew much about Pang Young and that he had been "one of the loneliest figures who ever waited out the hours in the death row of Ohio Penitentiary."[44]

LOUIS VERNON HAND; EXECUTED JANUARY 14, 1944[45]

Louis Hand was seventeen years old when he was executed and probably only sixteen at the time of his crime. He had been placed in a state children's home at the age of eighteen months when his parents separated. He spent the next fifteen years either in state-operated homes or in the Boy's Industrial School.

At the time of his crime he was on parole from a commitment to the school for automobile theft. He was working and apparently living on the Stober family farm near Celina, Ohio, in Mercer County. On July 3, 1943, he was reprimanded by Mr. Stober for not properly greasing a farm implement. Then Mr. Stober's six-year-old grandson, Richard, began to tease Hand about the error and the reprimand. In retaliation, Hand beat the child to death with a hammer and hid the body in the barn. When the child's body was found, Hand was reported missing. He was arrested in Greenville soon thereafter by the chief of police. Hand confessed that he had killed the child and was charged with first-degree murder.

In September 1943 Hand was tried in Celina. The jury convicted him of first-degree murder without a recommendation of mercy. This verdict made the death penalty mandatory, and on September 26, 1943, the trial judge sentenced Hand to death.

No record could be found of any appeals in Hand's case. He was put to death in Ohio's electric chair at 8:01 P.M., still calm and defiant, as he had been during his three and one-half months on death row.

WILLIAM HENRY HAGERT; EXECUTED OCTOBER 3, 1945[46]

William Hagert's crimes were perhaps the most sensational of all these Ohio juvenile crimes. Hagert was a violent psychopath who raped and murdered young boys. Nonetheless, his case took longer to get to execution that any of the other cases analyzed in this chapter.

Hagert, born September 15, 1925, was left emotionally disturbed after suffering brain fever and double pneumonia at age seven. His troubled childhood included an eleven-month stay at the Boy's Industrial School for automobile theft. It was at this institution that Hagert "learned bad sexual practices from other boys" and practiced "sexual perversion."[47]

After he was released from the school, Hagert lived for a short time with his family in Cleveland but had violent quarrels with his mother and fistfights with his father. He was committed by his mother to the psychopathic ward of the city hospital on July 7, 1943, but was released on August 9.

Hagert, seventeen years old, took his father's gun on the day he was released from the hospital and immediately began picking up young boys and either raping them or killing them or both. Within two days he had kidnapped and forcibly sodomized two local boys, age nine and twelve. On August 12 he picked up twin twelve-year-old boys who were hitchhiking to the country club to work as caddies. Using his father's gun to force them to acquiesce, he took them to a wooded area in suburban Bay Village near Cleveland. There he attempted to commit sodomy on one of the boys but was repulsed by him. He then shot and killed both boys and left their bodies in the woods. Later he said he killed them "for the heck of it."

The next day Hagert was observed at the scene of the kidnapping and sodomizing of the nine-year-old. Police became suspicious of Hagert and arrested him even before they learned of the deaths of the twins. Hagert not only confessed to the crimes with the nine-year-old but also led the police to the bodies of the twins. The next morning's newspaper devoted almost the entire front page to stories about the dangers of hitchhiking, the crimes of psychopaths, and the urgent need to curb degenerates.

Investigating detectives filed a complaint in juvenile court on August 14 and a hearing was held in that court on August 24. Although the juvenile court judge believed Hagert to be insane, he ordered him held for investigation by the grand jury. Hagert was indicted by the grand jury for first-degree murder of the twin boy that he had attempted to rape. Arraigned on this indictment, Hagert entered a plea of not guilty by reason of insanity. In addition, Hagert claimed that he was presently insane and thus could not be tried. The court appointed physicians to examine Hagert and conducted a preliminary hearing before a jury to determine this issue. The physicians differed in their opinions about Hagert's sanity, and the jury returned a unanimous verdict on October 27 that Hagert was sane at the time and thus could stand trial.

Hagert's trial began in late November and ended on December 1. At this trial on the merits the state was allowed to present as evidence the verdict of the jury finding that Hagert was sane at the time of the preliminary hearing. The two boys previously molested by Hagert were allowed to testify about their experiences, apparently as evidence of Hagert's mens rea in the crime at issue in the trial. On December 1 the jury rejected Hagert's insanity defense and found him guilty of first-degree murder without any recommendation of mercy. The trial judge overruled Hagert's motion for a new trial, entered judgement on the verdict, and sentenced him to death.

Hagert's case was the only one of these nineteen that involved appellate reversal of the first conviction. After his original conviction, Hagert's case came before Ohio's Court of Appeals, which confirmed both his conviction and his sentence on May 2, 1944. In a subsequent four-to-three decision on December 27, the Ohio Supreme Court found prejudicial error by the trial court in admitting the state's evidence on the insanity finding from the preliminary hearing. Although no other prejudicial error was found, the court reversed Hagert's conviction and remanded the case for trial.

Hagert's second trial was before three Common Pleas Court judges, a jury trial having been waived. Hagert was convicted again and this time his appeals and petitions for clemency were unsuccessful. He was executed in Ohio's electric chair at 7:08 P.M., almost twenty-six months after he killed the twins. He had reached age twenty.

DONALD EDWARD FROHNER; EXECUTED AUGUST 20, 1948[48]

Donald Frohner was a high school junior, hesitant in making friends and with a tendency to formulate schemes for gaining some desired end. One of his schemes was to steal an automobile and use it to kidnap for ransom a high school acquaintance. But the theft went awry, and Frohner's scheme led him to Ohio's electric chair.

Frohner was born May 9, 1930, in Youngstown, Ohio, and lived on a thirty-acre farm near there with his parents and older brother. He was doing well in school, had been a baby-sitter for neighbors, was a member of the Christian Science Church, and seemed to have no particular behavior problems. Testimony at his trial revealed, however, that Frohner's parents often quarreled and that his father was cruel toward Frohner, having ordered him out of the house at one point about two weeks before the crimes. When he embarked on the automobile theft and kidnapping scheme, Frohner took with him some poison to ingest if his adventure did not go well.

On Monday, January 13, 1947, Frohner brought a handgun to school that he had taken from his father's bedroom. After school that day, sixteen-year-old Frohner and his seventeen-year-old friend Arthur Chapman took buses and hitched rides to get to the outskirts of Youngstown. They finally hitched a ride in an automobile driven by William Spieth, with Chapman in the right front passenger seat and Frohner in the back seat. Frohner was well equipped for the planned activities, not only with his father's revolver and the poison but also with a blackjack, substitute license plates for the automobile to be stolen, and ransom notes for the kidnapping.

Frohner's plan went awry when he ordered Spieth to stop the automobile and Spieth refused to do so. Frohner then struck Spieth with his blackjack but it broke in his hands. Frohner began to strike Spieth with his gun. The weapon discharged and Spieth was shot twice—intentionally or unintentionally—in the back and fatally wounded.

A passing bus stopped near the automobile in response to the activity, prompting Frohner and Chapman to run from the automobile and across a field. After hiding in a wooded area for four hours, the boys were arrested walking down a nearby road. A search the next morning of the area in which they hid turned up the murder weapon, ransom notes, and other evidence.

Soon after their arrest and incarceration, first Chapman and then Frohner gave full confessions, prompted by intensive questioning by the sheriff and the prosecuting attorney. The day after the crime, complaints were filed against both Frohner and Chapman in the juvenile division of the Court of Common Pleas. Following two weeks of psychiatric evaluations and other investigations, they were found to be sane and were transferred to adult criminal court on January 18.

Frohner and Chapman were jointly indicted for first-degree murder while attempting a robbery. At their arraignment on February 3, both entered a plea of not guilty. They waived jury trials and elected to have a three-judge panel hear their case. That decision was largely in response to adverse public opinion aroused and maintained by various press coverage of the crime and the proceedings.

Although both defendants subsequently changed their pleas to guilty, the court nevertheless was required to "examine the witnesses, determine the degree of the crimes and pronounce sentence accordingly."[49] Following this evidentiary hearing on February 28 the trial court found both Frohner and Chapman guilty of first-degree murder but extended mercy only to Chapman. As a result, Frohner was sentenced to die in Ohio's electric chair.

On March 7 the trial court denied Frohner's motions for a new trial, to withdraw his guilty plea, and to retract his waiver of a jury trial. His subsequent appeals and petitions for clemency were described as "one of the most energetic attempts to rescue a condemned man ever staged in Ohio." His first appeal, to the court of appeals, resulted in reaffirmation of the conviction and death sentence.

Frohner's case was decided by the Ohio Supreme Court on July 21, 1948. In addition to deciding several lesser issues, the court held that Frohner entered his guilty plea knowingly and intelligently, that his waiver of trial by jury was valid, that he was not legally insane, and that the trial judges did not abuse their discretion in refusing to extend mercy to Frohner. Justice Hart dissented without opinion and in so doing became the only one of the thirteen judges who heard the case at the trial, court of appeals, and supreme court levels to vote against the death penalty for Frohner.

A major effort ensued to obtain clemency from the parole commission and the governor. These attempts were unsuccessful, and Frohner was executed on schedule in the electric chair at the Ohio Penitentiary Annex in Columbus at 9:09 P.M. The sixteen-year-old killer had turned eighteen while on death row.

BERNARD SCHREIBER; EXECUTED MARCH 15, 1956[50]

Bernard Schreiber was the last juvenile executed by Ohio, ending a practice that had begun over seventy-five years earlier. Schreiber, unlike most of the other juveniles executed, had never been in trouble before. He was a fairly typical seventeen-year-old high school senior.

Schreiber and a twelve-year-old boy companion made an indecent proposal to a seventeen-year-old girl as she rode past them on her bicycle on August 11, 1954. Rejected, they decided to be there when she rode by again the following day. When she arrived on August 12, they knocked her from her bicycle, chased her into a wooded area, and knocked her unconscious with a club. Schreiber raped her, then stabbed her to death with his pocketknife.

The victim's body was found that evening by a neighborhood search party. After a week of intensive investigation, Schreiber's twelve-year-old accomplice confessed to the police and implicated Schreiber. Schreiber was soon arrested, and after failing a lie-detector test he confessed. The rape apparently was motivated in part by some teasing Schreiber had been subjected to about his virginity. The killing followed because Schreiber feared the girl might identify him.

Indicted for first-degree murder, Schreiber waived a jury trial. His trial before a three-judge panel began on January 10, 1955. Three days later, he was convicted of first-degree murder and sentenced to death, with the execution set for June 1.

The date was stayed three times as Schreiber's appeals progressed. The court of appeals sustained his conviction and sentence, and on December 14 the Ohio Supreme Court refused to review his case. Schreiber's clemency appeal was considered at length by the governor but also was unsuccessful.

Schreiber died in the electric chair at the Ohio Penitentiary Annex in Columbus. Nineteen years old, he had spent the last thirteen months of his life on death row.

Although Ohio continued executing condemned prisoners for exactly seven more years, ending with the execution of Donald L. Reinbolt on March 15, 1963,[51] Schreiber was the last person the state executed for crimes committed while under age eighteen. While Ohio once again has a valid death penalty statute and had sixty-six persons on death row at this writing, the new statute excludes crimes committed while under age eighteen.

COMPARING OHIO CASES
WITH CASES NATIONWIDE

Ohio's nineteen executions for crimes committed while under age eighteen comprise 6.8 percent of the nationwide total of 281 such executions. In most ways these Ohio cases tend to parallel the rest of the cases but differ strikingly in some significant aspects.

Two-thirds of the Ohio juveniles were age seventeen when they committed their crimes. A different two-thirds of them were white, so far as could be determined from available reports. Four of these juveniles (but only one since 1890) were foreign-born. Approximately one-third of them lived in reasonably stable, lower-class homes, but more than half were orphans, runaways, or otherwise from substantially deprived backgrounds (table 7–1).

In comparing these nineteen Ohio offenders with the 281 offenders nationwide, the most striking difference is the race of the offenders (table 7–2). Blacks make up over two-thirds of all juveniles executed nationwide but only one-third of the Ohio juveniles executed. Ohio accounts for one of the three Chinese juveniles executed—an oddity, given the very low percentage of Chinese in Ohio's population.

Ohio matches the national experience fairly closely in the category of age of the offender. Most of the offenders in both groups were age seventeen when they committed their offenses. No record could be found that Ohio ever executed any person for a crime committed while younger than age fifteen, but twenty-three juveniles age ten to fourteen have been executed nationwide.

A review of Ohio's nineteen cases according to various facts about the crimes involved (table 7–3) shows that these crimes were scattered throughout the state, with five in or near Cleveland, three in or near Cincinnati, one near Columbus, one in Toledo, and one in Youngstown. The other eight crimes occurred in small towns or rural areas. In almost every case the victim was white, a fact that generally tends to increase the severity of the punishment in criminal cases and increases the probability of capital punishment. In only two cases were the victims black. One was a black police officer; the other was Pang Young's victim, a black laundryman working at the store Young robbed. The weapons used varied considerably, but after 1920 three-fourths of the murders were committed with handguns. Fourteen cases involved a felony-murder prosecution in which the offender was involved in the felony of robbery or rape when the killing occurred. Only five involved an isolated murder situation. Four involved multiple victims and three involved the murder of young children. Six involved sexual aggression by young boys against women or girls.

In comparison, only 81 percent of the nationwide cases involved murders

TABLE 7–1. Ohio Offenders by Race, Age, and Background

Offender	Race	Age at Offense	Background
Mann	W	16	Born in England; mother died; ran away; became hobo
Ohr	W	15	Born in Bavaria; father died; ran away; became hobo
Sammett	W	17	Born in Ohio; mother died; prior burglary
Leuth	W	16	Born in Germany; family epilepsy; parental beatings
Taylor	B	17	Born in Ohio; illegitimate and fatherless; dull mentality; farm worker
Hass	W	16	Orphan; ran away; lived with foster parents
Beard	W	17	Orphan; dull mentality; farm worker
Pupera	W	16	Born in Pennsylvania; raised in ghetto; prior auto theft and alcohol offense
Ross	B	17	Born in Mississippi; father deserted; dishwasher; prior crimes
Hewitt	W	16	Mental age of ten; lived on small farm
Coverson	B	17	Recently moved to black section of Cincinnati
Coleman	B	17	Born in North Carolina; recently moved to Ohio; prior thefts
Akers	B	17	Wanted in St. Louis for robbery and burglary
Murphy	B	17	Unknown
Young	O	17	Born in China; attempted suicide after crime
Hand	W	17	Raised in state children's homes; prior auto theft; on parole from Boy's School; farm worker
Hagert	W	17	Violent psychopath; homosexual; prior auto theft; just released from mental ward of hospital
Frohner	W	16	Born in Ohio; lived on family farm; minor quarrels with father
Schreiber	W	17	No prior trouble with authorities

(table 7–4). The nonhomicide cases are almost all limited to the southeastern states and to the period before 1880.

Ohio began using the electric chair at the Ohio Penitentiary Annex in 1897, so the fourteen executions from 1897 to 1956 all occurred there (table 7–5). The period the Ohio juveniles spent on death row, calculated from the sentencing decision by the trial judge to the execution, ranged from three to twenty-six months, with a generally longer period for the post-World War II cases. Hagert's lengthy period was due largely to the fact that his first conviction was overruled and he had to be retried and reconvicted.

The nineteen Ohio executions for crimes committed while under age eigh-

TABLE 7-2. Ohio and Nationwide Cases by Offender's Race and Age

Race	Ohio Cases		Nationwide Cases[a]		Age at Offense	Ohio Cases		Nationwide Cases	
Black	6	(32)	185	(69)	17	12	(63)	153	(55)
White	12	(63)	68	(25)	16	6	(32)	75	(27)
Other					15	1	(5)	28	(10)
Hispanic	0	(0)	6	(2)	14	0	(0)	11	(4)
American Indian	0	(0)	8	(3)	13	0	(0)	4	(1)
Chinese	1	(5)	3	(1)	12	0	(0)	5	(2)
Total	19	(100)	270	(100)[b]	11	0	(0)	1	(0)
					10	0	(0)	2	(1)
					Total	19	(100)	279	(100)[c]

Note: Figures in parentheses are percentages.
[a]See chapter four for more information about nationwide cases.
[b]Eleven offenders executed for crimes committed while under age 18 were of unknown race, making a total of 281 nationwide.
[c]Two offenders executed for crimes committed while under age 18 were of unknown precise age at the time of their crimes, making a total of 281 nationwide.

teen may be compared by decade with Ohio's total executions for offenders of any age and the nationwide executions of offenders whose crimes were committed while under age eighteen (table 7-6). While the cell size for the Ohio child executions is too small for much comparative analysis, a few differences appear within the Ohio data. The peak of child and adult executions in Ohio occurred in the 1920s and 1930s, with almost half of all executions in Ohio's history occurring then. Comparing Ohio juvenile executions with nationwide juvenile executions reveals a somewhat contrasting pattern. While the peak for Ohio juvenile executions came in the 1920s, the peak nationally did not come until the 1940s. The curves are about parallel, however, and Ohio seems to have been fairly congruous with the rest of the nation in the frequency with which it executed persons for crimes committed while under age eighteen.

CONCLUSIONS

The legal environment surrounding the issue of juvenile executions evolved for two centuries before reaching its present state. The advent of the juvenile justice system was a major effort to remove juveniles from the harsh sanctions of criminal law but was unsuccessful in terminating the death penalty for all juveniles. Ohio followed this legal progression with little deviation, even gaining some notoriety in the mid-1970s by sentencing an offender to death for a murder he committed when he was only sixteen years old; the U.S. Supreme Court reversed the case.[52]

Ohio has rather clearly joined the growing trend on this issue in the 1980s. Of the thirty-six states with presumptively valid post-*Furman*[53] death penalty

TABLE 7–3. Ohio Crimes by Date, Place, Category, Victim, and Weapon

Offender	Date	Place	Category	Victim	Weapon
Mann	6–27–1879	Alliance	Robbery-murder	W M adult	Club
Ohr	6–27–1879	Alliance	Robbery murder	W M adult	Club
Sammett	11–25–1879	Massillon	Murder	W M teenager	Rifle
Leuth	5–9–1889	Cleveland	Rape-murder	W girl	Hammer
Taylor	12–20–1894	Worthington	Robbery-murder	W M adult	Club
Hass	7–2–1896	Cloverdale	Rape-murder	W F adult	Razor, club
Beard	5–11–1914	Ironton	Murders	2 W F adults, W M adult	Razor, club
Pupera	12–31–1920	Cleveland	Robbery-murders	2 W M adults	Handgun
Ross	11–5–1925	Cleveland	Robbery-murder	W M adult	Handgun
Hewitt	2–14–1927	Conneaut	Attempted Rape-murder	W F adult, W boy	Club
Coverson	5–14–1927	Cincinnati	Murder	B policeman	Handgun
Coleman	2–6–1928	Portsmouth	Murder	W policeman	Handgun
Akers	12–25–1928	Cleveland	Robbery-murder	W M adult	Handgun
Murphy	10–8–1932	Silverton	Robbery-murder	W M adult	Handgun
Young	7–12–1938	Cincinnati	Robbery-murder	B M adult	Handgun
Hand	7–3–1943	Mercer County	Murder	W boy	Hammer
Hagert	8–12–1943	Bay Village	Murder	2 W boys	Handgun
Frohner	1–13–1947	Youngstown	Robbery-murder	W M adult	Handgun
Schreiber	8–12–1954	Toledo	Rape-murder	W F teenager	Club, knife

statutes, Ohio is one of ten that now prohibit capital punishment for crimes committed while under age eighteen.[54] Only ten states have no minimum age for capital punishment.[55]

Before Ohio enacted this new prohibition of the death penalty for juveniles,

TABLE 7–4. Ohio and Nationwide Cases by Offense

Offense		Ohio		Nationwide[a]	
Murder		19	(100)	226	(81)
Rape		0	(0)	43	(15)
Other		0	(0)	11	(4)
	Total	19	(100)	280	(100)[b]

Note: Figures in parentheses are percentages.
[a]See chapter four for more information about nationwide cases.
[b]One offender executed for a crime committed while under age 18 committed an unknown crime, making a total of 281 nationwide.

TABLE 7–5. Ohio Executions by Method, Time, Date, and Months on Death Row

Offender	Method	Time	Date	Months on Death Row
Mann	Hanging	11:35 A.M.	6–23–1880	6
Ohr	Hanging	11:35 A.M.	6–23–1880	6
Sammett	Hanging	11:35 A.M.	6–23–1880	4
Leuth	Hanging	12:05 A.M.	8–29–1890	8
Taylor	Hanging	12:06 A.M.	7–26–1895	6
Haas	Electrocution	12:30 A.M.	4–21–1897	6
Beard	Electrocution	12:10 A.M.	12–4–1914	6
Pupera	Electrocution	12:10 A.M.	5–9–1922	12
Ross	Electrocution	1:05 A.M.	11–26–1926	10
Hewitt	Electrocution	7:38 P.M.	1–6–1928	8
Coverson	Electrocution	7:37 P.M.	1–9–1928	3
Coleman	Electrocution	9:18 P.M.	7–5–1928	3
Akers	Electrocution	9:03 P.M.	6–13–1930	14
Murphy	Electrocution	8:50 P.M.	8–14–1933	9
Young	Electrocution	8:16 P.M.	7–12–1939	8
Hand	Electrocution	8:01 P.M.	1–14–1944	4
Hagert	Electrocution	7:08 P.M.	10–3–1945	26
Frohner	Electrocution	9:09 P.M.	8–20–1948	19
Schreiber	Electrocution	8:02 P.M.	3–15–1956	14

the state was responsible for nineteen executions for crimes committed while under age eighteen. Probably many times that number of juveniles were sentenced to death but were never actually executed.

While racial discrimination did not seem to be a factor in these Ohio executions, most of the juveniles executed were from deprived socioeconomic

TABLE 7–6. Ohio and Nationwide Executions by Decade

Decade	Ohio				Nationwide Juvenile[b]	
	Juvenile		Total[a]			
1880–1899	3	(16)	16	(5)[c]	20	(9)
1890–1899	3	(16)	28	(8)	20	(9)
1900–1909	0	(0)	25	(7)	23	(10)
1910–1919	1	(5)	26	(7)	24	(10)
1920–1929	5	(26)	85	(24)	27	(12)
1930–1939	3	(16)	82	(23)	41	(18)
1940–1949	3	(16)	51	(14)	53	(23)
1950–1959	1	(5)	32	(9)	16	(7)
1960–1969	0	(0)	7	(2)	3	(1)
1970–1979	0	(0)	0	(0)	0	(0)
1980—8-1-86	0	(0)	0	(0)	3	(1)
Total	19	(100)	352	(100)	230	(100)[d]

Note: Figures in parentheses are percentages.
[a]Source of data: W. BOWERS, LEGAL HOMICIDE 479–486 (1984).
[b]See chapter four for more information about nationwide cases.
[c]The data reported by BOWERS begin with 1885, with 8 executions reported for 1885–1889. To more accurately estimate the total executions for 1880–1889, that number has been doubled, to 16.
[d]Fifty-one offenders were executed before 1880 for crimes committed while under age 18, making a total of 281 in the nation's history.

backgrounds and had little support in the community in which they lived. In contrast, their victims were typically white citizens of the community who had significant social standing.

The nineteen executions were not limited to Ohio's several urban areas but were scattered around the state. The frequency pattern of these executions over the years from 1880 to 1956 matches fairly well the nationwide pattern and the pattern of Ohio executions of offenders of all ages. Unlike several other states, Ohio no longer sentences its juveniles to death.

EIGHT

Juveniles' Attitudes toward Impending Execution

American jurisdictions have executed 281 persons for crimes committed while under age eighteen.[1] Their ages at execution ranged from twelve to twenty-eight. All of them apparently were healthy young persons with no reason to contemplate their deaths from natural causes in the foreseeable future. All came to contemplate their deaths from impending execution during periods of waiting that lasted from a few weeks to over ten years.

The focus of this chapter is on the attitudes and perceptions of these persons concerning their impending executions. No attempt has been made to present this information for all 281 cases. Such an attempt would be doomed to failure, since for most cases this information either has never been recorded or, if recorded, is lost to current researchers. The cases selected for description are taken from those for which adequate information exists.

Chapters five, six, and seven present fairly detailed case studies of sixty persons executed for crimes committed while under age eighteen. This chapter selects from among these sixty in order to examine the much narrower issue of attitudes toward impending execution. While these cases are not necessarily a representative sample of the universe of 281 cases, they do tend to include offenders from different periods, of varying ages, and with differing attitudes.

CATEGORIES OF ATTITUDES

Analyses of the attitudes and perceptions of these juveniles is facilitated by a rough categorization. Such a categorization may obscure the uniqueness of each case and erroneously imply that members of a category behave in an identical manner. Nonetheless, members of the categories have expressed similar sentiments and manifested similar attitudes while facing lawful execution. In this spirit six categories have been formulated and cases are used for illustrative purposes. The categories are (1) indifference or lack of concern; (2) resignation and weariness with waiting; (3) fear, abandonment, and seeking rescue; (4) proud, defiant, boastful, and joking; (5) seeking forgiveness and acceptance and serving as an example to others; and (6) religious conversion.

Some of the condemned juveniles seemed expressionless or without apparent concern about their impending execution. That was particularly true for some during the trial and early post-trial stages of their cases. Their attitude sometimes changed dramatically as execution grew more imminent. This lack of concern or indifference may have stemmed from an unrealistic perception of death or from stoicism, but it was manifested in a fairly consistent manner.

One example is Hannah Ocuish, the twelve-year-old retarded girl executed by Connecticut in 1786.[2] At her trial for the murder of a six-year-old girl, Ocuish seemed unconcerned and reasonably content. In contrast, the presiding judge could barely speak and the spectators wept openly as she was sentenced to death.

James Guild was also executed at age twelve, in 1828 in New Jersey.[3] This servant boy murdered a prominent grandmother. Awaiting execution for fourteen months, he seemed not to fully comprehend his situation. To pass the time, he enacted a bizarre mock trial with mice captured in his cell. This trial, complete with twelve mice jurors, resulted in the ceremonial hanging of the mouse defendant, all to the indifferent bemusement of the young boy.

Another example is George Stinney, a fourteen-year-old executed in South Carolina in 1944 for the murder of two young girls.[4] As Stinney entered the death chamber and was strapped into the electric chair, he "appeared far more at ease than some of those who came to watch him die."[5] As the guards fumbled with the straps, they were relieved that he was calm and cooperative with their efforts.[6]

In 1947 Mississippi executed James Lewis, age fifteen, and Charles Trudell, age sixteen, who had murdered their employer.[7] During the sixteen months they awaited execution and endured the ups and downs of the appellate and clemency process, they seemed unconcerned about their fate. They continued to read their comic books and plunk their guitars, passing the time in the local jail.

Charles Rumbaugh, executed in Texas in 1985 for a robbery and murder committed over ten years earlier, ranged through several attitudes before finally meeting death.[8] His personal perception of the death penalty and its deterrent effect upon him prior to committing murder seems to put him in this unconcerned category: "I was 17 years old when I committed the offense for which I was sentenced to die, and I didn't even start thinking and caring about my life until I was at least 20."[9]

A final example is Terry Roach, executed in South Carolina in 1986.[10] A retarded seventeen-year-old when he raped and murdered, he deteriorated mentally from Huntington's chorea during his eight years on death row and had the mental age of a twelve-year-old. That prompted Supreme Court Justice Thurgood Marshall to observe that Roach's mental condition "raises substantial doubts as to whether Roach has any understanding that he is scheduled to die tomorrow."[11] Early the next morning, Roach seemed "calm and resigned as he shuffled into the death chamber."[12]

All seven of these young persons showed a lack of understanding and concern about the death penalty before committing their crimes or their impending executions after being condemned. For the younger ones and the more retarded ones, that may simply have stemmed from ignorance and immaturity. For the older ones, it may be illustrative of adolescents' lack of understanding of the nature of death.

RESIGNATION AND WEARINESS WITH WAITING

Some of these condemned juveniles concluded that they would rather die than spend their lives in prison. For some this attitude came quickly, stemming from a desire to be free of confinement. For others it dawned on them gradually, reaching full awareness only after many years in prison.

An example of the former is Joseph Nuana, executed in Washington Territory in 1874.[13] He had murdered a prominent farmer and the farmer's pregnant wife. Nuana spent less than four months awaiting execution but that was in a jail far away from his home. Before his trial he had seemed carefree and unconcerned but concluded rather quickly that an American jail was no place for a Hawaiian-Indian boy from San Juan Island to spend the rest of his life: "I would sooner be dead than live in jail here."[14] He made this life and death decision at the age of seventeen.

James (Sleepy) Coleman was executed in Ohio in 1928 for the murder of a police officer.[15] His crime was committed along with an older man, who gave him the gun and signaled Coleman when to shoot the officer. Both Coleman and his partner in crime were convicted and sentenced to death. Coleman's partner appealed repeatedly, and he vigorously sought clemency from the governor, all to no avail. In contrast, Coleman admitted his guilt and refused to seek either appellate review or executive clemency. The two murderers, one who fought fate and one who accepted it, died only minutes apart in Ohio's electric chair.

Charles Rumbaugh, described above as at first being unconcerned with death, spent almost ten years on death row (1976 to 1985), longer than any other juvenile in American history.[16] During that decade of waiting for death, Rumbaugh changed his attitude several times, finally becoming so weary of the vigil that he volunteered for execution and fought against any appeals on his behalf. This weariness began early, as illustrated by his words in a 1978 letter:

> You know, D.J., if they were to come to my cell and tell me I was going to be executed tomorrow, I would feel relieved, in a way. The waiting would be over. I would know what to expect. To me, the dying part is easy; its the waiting and not knowing that's hard.[17]

By 1982 Rumbaugh had instructed his attorneys not to appeal his case further. He even fought against a challenge filed by his parents. His frustration in not being able to end the process resulted in a plan to commit suicide. At a 1983 court hearing, he brandished a hidden knife and pointed it at a marshal, imploring him to shoot.[18] The marshal did, hitting Rumbaugh in the heart and lungs, but he recovered only to face another two and one-half years of waiting. By January 1984 he had sunk deeper into clinically diagnosed depression and psychosis:

> I feel like I have been traveling down a long, dark and winding tunnel for the past nine years—the length of time I have been on death row—and now I can see no end to the tunnel, no light at the end of it, just more long years of the same. I have reached the point where I no longer really care. . . . I'm so damn tired and disgusted with sitting here and watching my friends take that final trip to the execution chamber, one after the other, while I continue to wait and speculate about when my time will come. They're killing me a little bit each day.[19]

Each of the three cases in this category suggests more of a rejection of long-term confinement than a desire to die. If the option had been available to be released from prison or, in Rumbaugh's case, even to receive treatment for his spiraling depression and psychosis, death most probably would not have been seen as the preferable alternative. These cases do not illustrate some supposed desire to commit suicide by committing a capital crime and getting executed for it; they illustrate the lack of reasonable options once convicted and sentenced to death.

FEAR, ABANDONMENT, AND SEEKING RESCUE

The younger juveniles and most of the nine girls exhibited what can best be described as mortal fear and a feeling of being lost and abandoned. It appeared as uncontrollable crying, severe emotional depression, and childlike pleas for rescue to a parent or authoritative adult.

An example is Hannah Ocuish, who experienced her trial with indifference.[20] As her execution grew imminent, her attitude changed. Finally, when a visitor explained to Ocuish exactly what was going to happen to her, she wept uncontrollably for most of the day. Then the execution date arrived: "At the place of execution she said very little—appeared greatly afraid, and seemed to want somebody to help her."[21]

Fourteen years old and black, Brad Beard had experienced the lynching of his older brother for eloping with a white girl, a personal relationship quite forbidden at that time in Alabama.[22] When Beard was sentenced to death legally only a few months later for the rape of a young white girl, he barely avoided being lynched himself. He was terrified as he was moved from jail to jail to befuddle the lynch mobs. When he was hanged, in 1897, the ceremony was calm and peaceful for everyone except Beard. He remained terrified to the end.

Charles Oxnam was executed by California in 1916 for murdering his burglary victim.[23] His mental problems were so severe that he was described as feebleminded, with a mental age of eight. Although the debate about his sanity at the time of his crime raged to the end, the governor allowed the execution to occur. At age eighteen Oxnam "went to the scaffold at San Quentin penitentiary quivering and weeping. He sobbed until the drop fell."[24]

Ignatius (Sam) Pupera was a roaring twenties robber who died in Ohio's electric chair in 1922.[25] Only sixteen years old when the robbery and murders occurred, he turned seventeen before the police could arrest him. His concern was expressed in his plaintive question: "They'd never send a boy of seventeen to the chair in Ohio, would they?"[26] After being convicted and sentenced to death, he spent a year fighting for his life through court appeals and petitions to the governor. He lost his battle but won one small point. He was not sent to the chair in Ohio as a boy of seventeen. He celebrated his eighteenth birthday on death row, two and one-half months before being executed.

Pang Young, electrocuted in Ohio in 1939,[27] was variously described as "a childlike oriental" and a "sobbing Chinese." He seemed to have no friends or family. His intense fear and his remorse for the crime are indicated by his attempt at suicide soon afterward. Seventeen at the time of his crime and eighteen at his execution, Young was described by seasoned observers as "one of the loneliest figures who ever waited out the hours in the death row of Ohio Penitentiary."[28]

Edward Haight expressed more a feeling of loneliness and abandonment than of fear.[29] After eight months of waiting, he was executed by New York in 1943 for the kidnap-murder of two young girls. The day before he died he seemed anxious and lonely: "I guess this is my last day and I am only seventeen. I wish somebody would come and visit me. I'd like some company."[30]

George Stinney, executed in South Carolina in 1944, began his experience with an apparent lack of concern.[31] After this fourteen-year-old received the sentence of death and came to understand what he faced, his attitude changed. A few weeks before he died, he wrote to his mother, proclaiming innocence and begging her to help him. It was to no avail: "All she knew how to do was pray."[32]

The last illustration in this category is Terry Roach, the retarded and mentally deteriorating boy executed in South Carolina in 1986.[33] Given the nature of his brutal crimes, he was characterized by the state as mean and cruel.[34] But a reporter who interviewed Roach shortly before his execution saw him as "a terrified, cornered human being. He personified fear, not evil."[35]

These eight cases suggest a wide range of attitudes. Most of these juveniles simply were in mortal fear of the unknown and unknowable dimensions of death. Some seemed devastated by the uncaring attitudes and impotence of their family and friends. A few, including Hannah Ocuish and Pang Young, were truly alone in a hostile world and seemed crushed by their aloneness.

PROUD, DEFIANT, BOASTFUL, AND JOKING

These ways of contemplating one's execution seem consistent with the attitudes of many adolescent males. The examples for this category are all older males. They refused to admit fear or error, even playing joking games with the people intent upon executing them.

The first case is not an obvious example of this category and indeed is atypical in many of its attributes compared with the other 281 cases. David Dodd was hanged in Little Rock in 1864 for being a Confederate spy.[36] He had been gathering information about the Union Army behind the lines and was caught, convicted, and sentenced to death. When given the chance to save his life by identifying the other spies who had assisted him, he adamantly refused and remembered well his lessons from earlier days as a cadet in a private military school: ". . . and like Nathan Hale, my only regret is that I have but one life to give to my country."[37] He gave that one life at age seventeen and is remembered to this day in Arkansas as a war hero.

Edward Deacons, executed at sixteen by New York in 1888, was a boastful tough guy when he died.[38] He seemed to enjoy complicated lying schemes to befuddle those around him and cheerfully declared in open court that all witnesses against him were liars. Just days before the execution, the governor refused to intervene, evoking a bravado laugh from Deacons. On the scaffold, Deacons remained defiant to the end: "Friends, the law is about to take the life of an innocent man. That is all I have to say."[39]

Joseph Murphy and his older brother James were executed by Ohio in 1933 for a murder during a bank robbery.[40] They might never have been identified and arrested if they had not been boasting about their crime to anyone who would listen. They recanted these boasts once arrested and then denied the crime to the end. They were highly critical of the criminal justice process that brought them to Ohio's electric chair.

William Byers, executed by New York in 1956 at age nineteen,[41] had a similar attitude. He and his girl friend had murdered her mother two years earlier. As Byers awaited trial he wrote a letter to his girl friend, ridiculing his fate: "If I do get the electric chair, I hope that they do not burn me too badly. Maybe medium rare, or well done, but not to a crisp."[42] He made a concerted effort at trial to avoid the death penalty. Unsuccessful, he reverted to his fearless demeanor: "He went to his death at a slow, indifferent trot, chewing bubble gum."[43]

Charles Rumbaugh, executed in 1985, had hoped to become a notorious criminal.[44] Before depression descended upon him during the long wait on death row, he tended toward boastful claims about his exploits and intentions. An appellate court later interpreted this behavior as being "engaged in boasting and in making himself out to be a fearsome desperado in the eyes of his companions and in the face of peace officers."[45] One of his fearless boasts concerned his fate. When he was first arrested for the crime that led to his execution, he boasted to the police that "I ain't going nowhere but the electric chair."[46] The essence of his boast was to be fulfilled, though not exactly in the manner he had predicted: Texas was using lethal injection to kill prisoners by the time his execution date arrived ten years later. Rumbaugh went to the hospital gurney, not the electric chair.[47]

These five young males executed over a 101-year period personify the familiar tough young punk. Their words and actions illustrate the universally recognized defiant swagger of many adolescent males. As tough guys, all of them tried their best to camouflage any feelings of self-doubt or fear. They did so with differing degrees of success.

SEEKING FORGIVENESS AND ACCEPTANCE AND SERVING AS AN EXAMPLE TO OTHERS

Many executed juveniles approached death with a desire to be forgiven by family and friends and by the victims of their crimes. They politely thanked the prison guards for kindnesses to them while they awaited the execution date. They issued messages to other juveniles to look upon their own fate as the price for misdeeds. Some of these attitudes were undoubtedly prompted by the urgings of the various counselors who hovered around them near the end, but some apparently arose from deep-rooted childhood lessons.

An early example is William Battin, age seventeen when he was executed by Pennsylvania in 1722.[48] He had set fire to his master's house, killing three young children asleep within. Although he was mentally dull, ignorant, and illiterate, his last statement read for him at the gallows included the elaborate admonition: "I greatly desire all youth may take example by me, and have a care how they disobey their parents, which if I had not done, I should not have been here this day, and brought to this untimely end."[49] The statement was obviously written down and probably even composed by someone else. Perhaps Battin agreed with the essence of the admonition, since he did sign it with his mark.

Manuel Hernandez was executed in Arizona's gas chamber in 1934, sitting next to and holding the hand of his older brother.[50] They had been convicted and sentenced to death for killing an old prospector when Manuel was only seventeen years old. The night before their joint execution, Manuel tried to save his older brother's life by claiming that his brother had nothing to do with the murder. This desperate attempt was unsuccessful.

The fourteen-year-old boy executed by South Carolina in 1944, George Stinney, experienced attitudes ranging from indifference to fear but finally came to seek forgiveness.[51] Minutes before his execution, Stinney clutched his Bible tightly and told the sheriff he was sorry he had committed the crime and hoped God and his parents would forgive him. He seemed to be at peace with himself, if nonetheless afraid of what was about to happen to him.

In addition to being one of the loneliest juveniles ever executed, Frank Loveless sought one last time to get forgiveness and acceptance from his family.[52] Loveless had escaped from an Indiana reformatory and had killed a constable in Nevada, some 2,000 miles from his family home. He was executed by Nevada in 1944 at age seventeen after over two years on death row. The day before his execution he spent crying. The day of his execution he wrote long apologetic letters to his father, grandmother, and brother back in Indiana.

His last request to the prison warden was to "send some roses to my grandmother."[53]

James Echols, the last juvenile to die for rape, was executed in Texas in 1964.[54] Aging from seventeen to nineteen while awaiting execution, he maintained to the end that he had not raped the victim. Nevertheless, he came to accept his fate. As he entered the death chamber he expressed these thoughts: "I have no hard feelings against anyone and I want to thank everyone for what they have done for me."[55]

Charles Rumbaugh's careening path from boastfulness to indifference to weariness ended in a conciliatory gesture.[56] After waiting ten years for Texas to take his life, his last words were: "About all I can say is goodbye. For the rest of you, even though you don't forgive me my transgressions, I forgive you for yours against me. That's all I wish to say. I'm ready to begin my journey."[57]

Terry Roach spent the night before his execution trying to gain the approval of those around him and to understand what was about to happen to him.[58] He paid rapt attention to letters read to him by his attorney, not unlike a young child listening to a bedtime story. A key part of his last statement included a message to those he had injured: "To the families of the victims, my heart is still with you in your sorrow. May you forgive me just as I know that my Lord has done."[59]

The last juvenile to be executed, Jay Pinkerton in Texas in 1986, uttered perhaps the most touching last words of all.[60] Having waited six and one-half years, he was finally ushered into the death chamber and strapped onto the hospital gurney, where he endured the minor sting of insertion of intravenous tubes into his arms. His encouragement to the witnesses at his execution was "Be strong for me. I want you to know that I'm at peace with myself and with my God."[61] Pinkerton's father, in the death chamber with his condemned son, said, "Bye, Jay."[62] Jay Pinkerton's last words were private and personal but were overheard by all who came to see him die: "I love you, Dad."[63]

In all seven of these cases, the condemned juveniles made some last effort to set things right with others. They asked for forgiveness, understanding, acceptance, or even love while offering the same or more to the respondents. They were not particularly defiant or frightened but simply wanted to leave this world with their personal accounts in order.

RELIGIOUS CONVERSION

Probably the most common theme seen in the 281 cases is the last-minute conversion to an orthodox religion and a final prayer to God for salvation. Some of these conversions apparently were reaffirmations of childhood religious experiences. Others seemed to have no foundation that would have led one to predict them. Many undoubtedly stem from the fact that, unless the prisoner adamantly refuses, prison chaplains routinely counsel death row inmates and stay with them up to the moment of execution. If the condemned juvenile wants to discuss religion, he or she has someone right there with whom to do so.

Some executed juveniles seem simply to have accepted a prayer suggested by their religious counselor. A classic example is that of William Battin, the illiterate boy executed by Pennsylvania in 1722.[64] His last statement, signed by him with his witnessed mark, closed with this eloquent sentence: "I yield my body to this shameful and ignominious death this 15th day of August, 1722, being about seventeen years of age, hoping that God will have mercy upon my poor soul. Lord Jesus, receive my spirit."[65]

Irving Hanchett, just barely fifteen years old, was executed by Florida in 1910.[66] He had to wait only three months from crime through trial to execution for the murder of a teenage girl who had rejected his advances. Hanchett had just moved to Florida from Connecticut and had no friends or family in the area. While Hanchett was awaiting execution, a priest baptized him into the Catholic faith and Hanchett seemed buoyed by the hope of salvation. As he mounted the scaffold, he said: "Mercy, my Jesus; my Jesus, mercy. Goodbye everyone."[67]

Harley Beard was a slow-witted orphan executed in Ohio in 1914 for murdering the three people with whom he lived and for whom he worked.[68] He made a full confession and died less than seven months after his crime. His last words were "I think it is awful to send me to my Father this way."[69]

Willie Whitfield was executed in 1938 by Alabama for a robbery and murder.[70] He seemed defiant until near the end of his eleven-month wait from crime to execution. Then he began to consult regularly with the prison minister. His final words were: "I'm goin' on home. . . . tell 'em all I'm going on home to rest with Jesus. Preacher, all you all, goodbye. I'm ready to go. I've made up with the Good Master. If I hadn't did what I did I wouldn't be ready to go. . . . don't pull those straps so tight."[71]

Willie Francis, who killed a police chief's brother in Louisiana, holds the distinction of being sent to the electric chair twice, on dates over a year apart.[72] His first electrocution failed when a wire burned out in the electric chair. Francis saw that as divine intervention: "The Lord was with me."[73] When he was strapped in the chair, Francis recalled later, he was thinking about going to heaven and wondering what hell was like.[74] Thirteen months later the chair worked well and Francis was not spared.

James Echols was executed by Texas in 1964 for rape.[75] Only weeks before he died he was baptized as a Catholic by the prison chaplain. On the day before he died, Echols reflected upon his newly embraced religion: "No one wants to die, but I would rather die knowing God than not knowing him."[76]

The guilelessness and simplicity of the retarded and mentally deteriorating Terry Roach reveals the essence of cases in this category.[77] While he was afraid and confused about his rapidly approaching death, he nonetheless spent considerable time going over various prayer options with the prison chaplain and kept asking the chaplain which prayers were most likely to work—most likely to get him into heaven.[78]

The conversion of so many of these condemned juveniles to an orthodox religion, usually the Catholic faith, may be explained by several hypotheses.

Perhaps they were all resigned to face their death as true believers in what they saw as a powerful religion. Perhaps they were simply covering all bases, not certain about religion but thinking it couldn't hurt to embrace it just in case what was said about heaven and hell was true. Or perhaps these last-minute conversions came because the only counselors these juveniles had near the end were chaplains. When the chaplains were asked what to do about the frightening approach of death, they may have had only one answer—turn to God. If lay counselors had been equally available, the results might have been different.

CONCLUSIONS

This anecdotal but revealing collection of facts about the attitudes of executed juveniles can only serve to stimulate wonder at what their true, deeper feelings must have been. With the more recent cases, particularly those of Rumbaugh and Roach, fairly extensive and reliable information exists. As for the others, we are generally left with only a last comment to suggest an outline of their attitudes toward their impending execution.

PART III

The Future

NINE

Juvenile Death Sentences
in the 1980s

Despite a marked decline in the frequency with which juveniles are sentenced to death, this practice has not disappeared. A few juveniles are still sentenced to death each year and, as of November 1, 1986, thirty-eight persons were on death row for crimes committed while under age eighteen.

This chapter first describes the juvenile death sentencing practices of trial courts in various jurisdictions of the United States over the past few years. The focus is on what trial courts actually did from 1982 through late 1986 when faced with the opportunity to impose the death sentence for a juvenile crime. The second part of this chapter considers the cases of the thirty-seven juveniles on death row, including information about the offenders, their crimes, and the criminal processes that placed them on death row. Finally, six of these cases are presented in more detail as representative of certain categories of juveniles on death row.

SENTENCES, 1982 TO NOVEMBER 1986

From January 1, 1982, to November 1, 1986, sixteen states imposed death sentences for crimes committed while under age eighteen. These juvenile death sentences were imposed in thirty-seven separate instances on a total of thirty-two offenders. Several of these offenders received more than one death sentence for the same crime during this period, an earlier death sentence having been reversed and then subsequently reimposed. Thus, on thirty-seven separate occasions a state trial court decided to sentence an offender to death for a crime committed while under age eighteen.

The number of juvenile death sentences declined significantly during this period (table 9–1). Eleven such sentences were imposed in 1982, nine in 1983, six in 1984, four in 1985, and seven during the first ten months of 1986. While the number of juvenile death sentences was thus declining, the number of adult death sentences remained fairly constant at 250 to 300 each year.[1]

TABLE 9–1. Juveniles Sentenced to Death, 1982 to November 1, 1986

Year	Offender	Age at Offense	Race	State	Status 11–1–86
1982	Barrow, Lee Roy[2]	17	W	Tex.	Reversed in 1985
	Cannon, Joseph J.[3]	17	W	Tex.	On death row
	Carter, Robert A.[4]	17	B	Tex.	On death row
	Garrett, Johnny F.[5]	17	W	Tex.	On death row
	Johnson, Lawrence[6]	17	B	Md.	Reversed twice but resentenced to death in 1983 and 1984
	Lashley, Frederick[7]	17	B	Mo.	On death row
	Legare, Andrew[8]	17	W	Ga.	Reversed in 1983; resentenced to death in 1984; reversed in 1986
	Stanford, Kevin[9]	17	B	Ky.	On death row
	Stokes, Freddie[10]	17	B	N.C.	Reversed in 1982 but resentenced to death in 1983
	Thompson, Jay[11]	17	W.	Ind.	Reversed in 1986
	Trimble, James[12]	17	W	Md.	On death row
1983	Bey, Marko[13]	17	B	N.J.	On death row
	Cannaday, Attina[14]	16	W	Miss.	Reversed in 1984
	Harris, Curtis P.[15]	17	B	Tex.	On death row
	Harvey, Frederick[16]	16	B	Nev.	Reversed in 1984
	Hughes, Kevin[17]	16	B	Pa.	On death row
	Johnson, Lawrence[18]	17	B	Md.	Reversed in 1983 but resentenced to death in 1984
	Lynn, Frederick[19]	16	B	Ala.	Reversed in 1985 but resentenced to death in 1986
	Mhoon, James[20]	16	B	Miss.	Reversed in 1985
	Stokes, Freddie[21]	17	B	N.C.	On death row
1984	Aulisio, Joseph[22]	15	W	Pa.	On death row
	Brown, Leon[23]	15	B	N.C.	On death row
	Johnson, Lawrence[24]	17	B	Md.	On death row
	Legare, Andrew[25]	17	W	Ga.	On death row
	Patton, Keith[26]	17	B	Ind.	On death row
	Thompson, Wayne[27]	15	W	Okla.	On death row

TABLE 9–1. (Cont'd)

Year	Offender	Age at Offense	Race	State	Status 11–1–86
1985	Livingston, Jesse[28]	17	B	Fla.	On death row
	Morgan, James[29]	16	W	Fla.	On death row
	Ward, Ronald[30]	15	B	Ark.	On death row
	Williams, Raymond[31]	17	B	Pa.	On death row
1986[a]	Comeaux, Adam[32]	17	B	La.	On death row
	Cooper, Paula R.[33]	15	B	Ind.	On death row
	LeCroy, Cleo D.[34]	17	W	Fla.	On death row
	Lynn, Frederick[35]	16	B	Ala.	On death row
	Sellers, Sean R.[36]	16	W	Okla.	On death row
	Wilkins, Heath[37]	16	W	Mo.	On death row
	Williams, Alexander[38]	17	B	Ga.	On death row

[a]First ten months only.

Four of the juvenile offenders sentenced to death during this period subsequently had their death sentences reversed in a manner having significant long-term effects. Lee Roy Barrow, sentenced to death in Texas in 1982, had his conviction and sentence reversed in 1985 and was awaiting retrial.[39] Mississippi's Attina Cannaday and James Mhoon and Nevada's Frederick Harvey were resentenced to life imprisonment after their 1983 death sentences were reversed.[40] Jay Thompson in Indiana also had his death sentence reversed and was awaiting resentencing.[41]

During this period, thirty-six states had death penalty statutes that apparently were valid. Statutes in as many as thirty of these states permitted imposition of the death penalty for crimes committed while under age eighteen. Only about half (sixteen states) actually imposed such a sentence (table 9–2). These sixteen states represented a broad spectrum of the United States, ranging from New Jersey to Texas and from Missouri to Florida.

States in the South predominated in this juvenile death sentencing practice, as they did also in adult death sentencing. Three-quarters of the juvenile death sentences (twenty-seven of thirty-seven) were imposed in the South, and eleven of the sixteen states (69 percent) that imposed juvenile death sentences were in the South. Texas was the leader with five sentences, but all five of its offenders were seventeen at the time of their crimes, since Texas law establishes seventeen as the juvenile court cutoff age and the minimum age at crime for the death penalty.[42] Other states with more than two juvenile death sentences were Maryland with four and Florida, Georgia, Indiana, North Carolina, and Pennsylvania with three each.

Of the thirty-seven juvenile death sentences imposed, five (14 percent)

TABLE 9-2. Characteristics of Juveniles Sentenced to Death, 1982 to November 1, 1986

Region and State	Sentences[a]	Offenders[a]	Age at Offense			Race		Sex	
			15	16	17	B	W	M	F
Northeast									
New Jersey	1	1	0	0	1	1	0	1	0
Pennsylvania	3	3	1	1	1	2	1	3	0
Total	4	4	1	1	2	3	1	4	0
North Central									
Indiana	3	3	1	0	2	2	1	2	1
Missouri	2	2	0	1	1	1	1	2	0
Total	5	5	1	1	3	3	2	4	1
South									
Alabama	2	1	0	2	0	2	0	2	0
Arkansas	1	1	1	0	0	1	0	1	0
Florida	3	3	0	1	2	1	2	3	0
Georgia	3	2	0	0	3	1	2	3	0
Kentucky	1	1	0	0	1	1	0	1	0
Louisiana	1	1	0	0	1	1	0	1	0
Maryland	4	2	0	0	4	3	1	4	0
Mississippi	2	2	0	2	0	1	1	1	1
North Carolina	3	2	1	0	2	3	0	3	0
Oklahoma	2	2	1	1	0	0	2	2	0
Texas	5	5	0	0	5	2	3	5	0
Total	27	22	3	6	18	16	11	26	1
West									
Nevada	1	1	0	1	0	1	0	1	0
Total	1	1	0	1	0	1	0	1	0
Grand Total	37	32[b]	5	9	23	23	14	35	2

[a]Five cases involve resentencing of offender to death after reversal of previous death sentence.
[b]Six other juveniles also on death row on November 1, 1986, were sentenced before 1982.

were for crimes committed while only age fifteen. These exceptionally youthful offenders were sentenced across the country, in Arkansas, Indiana, North Carolina, Oklahoma, and Pennsylvania. Perhaps surprisingly, all these death sentences for crimes committed at age fifteen were imposed in the last two years of the period. Nine death sentences were imposed for crimes committed while age sixteen, but the majority of sentences (23 of 37, of 62 percent) went to offenders who were seventeen at the time of their crimes.

The racial split of these offenders is somewhat surprising. Twenty-three of the sentences (62 percent) were given to blacks and fourteen (38 percent) to whites. The overrepresentation of blacks was not due particularly to the sentences in the South, where sixteen of twenty-seven, or 59 percent of the sentences went to blacks. Outside the South, 70 percent (seven of ten) of the sentences went to blacks. Death sentences for female juvenile offenders were quite rare, comprising only two (5 percent) of the thirty-seven sentences. They occurred in Indiana and Mississippi. The girls were ages fifteen and sixteen at the time of their crimes.

Seven of the thirty-seven sentences involved multiple victims, and the total number of victims involved was forty-seven (table 9–3). Three of the cases (Ward in Arkansas, Sellers in Oklahoma, and Mhoon in Mississippi) involved three victims each. Eighty-one percent (thirty of thirty-seven) of the juvenile death sentences were imposed for crimes involving a single victim.

Overall, 83 percent (thirty-eight of forty-six) of the victims were white, excluding the one victim for whom the race is unknown. All multiple victim cases involved only white victims. In the South, 89 percent (thirty-one of thirty-five) of the victims were white. Outside the South, only 64 percent (seven of eleven) of the victims were white. Even given this difference by region of the country, the nationwide overrepresentation of whites among the victims is striking.

Analysis of the sex of the victims reveals another imbalance. For the forty-seven victims nationwide, twenty-eight (60 percent) were female. Here the Southern states were not particularly the cause of the imbalance, since the victims were female in only twenty-one of thirty-five (60 percent) of the instances there. Outside the South, 58 percent (seven of twelve) of the victims were female.

The thirty-seven juvenile death sentences during these nearly five years fit a rough pattern. The sentences were imposed primarily in the earlier years but in a wide variety of states. The offenders were likely to have been black males who were age seventeen at the time of their crimes. They almost always killed a single victim, typically a white female.

JUVENILES ON DEATH ROW, NOVEMBER 1, 1986

Of the thirty-seven death sentences described in the preceding section and the fifty or more other death sentences imposed between 1972 and 1982, only

TABLE 9–3. Characteristics of Victims of Juveniles Sentenced to Death, 1982 to November 1, 1986

Region and State	Sentences	Victims	Race				Sex	
			B	Hᵃ	W	Uᵇ	M	F
Northeast								
New Jersey	1	1	1	0	0	0	0	1
Pennsylvania	3	4	1	0	3	0	2	2
Total	4	5	2	0	3	0	2	3
North Central								
Indiana	3	4	1	0	3	0	2	2
Missouri	2	2	1	0	1	0	0	2
Total	5	6	2	0	4	0	2	4
South								
Alabama	2	2	0	0	2	0	0	2
Arkansas	1	3	0	0	3	0	1	2
Florida	3	4	0	0	4	0	1	3
Georgia	3	3	2	0	1	0	2	1
Kentucky	1	1	0	0	1	0	0	1
Louisiana	1	2	0	0	2	0	0	2
Maryland	4	4	0	0	4	0	0	4
Mississippi	2	4	0	0	4	0	3	1
North Carolina	3	3	1	0	2	0	2	1
Oklahoma	2	4	0	0	4	0	3	1
Texas	5	5	0	1	4	0	2	3
Total	27	35	3	1	31	0	14	21
West								
Nevada	1	1	0	0	0	1	1	0
Total	1	1	0	0	0	1	1	0
Grand Total	37	47	7	1	38	1	19	28

ᵃH = Hispanic.
ᵇU = Unknown.

thirty-eight persons remained on death row on November 1, 1986, for crimes committed while under age eighteen. Fifteen states were holding such persons and apparently were ready, willing, and able to execute them.

From January 1, 1982, to November 1, 1986, the total death row population in the United States grew from 860 to 1,800.[43] That was an increase of 109 percent during this period, and the total of 1,800 was the greatest number of persons on death row in U.S. history. During this same period the number of persons on death row for crimes committed while under age eighteen grew from approximately thirty to thirty-eight, only a 27 percent increase (table 9–4).

The original death sentencing dates for these thirty-eight persons ranged over more than eleven years, from March 19, 1975, for Larry Jones in Mississippi to October 2, 1986, for Sean Sellers in Oklahoma. Their ages on November 1, 1986, ranged from seventeen (Ronald Ward in Arkansas, Paula Cooper in Indiana, Heath Wilkins in Missouri, and Sean Sellers in Oklahoma) to twenty-nine (Larry Jones in Mississippi). Most of them were sentenced to death only once for their crimes as juveniles. Six, however, received two death sentences and three received three. These nine had their sentences reversed on appeal and were sentenced to death again at subsequent trial court sentencing hearings.

Only two of the thirty-eight (Dalton Prejean in Louisiana, who murdered a state police officer in 1977, and Sean Sellers in Oklahoma, who murdered a store clerk in 1985 and his parents in 1986) were under sentences of death for murders unconnected to other major felonies. Most commonly (seventeen cases) the other crime was robbery. The other commonly connected crime was rape, in thirteen of the cases. Three cases involved burglary and three involved kidnapping. In 95 percent of the cases (thirty-six of thirty-eight) the states used a felony-murder prosecution, in which the seriousness of the homicide was proved primarily by proving its connection with another serious felony.

TABLE 9–4. Juvenile Offenders on Death Row, November 1, 1986

ALABAMA

Davis, Timothy. White male; 17 at crime and now age 25; robbery of store and rape and murder of white female age 60 in Coosa County in 1978; sentenced 7–28–80.[44]

Jackson, Carnel. Black male; 16 at crime and now age 23; rape and murder of white male and female in Birmingham on 1–6–80; sentenced on 11–20–81.[45]

Lynn, Frederick. Black male; 16 at crime and now age 22; burglary and murder of elderly white female in Eufaula on 2–5–81; sentenced on 5–31–83 and 4–9–86.[46]

ARKANSAS

Ward, Ronald. Black male; 15 at crime and now age 17 (DOB:[a]10–14–69); murder of two white females ages 72 and 75 and of white male age 12 and rape of one of the females in Crittendon County on 4–12–85; sentenced on 9–20–85.[47]

TABLE 9–4. Juvenile Offenders on Death Row, November 1, 1986

FLORIDA

LeCroy, Cleo Douglas.   White male; 17 at crime and now age 23; robbery and murder of white male adult and white female adult in Palm Beach County on 1–4–81; sentenced on 10–1–86.[48]

Livingston, Jesse James.   Black male; 17 at crime and now age 19 (DOB: 6–20–67); robbery of store and murder of white female age 50 in Perry in February 1985; sentenced on 10–23–85.[49]

Magill, Paul Edward.   White male; 17 at crime and now age 27 (DOB: 2–21–59); robbery of store and rape and murder of white female age 25 on 12–23–76; sentenced on 4–25–77 and 1–26–81.[50]

Morgan, James A.   White male; 16 at crime and now age 26; rape and murder of white female age 66 in Martin County on 6–6–76; sentenced on 12–30–77, 12–7–81, and 6–7–85.[51]

GEORGIA

Burger, Christopher.   White male; 17 at crime and now age 26 (DOB: Jan 1960); robbery and murder of white male cab driver in Wayne County on 9–4–77; sentenced 1–25–78 and 7–17–79.[52]

Buttrum, Janice: White female; 17 at crime and now age 23 (DOB: 1–17–63); rape and murder of white female in Whitfield County on 9–3–80; sentenced on 8–31–81.[53]

[High, Jose Martinez].[b]   Black male; 16 at crime and now age 27 (DOB: 8–16–59); kidnap and murder of white male age 11 in Crawfordville on 7–26–76; sentenced on 12–1—78 but sentence reversed on 11–19–85.[54]

Legare, Andrew Phillip.   White male; 17 at crime and now age 26 (DOB: 3–24–60); burglary and murder of black male in Baldwin County on 5–27–77; sentenced on 11–23–77, 9–4–82, and 12–1–84.[55]

Williams, Alexander.   Black male; 17 at crime and now age 18; rape and murder of white female age 16 in Richmond County on 3–4–86; sentenced on 8–29–86.[56]

INDIANA

Cooper, Paula R.   Black female; 15 at crime and now age 17 (DOB: 8–25–69); robbery and murder of white female age 78 in Gary on 5–14–85; sentenced on 7–11–86.[57]

Patton, Keith.   Black male; 17 at crime and now age 20; murder of black male age 19 and rape of black female age 19 in Indianapolis on 10–22–83; sentenced on 7–18–84.[58]

[Thompson, Jay R.].[b]   White male; 17 at crime and now age 22; burglary and murder of elderly white couple in Petersburg on 3–8–81; sentenced on 3–18–82 but sentence reversed on 4–25–86.[59]

TABLE 9–4. Juvenile Offenders on Death Row, November 1, 1986

KENTUCKY

Stanford, Kevin. Black male; 17 at crime and now age 23; rape and murder of young white female in Jefferson County on 1–7–81; sentenced on 9–28–82.[60]

LOUISIANA

Comeaux, Adam. Black male; 17 at crime and now age 23; rape and murder of two white females in Rapides Parish on 9–1–85; sentenced on 2–14–86.[61]

Prejean, Dalton. Black male; 17 at crime and now age 26 (DOB: Dec. 1959); murder of white male police officer in Lafayette Parish on 7–2–77; sentenced on 5–3–78.[62]

MARYLAND

Johnson, Lawrence. Black male; 17 at crime and now age 25; robbery and murder of white female age 78 in Baltimore on 1–9–79; sentenced on 10–6–82, 7–29–83, and 2–17–84.[63]

Trimble, James Russell. White male; 17 at crime and now age 22 (DOB: 11–5–63); rape and murder of white female age 22 in Baltimore on 7–3–81; sentenced on 3–19–82.[64]

MISSISSIPPI

Jones, Larry. Black male; 17 at crime and now age 29; robbery of store and murder of white male age 75 in Harrison County on 12–2–74; sentenced on 3–19–75 and 12–15–77.[65]

Tokman, George David. White male; 17 at crime and now age 23; robbery and murder of black male age 65 in Hinds County on 8–24–80; sentenced on 9–10–81.[66]

MISSOURI

Lashley, Frederick. Black male; 17 at crime and now age 22 (DOB: 3–10–64); robbery and murder of foster mother, black female age 55, in St. Louis on 4–9–81; sentenced on 4–26–82.[67]

Wilkins, Heath A. White male; 16 at crime and now age 17; robbery of store and murder of white female age 26 near North Kansas City on 7–27–85; sentenced on 6–27–86.[68]

NEW JERSEY

Bey, Marko. Black male; 17 at crime and now age 21 (DOB: 4–11–65); rape and murder of black female age 19 in Monmouth County on 4–1–83; sentenced on 9–15–83.[69]

TABLE 9–4. Juvenile Offenders on Death Row, November 1, 1986

NORTH CAROLINA

Brown, Leon. Black male; 15 at crime and now age 18 (DOB: 12–24–67); rape and murder of black female age 11 in Robeson County on 9–21–83; sentenced on 10–26–84.[70]

Stokes, Freddie Lee. Black male; 17 at crime and now age 21; robbery and murder of white male adult in Wilmington on 12–28–81; sentenced on 6–2–82 and 3–15–83.[71]

OKLAHOMA

Sellers, Sean Richard. White male; 16 at crime and now age 17 (DOB: 5–18–69); murder of white male age 35 in Oklahoma City on 9–8–85 and murder of mother age 32 and stepfather age 43 in Oklahoma City on 3–5–86; sentenced on 10–2–86.[72]

Thompson, Wayne. White male; 15 at crime and now age 19 (DOB: 3–4–67); kidnap and murder of white male adult in Grady County on 1–23–83; sentenced on 1–6–84.[73]

PENNSYLVANIA

Aulisio, Joseph. White male; 15 at crime and now age 20 (DOB: March 1966); kidnap and murder of white female age 8 and white male age 4 near Old Forge on 7–26–81; sentenced on 5–17–84.[74]

Hughes, Kevin. Black male; 16 at crime and now age 23; rape and murder of black female age 9 in Philadelphia in 1979; sentenced on 10–27–83.[75]

Williams, Raymond. Black male; 17 at crime and now age 20 (DOB: 9–27–66); robbery and murder of white male age 33 in Butler County on 8–5–84; sentenced on 1–28–85.[76]

TEXAS

Cannon, Joseph John. White male; 17 at crime and now age 26; robbery and murder of adult white female in Bexar County on 9–30–77; sentenced on 2–22–82.[77]

Carter, Robert Anthony. Black male; 17 at crime and now age 22; robbery of store and murder of teenage Hispanic female on 6–24–81; sentenced on 3–10–82.[78]

Garrett, Johnny Frank. White male; 17 at crime and now age 22; rape and murder of white female nun age 76 in Amarillo convent on 10–31–81; sentenced on 9–2–82.[79]

Graham, Gary L. Black male; 17 at crime and now age 22; robbery of store and murder of black male adult in Houston on 5–13–81; sentenced on 10–26–81.[80]

[Harris, Curtis Paul,][b] Black male; 17 at crime and now age 25; robbery and murder of white male adult in Bryan County on 12–12–78; sentenced on 6–7–79 and 8–6–83 but sentence reversed in 1986.[81]

[a]DOB = date of birth.
[b]Name bracketed because death sentence had been reversed and prisoner was awaiting resentencing on 11–1–86.

Twenty-nine (76 percent) of the thirty-eight received their sentences from states in the South (table 9–5). Georgia and Texas had the greatest number with five; four were in Florida. The juveniles in Texas comprised only 2 percent (5 of 218) of the total death row population in that state.[82] In terms of proportion, Georgia was the leader; its persons under a juvenile death sentence comprised 5 percent (5 of 105) of its total death row population.[83] Although Florida had four persons under a juvenile death sentence, they represented only 2 percent (4 of 247) of the Florida death row population.[84] Nationwide, persons under a juvenile death sentence accounted for only 2.1 percent (38 of 1,800) of the total death row population.[85]

The age of the offenders at the time of their crimes ranged from fifteen to seventeen. Five were fifteen-year-olds, only 13 percent of the total. They were under sentences of death in Arkansas, Indiana, North Carolina, Oklahoma, and Pennsylvania. Seven (18 percent) were sixteen at the time of their crimes and the other twenty-six (68 percent) were seventeen.

Black offenders were 58 percent (twenty-two of thirty-eight) of the total. That may be compared with the total death row population, of whom only 41 percent (741 of 1,800) were black.[86] This overrepresentation of blacks among those under juvenile death sentences seemed not to have been caused by the South. In the South, 55 percent (sixteen of twenty-nine) were black; outside the South, 67 percent (six of nine) were black. The sex of these offenders was overwhelmingly male (thirty-six of thirty-eight, or 95 percent). This overrepresentation of males, as of blacks, seemed evenly distributed among the regions. One female (Janice Buttrum) was in Georgia and one (Paula Cooper) in Indiana.

There were forty-seven victims of these thirty-eight offenders (table 9–6). Six cases involved multiple victims, while thirty-two (84 percent) involved only one victim. The multiple victim cases were spread out across the country, in Alabama, Arkansas, Florida, Indiana, Oklahoma, and Pennsylvania. Thirty-eight (81 percent) of the victims were white. The region of the country may have been a factor in this overrepresentation of whites among the victims, since 86 percent (thirty-one of thirty-six) of the Southern victims were white. Outside the South, 64 percent (seven of eleven) were white.

The victims were female in 60 percent (twenty-eight of forty-seven) of the cases overall. The South was not the major cause of this overrepresentation of female victims, since only 58 percent (twenty-one of thirty-six) of the Southern victims were female. In cases outside the South, 64 percent (seven of eleven) of the victims were female.

In summary, the thirty-eight persons under a juvenile death sentence on November 1, 1986, were alike in some ways but quite different in others. While all were age fifteen to seventeen at the time of their crimes, these crimes were committed from 1974 through 1986 and the ages of the offenders in 1986 ranged from seventeen to twenty-nine. They had been under sentences of death from a few weeks to over eleven years. The typical person under a juvenile death

TABLE 9-5. Characteristics of Juvenile Offenders on Death Row, November 1, 1986

Region and State	Offenders	Age at Crime			Race		Sex	
		15	16	17	B	W	M	F
Northeast								
New Jersey	1	0	0	1	1	0	1	0
Pennsylvania	3	1	1	1	2	1	3	0
Total	4	1	1	2	3	1	4	0
North Central								
Indiana	3	1	0	2	2	1	2	1
Missouri	2	0	1	1	1	1	2	0
Total	5	1	1	3	3	2	4	1
South								
Alabama	3	0	2	1	2	1	3	0
Arkansas	1	1	0	0	1	0	1	0
Florida	4	0	1	3	1	3	4	0
Georgia	5	0	1	4	2	3	4	0
Kentucky	1	0	0	1	1	0	1	1
Louisiana	2	0	0	2	2	0	2	0
Maryland	2	0	0	2	1	1	2	0
Mississippi	2	0	0	2	1	1	2	0
North Carolina	2	1	0	1	2	0	2	0
Oklahoma	2	1	1	0	0	2	2	0
Texas	5	0	0	5	3	2	5	0
Total	29	3	5	21	16	13	28	1
West								
Total	0	0	0	0	0	0	0	0
Grand Total	38	5	7	26	22	16	36	2

TABLE 9–6. Characteristics of Victims of Juvenile Offenders on Death Row, November 1, 1986

Region and State	Offenders	Victims	Race of Victim			Sex	
			B	H[a]	W	M	F
Northeast							
New Jersey	1	1	1	0	0	0	1
Pennsylvania	3	4	1	0	3	2	2
Total	4	5	2	0	3	2	3
North Central							
Indiana	3	4	1	0	3	2	2
Missouri	2	2	1	0	1	0	2
Total	5	6	2	0	4	2	4
South							
Alabama	3	4	0	0	4	1	3
Arkansas	1	3	0	0	3	1	2
Florida	4	5	0	0	5	1	4
Georgia	5	5	1	0	4	3	2
Kentucky	1	1	0	0	1	0	1
Louisiana	2	3	0	0	3	1	2
Maryland	2	2	0	0	3	2	0
Mississippi	2	2	1	0	1	2	0
North Carolina	2	2	1	0	1	1	0
Oklahoma	2	4	0	0	4	3	1
Texas	5	5	1	1	3	2	3
Total	29	36	4	1	31	15	21
West							
Total	0	0	0	0	0	0	0
Grand Total	38	47	8	1	38	19	28

[a]H = Hispanic.

sentence was a black male age seventeen at the time of his crime. He was sentenced to death in the South for a murder connected to robbery or rape. He had only one victim, a white female. He had been on death row over four years.

SELECTED CASE STUDIES

A few of these thirty-eight persons under juvenile death sentences represent extremes and thus are of particular interest. Taken as a group, the following six cases touch most of the dimensions of cases involving the death penalty for juveniles.

RONALD WARD: YOUNGEST JUVENILE ON DEATH ROW[87]

Born on October 14, 1969, Ronald Ward was seventeen years old in November 1986 and thus was the youngest person under a sentence of death in the United States. When he was only three months old, his mother abandoned him. He was raised by his grandmother. In 1984 he overdosed on drugs and continued to have a variety of personal problems. In the spring of 1985 he was repeating the seventh grade for the third time.

On April 12, 1985, a crime occurred in West Memphis, Arkansas, for which Ward, a black, was arrested, tried, convicted, and sentenced to death. One of Ward's classmates, a twelve-year-old white boy, and the boy's two aunts, ages seventy-two and seventy-five, were stabbed to death. One of the elderly women was also raped. Ward was arrested six days later and came to trial in early September 1985.

The jury convicted him of the murders and then needed only thirty minutes to decide that he should receive the death penalty for his crimes. The trial judge formally pronounced sentence on September 20, and the fifteen-year-old boy was taken away to Arkansas's overcrowded adult prison. He celebrated his sixteenth and seventeenth birthdays on death row and in late 1986 was marking time while his attorneys carried his case through the long appellate process for capital cases.

PAULA COOPER: GIRL ON DEATH ROW[88]

Indiana's Paula Cooper, a black, was less than two months older than Ronald Ward and also was only fifteen when she committed her capital crime. Unlike Ward, Cooper was raised by her parents but in a most unfortunate home life. Her father physically abused Cooper, her sister, and her mother over a period of years, causing Cooper to be a chronic runaway. When Cooper was only eleven, her mother unsuccessfully tried to commit suicide and to take her daughters with her.

On May 14, 1985, Cooper and three girl friends from school went to the home of a neighbor, a seventy-eight-year-old white woman, gaining entrance on the pretense of wanting Bible lessons. They ransacked the house for things to steal and stabbed the woman to death. The girls took the victim's car and drove it for a day or two before police arrested them.

The other three girls each received long prison sentences for their part in the crime. Cooper, seen as the most centrally involved, followed her attorney's advice and pleaded guilty, throwing herself on the mercy of the court. The court was presided over by a black judge who had never imposed the death penalty on any offender. He sentenced Cooper to death on July 11, 1986. No trial had been conducted, and no jury had considered Cooper's case.

Cooper turned sixteen in the Gary jail. In late August 1986 she celebrated her seventeenth birthday, hoping the appellate courts, the governor, or someone would intervene on her behalf.

LARRY JONES: OLDEST AND LONGEST ON DEATH ROW[89]

On the evening of December 2, 1974, three black men robbed a store in Biloxi, Mississippi. During the robbery the owner, a white man in his seventies, was beaten to death. One of the perpetrators, Larry Jones, was only seventeen years old. He and his co-felons were arrested soon after the crime.

Jones was brought to trial three months later. Convicted of murder, he was sentenced to death on March 19, 1975. The conviction and the resulting death sentence were reversed by the Mississippi Supreme Court on February 9, 1977. The state brought Jones to trial again, reconvicted him, and on December 15, 1977, resentenced him to death.

Jones fought this second death sentence through the state and federal courts without success until September 17, 1984, when the U.S. Court of Appeals for the Fifth Circuit ordered the lower court to reverse Jones's death sentence and resentence him to a penalty less than death. His relief following this decision lasted for a year and a half. On February 24, 1986, the U.S. Supreme Court vacated the Fifth Circuit ruling and reinstated Jones's death penalty.

In November 1986, nearly twelve years after the crime, Jones was twenty-nine years old and had resided on death row for eleven and a half years.

JAMES A. MORGAN: SENTENCED TO DEATH THREE TIMES[90]

James Morgan is one of the three persons who were sentenced to death three successive times for crimes committed while they were juveniles. On June 6, 1976, in Martin County, Florida, Morgan raped, beat, and stabbed to death a white woman age sixty-six. Morgan was a white illiterate sixteen-year-old with an I.Q. of 80 and minor brain damage from his practice of sniffing gasoline fumes.

Morgan's insanity plea was unsuccessful at trial. He was convicted and sentenced to death the first time on December 30, 1977. After Morgan had spent over three years on death row, the Florida Supreme Court reversed this death sentence on January 15, 1981. He was resentenced to death eleven months later, on December 7, 1981. This death sentence lasted two and one-half years, being reversed on July 12, 1984. A third sentencing hearing was convened, and he was again sentenced to death on June 7, 1985. Again under appeal in 1986, this death sentence seemed likely to be his last. Over ten years after his crime, he was twenty-six years old and one of 247 persons on Florida's death row.

JOSE MARTINEZ HIGH: "ARE YOU READY TO DIE?"[91]

Jose Martinez High is listed as black but, with his Hispanic given names, it seems reasonable to assume that he is at least partly Hispanic. If so, he was apparently the only Hispanic under a juvenile death sentence in 1986. At the time of his crime, July 26, 1976, he appeared fiercely proud of his black heritage, bragging that "he wanted to be the most famous black ringleader in the world."[92]

His crime was robbing and kidnapping two persons in Georgia and killing one of them. The homicide victim was a white boy only eleven years old. High was convicted and sentenced to death on December 1, 1978. On November 19, 1985, this death sentence was set aside by the Federal District Court and he was expected to undergo resentencing if a higher court did not reverse this ruling.

The sentencing and appellate courts gave particular significance to High's taunting of the helpless young victim. As High and his co-felons drove to a rural area, High repeatedly asked the terrified boy: "Are you ready to die? Do you want to die? Well, you're going to die."[93] This action by High was deemed to "support a finding of depravity of the mind of the defendant."[94] Nonetheless, since December 1, 1978, the state of Georgia had been making the same threats to Jose High.

HEATH A. WILKINS: "I PREFER THE DEATH PENALTY"[95]

Heath Wilkins, a white male, was sixteen years old when he robbed a liquor store in Avondale, Missouri, on July 27, 1985. Apparently in order to leave no witnesses to his crime, he repeatedly stabbed the clerk, a twenty-six-year-old white female. After he was caught and was facing a capital murder prosecution, Wilkins decided to fire his public defender, to represent himself, and to confess everything.

Wilkins pleaded guilty in May 1986 and represented himself at a sentencing hearing the next month. At this hearing he agreed fully with the prosecutor's evidence of aggravating factors in the crime. Asked by the judge which sentence he preferred, Wilkins was unequivocal: "I prefer the death penalty. One I fear, and one I don't."[96]

CONCLUSIONS

The practice of sentencing persons to death for crimes committed while under age eighteen is fading from the criminal justice scene in the United States. In a period of unprecedented popularity of the death penalty, when some 250 to 300 adult death sentences are imposed each year, juvenile death sentences are extremely rare. As of 1986 the annual juvenile death sentencing rate was five or six.

Of the 1,800 persons on death row on November 1, 1986, only thirty-eight were under juvenile death sentences. While only 41 percent of the total death row population was black, 58 percent of those under a juvenile death sentence were black. For juveniles and adults alike, almost all persons under a death sentence were male and poor.

Most persons under a juvenile death sentence (twenty-two of thirty-eight) had received their original sentence more than four years earlier. Five had been on death row more than eight years. Many of these longtime death row inmates were nearing the end of their ability to stave off execution. The average time between sentence and execution for the three juveniles executed in 1985 and 1986 was just over seven years.[97]

TEN

Prognosis for Progress

The preceding chapters describe the history of juvenile death sentences and the status of this practice in late 1986. A more important and more difficult issue is where it will lead in the years to come. Will the laws continue to change in ways that minimize or prohibit juvenile death sentences? Will the practice of imposing juvenile death sentences and executing juveniles continue to fade away? As the people and their legislative and judicial officers consider these questions, what fundamental issues should they address? This chapter attempts to provide answers to these questions while keeping in mind that the future is difficult to predict for such a volatile phenomenon.

A BRIEF RETROSPECTION

Most reliable predictions must be based on a sober assessment of the past and present, and juvenile death penalty predictions are no exception. Using the comparative clarity of hindsight, the treatment of these issues in our society can and must be analyzed to determine what they suggest about future evolution in this area. The foregoing chapters have presented detailed information on these past and present practices. From these presentations, conclusions are distilled that have varying impacts on future developments.

Persons who have not reached the age of majority have always been treated differently in our society. This fundamental principle permeates American law, stemming from general agreement that "children have a very special place in life which law should reflect."[1] The manifestations of this fundamental principle include the creation and maintenance of the juvenile justice system for young offenders, the institution of special legal protections against victimization of children, and the imposition of limitations on the legal rights and privileges young persons may enjoy.[2]

The underlying reason for such a "special place" for children in law is not their inability to act and to harm themselves or others. Even the toddler can discharge a firearm and kill an intended victim. The toddler can engage in sexual intercourse, pull the lever in the voting booth, make an identifiable mark on the signature line of a contract, or take a sip of beer. It seems clear that even very young children can commit adult acts, including criminal acts.

The difference that separates children from adults for most purposes of the law is children's immature, undeveloped abilty to reason in an adultlike manner. Even though they can intentionally commit most adult acts, they are not able to control their acts or to foresee the consequences of such acts, at least not to the same degree that an adult can.[3] For this reason, Anglo-American law throughout history has either ascribed no adult responsibility to such child actors or has placed limitations on the degree to which they can be held to adult standards of behavior.[4] That holds true in the law of the death penalty.

Law stemming from federal and state constitutional requirements is of paramount authority in our legal system. While no U.S. court has yet found such constitutional requirements to prohibit juvenile death sentences, the historical premises on which these constitutional requirements developed suggest that such a ruling can and should be made. That is most certainly true if the recognition of "evolving standards of decency"[5] still guides the courts.

All the guidelines for assessing such evolving standards suggest that these are bases for a constitutional prohibition. The changing attitude of legislators is revealed by recent amendments to their statutes, establishing minimum ages for the death penalty. Jury decisions demonstrate a growing distaste for juvenile death sentences. These and other factors have become stronger and stronger in recent years, suggesting the need for courts to reconsider their previous reluctance to impose constitutional prohibitions on this practice.

Statutory law has been moving steadily toward the abolition of juvenile death sentences. In 1962 nearly 54 percent (twenty-two of forty-one) of the death penalty statutes permitted the death penalty for crimes committed while age ten or younger.[6] By 1986 the percentage of statutes in that category had dropped to 28 (ten of thirty-six).[7] The changes since 1980 included five states placing a minimum age of eighteen in their statutes.[8] Other states' legislatures were considering similar amendments to their statutes.

The practice of imposing death sentences and actually executing persons for crimes committed while under age eighteen has followed a similar path. Public support is the touchstone for such sentences and executions. This support apparently has never been found among a majority of persons and is declining. A poll conducted in 1936, when the execution rate in the United States was quite high, showed that less than half the respondents favored death sentences for crimes committed while under age twenty-one.[9] Half a century later, at the height of support for the death penalty in general, polls showed that less than one-third of the respondents favored death sentences for crimes committed while under age eighteen.[10]

In keeping with the apparent public opposition to juvenile death sentences, fewer and fewer judges and juries are imposing such sentences. From 1982 to 1986 the juvenile death sentencing rate dropped from eleven per year to about half that rate.[11] Although the adult death sentencing rate of 250 to 300 per year remained fairly constant, juvenile death sentences dropped from 4 percent to 1 or 2 percent of the total.[12]

With fewer juvenile death sentences being imposed and with the reversal rate high for such sentences once imposed, the number of juveniles on death row has dropped significantly. The thirty-eight juvenile death row inmates in

1986 constituted the lowest number in recent years.[13] In fact, in the period from December 1983 to November 1986 the juvenile death row population remained constant while the adult death row population increased by 44 percent (from 1,252 to 1,800).[14]

Finally, the number and proportion of executions authorized by juvenile death sentences has dropped. In the 1940s fifty-three juvenile executions occurred, an all-time high in number and proportion (4.1 percent) of all executions.[15] The number dropped precipitously in the next twenty years to a minuscule level.[16] No juvenile executions at all occurred from 1964 to 1985. Although three (4.5 percent) of the sixty-six executions from 1977 to late 1986 were juvenile executions, it seems clear that this comparatively high proportion resulted from the chance order of execution rather than from any long-term trend toward increased juvenile executions.[17] Only 2 percent (thirty-eight of 1,800) of those on death row in 1986 were under a juvenile death sentence.[18]

AN EVOLUTION TOWARD DECENCY

Whether or not the death penalty for juveniles will be banned as unacceptable in our society is largely to be determined by appraisal of "the evolving standards of decency that mark the progress of a maturing society."[19] Such progress is halting at best, and to precisely determine the level of progress at any one time is extremely difficult. Nevertheless, can it now be said that our society has reached the level at which it will reject the death penalty for juveniles?

The simplest way for a rejection of juvenile death sentences to occur would be for the U.S. Supreme Court to declare them unconstitutional. In 1982, in *Eddings v. Oklahoma*,[20] the Court had this opportunity but did not take advantage of it. Even though a slim, five-justice majority reversed the case on other grounds, the four justices in dissent were not ready or willing to find any constitutional bar to the death penalty for a crime committed at age sixteen.[21] With one more vote they would have settled the issue. If and when it comes before the Court again, will this four-justice minority become a five-justice majority? Given the recent changes in Court personnel, this question is difficult to answer.

Much more likely is a state-by-state consideration of this issue, resulting in even more statutory amendments establishing a minimum age for the death penalty. This minimum age in the vast majority of instances is being set at age eighteen.[22] State legislators such as those in Georgia are being sensitized to the wishes of their voting constituencies, and the message from these constituencies is relatively clear.[23] Thus the major indicator in law of having reached the level of decency that rejects juvenile death sentences will be the continuing trend toward statutory minimum ages, typically age eighteen.

As is so common in the frustratingly slow progression of law, the general public is reaching this level of decency long before the law catches up. A strong majority of the public opposes the death penalty for crimes committed while under age eighteen, and that has been true for at least a half-century.[24] This majority opposition is not only growing but is being identified in more and more locations.

Since trial juries and judges are drawn from this population, it is not surprising to see a continuing decline in the juvenile death sentencing rate. As public rejection grows stronger and gets more publicity, the rate will decline even more. It is already extremely low and may almost disappear in the next few years.

The number of persons on death row for crimes committed while under age eighteen necessarily will follow this trend. Not only will minimal new sentences add few to the total but the high reversal rate will continue. Such reversals will be for a variety of reasons but all will be increasingly controlled by concern for the youth of the offender.[25]

An apparently inconsistent indicator of the achievement of this level of decency is the probable continuation of executions of persons now under juvenile death sentences. Many of these presently condemned persons have been on death row for so many years and have exhausted so many avenues of appeal that little remains to stave off execution. In grass-roots evolutions like this one the governmental system usually continues to go through its assigned tasks long after the people want it to stop. Even after the people have made up their mind, it takes time to shut down the machinery.

APPROPRIATE CRITERIA
FOR FUTURE DECISIONS

During this accelerating change in societal acceptance of the juvenile death penalty, many individuals and groups are being asked to decide where they stand. Many are considering making an exception for juveniles in their otherwise unwavering support for the death penalty. Several key criteria should be addressed in making such decisions.

First, the choice of criminal punishment should be based on both the harm inflicted and the criminal intent of the offender. That fundamental legal principle underlies the conflict between the simplistic slogans of "Old enough to kill, old enough to die!" and "But he is only a boy!" For such crimes as murder, Anglo-American criminal law has consistently required a focus on the criminal intent of the offender. For all homicide crimes, the harm inflicted is the death of an innocent person. The difference between the less serious level, such as negligent manslaughter, and the capital level of first-degree murder is typically the criminal intent of the offender. Therefore, in deciding the basis for imposition of criminal punishment, one must consider in part the harm inflicted but primarily the criminal intent involved. It seems generally accepted that adolescents typically do not have an adult level of maturity and sophistication in their thought processes. While they can intend behavior, it is unlikely they have thought about it with insight and understanding. While they may have the criminal intent required for first-degree murder, they seldom have such intent to the fullest extent. They fall short in this critical criterion and thus their punishment should be a little short of the punishment for a comparable adult's acts. Given this criterion, they should receive long-term imprisonment rather than the death penalty.

Second, retribution does not demand the death penalty for juvenile crimes. The harm these juveniles have inflicted is tragically enormous, giving rise to strong emotional feeling in the community. Nevertheless, anger at the misdeeds of children is always blunted somewhat, at least for reasonable persons, by the knowledge that children cannot be expected to behave like adults all the time. The strong if blunted need for retribution cannot be ignored, but it can be satisfied by long-term imprisonment. The death penalty is simply an excessive and overly emotional response to this undeniable feeling.

Third, deterrence is not enhanced by choosing the death penalty. If the alternative were nothing or just a slap on the wrist, then of course the death penalty might be necessary for deterrence. But the alternative, long-term imprisonment, is a punishment even more dreaded than death by many adolescents. The death penalty is not a greater deterrent than long-term imprisonment to violent juvenile crime. The only question left open in this regard is how long the imprisonment must be in order to provide satisfactory deterrence, a question answered in widely varying ways by different jurisdictions.

Fourth, it is unreasonable to totally disregard the goals of reform and rehabilitation for juvenile offenders. Behavior patterns change significantly as persons mature from adolescence to adulthood and into middle age. Most persons mellow in their behavior after the teen years and many are later embarrassed to recall some of the wilder acts they committed during that stage of life. Given long-term imprisonment, juvenile murderers also would change their behavior, most probably in ways more acceptable to society. Imposing the death penalty for juvenile crimes totally disregards these universally accepted truisms about maturation. Long-term imprisonment holds out the possibility that a destructive teenager will become a productive adult.

Fifth, the message juveniles receive from the imposition of juvenile death sentences is not the one society intends to convey. The crimes juveniles commit often involve the killing of a person in order to solve some problem the offender perceives as otherwise unsolvable. The girl with whom they wish to have sexual relations or the victim they wish to rob struggles and causes them major problems. Their solution is to kill the person who is causing the problem. Now they see the government struggling with a problem of its own, a person whose behavior is unacceptable. How does the government solve its problem? It kills the person who is causing the problem. Is it wrong to kill someone to solve a problem? It is difficult to convince teenagers not to do something if they see government officials doing it with the apparent blessings of society.

Sixth, abolition of the death penalty for juveniles is a common ground on which death penalty proponents and opponents can meet and agree. The acrimonious and interminable debate about the death penalty in general has resulted in deep divisions between the opposing camps. Such debates often end in name-calling, angry shouting matches, and bumper-sticker slogans. The death penalty for juveniles is a point on which the warring parties can come together. It appears that a majority would agree that at least this branch of the death penalty laws should be trimmed back. If everyone can reason together on this one issue, avenues of dialogue and understanding can be opened for more rational and constructive discussion of the death penalty for adults and for the appropriate application of criminal punishment in general.

Finally, if we discard the death penalty for juveniles, what can be done about violent juvenile crime? Many persons support the death penalty for juveniles from fear of and outrage over violent juvenile crime. This fear and outrage is shared by all reasonable persons, whether they are for or against the death penalty. Two answers to this problem suggest themselves. The temporary solution is to impose long-term prison sentences on such violent juveniles. That would ensure that they were reasonably mature adults and had been subjected to whatever rehabilitative programs were available before they were set free again. Life imprisonment without possibility of parole seems an unwise choice, like any personal or business decision that we vow never to reconsider regardless of future events. Few of the violent juveniles would be good candidates for parole in less than ten or twenty years, but that option should be left open for them to work toward.

The long-term solution to violent juvenile crime—or all crime, for that matter—cannot come from harsh criminal punishment, whether it is imprisonment or death. Given the individual freedom enjoyed in our society, the resultant ample opportunities for violent juvenile crime, and the low probability of being caught and punished, prevention through threatened punishment will always be insufficiently effective.

Our society must be willing to devote enormous resources to a search for the causes and cures of violent juvenile crime, just as we have done in the search for the causes and cures of such killer diseases as cancer. And we must not demand a complete cure in a short time, since no one knows how long it will take. We must at the same time beware of those persons who loudly proclaim that they have the cure now. Unfortunately, no one yet has the cure for violent juvenile crime. It seems clear, however, that the death penalty for juveniles has been given a long trial period and has been found wanting. Its societal costs are enormous, and it delays our search for a rational and acceptable means of reducing violent juvenile crime.

APPENDIX

Persons Executed for Crimes Committed while under Age Eighteen: An Inventory of Names, Dates, and Other Information

This list of executed juvenile offenders is arranged by jurisdiction in which they were executed. The list includes all 281 persons who were executed for crimes committed while under age eighteen in a total of thirty-six jurisdictions. The period covered is 1642 through 1986. The range of ages at the time of the crimes is from ten to seventeen or eighteen years. The race of these executed persons was black, 69 percent; white, 25 percent; and other, 6 percent. The crimes for which they were executed were murder, 81 percent; rape, 15 percent; and other, 4 percent.

KEY TO SYMBOLS AND ABBREVIATIONS USED IN INVENTORY

AGE AT TIME OF CRIME AND AT EXECUTION

Exact age given unless uncertain, then given as range, e.g., 16/17, 17/18.

RACE OF OFFENDER

0   B = black, C = Chinese, I = American Indian, M = Mexican or Mexican-American, U = unknown, W = white. (White includes a variety of ethnic groups, including Italian, Puerto Rican, etc.)

CRIMES

A = arson, A & B = assault and battery, Am = attempted murder, Ar = attempted rape, Be = Bestiality, Br = burglary, K = kidnapping, M = murder, Ra = rape, Ro = robbery, S = spying, T = theft. (The most serious crime is listed first, then other crimes committed at the same time as the most serious crime.)

VICTIMS

First letter is race (B = black, W = white, U = unknown). Second letter is sex (M = male, F = female, U = unknown). Third entry is age in years, or adult (A) or child (C). Fourth entry is law enforcement officer (LE) if applicable.

A L A B A M A (11)

Period of Executions: 1858–1961   Race: black, 11
Age at Crime: 12 to 17   Crime: murder, 7; rape, 4

Date of Execution	Name	Age at Time of Crime & Exec.	Race	Crime	Victims
7–16–1858	Alfred (Godfrey)	11 & 12	B	M	WM4
4–20–1866	Henry	15 & 15	B	MT	WM13
3–12–1869	Johnson, Isaac	17/18 & 18	B	MRo	WMA
12–17–1897	Beard, Brad	14 & 14	B	Ra	WF17
1–28–1938	Millhouse, Frank	15 & 18	B	MRo	WMA
8–19–1938	Whitfield, Willie James	16 & 17	B	M	WMA
1–7–1941	Clark, William	16 & 18	B	RaBr	WFA
1–25–1946	Johnson, Ernest	16/17 & 17	B	MRo	WM63
9–18–1956	Jackson, Melvin	16 & 18	B	Ra	WF21
3–28–1958	Reeves, Jeremiah, Jr.	17 & 23	B	RaBr	WFA
11–24–1961	Johnson, Joe Henry	17 & 19	B	MRa, A & B	WF62, WF89

A L A S K A (0)

A R I Z O N A (2)

Period of Executions: 1880–1934   Race: Mexican-American, 2
Age at Crime: 16 to 17   Crime: murder, 2

Date of Execution	Name	Age at Time of Crime & Exec.	Race	Crime	Victims
11–26–1880	Dominquez, Demetrio	16 & 17	M	M	UMA
7–6–1934	Hernandez, Manuel	17 & 18	M	MRo	UM65

ARKANSAS (6)

Period of Executions: 1879–1927   Race: black, 4; white, 1; unknown, 1
Age at Crime: 14 to 17/18   Crime: murder, 5; rape, 1

Date of Execution	Name	Age at Time of Crime & Exec.	Race	Crime	Victims
10–3–1879	Kemp, David	14 & 25	W	M	UMA
3–20–1903	Greene, Jay	15 & 17	B	M	BMA
9–2–1910	Poe, Harry	17 & 17	B	Ra	WF10
9–11–1913	Davis, Omer	17/18 & 18	U	M	UFA
3–10–1922	Wells, James	17/18 & 18	B	MRo	UMA
6–24–1927	Dixon, Lonnie	17 & 18	B	M	WF12

CALIFORNIA (6)

Period of Executions: 1864–1923   Race: Indian, 2; white, 2; unknown, 2
Age at Crime: 15 to 17/18   Crime: murder, 6

Date of Execution	Name	Age at Time of Crime & Exec.	Race	Crime	Victims
12–7–1864	(Yuki Indian)	15 & 16	I	M	UMA
9–7–1906	Brown, Henry	16/17 & 18	U	MRo	WMA
7–31–1908	Dabner, Louis	17/18 & 18	W	MRo	3UUA
1–20–1911?	Augustine, Louis	16/17 & 17	I	MRo	UMALE
3–3–1916	Oxnam, Charles E.T.	17 & 18	W	MBr	WMA
6–22–1923	Campbell, Lawrence C.	17/18 & 18	U	M	UMA

COLORADO (0)

CONNECTICUT (3)

Period of Executions: 1786–1900   Race: Indian, 1; white, 2
Age at Crime: 12 to 17/18   Crime: murder, 3

Date of Execution	Name	Age at Time of Crime & Exec.	Race	Crime	Victims
12–20–1786	Ocuish, Hannah (female)	12 & 12	I	M	WF6
7–11–1854	Jennings, Michael	17 & 18	W	MRo	WFA
7–20–1900	Cross, Charles B.	17 & 18	W	MRa	WFA

DELAWARE (2)

	Period of Executions: 1866–1891		Race: black, 2		
	Age at Crime: 16 to 16/17		Crime: murder, 2		

Date of Execution	Name	Age at Time of Crime & Exec.	Race	Crime	Victims
12–16–1866?	Green, John	16 & 16	B	M	BMA
2–13–1891	Young, Frederick	16/17 & 17	B	MRo	UMA

DISTRICT OF COLUMBIA (0)

FLORIDA (12)

	Period of Executions: 1910–1954		Race: black, 11; white, 1		
	Age at Crime: 13/14 to 17		Crime: murder, 8; rape, 4		

Date of Execution	Name	Age at Time of Crime & Exec.	Race	Crime	Victims
5–6–1910	Hanchett, Irving	14 & 15	W	M	WF15
4–27–1927	Ferguson, Fortune	13/14 & 16	B	Ra	WF8
9–16–1935	Hasty, Monroe,	16 & 17	B	M	WFA
7–23–1937	Hinds, Robert	17 & 17	B	Ra	WFA
11–11–1940	Williams, Ivory Lee	17 & 18	B	MRa	UFA
12–29–1941	Clay, Willie B.	15 & 19	B	MRo	WF59
12–29–1941	Powell, Edward	15 & 18	B	MRo	WF59
12–29–1941	Walker, Nathaniel	14 & 18	B	MRo	WF59
10–9–1944	Davis, James	16 & 16	B	RaAm	WF22
10–25–1948	Stewart, Lacy	17 & 19	B	MRo	WM64
9–28–1954	Johnson, Orion Nathaniel	16 & 19	B	M	WMALE
11–8–1954	Beard, Abraham	16 & 18	B	Ra	WFA

GEORGIA (41)

	Period of Executions: 1848–1957		Race: black, 39; white, 2		
	Age at Crime: 13 to 17/18		Crime: murder, 30; Rape, 11		

Date of Execution	Name	Age at Time of Crime & Exec.	Race	Crime	Victims
8–25–1848	(slave)	17 & 17	B	2M	WMA, WFA
4–29–1876	Sally, Ed	U & U	B	M	BMA

GEORGIA (41) (Cont'd)

Date of Execution	Name	Age at Time of Crime & Exec.	Race	Crime	Victims
7-6-1877	Thomasson, Jack	15 & 15	B	2M	BF2, BF8
11-7-1884	Perry, Homer	14 & 15	B	Ra A & B	BF8
8-31-1892?	O'Neal, Reuben	13 & 16	B	Ra	WF11
11-29-1892	Bell, Willie	14 & 15	B	M	WMALE
5-3-1895	Brooks, Edward	17/18 & 18	B	M	BMU
1-5-1900	Harris, Sam "Bud"	16 & 17	B	M	BMU
5-29-1907	High, Buck	15 & 15	B	Ra	WF4
1-12-1917	Sutton, Harris A.	16 & 16	B	Ra	WF10
10-8-1926	Williams, Pringle	17 & 17	B	Ra	UFU
1-18-1929	Capers, Ed	17/18 & 19	B	M	BMU
11-21-1930	Smith, Wash	17 & 19	W	M	UMA
5-18-1931	Griffin, Fred	17/18 & 18	B	M	UUU
2-9-1932	March, Eddie	15/16 & 16	B	M	UUU
8-11-1933	Morris, Richard	16/17 & 18	B	MRo	WMALE
8-11-1933	Sims, Richard	16/17 & 18	B	MRo	WMALE
8-11-1933	White, Tom (Moses)	16/17 & 18	B	MRo	WMALE
1-12-1934	Osborne, Will	17/18 & 18	B	Ra	WFA
1-21-1935	Dodson, Charlie	17 & 17	B	M	UUU
3-6-1936	Bowen, Eddie B.	17 & 18	B	M	UMA
5-24-1937	Brown, Leonard	17/18 & 18	B	M	UMA
12-9-1938	Rucker, Charlie	17/18 & 18	B	MRo	WMALE
5-28-1943	Franklin, Bernice	17 & 17	B	M	WFA
8-20-1943	Sexton, Charlie	16 & 16	B	MRo	BMA
12-11-1943	Allison, S.A.	17 & 17	B	M	UUU
2-3-1944	Hicks, Willie	17/18 & 18	B	Ra	WFA
5-11-1945	Watkins, David	17 & 18	B	MRo	WF70
11-15-1946	Allen, Lee James	15 & 16	B	Ra	WF41
11-22-1946	Stevenson, Willie	16/17 & 17	B	MRo	UUU
12-20-1946	Hill, J.C.	17/18 & 19	B	MBr	WF72
6-30-1947	Reddick, Herbert Lee	16 & 17	B	MRo	WMA
3-5-1948	Mangum, James	16/17 & 18	B	Ra	WF70
9-12-1949	Jones, John Albert, Jr.	16/17 & 17	B	MRo	UMA
9-12-1949	Jones, Wilbur G.	17/18 & 18	B	MRo	UMA

GEORGIA (41) (Cont'd)

Date of Execution	Name	Age at Time of Crime & Exec.	Race	Crime	Victims
6–15–1954	Jackson, Willie, Jr.	16 & 17	B	Ra	WF18
6–15–1954	Miller, Herman Lee	17 & 18	B	Ra	WF18
11–19–1954	Jones, Joe Lee	16 & 17	B	MRo	WM65
11–19–1954	King, Charles L.	17 & 19	B	MRo	WM65
1–7–1955	Morgan, James Willie	17/18 & 18	W	MRo	UMA
3–19–1957	Colman, Don Mitchell	17 & 18	B	MRo	UFA

HAWAII (0)

IDAHO (0)

ILLINOIS (1)

Period of Executions: 1929   Race: white, 1
Age at Crime: 17   Crime: murder, 1

Date of Execution	Name	Age at Time of Crime & Exec.	Race	Crime	Victims
2–20–1929	Walz, Charles	17 & 18	W	M	WMALE

INDIANA (3)

Period of Executions: 1871–1920   Race: black 2; white, 1
Age at Crime: 17   Crime: murder, 3

Date of Execution	Name	Age at Time of Crime & Exec.	Race	Crime	Victims
2–10–1871	(black male)	17 & 17	B	M	UUU
1–25–1884	Anderson, John	17 & 17	W	MRo	WM17
8–5–1920	Ray, William	17 & 18	B	M	WF14

IOWA (1)

Period of Executions: 1894   Race: white, 1
Age at Crime: 16   Crime: murder, 1

Date of Execution	Name	Age at Time of Crime & Exec.	Race	Crime	Victims
10–19–1894	Dooley, James O.	16 & 18	W	2M,Ra	WFA, WF10

KANSAS (0)

KENTUCKY (11)

Period of Executions: 1847–1945   Race: black, 9; white, 2
Age at Crime: 12 to 17/18   Crime: murder, 6; rape, 5

Date of Execution	Name	Age at Time of Crime & Exec.	Race	Crime	Victims
6–5–1847	Stepter, William H.	17 & 17	W	M	WFA (mother)
2–7–1868	Eliza (Susan) (female)	12 & 13	B	M	WFC
2–5–1892	Charlton, Robert	17/18 & 19	B	M	BF25
2–3–1899	Miller, William	16 & 16	B	Ra	WFA
7–31–1906	Mathis, Allen	16 & 16	B	Ra	WFA
1–7–1910	Thompson, Earl	17 & 17	B	Ra	WFA
3–21–1913	Williams, Silas	17 & 17	B	2M,Ra	WF80, WFA
3–27–1942	Burnam, Eugene	15 & 18	B	Ra	WF22
1–15–1943	Sexton, Burnette	17 & 18	W	M	WMU
6–25–1943	Gray, William Carson	17 & 18	B	MRo	WM66
4–6–1945	Fox, Carl	17 & 19	B	Ra	WFU

LOUISIANA (9)

Period of Executions: 1855–1948   Race: black, 8; unknown, 1
Age at Crime: 10 to 17   Crime: murder, 7; rape, 1; unknown, 1

Date of Execution	Name	Age at Time of Crime & Exec.	Race	Crime	Victims
9–?–1855	(male child)	10 & 10	U	U	U
4–22–1878	Turner, Wesley	15 & 17	B	M	WMA

LOUISIANA (9) (Cont'd)

Date of Execution	Name	Age at Time of Crime & Exec.	Race	Crime	Victims
2–3–1888	Conelm, Jim	13 & 14	B	M	WM4
10–11–1907	Young, Lewis	17 & 17	B	Ra	WFU
12–7–1945	Riley, Henry	17 & 17	B	M	UFU
6–7–1947	Francis, Willie	15 & 18	B	MRo	WM54
1–9–1948	Mattio, Irvin	15 & 18	B	M	UFU
4–23–1948	Bessar, James, Jr.	17 & 20	B	M	UFA
4–23–1948	Powell, Wilbert	17 & 20	B	M	UFA

MAINE (0)

MARYLAND (7)

Period of Executions: 1871–1959   Race: black, 7
Age at Crime: 15 to 17/18   Crime: murder, 6; rape, 1

Date of Execution	Name	Age at Time of Crime & Exec.	Race	Crime	Victims
2–10–1871	Wallis, Mary (female)	16 & 17	B	M	WUC
12–5–1879	Waters, Medford	17 & 18	B	M	BMA
8–12–1898	Dennis, Sommerfield	16 & 16	B	M	BMA (stpfthr)
6–16–1899	Berry, John	15 & 15	B	MRo, Am	WF52, WF55
5–31–1901	Kirk, Wiley	17/18 & 18	B	Ra	WFA
8–1–1947	Jones, Weldon, Jr.	15/16 & 18	B	MRo	UMA
4–10–1959	Shockley, Leonard M.	16 & 17	B	MRo	WF39

MASSACHUSETTS (8)

Period of Executions: 1642–1942   Race: black, 1; Chinese, 1; white, 6
Age at Crime: 13 to 17   Crime: arson, 2; bestiality, 2; murder, 4

Date of Execution	Name	Age at Time of Crime & Exec.	Race	Crime	Victims
?–?–1642	Graunger, Thomas	16/17 & 16/17	W	Be	horse, cow

MASSACHUSETTS (8) (Cont'd)

Date of Execution	Name	Age at Time of Crime & Exec.	Race	Crime	Victims
4–2–1674	Gourd, Benjamin	17 & 17	W	Be	horse
12–1–1763	Bristol	16 & 16	B	M	WFA
5–10–1821	Clark, Stephen M.	15 & 16	W	A	UUU
?–?–1837	(male child)	13 & 13	W	A	UUU
1–20–1888	Nowlin, James E.	16 & 17	W	MRo	WMA
10–12–1909	Gong, Leon	17 & 19	C	4M	4CMA
6–30–1942	Giacomazza, Paul	17 & 19	W	MRo	UM74

MICHIGAN (0)

MINNESOTA (2)

Period of Executions: 1889   Race: white, 2
Age at Crime: 15 to 16/17   Crime: murder, 2

Date of Execution	Name	Age at Time of Crime & Exec.	Race	Crime	Victims
3–22–1889	Barrett, Peter	15 & 16	W	MRo	UMA
3–22–1889	Barrett, Timothy	16/17 & 17/18	W	MRo	UMA

MISSISSIPPI (6)

Period of Executions: 1880–1950   Race: black, 5; unknown, 1
Age at Crime: 14 to 17/18   Crime: murder, 6

Date of Execution	Name	Age at Time of Crime & Exec.	Race	Crime	Victims
12–31–1880	Washington, Henry	17/18 & 18	B	M	UMA
5–8–1931	Nelson, Cleveland	17/18 & 18	B	M	WMA
7–1–1943?	Parker, Elijah	17 & 17/18	U	M	UMA
7–23–1947	Lewis, James, Jr.	14 & 15	B	MRo	WMA
7–23–1947	Trudell, Charles	14 & 16	B	MRo	WMA
5–25–1950	Pulliam, John West	16 & 17	B	MBr	WM70

MISSOURI (6)

Period of Executions: 1838–1921   Race: black, 3; white 1; unknown, 2
Age at Crime: 12 to 17/18   Crime: murder, 6

Date of Execution	Name	Age at Time of Crime & Exec.	Race	Crime	Victims
9–30–1838	Mary (female)	16 & 19	B	M	WUC
12–11–1873	Orr, Samuel	12 & 15	U	M	WMA
3–26–1880	Barton, William	15 & 16	B	M	WMA
7–22–1881	Talbot, Charles E.	16 & 16	W	M	WMA (father)
2–16–1897	Schmidt, Peter (Cotton)	15 & 16	B	MRo	UMA
8–12–1921	Jacoy, Charles W.	17/18 & 18	U	M	UMA

MONTANA (1)

Period of Executions: 1878   Race: white, 1
Age at Crime: 16   Crime: murder, 1

Date of Execution	Name	Age at Time of Crime & Exec.	Race	Crime	Victims
10–31–1878	Roberts, Frank	16 & 17	W	M	WMA

NEBRASKA (0)

NEVADA (3)

Period of Executions: 1905–1949   Race: white, 2; unknown, 1
Age at Crime: 15 to 16   Crime: murder, 3

Date of Execution	Name	Age at Time of Crime & Exec.	Race	Crime	Victims
11–17–1905	Roberts, Fred	16 & 18	U	MRo	UMA
9–29–1944	Loveless, Floyd	15 & 17	W	MT	WM56LE
4–22–1949	Blackwell, David	16 & 18	W	2MRo	UM56LE, UM36LE

NEW HAMPSHIRE (0)

NEW JERSEY (5)

Period of Executions: 1828–1915   Race: black 4; white, 1
Age at Crime: 12 to 16/17   Crime: murder, 5

Date of Execution	Name	Age at Time of Crime & Exec.	Race	Crime	Victims
11–28–1828	Guild, James	12 & 13	B	M	WF60
4–26–1844	Keen, Rosan (female)	16 & 16	B	M	WMA
12–2–1884	Sullivan, Howard	U & U	B	MRoRa	WF15
12–22–1914	Ruggierri, Stefano	16/17 & 17	W	M	UUU
1–5–1915	Sparks, Richard (Michael)	16 & 16	B	M	UUU

NEW MEXICO (1)

Period of Executions: 1883   Race: Mexican-American, 1
Age at Crime: 17   Crime: murder, 1

Date of Execution	Name	Age at Time of Crime & Exec.	Race	Crime	Victims
2–2–1883	Romero	17 & 18	M	M	UMA

NEW YORK (18)

Period of Executions: 1817–1956   Race: black, 5; Chinese, 1; Indian, 1; white, 11
Age at Crime: 16 to 17/18   Crime: murder, 18

Date of Execution	Name	Age at Time of Crime & Exec.	Race	Crime	Victims
7–25–1817	Tuhi, John	17 & 17	I	M	IMA
7–26–1838	Baron, Octavius	17/18 & 18	W	MRo	UMA

NEW YORK (18) (Cont'd)

Date of Execution	Name	Age at Time of Crime & Exec.	Race	Crime	Victims
7–26–1844	Denny, George	17 & 18	W	M	UM80
7–10–1888	Deacons, Edward Alonzo	16 & 16	W	MAr	WFA
8–26–1926	Brescia, Cosimo	17/18/19 & 19	W	M	WMA
8–26–1926	Garguila, John	17/18/19 & 19	W	MRo	UMA
4–25–1935	Pluzdrak, Stanley	16/17 & 17	W	M	UUU
1–21–1937	Fowler, Frederick	17/18 & 18	B	MRo	UMA
1–26–1939	Guariglia, Dominick	17 & 18	W	MRo	WMALE
9–17–1942	Edwards, Lawrence	17/18 & 18	B	M	UUU
7–8–1943	DeJesus, Benitez	17/18 & 18	B	M	UUU
7–8–1943	Diaz, William	17/18 & 18	B	M	UUU
7–8–1943	Haight, Edward	16 & 17	W	2M, 2K	WF7, WF8
8–31–1944	Bing, Lew York	17/18 & 18	C	M	UUU
1–8–1948	Jackson, Jauvhan	17/18 & 18	B	M	UUU
2–10–1955	Matthews, Henry	16 & 18	W	M	WF85
1–12–1956	Byers, William Snyder	17 & 19	W	M	WF43
1–9–1956	Roye, Norman	16/17 & 17	B	M	UUU

NORTH CAROLINA (19)

Period of Executions: 1852–1944   Race: black, 17; white, 1; unknown, 1
Age at Crime: 15 to 17/18   Crime: murder, 14; rape, 5

Date of Execution	Name	Age at Time of Crime & Exec.	Race	Crime	Victims
5–21–1852?	Arnold	17 & 17	U	M	UUU
6–1–1886	McNair, George	17 & 19	B	Ra	WF9

NORTH CAROLINA (19) (Cont'd)

Date of Execution	Name	Age at Time of Crime & Exec.	Race	Crime	Victims
1–22–1892	Shipp, Caroline (female)	17/18 & U	B	M	BUC
5–22–1903?	Broadnax, John	16 & 16	B	MBr	UMA
12–20–1905	Carter, Will	17 & 17	B	Ra	WF6
7–21–1916	Black, Willie	16 & 16	B	Ra	WF6
10–12–1922	Burnette, McIver	16 & 16	B	M	UUU
1–5–1925	Hale, Kenneth	17 & 17	B	MRo	UMA
6–28–1929	Willey, Freddie	16/17 & 17	B	Ra	WFA
12–11–1931	Ballard, J.W.	17 & 17	B	M	UUU
7–6–1934	Edwards, James Lewis	16 & 17	B	M	UMA
9–6–1935	Miller, Caesar	17/18 & 18	B	M	UUU
10–4–1935	Gosnell, Arthur	17/18 & 18	W	M	UUU
7–9–1937	Brown, Robert Glenn	17/18 & 18	B	M	UUU
8–13–1937	McNeill, Leroy	15 & 17	B	M	UMA
12–10–1937	Perry, William	17/18 & 18	B	MAr	WFA
9–23–1938	Jefferson, L.J.	17 & 17	B	M	UUU
2–16–1940	Bryant, Nathaniel	17 & 17	B	MBr	UMA
10–30–1942	Harris, Otis	17 & 17	B	Ra	WFA

NORTH DAKOTA (0)

OHIO (19)

Period of Executions: 1880–1956   Race: black, 6; Chinese, 1; white, 12
Age at Crime: 15 to 17   Crime: murder, 19

Date of Execution	Name	Age at Time of Crime & Exec.	Race	Crime	Victims
6–25–1880	Mann, George E.	16 & 17	W	MRo	WMA
6–25–1880	Ohr, Gustave A.	15 & 16	W	MRo	WMA

OHIO (19) (Cont'd)

Date of Execution	Name	Age at Time of Crime & Exec.	Race	Crime	Victims
6–25–1880	Sammett, John	17 & 18	W	M	WM16
8–29–1890	Leuth, Otto	16 & 17	W	MRa	WF7
7–26–1895	Taylor, William	17 & 18	B	MRo	WMA
4–21–1897	Haas, William	16 & 17	W	MRa	WFA
12–4–1914	Beard, Harley	17 & 18	W	3M	WM45, WF46, WF80
5–9–1922	Pupera, Ignatius (Sam)	16 & 18	W	2MRo	2WMA
11–26–1926	Ross, Emanuel	17 & 18	B	MRo	WMA
1–6–1928	Hewitt, Floyd	16 & 17	W	2MAr	WM5, WF24
1–9–1928	Coverson, John	17 & 18	B	M	BMALE
7–5–1928	Coleman, James	17 & 18	B	M	UMALE
6–13–1930	Akers, Lee	17 & 18	B	MRo	UMA
8–14–1933	Murphy, Joseph	17 & 18	B	MRo	UMA
7–12–1939	Young, Pang	17 & 18	C	MRo	BMA
1–14–1944	Hand, Louis Vernon	16 & 17	W	M	WM6
10–3–1945	Hagert, William Henry	17 & 20	W	2M	2WM12
8–20–1948	Frohner, Donald Edward	16 & 18	W	MRo	WMA
3–15–1956	Schreiber, Bernard	17 & 19	W	MRa	WF17

OKLAHOMA (0)

OREGON (1)

Period of Executions: 1942   Race: white, 1
Age at Crime: 16   Crime: murder, 1

Date of Execution	Name	Age at Time of Crime & Exec.	Race	Crime	Victims
3–20–1942	Soto, John A.	16 & 17	W	3MRo	WM25, WM45, WF68

PENNSYLVANIA (5)

Period of Executions: 1722–1916   Race: white, 4; unknown, 1
Age at Crime: 15 to 17   Crime: murder, 5

Date of Execution	Name	Age at Time of Crime & Exec.	Race	Crime	Victims
8–15–1722	Battin, William	17 & 17	W	3MA	3WMC
10–16–1784	Burke, James	17 & 17	W	M	WMA
7–14–1908	Sergi, Rosario	17 & 18	W	M	WMA
11–18–1909	Marcavich, Stanley	15 & 17	U	M	UMA
12–4–1916	Digeso, Dominick	17 & 18	W	M	WMA

RHODE ISLAND (0)

SOUTH CAROLINA (11)

Period of Executions: 1865–1986   Race: black, 10; white, 1
Age at Crime: 14 to 17/18   Crime: murder, 8; rape, 2; robbery, 1

Date of Execution	Name	Age at Time of Crime & Exec.	Race	Crime	Victims
3–10–1865	Spain, Amy (female)	17 & 17	B	T	WMA (master)
7–11–1890	Jones, Armstead	16 & 16	B	M	BFA (stpmthr)
10–7–1892	Brown, Milbry (female)	14 & 14	B	M	WU1
6–16–1905	Johnson, William	17 & 17	B	Ra	WF8
1–18–1908	Kenny, George	17 & 19	B	M	WMA (guard)
2–2–1923	Johnson, Thomas	16 & 16	B	M	WFA
7–20–1934	Jones, Reuben	17/18 & 18	B	MRo	WMA
6–26–1936	Ashley, Robert	17 & 17	B	MRo	UM40
6–16–1944	Stinney, George Junius, Jr.	14 & 14	B	MAr	WF11
12–3–1948	Jamison, Matthew	17/18 & 18	B	Ra	WFA
1–10–1986	Roach, James Terry	17 & 25	W	MRa	WM17, WF14

SOUTH DAKOTA (0)

TENNESSEE (11)

Period of Executions: 1818–1947   Race: black, 9; white, 2
Age at Crime: 14 to 17/18   Crime: murder, 10; rape, 1

Date of Execution	Name	Age at Time of Crime & Exec.	Race	Crime	Victims
?–?–1818	(slave)	14 & 14	B	4M	WFA, WUC, WUC, BUC
9–5–1878	Howell, George	16 & 16	B	M	UMA
12–22–1894	Cox, Clarence	15 & 16	W	2MRo	WM90, WF76
1–11–1895	Mapp, George	15 & 17	B	M	WMA
12–19–1912	Temples, Leo	17 & 17	B	Ra	WF7
8–3–1921	Jackson, Cyrenus	17 & 18	B	MRo, Ra	WM19, WFA
8–3–1921	Neal, Taylor	17 & 19	B	MRo, Ra	WM19, WFA
7–25–1922	Dwight, William	17 & 18	B	MRo	UMA
1–21–1936	Kennedy, Walter	17/18 & 18	W	2M	WM65, WMA
4–10–1936	Womack, Ernest	17/18 & 18	B	M	UMA
8–11–1947	Jackson, Fred	16 & 18	B	2M, RaA	WM1, WM3, WF37

TEXAS (18)

Period of Executions: 1859–1986   Race: black, 12; Mexican-American, 3; white, 3
Age at Crime: 16 to 17/18   Crime: murder, 13; rape, 4; robbery 1

Date of Execution	Name	Age at Time of Crime & Exec.	Race	Crime	Victims
1–27–1859	Peter	16 & 16	B	M	WFA
12–21–1888	Johnson, John Andrew	17 & 17	B	Ra	WFA

TEXAS (18) (Cont'd)

Date of Execution	Name	Age at Time of Crime & Exec.	Race	Crime	Victims
3–18–1896	Chappell, Buck	17/18 & 18	B	M	UUU
5–7–1900	Brown, Henry	17 & 18	B	M	BFA
6–28–1908	Gibson, Monk	17 & 19	B	5MRa	WFA, WM3, WM6, WM10, WF12
5–11–1914	Martinez, Leon Cardenas, Jr.	16 & 19	M	M	WF28
3–3–1915	Sanchez, Federico	17 & 17	M	M	UMALE
7–21–1921	Flores, Jose	16/17 & 17	M	M	WMALE
5–24–1929	Jarman, Silas	17 & 18	B	RoAr, A&B	WFA
8–5–1932	Green, John L.	17 & 18	B	MRo	WMA
12–15–1933	Thomas, Clarence	17/18 & 18	B	M	UMALE
6–17–1938	Calhoun, Mark Henry	17/18 & 18	B	Ra	WF13
7–9–1944	Williams, David	17 & 18	B	Ra	WF16
4–16–1949	Northern, Buster	17 & 20	W	MRo	WF70
4–19–1962	Johnson, Adrian	17 & 19	B	MRa	WM12
5–7–1964	Echols, James Andrew	17 & 19	B	Ra	WF18
9–11–1985	Rumbaugh, Charles	17 & 28	W	MRo	WM54
5–15–1986	Pinkerton, Jay Kelly	17 & 24	W	MRa	WF30

UTAH (1)

Period of Executions: 1869 Race: white, 1
Age at Crime: 17 Crime: murder, 1

Date of Execution	Name	Age at Time of Crime & Exec.	Race	Crime	Victims
1–29–1869	Millard, Chauncey	17 & 17	W	MRo	UUU

VERMONT (1)

Period of Executions: 1871   Race: white, 1
Age at Crime: 17   Crime: murder, 1

Date of Execution	Name	Age at Time of Crime & Exec.	Race	Crime	Victims
1–20–1871	Welcome, Henry	17 & 19	W	MRo	WM72

VIRGINIA (18)

Period of Executions: 1787–1932   Race: black, 18
Age at Crime: 12 to 17/18   Crime: assault & battery, 1; attempted rape,
                                    2; murder, 10; rape, 4; robbery, 1

Date of Execution	Name	Age at Time of Crime & Exec.	Race	Crime	Victims
5–11–1787	Clem	12 & 12	B	2M	2WMU
6–5–1857	Arthur	17 & 17	B	A&B	WFA
3–30–1883	Beaver, Charles William	16 & 16	B	Ra	WF10
6–8–1906	Battaile, Gabriel	16 & 16	B	Ra	WFA
10–30–1908	Green, Winston	17 & 17	B	Ar	WFC
3–22–1909	Christian, Arthlius	17 & 17	B	MRa	WF14
1–14–1910	Spinher, Thurman	17/18 & 18	B	M	UUU
11–11–1910	Eccles, John	17 & 17	B	M	BMA
12–16–1910	Sitlington, Harry	17 & 17	B	M	WF70
6–21–1912	Jackson, Byrd	17/18 & 18	B	Ro	UUU
8–16–1912	Christian, Virginia (female)	16 & 17	B	M	WF60
9–17–1915	Stanfield, Sherman	17/18 & 18	B	Ar	UFU
3–15–1916	Ellis, Percy	16 & 16	B	M	UUU
7–2–1918	Bailey, Tolson	17 & 17	B	MRo	WMA
9–30–1921	Haskins, Raleigh	17/18 & 18	B	M	WMA
9–12–1924	Lewis, Fritz	17 & 17	B	MRoA	WM68
6–26–1931	Groome, Calvin	17/18 & 18	B	Ra	WFU
5–20–1932	Pannell, Sam	17/18 & 18	B	Ra	WFU

WASHINGTON (3)

Period of Executions: 1874–1932   Race: Indian, 1; white, 2
Age at Crime: 16 to 17   Crime: murder, 3

Date of Execution	Name	Age at Time of Crime & Exec.	Race	Crime	Victims
3–6–1874	Nuana, Joseph	16 & 17	I	3MRo	WMA, WM35 WF20 (preg)

WASHINGTON (3) (Cont'd)

Date of Execution	Name	Age at Time of Crime & Exec.	Race	Crime	Victims
3–2–1906	White, William	17 & 18	W	MRo	UMA
4–15–1932	Dubuc, Walter	17 & 17	W	MRo	WM86

WEST VIRGINIA (1)

Period of Execution: 1879　　　　Race: unknown, 1
Age at Crime: 17　　　　Crime: murder, 1

Date of Execution	Name	Age at Time of Crime & Exec.	Race	Crime	Victims
11–28–1879	Walker, Laban P.	17 & 18	U	M	UMA

WISCONSIN (0)

WYOMING (0)

FEDERAL (8)

Period of Executions: 1864–1885　　　Race: Indian, 3; white, 5
Age at Crime: 10 to 17　　　　Crime: murder, 7; spying, 1

Date and Place of Execution	Name	Age at Time of Crime & Exec.	Race	Crime	Victims
1–8–1864 (Ark.)	Dodd, David O.	17 & 17	W	S	Union Army
1–26–1866 (Tenn.)	Crab, George	17 & 17	W	M	WMA
1–26–1866 (Tenn.)	Ferry, Thomas	17 & 17	W	M	WMA
1–26–1866 (Tenn.)	Knight, James	17 & 17	W	M	WMA
1–26–1866 (Tenn.)	Lysaught, James	17 & 17	W	M	WMA
4–3–1874 (Ark.)	Fillmore, Isaac	17 & 18	I	M	WMA
9–8–1876 (Ark.)	Wilson, Sinker	15 & 24	I	M	WMC
6–26–1885 (Ark.)	Arcene, James	10 & 23	I	MRo	WMA

NOTES

1. JUVENILES IN LAW AND SOCIETY

Information in this chapter is based largely on the author's article "Juvenile Law," in ENCYCLOPEDIA OF THE AMERICAN JUDICIAL SYSTEM (R. Janosik ed. 1987).

1. May v. Anderson, 345 U.S. 528, 536 (1953).
2. S. DAVIS, RIGHTS OF JUVENILES 1–1 (2d ed. 1985).
3. In re Gault, 387 U.S. 1, 16 (1967); 4 W. BLACKSTONE, COMMENTARIES ON THE LAW OF ENGLAND 23–24 (1792).
4. *Id.*
5. JUVENILE OFFENDERS FOR A THOUSAND YEARS (W. Sanders ed. 1970).
6. Fox, "Juvenile Justice Reform: An Historical Perspective," 22 STAN. L. REV. 1187 (1970); and Mennel, "Origins of the Juvenile Court: Changing Perspectives on the Legal Rights of Juvenile Delinquents," 18 CRIME & DELINQ. 68 (1972).
7. Schultz, "The Cycle of Juvenile Court History," 19 CRIME & DELINQ. 457 (1973).
8. A. PLATT, THE CHILD SAVERS (2d ed. 1972).
9. V. STREIB, JUVENILE JUSTICE IN AMERICA 6 (1978).
10. S. FOX, THE LAW OF JUVENILE COURTS IN A NUTSHELL 8 (3d ed. 1984).
11. 387 U.S. 1 (1967).
12. STREIB, *supra* note 9, at 7–9; and JUVENILE JUSTICE PHILOSOPHY 145 (F. Faust & P. Brantingham eds. 1974).
13. Faust & Brantingham, *supra* note 12, at 147.
14. Commonwealth v. Fisher, 213 Pa. 48, 62 A. 198 (1905).
15. 387 U.S. 1 (1967).
16. Kent v. United States, 383 U.S. 541 (1966).
17. 397 U.S. 358 (1970).
18. 403 U.S. 528 (1971).
19. Schall v. Martin, 467 U.S. 253, 263 (1984).
20. See, e.g., STREIB, *supra* note 9.
21. L. FORER, "NO ONE WILL LISSEN": HOW OUR LEGAL SYSTEM BRUTALIZES THE YOUTHFUL POOR (1970).
22. S. FOX, MODERN JUVENILE JUSTICE 40–79 (1981).
23. See generally INTRODUCTION TO JUVENILE DELINQUENCY (P. Cromwell, G. Killinger, R. Sarri & H. Solmon eds. 1978).
24. FOX, *supra* note 10, at 49.
25. *Id.* at 48.
26. *Id.* at 49.
27. Breed v. Jones, 421 U.S. 519 (1975).
28. F. MCCARTHY & J. CARR, JUVENILE LAW AND ITS PROCESSES (1980).
29. Garlock, " 'Wayward' Children and the Law: The Genesis of the Status Offense Jurisdiction of the Juvenile Court," 13 GA. L. REV. 341 (1979).
30. DAVIS, *supra* note 2, at 2-11–2-12.
31. *Id.* at 2-13–2-15.
32. *Id.* at 2-12–2-13.
33. FOX, *supra* note 10, at 39–40.
34. DAVIS, *supra* note 2, at 2–16. See chapter three, *supra*, for a detailed discussion of these statutes.
35. FOX, *supra* note 10, at 39.
36. *Id.* at 38.

37. R. TROJANOWICZ, JUVENILE DELINQUENCY: CONCEPTS AND CONTROLS (2d ed. 1978).

38. See, e.g., LA. REV. STAT. ANN. sec. 13:1570 (A) (5) (1983); State v. Leach, 425 So.2d 1232 (La. 1983); and State v. Perique, 439 So.2d 1060 (La. 1983).

39. See, e.g., N.C. Gen. Stat. sec. 7A-608 (1981) and chapter three, *supra*.

40. DAVIS, *supra* note 2, at 2-17–2-18; Paulsen, "The Delinquency, Neglect and Dependency Jurisdiction of the Juvenile Court," in JUSTICE FOR THE CHILD 44, 62 (M. Rosenheim ed. 1962).

41. THE DEATH PENALTY IN AMERICA 93–185 (H. Bedau ed. 3d ed. 1982).

42. FOX, *supra* note 10, at 45–48.

43. W. LAFAVE & A. SCOTT, CRIMINAL LAW, 304–332 (2d ed. 1986).

44. F. MCCARTHY & J. CARR, *supra* note 28.

45. DAVIS, *supra* note 2, at 2–2.

46. See note 3, *supra* and accompanying text, and DAVIS, *supra* note 2, at 2-4-2-6.

47. In re Gladys, 1 Cal.3d 855, 464 P.2d 127, 83 Cal. Rptr. 671 (1970).

48. Sametz, "Revamping the Adolescent's Justice System to Serve the Needs of the Very Young Offender," 34 JUV. & FAM. CT. J. 21 (1983).

49. T. JOHNSON, INTRODUCTION TO THE JUVENILE JUSTICE SYSTEM (1975).

50. FOX, *supra* note 10, at 80–85.

51. L. SIEGEL & J. SENNA, JUVENILE DELINQUENCY (1981).

52. D. BESHAROV, JUVENILE JUSTICE PRACTICE 107–11 (1974).

53. W. LAFAVE, ARREST: THE DECISION TO TAKE A SUSPECT INTO CUSTODY (1965).

54. Chimel v. California, 395 U.S. 752 (1969).

55. Fare v. Michael C., 442 U.S. 707 (1979).

56. DAVIS, *supra* note 2, at 3-44.2–3-64.1; FOX, *supra* note 10, at 114–28.

57. DAVIS, *supra* note 2, at 3-64.1–3-69; FOX, *supra* note 10, at 136–40.

58. Kirby v. Illinois, 406 U.S. 682 (1972).

59. In re Lynette G., 54 Cal. App. 3d 1087, 126 Cal. Rptr. 898 (1976).

60. DAVIS, *supra* note 2, at 3-41–3-44.2.

61. FOX, *supra* note 10, at 146–53.

62. Schall v. Martin, 467 U.S. 253 (1984).

63. FOX, *supra* note 10, at 146–53.

64. Streib, "The Informal Juvenile Justice System: A Need for Procedural Fairness and Reduced Discretion," 10 J. MAR. J. PRAC. & PROC. 41 (1976).

65. *Id.*

66. FOX, *supra* note 10, at 153–59.

67. F. ZIMRING, THE CHANGING LEGAL WORLD OF ADOLESCENCE xii (1982).

68. FOX, *supra*, note 10, at 64–65.

69. DAVIS, *supra* note 2, at 2-22–2-25.

70. *Id.* at 4-1–4-5.

71. 383 U.S. 541 (1966).

72. BESHAROV, *supra* note 52, at 311–34.

73. 387 U.S. 1 (1967).

74. In re Winship, 397 U.S. 358 (1970).

75. McKeiver v. Pennsylvania, 403 U.S. 528 (1971).

76. FOX, *supra* note 10, at 185–86.

77. Streib, "The Juvenile Justice System and Children's Law: Should Juvenile Defense Attorneys Be Replaced with Children's Lawyers?" 31 JUV. & FAM. CT. J. 53 (1980).

78. JOHNSON, *supra* note 49, at 117.

79. STREIB, *supra* note 9, at 41–43.

80. Fox, "Philosophy and the Principles of Punishment in the Juvenile Court," 8 FAM. L. Q. 373 (1974).

81. DAVIS, *supra* note 2, at 6–10.

82. P. MURPHY, OUR KINDLY PARENT—THE STATE: THE JUVENILE JUSTICE SYSTEM AND HOW IT WORKS (1974).

83. FOX, *supra* note 10, at 225–31.

84. *Id.* at 231–41.

85. *Id.* at 231.

86. DAVIS, *supra* note 2, at 6-20.1–6-20.3.

87. W. ARNOLD, JUVENILES ON PAROLE: A SOCIOLOGICAL PERSPECTIVE (1970).

88. DAVIS, *supra* note 2, at 2-10–2-11.

89. FOX, *supra* note 10, at 51–52.

90. R. MNOOKIN, CHILD, FAMILY AND STATE 306–40 (1978).

91. Katz, "Child Neglect Laws in America," 9 FAM. L. Q. 1 (1975).

92. *Id.*

93. *Id.*

94. FOX, *supra* note 10, at 57.

95. *Id.* at 57–59.

96. Lassiter v. Department of Social Services, 452 U.S. 18 (1981); Santosky v. Kramer, 455 U.S. 745 (1982).

97. Lassiter v. Department of Social Services, 452 U.S. 18 (1981).

98. MNOOKIN, *supra* note 90, at 312.

99. FOX, *supra* note 80.

100. See generally notes 6 and 7, *supra*, and accompanying text.

101. FOX, *supra* note 22, at 507–35.

2. CONSTITUTIONAL LAW
AND THE JUVENILE DEATH PENALTY

Information in this chapter is based largely on the author's article "The Eighth Amendment and Capital Punishment of Juveniles," 34 CLEVE. ST. L. REV. 363 (1986).

1. "The courts have never drawn a line to protect juveniles as such from the reach of death sentences . . . on the grounds of the unconstitutional cruelty and unusualness of such [sentences]." H. BEDAU, THE COURTS, THE CONSTITUTION, AND CAPITAL PUNISHMENT 33 (1977). Eddings v. Oklahoma, 455 U.S. 104 (1982), considered the constitutionality issue but was decided on another basis.

2. 428 U.S. 153 (1976).

3. *Id.* at 169 (Stewart, J., plurality opinion) and at 226 (White, J., concurring).

4. *Id.* at 196–98 (Stewart, J., plurality opinion).

5. *Id.* at 197.

6. Jurek v. Texas, 428 U.S. 262, 273 (1976) (Stewart, J., plurality opinion), quoting with approval Jurek v. Texas, 522 S.W.2d 934, 940 (Tex. Crim. App. 1975).

7. 431 U.S. 633 (1977).

8. *Id.* at 637.

9. 438 U.S. 536 (1978).

10. *Id.* at 608.

11. 438 U.S. 637 (1978).

12. *Id.* at 639.

13. *Id.* at 642–43.

14. *Id.* at 642–43 n. *.

15. Eddings v. Oklahoma, 455 U.S. 104 (1982), *cert. granted*, 450 U.S. 1040 (1981).

16. *Id.* at 117.

17. *Id.* at 115–16 (footnotes omitted).

18. See *id.* at 119 (O'Connor, J., concurring).

19. *Id.* at 128 (Burger, C.J., dissenting).

20. See, e.g., Roach v. Martin, 757 F.2d 1463 (4th Cir. 1985), *cert. denied,* 106 S.Ct. 645 (1986); Trimble v. State, 300 Md. 387, 478 A.2d 1143 (Md. 1983), *cert. denied,* 105 S.Ct. 1231 (1985); Cannaday v. State, 455 So.2d 713 (Miss. 1984), *cert. denied,* 105 S.Ct. 1209 (1985); High v. Zant, 250 Ga. 693, 300 S.E.2d 654 (1983), *cert. denied,* 104 S.Ct. 2669 (1984); and Tokman v. State, 435 So.2d 664 (Miss. 1983), *cert. denied.* 104 S.Ct. 3574 (1984).

21. Lockett v. Ohio, 438 U.S. 586, 605 (1978) (Burger, C.J., plurality opinion) and Coker v. Georgia, 433 U.S. 584, 592 (1977) (White, J., plurality opinion).

22. See, e.g., Furman v. Georgia, 408 U.S. 238 (1972); Woodson v. North Carolina, 428 U.S. 280 (1976); Lockett v. Ohio, 438 U.S. 586 (1978).

23. Eddings v. Oklahoma, 455 U.S. 104, 115–17 (1982).

24. Bellotti v. Baird, 443 U.S. 622, 635 (1979).

25. F. ZIMRING, THE CHANGING LEGAL WORLD OF ADOLESCENCE (1982).

26. May v. Anderson, 345 U.S. 528, 536 (1953) (Frankfurter, J., concurring).

27. See, e.g., Eddings v. Oklahoma, 455 U.S. 104, 115–16 (1982).

28. Haley v. Ohio, 332 U.S. 596, 599 (1948).

29. See In re Gault, 387 U.S. 1 (1967); and McKeiver v. Pennsylvania, 403 U.S. 528 (1971).

30. In re Gault, 387 U.S. 1, 15 (1967).

31. See Kent v. United States, 383 U.S. 541 (1966).

32. See chapter one for more information on waiver.

33. McKeiver v. Pennsylvania, 403 U.S. 528, 544 (1971).

34. "In some jurisdictions, the question of whether a 16-year-old accused of murder will stay in juvenile court, or be tried in the criminal courts for a capital crime, will depend on an individual judge assessing whether that 16-year-old is 'mature' and 'sophisticated.' If he is found to be 'sophisticated,' his reward can be eligibility for the electric chair." F. ZIMRING, *supra* note 25, at xii.

35. See generally Note, "*Eddings v. Oklahoma*: A Stay of Execution for Juveniles?" 9 NEW ENGLAND J. CRIM. & CIV. CONFINEMENT 407 (1983).

36. Robinson v. California, 370 U.S. 660, 666 (1962).

37. Trop v. Dulles, 356 U.S. 86, 101 (1958) (Warren, C.J., plurality opinion).

38. Gregg v. Georgia, 428 U.S. 153, 173 (1976) (Stewart, J., plurality opinion), quoting Trop v. Dulles, 356 U.S. 86, 100 (1958) (Warren, C.J., plurality opinion).

39. Coker v. Georgia, 433 U.S. 584, 592 (White, J., plurality opinion).

40. In re Gault, 387 U.S. 1, 15–16 (1967).

41. See, e.g., Fox, "Juvenile Justice Reform: An Historical Perspective," 22 STAN. L. REV. 1187 (1970).

42. See generally J. LAURENCE, THE HISTORY OF CAPITAL PUNISHMENT 16–18 (1960).

43. Knell, "Capital Punishment: Its Administration in Relation to Juvenile Offenders in the Nineteenth Century and Its Possible Administration in the Eighteenth," 5 BRIT. J. CRIMINOLOGY 198, 199 (1965). England's Old Bailey is the primary criminal court in London.

44. *Id.* at 202.

45. *Id.* at 203.

46. *Id.* at 202.

47. See, e.g., THE DEATH PENALTY IN AMERICA 52–56 (H. Bedau ed. 1964). Chapter four, *infra,* provides detailed information about executions of juveniles in the United States.

48. Bedau, "Death Sentences in New Jersey: 1907–1960," 19 RUTGERS L. REV. 1, 25 (1964).

49. See generally Echols v. State, 370 S.W.2d 892 (Tex. Crim. App. 1963), affirming conviction and death sentence. Echols was executed on May 7, 1964. W. BOWERS, LEGAL HOMICIDE 512 (1984).

50. BOWERS, *supra* note 49, at 419 and 513.

51. NAACP LEGAL DEFENSE AND EDUCATIONAL FUND, INC., DEATH ROW, U.S.A. 4 (Aug. 1, 1986). See chapter six, *infra*, for more information about the Rumbaugh, Roach, and Pinkerton cases.

52. ZIMRING, *supra* note 25.

53. S. DAVIS, RIGHTS OF JUVENILES: THE JUVENILE JUSTICE SYSTEM app. B (2d ed., release #6, June 1986).

54. See chapter one for more information about juvenile waiver.

55. See chapter three for more information about state death penalty laws.

56. N.Y. Times, Jan. 7, 1962, at 81, col. 1.

57. *Id.*

58. California (CAL. PENAL CODE sec. 190.5 [West Supp. 1985]); Colorado (COLO. REV. STAT. sec. 16–11–103(1)(a) [1985]); Connecticut (CONN. GEN. STAT. ANN. sec. 53a–46a [h] [West Supp. 1985]); Georgia (GA. CODE ANN. sec. 17–9–3 [1982]); Illinois (ILL. ANN. STAT. ch. 38, sec. 9–1[b] [Smith–Hurd Supp. 1985]); Nebraska (NEB. REV. STAT. sec. 28–105.01 [1984]); Nevada (NEV. REV. STAT. sec. 176.025 [1979]); New Hampshire (N.H. REV. STAT. ANN. sec. 630:5 (IX) (1986); New Jersey (N.J. STAT. ANN. sec. 2C:11–3f [West 1986]); New Mexico (N.M. STAT. ANN. sec. 31–18–14 [1979]); Ohio (OHIO REV. CODE ANN. sec. 2929.02[E] [Page 1984]); Oregon (ORE. REV. STAT. sec. 161.615 [1985]); Tennessee (TENN. CODE ANN. sec. 37–1–134[1] [1984]); and Texas (TEX. PENAL CODE ANN. sec. 8.07[d] [Vernon Supp. 1985]).

This list totaled fifteen states with Kentucky. Kentucky repealed its new juvenile code in 1984 because of funding problems. That code, passed originally in 1980, prohibited the death penalty for juveniles under age eighteen. KY. REV. STAT ANN. sec. 208F.040 (1980) (repealed 1984).

59. TEX. PENAL CODE ANN. sec. 8.07 (d) (Vernon Supp. 1982).

60. Ohio's 1954 capital punishment statute was declared unconstitutional in State v. Leigh, 31 Ohio St. 2d 97, 285 N.E.2d 333 (Ohio 1972), and Ohio's 1975 capital punishment statute was declared unconstitutional in Lockett v. Ohio, 438 U.S. 536 (1978).

61. OHIO REV. CODE ANN. sec. 2929 (Page 1982) (effective Oct. 1, 1981). This statute has been upheld in two Ohio Supreme Court decisions. State v. Jenkins, 15 Ohio St. 3d 164, 473 N.E.2d 264 (1984), and State v. Maurer, 15 Ohio St. 3d 209, 473 N.E.2d 768 (1984).

62. See OHIO REV. CODE ANN. sec. 2929.02 (Page 1982). Chapter seven, *infra*, provides more information about the Ohio experience with the death penalty for juveniles.

63. NEB. REV. STAT. sec. 28–105.01 (1982).

64. COLO. REV. STAT. sec. 16–11–103(1)(a) (1985).

65. ORE. REV. STAT. sec. 161–620 (1985).

66. N.J. STAT. ANN. sec. 2C:11–3f (West 1986) (P.L. 1985, ch. 478, approved Jan. 17, 1986).

67. Ky. Rev. Stat. sec. 208F.040(1) (1980) (repealed 1984).

68. See Ice v. Commonwealth, 667 S.W.2d 671 (Ky. 1984).

69. Alabama (ALA. CODE sec. 12–15–34[a] [1977]); Arkansas (ARK. STAT. ANN. sec. 41–617(2) [Supp. 1985]); Idaho (IDAHO CODE sec. 16–1806A[1] [Supp. 1984]); Indiana (IND. CODE ANN. sec. 31–6–2–4[c] [Burns Supp. 1982]); Kentucky (KY. REV. STAT. ANN. sec. 208E.070[2] [Baldwin 1980]); Louisiana (LA. REV. STAT. ANN. sec. 13:1570[a][5] [1983]); Mississippi (MISS. CODE ANN. sec. 43–21–151 [1985]); Missouri (MO. ANN. STAT. sec. 211.071 [Vernon Supp. 1985]); Montana (MONT. CODE ANN. sec. 41–5–206(1)(a) [1985]); North Carolina (N.C. GEN. STAT. sec. 7A–608 [1986]); Utah (UTAH CODE ANN. sec. 78–3a–25[1] [Supp. 1985]); and Virginia (VA. CODE ANN. sec. 16.1–269[A] [1982]).

70. Arizona (ARIZ. REV. STAT. ANN. sec. 13–703[G][5] [Supp. 1985]); Florida (FLA. STAT. ANN. sec. 921.141[6][g] [West Supp. 1984]); Maryland (MD. CODE art. 27, sec.

413[g][5] [Supp. 1985]); Pennsylvania (PA. CONS. STAT. ANN. art. 42, sec. 9711[e][4][1982]); South Carolina (S.C. CODE ANN. sec. 16–3–20[c][b][7] [1985]); Washington (WASH. REV. CODE sec. 10.95.070[7] [Supp. 1986]); and Wyoming (WYO. STAT. sec. 6–2–102[j][vii] [Repl. 1983]).

71. Alaska, District of Columbia, Hawaii, Iowa, Kansas, Maine, Massachusetts, Michigan, Minnesota, New York, North Dakota, Rhode Island, Vermont, West Virginia, and Wisconsin. NAACP LEGAL DEFENSE AND EDUCATIONAL FUND, INC., DEATH ROW, U.S.A. 1 (Oct. 1, 1986). Vermont should be included in this list because its death penalty statute has not been amended since Furman v. Georgia, 408 U.S. 238 (1972), and is clearly invalid.

72. Delaware (DEL. CODE. ANN. tit. 11 sec. 4209[c] [Repl. 1979]); Oklahoma (OKLA. STAT. ANN. tit. 21, sec. 701.01 [West 1983]); and South Dakota (S.D. CODIFIED LAWS ANN. 23A–27A–1 [Supp. 1984]).

73. See table 9–4.

74. U.S. DEPARTMENT OF JUSTICE, CAPITAL PUNISHMENT 1984 6 (1986).

75. See FEDERAL BUREAU OF INVESTIGATION, U.S. DEPARTMENT OF JUSTICE, UNIFORM CRIME REPORTS: CRIME IN THE UNITED STATES 179 (1983), 176 (1982), 171 (1981), 200 (1980), 196 (1979), 194 (1978), 180 (1977), 181 (1976), 188 (1975), 186 (1974), and 128 (1973).

76. Furman v. Georgia, 408 U.S. 238, 300 (1972) (Brennan, J., concurring).

77. Id. at 331–32 (Marshall, J., concurring).

78. But see Hill, "Can the Death Penalty Be Imposed on Juveniles: The Unanswered Question in *Eddings v. Oklahoma*," 20 CRIM. L. BUL. 5 (1984).

79. See Time, Feb. 2, 1968, at 64–65.

80. Model Penal Code sec. 210.6 commentary at 133 (Official Draft and Revised Comments 1980).

81. NATIONAL COMMISSION ON THE REFORM OF CRIMINAL LAW, FINAL DRAFT OF THE NEW FEDERAL CODE sec. 3603 (1971).

82. See "ABA Opposes Capital Punishment for Persons under 18," 69 A.B.A.J. 1925 (1983); and Recommendation and Report to the ABA House of Delegates by the Section of Criminal Justice, August 1983 (proposing that this resolution be adopted by the American Bar Association).

83. Washington Post, Nov. 8, 1983, sec. A, at 18, col. 1.

84. AMNESTY INTERNATIONAL, THE DEATH PENALTY (1979); Note, "Juvenile Offenders and the Electric Chair: Cruel and Unusual Punishment or Firm Discipline for the Hopelessly Delinquent?" 35 U. FLA. L. REV. 344, 345 (1983).

85. Patrick, "The Status of Capital Punishment: A World Perspective," 56 J. CRIM. L., CRIMINOLOGY & POLICE SCI. 397, 398–404 (1965).

86. International Covenant on Civil and Political Rights, *entered into force* Mar. 23, 1976, G.A. Res. 2200A, 21 U.N. GAOR, Supp. (No. 16) at 49, 52, U.N. Doc. A/ 6316 art. 6(5) (1967) (signed by over sixty countries). See Hartman, " 'Unusual' Punishment: The Domestic Effects of International Norms Restricting the Application of the Death Penalty," 52 CIN. L. REV. 655 (1983).

87. N.Y. Times, Jan. 16, 1983, at 5, col. 2.

88. Article 68 of the Geneva Convention Relative to the Protection of Civilian Persons in Times of War, Aug. 12, 1949, 6 U.S.T. 3516, T.I.A.S. No. 3365, 75 U.N.T.S. 287, as cited in INTERNATIONAL RED CROSS HANDBOOK 157 (12th ed. July 1983).

89. The Gallup Report 10–16 (Jan.–Feb. 1986).

90. H. CANTRIL, PUBLIC OPINION: 1935–1946 94 (1951).

91. Id.

92. Erskine, "The Polls: Capital Punishment," 34 PUB. OPINION Q. 290 (1970), cited in Vidmar and Ellsworth, "Public Opinion and the Death Penalty," 26 STAN. L. REV. 1245, 1250 (1974).

93. Reskin, "Majority of Lawyers Support Capital Punishment," 71 A.B.A.J. 44 (Apr. 1985); "Lawyers Strongly Favor the Death Penalty," 69 A.B.A.J. 1218 (Sept. 1983).

94. Reskin (1985), *supra* note 93.

95. Reskin, "A Portrait of America's Law Students," 71 A.B.A.J. 43, 44 (May 1985).

96. "SCJP Poll Results: Don't Execute Juveniles," 13/1 Southern Coalition Report on Jails & Prisons 1 (Spring 1986).

97. Tuckel & Greenberg, Capital Punishment in Connecticut (May 1986) (Unpublished report prepared for the Archdiocese of Hartford by the Analysis Group, Inc., New Haven).

98. *Id.*

99. Furman v. Georgia, 408 U.S. at 278–79 (Brennan, J., concurring).

100. Bruck, "Executing Juveniles for Crime," N.Y. Times, June 16, 1984, at 17, col. 1.

101. Gregg v. Georgia, 428 U.S. at 183 (Stewart, J., plurality opinion).

102. Williams v. New York, 337 U.S. 241, 248 (1949).

103. Gregg v. Georgia, 428 U.S. at 183 (Stewart, J., plurality opinion); and Furman v. Georgia, 408 U.S. at 394–95 (Burger, C.J., dissenting).

104. Furman v. Georgia, 408 U.S. at 342–45 (Marshall, J., concurring).

105. For an excellent summary of the various interpretations, see Note, "Capital Punishment for Minors: An Eighth Amendment Analysis," 74 J. CRIM. LAW & CRIMINOLOGY 1471 (1983).

106. *Id.* and Gregg v. Georgia, 428 U.S. at 183–84.

107. 458 U.S. 782 (1982).

108. *Id.* at 800–01 (citations omitted).

109. See, e.g., Frazier, Juvenile Executions: The Folly of the Inevitable (March 1985) (Paper presented at the Annual Meeting of the Academy of Criminal Justice Sciences) (available from the author, Prof. Harriet C. Frazier, Criminal Justice Administration Dept., Central Missouri State University, Warrensburg, Mo. 64093).

110. TWENTIETH CENTURY FUND TASK FORCE ON SENTENCING POLICY TOWARD YOUNG OFFENDERS, CONFRONTING YOUTH CRIME 7 (1978), cited with approval in Eddings v. Oklahoma, 455 U.S. 104, 115 n.111. On the issue of youth crime being caused at least in part by such outside influences, see particularly Note, *supra* note 105, at 1492–1503.

111. See, THE DEATH PENALTY IN AMERICA 93–185 (H. Bedau ed. 3d ed. 1982).

112. Furman v. Georgia, 408 U.S. at 302 (Brennan, J., concurring) and at 353–54 (Marshall, J., concurring).

113. Gregg v. Georgia, 428 U.S. at 185–86 (Stewart, J., plurality opinion).

114. Bellotti v. Baird, 443 U.S. 622, 635 (1979); *accord*, Parham v. J.R., 442 U.S. 584, 603 (1979).

115. Haley v. Ohio, 332 U.S. 596, 599 (1948).

116. Eddings v. Oklahoma, 455 U.S. 104, 115–16 (1982).

117. *Id.* at 115.

118. Kastenbaum, "Time and Death in Adolescence," in THE MEANING OF DEATH 99 (H. Feifel ed. 1959). In a news story, "Children on Death Row," aired by ABC's World News Tonight on Apr. 15, 1985, correspondent Karen Burns interviewed Wayne Thompson on Oklahoma's death row. Thompson was only fifteen years old at the time of his crime. After Burns reminded Thompson that he had been sentenced to death for his crime, she asked him if he had ever thought about the death penalty before committing his crimes. He responded that he had not, that his only thoughts then were of playing ball or just hanging around with his friends.

119. Fredlund, "Children and Death from the School Setting Viewpoint," 47 J. SCHOOL HEALTH 533 (1977); and Miller, "Adolescent Suicide: Etiology and Treatment," in ADOLESCENT PSYCHIATRY 327 (S. Feinstein, J. Looney, A. Schwartzberg & A. Sorosky eds. 1981). See generally ADOLESCENCE AND DEATH (C. Corr & J. McNeil eds. 1986).

120. Knell, *supra* note 43, at 202 n.8.

121. See. e.g., Rest, Davidson & Robbins, "Age Trends in Judging Moral Issues: A

Review of Cross–Sectional Studies of the Defining Issues Test," 49 CHILD DEVELOP-
MENT 263 (1978); M. RITTER, CHANGING YOUTH IN A CHANGING SOCIETY 83 (1980);
and E. PEEL, THE NATURE OF ADOLESCENT JUDGMENT 131–34 (1971).

122. Kohlberg, "Development of Moral Character and Moral Ideology," in REVIEW
OF CHILD DEVELOPMENT RESEARCH 404–05 (Hoffman & Hoffman eds. 1964).

123. Bellotti v. Baird, 443 U.S. 622, 635 (1979).

124. Gregg v. Georgia, 428 U.S. at 186 (Stewart, J., plurality opinion).

125. See the section on Arbitrary, Capricious, and Freakish Manner in this chapter.

126. See, e.g., H. BEDAU, THE CASE AGAINST THE DEATH PENALTY (1985) (published by and available from the American Civil Liberties Union, 132 W. 43d St., New
York, N.Y. 10036).

127. Furman v. Georgia, 408 U.S. at 355 (Marshall, J., concurring).

128. Vitello, "Constitutional Safeguards for Juvenile Transfer Procedure: The Ten
Years since Kent v. United States," 26 DEPAUL L. REV. 23, 32–34 (1976). See also D.
HAMPARIAN, R. SCHUSTER, S. DINITZ & J. CONRAD, THE VIOLENT FEW 52 (1978),
and T. SELLIN, THE DEATH PENALTY 102–20 (1982).

129. See, e.g., People v. Hiemel, 49 A.D.2d 769, 372 N.Y.S.2d 730 (1975). The court
reduced the murder sentence of a sixteen-year-old who had used the time in prison to
become "a classic example of the rehabilitation heights attainable within our existing
penal system by an inmate desirous of taking advantage of the educational facilities
available." Id. at 770, 372 N.Y.S.2d at 731.

130. Workman v. Commonwealth, 429 S.W.2d 374, 378 (Ky. 1968).

131. See generally Note, supra note 105.

132. See Furman v. Georgia, 408 U.S. at 309 (Stewart, J., concurring).

133. Lockett v. Ohio, 438 U.S. 586, 620 (1978) (Marshall, J, concurring).

134. See Greenberg, "Capital Punishment as a System," 91 YALE L.J. 908 (1982).

135. The execution of Charles Rumbaugh in Texas on Sept. 11, 1985, prompted in-
depth coverage by the news media. See, e.g., N.Y. Times, Sept. 10, 1985, at 8, col. 1
(four-column article on "Execution for Juveniles: New Focus on Old Issue"), and Sept.
12, 1985, at 11, col. 4 (two-column article on the execution of Rumbaugh); and National
Catholic Reporter, Nov. 8, 1985, at 11–22 (forum section with six articles on Rumbaugh).
Similar news media coverage was devoted to the execution of James Terry Roach in
South Carolina on Jan. 10, 1986. See, e.g., Newsweek, Jan. 13, 1986, at 74 (two-column
article); Time, Jan. 20, 1986, at 22 (one and one-half page article); and N.Y. Times, Jan.
9, 1986, at 22, col. 1 (editorial opposing executions of juveniles).

136. See supra, note 74.

137. Id. at 6.

138. Id.

139. See tables 2–3 and 2–4.

140. Streib, "Executions under the Post–Furman Capital Punishment Statutes: The
Halting Progression from 'Let's do it' to 'Hey, there ain't no point in pulling so tight,' "
15 RUTGERS L.J. 443, 486 (1984).

141. Pulley v. Harris, 465 U.S. 37, 60 (1984) (Brennan, J., dissenting).

142. DAVIS, supra note 53.

143. See chapter three.

144. See supra note 80 and accompanying text.

145. Patrick, supra note 85, at 398–404.

sm146. See supra note 86.

147. See supra, note 88.

148. See chapter three.

149. A fundamental premise of Anglo-American criminal law is that persons under
age seven are conclusively presumed to be incapable of entertaining criminal intent and
thus cannot have criminal liability imposed on them. For the historical roots of this
premise, see 4 W. BLACKSTONE, COMMENTARIES ON THE LAW OF ENGLAND 23–24

(1792), and 1 M. HALE, PLEAS OF THE CROWN 25–28 (1682). For a recent American acceptance of this premise, see In re Gault, 387 U.S. 1, 16 (1967).

3. STATE LAWS AND
THE JUVENILE DEATH PENALTY

Information in this chapter is based in part on the author's article "The Eighth Amendment and Capital Punishment of Juveniles," 34 CLEVE. ST. L. REV. 363 (1986).

1. "The courts have never drawn a line to protect juveniles as such from the reach of death sentences . . . on the grounds of the unconstitutional cruelty and unusualness of such [sentences]." H.BEDAU, THE COURTS, THE CONSTITUTION, AND CAPITAL PUNISHMENT 33 (1977).

2. Eddings v. Oklahoma, 455 U.S. 104, 116 (1982) ("the chronological age of a minor is itself a relevant mitigating factor of great weight. . . ."); and Lockett v. Ohio, 438 U.S. 536, 608 (1978).

3. Furman v. Georgia, 408 U.S. 238 (1972).

4. Gregg v. Georgia, 428 U.S. 153 (1976).

5. Federal statutes authorize the death penalty for a variety of crimes. See, e.g., 18 U.S.C.A. sec. 1111 (1969) (murder), 18 U.S.C.A. sec. 2031 (1969) (rape), and 18 U.S.C.A. sec. 2113 (1969) (bank robbery). However, they do not provide for the guided discretion in sentencing required by the Supreme Court in Gregg and thus are clearly unconstitutional. No persons are presently under a sentence of death for violation of federal laws.

6. Report of the Committee on the Judiciary . . . to Accompany H.R. 6915, 25 Sept. 1980, p. 434, citing United States v. Weedell, 567 F.2d 767 (8th Cir.1977).

7. S. REP. NO. 239, 99th Cong., 2d Sess. 3591 (1986). An amendment placed in the original bill states "that no person may be sentenced to death who was less than eighteen years of age at the time of the offense." This bill as amended was ordered out of the Senate Judiciary Committee on Feb. 20, 1986, and placed on the Senate's legislative calendar on Apr. 16, 1986. I Cong. Index 20,501 (1985–1986).

8. N.Y. Times, Feb. 7, 1985, at 13, col. 4.

9. NAACP LEGAL DEFENSE AND EDUCATIONAL FUND, INC., DEATH ROW U.S.A. 1 (Aug. 1, 1986), lists fourteen non–death penalty states. For the purposes of the analysis in this chapter Vermont has been included as a non–death penalty state for reasons noted in table 3-1.

10. THE DEATH PENALTY IN AMERICA 23 (H. Bedau ed. 3d ed. 1982).

11. Supra, chapter two note 58.

12. CAL. PENAL CODE sec. 190.5 (1985).

13. GA. CODE ANN. sec. 17-9-3 (1982).

14. Alabama (ALA. CODE sec. 12-15-34[a] 1977]); Indiana (IND. CODE ANN. sec. 31-6-2-4[c] [Burns Supp. 1982]); Kentucky (KY. REV. STAT. ANN. sec. 208E.070[2] [Baldwin 1980]); Mississippi (MISS. CODE ANN. sec. 43-21-151 [1985]); Missouri (MO. ANN. STAT. sec. 211.071 [Vernon Supp. 1985]); Montana (MONT. CODE ANN. sec. 41-5-206(1)(a) [1985]); Utah (UTAH CODE ANN. sec. 78-3a-25[1] [Supp. 1985]); and Virginia (VA. CODE ANN. sec. 16.1-269[A] [1982]).

15. Alabama, Kentucky, Missouri, and Utah. Id.

16. See Supra note 14.

17. See generally Kent v. United States, 385 U.S.541 (1966).

18. Arkansas (ARK. STAT. ANN. sec. 41-617(2)[Supp. 1985]); Idaho (IDAHO CODE sec. 16-1806A[1] [Supp. 1986]); Louisiana (LA. REV. STAT. ANN. sec. 13:1570[a] [5] [1983]); and North Carolina (N.C. GEN. STAT. sec.7A-608 [1986].

19. Id.

20. *Supra* chapter two note 70.
21. *Supra* note 2.
22. *Supra* chapter two note 72.
23. 455 U.S. 104 (1982).
24. Table 9-4 provides more information about the Thompson case.
25. Eddings v. Oklahoma, 455 U.S. 104 (1982) Lockett v. Ohio, 438 U.S. 536 (1978)
26. 429 S.W.2d 374 (Ky. 1968).
27. *Id.* at 378.
28. 197 Neb. 497, 250 N.W.2d 849 (1977).
29. *Id.* at 526, 250 N.W.2d at 866.
30. 246 Ga. 101, 268 S.E.2d 915 (1980).
31. GA. CODE ANN. sec. 17-9-3 (1982).
32. Lewis v. State, 246 Ga. at 107, 268 S.E.2d at 921 (Hill, J., concurring).
33. 29 Cal.3d 814, 176 Cal. Rptr. 521, 633 P.2d 186 (1980).
34. See, e.g., Bracewell v. State, 401 So.2d 124 (Ala. Ct. App. 1980) ("[W]e would likewise direct the trial court to carefully reconsider the imposition of the death penalty where two mitigating circumstances weigh heavily in the appellant's favor, i.e., her young age and the dominance of her husband. . . . "*Id.* at 125) State v. Maloney, 105 Ariz. 348, 464 P.2d 793 (1970), *cert. denied*, 400 U.S. 841 (1970) ("The defendant has committed a heinous crime. . . . Had he been of mature age the death penalty would have gone undisturbed by this Court. . . . Because of his immaturity [age fifteen] we are persuaded that he should not die. . . ." *Id.* at 360, 464 P.2d at 805.); Vasil v. State, 374 So.2d 465 (Fla. 1979), *cert. denied*, 446 U.S. 967 (1980) (court reduced fifteen-year-old's death sentence); Coleman v. State, 378 So.2d 640 (Miss. 1979) (court reduced sixteen-year-old's death sentence); Commonwealth v. Green, 396 Pa. 137, 151 A.2d 241 (1959) (court vacated a fifteen-year-old's death sentence because "age is an important factor in determining the appropriateness of the penalty and should impose upon the sentencing court the duty to be ultra vigilant in its inquiry into the makeup of the convicted murderer." *Id.* at 147, 151 A.2d at 246).
35. 455 U.S. 104 (1982).
36. *Id.* at 119 (O'Connor, J., concurring).
37. 250 Ga. 693, 300 S.E.2d 654 (1983), *cert. denied*, 104 S.Ct. 2669 (1984).
38. 661 S.W.2d 487 (Mo. 1983) (en banc), *cert. denied*, 104 S.Ct. 2325 (1984).
39. Eddings v. Oklahoma, 455 U.S. 104, 128 (1982) (Burger, C.J., dissenting).
40. *Id.* at 119 (O'Connor, J., concurring).
41. 570 F.Supp. 985 (W.D. La. 1983), *aff'd*, 743 F.2d 1091 (5th Cir. 1984).
42. 300 Md. 387, 478 A.2d 1143 (Md. 1984).
43. Prejean v. Blackburn, 570 F.Supp. at 999.
44. Trimble v. State, 300 Md. at 387, 478 A.2d at 1146.
45. Brief for Appellant at 41-54, Trimble v. State, 300 Md. 387, 478 A.2d 1143 (Md. 1984).
46. Trimble v. State, 300 Md. at 417, 478 A.2d at 1158.
47. *Id.* at 420, 478 A.2d at 1160.
48. *Id.* at 421, 478 A.2d at 1161.
49. See chapter two for a discussion of the factors that should be considered in assessing society's evolving standards of decency.
50. Trimble v. State, 300 Md. at 428, 478 A.2d at 1164.
51. 455 So.2d 713 (Miss. 1984).
52. *Id.* at 725.
53. 667 S.W.2d 671 (Ky. 1984).
54. 435 So.2d 644 (Miss. 1983) (Hawkins, J., dissenting).
55. *Id.* at 672.
56. *Id.* at 674.

57. 132 Ariz. 248, 645 P.2d 239 (1982).

58. State v. Valencia, 121 Ariz. 191, 589 P.2d 434 (1979); State v. Valencia, 124 Ariz. 139, 602 P.2d 807 (1979); and State v. Valencia, 132 Ariz. 248, 645 P.2d 239 (1982).

59. State v. Valencia, 132 Ariz. at 250, 645 P.2d at 242.

60. *Id.* at 249, 645 P.2d at 241.

61. 428 So.2d 649 (Fla. 1983), *cert. denied*, 104 S. Ct. 198 (1983).

62. On Oct. 1, 1986, Florida had 247 persons on death row. NAACP LEGAL DEFENSE AND EDUCATIONAL FUND, INC., DEATH ROW, U.S.A. 9-11 (Oct. 1, 1986).

63. Magill v. State, 428 So.2d at 654 (Boyd, J., dissenting).

64. 682 P.2d 1384 (Nev. 1984). Nevada's minimum age for capital punishment is sixteen, and defendant Harvey was sixteen at the time of his robbery and murder. See NEV. REV. STAT. sec. 176.025 (1979).

65. See *supra* note 34.

66. See *supra* note 2.

4. JUVENILE EXECUTIONS, 1642 TO 1986

Information in this chapter is based in part on the author's article "Death Penalty for Children: The American Experience with Capital Punishment for Crimes Committed while under Age Eighteen," 36 OKLA. L. REV. 613 (1983). The data presented and analyzed herein are refined and updated from those presented in that article.

1. W. BOWERS, LEGAL HOMICIDE 45 (1984). Espy, "15,000 Confirmed Executions in America since Colonial Times: An Historical Data-Base" (Paper presented at the Annual Meeting of the American Society of Criminology, Atlanta, Oct. 30, 1986).

2. N. TEETERS & J. HEDBLOM " . . . HANG BY THE NECK . . . " 111 (1967). Chapter five, *infra*, provides a detailed description of the Graunger case.

3. N.Y. Times, May 16, 1986, at 11, col. 1.

4. See chapter six for a detailed description of the Pinkerton case.

5. BOWERS, *supra* note 1, at 53-57.

6. James Echols was executed on May 7, 1964, and Charles Rumbaugh on Sept. 11, 1985. See chapter six for detailed descriptions of these cases.

7. See chapter ten for a more complete exploration of this hypothesis.

8. See chapter five for a detailed description of the Arcene case.

9. Florida executed Fortune Ferguson on Apr. 27, 1927, for a rape committed when he was only thirteen years old. See chapter five for a detailed description of this case.

10. 4 W. BLACKSTONE, COMMENTARIES ON THE LAW OF ENGLAND 23-24 (1792); 1 M. HALE, PLEAS OF THE CROWN 25-28 (1682); In re Gault, 387 U.S. 1, 16 (1967).

11. See chapter nine and table 9-4 for detailed descriptions of the cases of Janice Buttrum in Georgia and Paula Cooper in Indiana.

12. See the appendix and chapter five for further information about these cases.

13. BOWERS, *supra* note 1, at 74.

14. *Id.* at 355-58. A recent case dealing with this issue is McClesky v. Kemp, 753 F.2d 877 (11th Cir. 1985), which was to be decided by the U.S. Supreme Court during its 1986-1987 term; the court heard oral argument on Oct. 15, 1986. N.Y. Times, Oct.16, 1986, at 15, col. 1.

15. See BOWERS, *supra* note 1, at 407-17.

16. See chapter seven for detailed descriptions of the Ohio cases.

17. TEX. PENAL CODE ANN. sec. 8.07 (d) (Vernon Supp. 1985).

18. See the appendix.

5. EARLY CASE STUDIES, 1642 TO 1930

1. Sources of information for the Graunger case are II Plymouth Colony Records 44 (1742); W. Bradford, Bradford's History of Plymouth Plantation, 1606-1646 474 (W. Davis ed. 1908); and N. Teeters & J. Hedblom," . . . Hang by the Neck" 111 (1967).

2. Sources of information about the Battin case are N.Teeters & J. Hedblom, *supra* note 1, at 84; and American Weekly Mercury (Philadelphia), Aug. 16-23, 1722, at 2, col. 2.

3. American Weekly Mercury, *supra* note 2, at 3, col. 1.

4. *Id.* at 3, col. 2.

5. *Id.*

6. Sources of information for the Ocuish case are J. Bolles, Genealogy of the Bolles Family 12 (1865); F. Caulkins, History of New London, Connecticut 576 (1895); Juvenile Offenders for a Thousand Years 320 (W. Sanders ed. 1970); T. McDade, The Annals of Murder 720 (1961); J. Nash, Murder, America 312 (1980); N. Teeters & J. Hedblom, *supra* note 1, at 16-17; J. Nash, Blood Letters and Bad Men 418 (1973); Channing, "God Admonishing his People of their Duty, as Parents and Masters. A Sermon, Preached at New London, December 20th, 1786, Occasioned by the Execution of Hannah Ocuish, a Mulatto Girl, Aged 12 Years and 9 Months. For the Murder of Eunice Bolles, Aged 6 years and 6 Months" (1786) (Pamphlet published in New London, Conn., by T. Green); Connecticut Gazette and Universal Intelligencer (New London), Oct. 20, 1786, at 2, col. 1, Oct. 13, 1786, at 3, col. 1, and July 28, 1786, at 3, col. 2; and Interview with Elizabeth B. Knox, Secretary and Curator of the New London County Historical Society, in New London (Aug. 15, 1985).

7. F. Caulkins, *supra* note 6.

8. Connecticut Gazette and Universal Intelligencer, Oct. 20, 1786, at 2, col. 1.

9. *Id.*

10. F. Caulkins, *supra* note 6, at 576-77.

11. Connecticut Gazette and Universal Intelligencer, *supra* note 8.

12. *Id.* at 2, col. 2.

13. Juvenile Offenders for a Thousand Years, *supra* note 6, at 323.

14. Channing, *supra* note 6, at 5.

15. Sources of information for the Clem case are Commonwealth v. Hartwell Seat's Clem (1787) (Deposition of Clem taken by Col. David Mason, Coroner, and Report of Corner's Inquisition, Apr. 14, 1787, at the Plantation of Hartwell Seat in Sussex County, Loose Court Papers of Sussex County, Va., 1754-1870, and Order Book, Court of Oyer and Terminer, Sussex County, 1754-1801, at 46); Letter from Watt Espy, University of Alabama, to Victor L. Streib (Oct. 15, 1984); and Letter from Gary M. Williams, Clerk, Circuit Court of Sussex County, Va., to Espy (Oct. 11, 1984).

16. Sources of information for the Guild case are State v. Guild, 10 N.J.L. Rep. 163 (1828); J. Snell, History of Hunterdon and Somerset Counties, New Jersey 200 (1881); J. Lequear, The Tradition of Hunterdon: A History of the County 75 (1957); N.Teeters & J. Hedblom, *supra* note 1, at 15; and Bag, "A Tragic New Jersey Case," 24 N.J.L.J. 681 (Oct. 1901).

17. Bag, *supra* note 16.

18. *Id.*

19. State v. Guild, 10 N.J.L. Rep. at 167.

20. *Id.* at 170

21. Sources of information for the Godfrey case are Godfrey v. State, 31 Ala. 323 (1858), and Mobile (Ala.) Daily Register, July 17, 1858.

22. Sources of information for the Dodd case are B. Wright, Burials and Deaths Reported in the Columbus (Georgia) Enquirer, 1832-1872, 127 (1984); Parham,

"David O. Dodd: The Nathan Hale of Arkansas," in Collection of Papers by the Arkansas Historical Association, Vol. II, 531 (J. Reynolds ed. 1908), first published in Benton (Ark.) Times Courier, Jan. 18, 1906, and Columbus (Ga.) Enquirer, Mar. 16, 1864.

23. Parham, *supra* note 22, at 533.

24. *Id.*

25. *Id.*

26. Sources of information for the Eliza case are Commonwealth v. Eliza, Henry County, Ky. (Arraignment Entry in Transcript, Circuit Court Book No. 22, at 39, Sept. 5, 1867; Defense Motion for New Trial, Sept. 6, 1867; Indictment for Murder, Grand Jury of Henry County, Sept. 4, 1867; Order for Extra Jail Guards, Book No. 11, at 630, Feb. 5, 1868; Preliminary Hearing Transcript, Aug. 16, 1867; Sentencing Entry in Transcript, Book No. 22, Sept. 30, 1867; and Verdict Entry in Transcript, Book No. 22, Sept. 6, 1867); Louisville (Ky.) Daily Courier, Feb. 9, 1868, at 2, col. 3; and N.Y. Times, Feb. 14, 1868, at 6, col. 1.

27. Louisville Daily Courier, *supra* note 26.

28. Sources of information for the Nuana case are D. RICHARDSON, PIG ISLAND WAR 159 (1971); Herberg, "Kanaka Joe," 48 (4) Frontier Times 32 (June-July 1974); Paterson, "Did They Get the San Juan Killer?" Western Frontier 26 (Mar. 1976); and Olympia (Wash.) Transcript, Mar. 14, 1874, at 2.

29. D. RICHARDSON, *supra* note 28, at 173.

30. *Id.* at 161.

31. Paterson, *supra* note 28, at 49.

32. Olympia Transcript, *supra* note 28.

33. Sources of information for the Arcene case are G. SHIRLEY, LAW WEST OF FORT SMITH 218 (1968); Daily Arkansas Gazette (Little Rock), June 27, 1885, at 3, col. 1, and Mar. 29, 1885, at 1, col. 4; and Galveston (Tex.) Daily News, June 27, 1885.

34. Sources of information for the Deacons case are People v. Deacons, 109 N.Y. 374, 16 N.E. 676 (1888); Galveston (Tex.) Daily News, July 11, 1888; and Union and Advertiser (Rochester, N.Y.), July 10, 1888.

35. Galveston Daily News, *supra* note 34.

36. Sources of information for the Beard case are N. TEETERS & J. HEDBLOM, *supra* note 1, at 18; Birmingham (Ala.) News, Dec. 22,1897, Dec. 18, 1897, Dec. 10, 1897, and Nov.5, 1897; and Letter from Madge D. Barefield, Executive Secretary, Birmingham Historical Society, to Victor L. Streib (Aug. 3, 1985).

37. Sources of information for the Gibson case are Gibson v. State, 53 Tex. Cr. R. 349, 110 S.W. 41 (1908); W. STERLING, TRAILS AND TRIALS OF A TEXAS RANGER 340 (1959); Old West, Winter 1970, at 91; Galveston (Tex.) News, June 29, 1908, at 1, col.7; and Letter from Maurice S. Shelby, Historian, Jackson County Historical Society, Edna, Tex., to Watt Espy, University of Alabama (Apr. 25, 1975).

38. STERLING *supra* note 37, at 342.

39. Gibson v. State, 110 S.W. at 51.

40. Sources of information for the Hanchett case are Transcript of Record of Proceedings in the Circuit Court of Volusia County, Fla., State v. Hanchett (Indictment, Apr. 6, 1910; Arraignment, Apr. 8, 1910; Trial Transcript, Apr. 8-9, 1910; Jury Charge, Apr. 9, 1910; Verdict, Apr. 11, 1910; Sentence, Apr. 11, 1910); Death Warrant for Irving Hanchett, signed by Gov. Gilchrist on Apr. 22, 1910, and executed by Sheriff Smith on May 6, 1910; Journal (Atlanta, Ga.), May 7, 1910, at 4, col. 5; and Times-Union (Jacksonville, Fla.), May 7, 1910, at 1, col. 1.

41. Transcript of Record, *supra* note 40, at 99 (Trial Transcript).

42. Times-Union, *supra* note 40.

43. Transcript of Record, *supra* note 40, at 109 (Sentence).

44. Times-Union, *supra* note 40.

45. *Id.*

46. Sources of information for the Christian case are W. BOWERS, LEGAL HOMICIDE

515 (1984), and "Christian Virginia vs. Virginia Christian," NAACP, THE CRISIS: A RECORD OF THE DARKER RACES, Sept. 1912, Vol. 3 (11), at 237.

47. NAACP, THE CRISIS, *supra* note 46, at 238.

48. *Id.* at 239.

49. VA. CODE ANN. sec. 16.1-269(A) (1982) (minimum age of fifteen for adult criminal court jurisdiction and the death penalty).

50. Sources of information for the Martinez case are Martinez v. State, 232 U.S. 714 (1914); Ex Parte Martinez, 66 Tex. Crim. 1, 145 S.W. 959 (1912); and A. HUGHES, PECOS: A HISTORY OF THE PIONEER WEST 193 (1978).

51. A. HUGHES, *supra* note 50.

52. Ex Parte Martinez, 66 Tex. Crim. at 16, 145 S.W. at 974.

53. A. HUGHES, *supra* note 50, at 973.

54. Ex Parte Martinez, 66 Tex. Crim. at 62, 145 S.W. at 1020.

55. Sources of information for the Oxnam case are People v. Oxnam, 170 Cal. 211, 149 P. 165 (1915); W. BOWERS, *supra* note 46, at 411; and Los Angeles Daily Times, Mar. 4, 1916, and Mar. 3, 1916, at 9, col. 5.

56. Los Angeles Daily Times, Mar. 3, 1916, at 9, col. 5.

57. People v. Oxnam, 170 Cal. 212, 149 P. 166.

58. Los Angeles Daily Times, Mar. 4, 1916.

59. Sources of information for the Ferguson case are Ferguson v. Florida, 273 U.S. 663 (1927); Ferguson v. State, 105 So. 840 (Fla. 1925); Death Warrant for Fortune Ferguson, signed on Apr. 13, 1927, and executed on Apr. 27, 1927; Mandate from the Supreme Court of Florida to the Judge of the Circuit Court for the Eighth Judicial Circuit (Nov. 23, 1925); Transcript of Proceedings, Circuit Court of the Eighth Judicial Circuit of the State of Florida for Alachua County, State of Florida v. Fortune Ferguson, Jr. (Indictment, June 9, 1924; Arraignment, June 11, 1924; Order Appointing Defense Counsel, June 16, 1924; Verdict, June 16, 1924; Judgment and Sentence, June 16, 1924); W. BOWERS, *supra* note 46, at 424; and Letters from Helen Cubberly Ellerbe, Alachua County Historical Commission, Gainesville, Fla., to Victor L. Streib (Jan. 25, 1985, and Oct. 22, 1984).

6. RECENT CASE STUDIES, 1930 TO 1986

1. Sources of information for the Hernandez case are Hernandez v. State, 32 P.2d 18 (1934); W. BOWERS, LEGAL HOMICIDE 402 (1984); Los Angeles Times, May 17, 1933, at 3, col. 6; and Times-Picayune (New Orleans), July 7, 1934, at 15, col. 4.

2. Hernandez v. State, 32 P.2d at 22.

3. *Id.*

4. Sources of information for the Hasty case are Hasty v. State, 162 So. 910 (Fla. 1935); Death Warrant for Monroe Hasty, signed on Sept. 10, 1935, and executed on Sept. 16, 1935; Indictment for Murder, State of Florida v. Monroe Hasty (July 18, 1934); Transcript of Record, Seventh Judicial Circuit Court in and for Volusia County, State of Florida v. Monroe Hasty (dated Nov. 4, 1934); and W. BOWERS, *supra* note 1, at 424.

5. Sources of information for the Whitfield case are Whitfield v. State, 236 Ala. 312, 182 So. 42 (Ala. 1938); W. BOWERS, *supra* note 1, at 400; Alabama Journal (Montgomery), Sept. 20, 1937, at 1, col. 4, Sept. 18, 1937, at 1, col. 6, and Sept. 17, 1937, at 1, col. 6; Birmingham (Ala.) News, Aug. 19, 1938, at 26, col. 4; and Montgomery (Ala.) Advertiser, Aug. 19, 1938, at 1, col. 6.

6. Montgomery Advertiser, *supra* note 5.

7. *Id.*

8. Sources of information for the Guariglia case are People v. Ertel, 283 N.Y. 519,

29 N.E.2d 70 (1940); People v. Guariglia, 279 N.Y. 707, 18 N.E.2d 324 (1938); W. BOWERS, *supra* note 1, at 468; R. ELLIOT, AGENT OF DEATH 171 (1940); and N.Y. Times, Jan. 27, 1939, at 42, col. 1, and Apr. 11, 1937, at 21, col. 1.

9. Sources of information for the Clay, Powell, and Walker cases are Clay v. State, 196 So. 462 (Fla. 1940); Death Warrants for Willie B. Clay, Edward Powell, and Nathaniel Walker, signed by Gov. Holland on Dec. 17, 1941, and executed by Prison Supt. Chapman on Dec. 29, 1941; Court Record, Circuit Court, Fourth Judicial Circuit of Florida, in and for Duval County, Fla., Spring Term, 1938, State of Florida vs. Willie B. Clay, Nathaniel Walker, and Edward Powell (Indictment, Oct. 18, 1938; Arraignment, Nov. 8, 1938; Jury Charge, undated; Jury Verdict, Dec. 8, 1938; Denial of Defense Motion for New Trial, Jan. 13, 1939; and Sentence, Jan. 13, 1939); W. BOWERS, *supra* note 1, at 425; and Florida Times-Union (Jacksonville), Dec. 30, 1941, Jan. 14, 1939, Dec. 9, 1938, and Aug. 8, 1938.

10. Clay v. State, 196 So. at 465.

11. Sources of information for the Burnam case are Burnam v. Commonwealth, 289 Ky. 312, 158 S.W.2d 131 (Ky. Ct. App. 1941); Burnam v. Commonwealth, 283 Ky. 361, 141 S.W.2d 282 (Ky. Ct. App. 1940); W. BOWERS, *supra* note 1, at 444; and Lexington (Ky.) Herald, Mar. 27, 1942, at 1, col. 2, Mar. 26, 1942, at 1, col. 7, Jan. 26, 1941, at 1, col. 2, Nov. 13, 1940, at 12, col. 8, Nov. 22, 1939, at 2, col. 4, June 6, 1939, at 12, col. 8, May 16, 1939, at 14, col. 1, Apr. 23, 1939, at 1, col. 2, Apr. 21, 1939, at 1, col. 8, Apr. 14, 1939, at 20, col. 1, Apr. 8, 1939, at 3, col. 7, and Apr. 7, 1939, at 1, col. 1.

12. Lexington Herald, Apr. 21, 1939, at 1, col. 8.

13. *Id.*

14. *Id.*, Mar. 27, 1942, at 1, col. 2.

15. Sources of information for the Giacomazza case are Commonwealth v. Giacomazza, 42 N.E.2d 506 (Mass. 1942); W. BOWERS, supra note 1, at 449; S. EHRMANN, FOR WHOM THE CHAIR WAITS 207 (1957); and Boston Globe, June 30, 1942, at 1, col. 4, June 29, 1942, at 20, col. 4, June 28, 1942, at 1, col. 3, June 25, 1942, June 23, 1942, at 14, col. 4, and Sept. 10, 1940, at 1, col. 2.

16. Sources of information for the Haight case are People v. Haight, 290 N.Y. 833, 50 N.E.2d 237 (1943); W. BOWERS, *supra* note 1, at 469; A. DEUTSCH, OUR REJECTED CHILDREN 200 (1950); Katonah (N.Y.) Record, July 29, 1943, Nov. 19, 1942, and Sept. 17, 1942; North Westchester (N.Y.) Times, Nov. 19, 1942, at 1, col. 3, Nov. 12, 1942, at 1, col. 3, Nov. 5, 1942, at 1, col. 1, Oct. 29, 1942, at 1, col. 6, Oct. 22, 1942, at 1, col. 2, and Sept. 24, 1942, at 1, col. 6; and Letter from Thomas McDade to Watt Espy, University of Alabama (June 27, 1978).

17. A. DEUTSCH, *supra* note 16, at 200.

18. North Westchester Times, Nov. 12, 1942, at 1, col. 3.

19. *Id.*, Nov. 29, 1942, at 1, col. 3.

20. Letter, *supra* note 16.

21. Sources of information for the Stinney case are Electrocution Record of George Stinney, Jr., South Carolina Penitentiary (June 16, 1944); W. BOWERS, *supra* note 1, at 500; N. TEETERS & J. HEDBLOM, ". . . HANG BY THE NECK . . ." 13 (1967); Bruck, "Executing Juveniles for Crime," N.Y. Times, June 16, 1984, at 17, col. 1; Bruck, "Executing Teen Killers Again," Washington Post, Sept. 15, 1985, sec. D, at 1, col. 1; Stout, "A Life for a Life, Even at Age 14," Sunday Record (Bergen/Passaic/Hudson Counties, N.J.), Mar. 28, 1982, sec. E, at 1, col. 1; Columbia (S.C.) Record, June 16, 1944, at 1, June 15, 1944, at 1, June 13, 1944, at 1, and Mar. 30, 1944, at 1; Manning (S.C.) Times, June 21, 1944, at 1, col. 5, Apr. 26, 1944, at 1, col. 5, Mar. 29, 1944, at 1, Mar. 27, 1944, at 1, and Mar. 25, 1944, at 1; News & Courier (Charleston, S.C.), Dec. 31, 1984, sec. 4, at 2, col. 4, June 17, 1944, at 1, col. 4, June 17, 1944, at 4, col. 1 (editorial), June 16, 1944, at 1, col. 1, Mar. 30, 1944, at 2, col. 1, Mar. 28, 1944, at 5, col. 4, and Mar. 26, 1944, at 1, col. 2; and State (Columbia, S.C.), June 17, 1944,

at 1, col. 2, June 14, 1944, at 2, col. 4, June 13, 1944, at 6, col. 3, June 12, 1944, at 2, col. 2, June 11, 1944, at 1, col. 6, June 10, 1944, at 1, col. 3, June 9, 1944, at 1, col. 1, June 8, 1944, at 11, col. 4, Mar. 30, 1944, at 1, col. 7, and Mar. 26, 1944, at 1, col. 4.

22. Bruck, N.Y. Times, *supra* note 21.

23. Stout, *supra* note 21.

24. State (Columbia, S.C.), June 14, 1944, at 2, col. 4 (Letter to the editor from Ensign Frank Williams, USNR).

25. *Id.* (Letter to the editor from Silas A. Frick, Sr.).

26. Columbia Record, June 16, 1944, at 1, col. 1.

27. Sunday Record, *supra* note 21.

28. *Id.*

29. *Id.*

30. Sources of information for the Loveless case are State v. Loveless, 150 P.2d 1015 (Nev. 1944); State v. Loveless, 62 Nev. 17, 36 P.2d 236 (Nev. 1943); W. BOWERS, *supra* note 1, at 452; and Elko (Nev.) Daily Press, Oct. 2, 1944, at 1, col. 3, Sept. 29, 1944, at 1, col. 1, Sept. 26, 1944, at 1, col. 5, Aug. 24, 1942, at 1, col. 8, Aug. 21, 1942, at 1, col. 8, and Aug. 20, 1942, at 1, col. 8.

31. State v. Loveless, 150 P.2d at 1019.

32. Elko Daily Press, Aug. 24, 1942 (editorial).

33. *Id.*, Sept. 29, 1944, at 1, col. 1.

34. Sources of information for the Francis case are State ex rel. Francis v. Resweber, 212 La. 143, 31 So.2d 697 (1947); B. PRETTYMAN, JR., DEATH AND THE SUPREME COURT 83 (1961); M. MELTSNER, CRUEL AND UNUSUAL: THE SUPREME COURT AND CAPITAL PUNISHMENT 177–178 (1973); Pittsburgh (Pa.) Courier, May 17, 1947; and Weekly Messenger (St. Martinsville, La.), May 9, 1947, at 1, col. 6, May 2, 1947, at 1, col. 1, Apr. 25, 1947, Apr. 18, 1947, Apr. 11, 1947, Jan. 17, 1947, at 1, col. 6, June 14, 1946, at 1, col. 6, May 10, 1946, at 1, col. 4, Sept. 14, 1945, at 1, col. 6, Aug. 10, 1945, at 1, col. 6, Nov. 17, 1944, at 6, col. 2, and Nov. 10, 1944, at 1, col. 3.

35. Weekly Messenger, May 10, 1946, at 1, col. 4.

36. *Id.*

37. *Id.*, June 14, 1946, at 1, col. 6.

38. *Id.*, May 10, 1946, at 1, col. 4.

39. *Id.*, May 9, 1947, at 1, col. 6.

40. Sources of information for the Lewis and Trudell cases are Lewis v. Mississippi and Trudell v. Mississippi, 331 U.S. 785 (1947); Lewis v. State, 28 So.2d 122 (Miss. 1946); Trudell v. State, 28 So.2d 124 (Miss. 1946); Catholic Action (Natchez, Miss.), July 31, 1947; Clarion (Miss.) Ledger, Jan. 5, 1947; Jackson (Miss.) Daily News, June 14, 1947, June 9, 1947, Jan. 15, 1947, and Dec. 10, 1946; Tribune (Berkeley, Cal.), Jan. 4, 1947, at 1, col. 1; and Woodville (Miss.) Republican, July 25, 1947, at 1, col. 6, June 6, 1947, at 1, col. 4, Mar. 21, 1947, at 1, col. 4, Jan. 17, 1947, at 1, col. 7, and Nov. 15, 1946, at 1, col. 6.

41. Trudell v. State, 28 So.2d at 124–25.

42. Lewis v. State, 28 So.2d at 123.

43. *Id.* at 124.

44. Catholic Action, *supra* note 40.

45. *Id.*

46. Clarion Ledger, *supra* note 40.

47. Sources of information for the Jackson and Miller cases are Jackson v. Balkcom, 210 Ga. 412, 80 S.E.2d 319 (1954); Miller v. Balkcom, 210 Ga. 415, 80 S.E.2d 321 (1954); W. BOWERS, *supra* note 1, at 434; Milledgeville (Ga.) Union Recorder, June 17, 1954; and Letter from Dr. James C. Bonner, Milledgeville, Ga., to Watt Espy, University of Alabama (Jan. 3, 1977).

48. Sources of information for the Byers case are People v. Byers, 309 N.Y. 908,

131 N.E.2d 580 (1955); W. BOWERS, *supra* note 1, at 471; F. LIPSIG, MURDER—FAMILY STYLE 147 (1962); and N.Y. Times, Jan. 13, 1956, at 7, col. 4.

49. F. LIPSIG, *supra* note 48, at 150.

50. *Id.* at 153.

51. *Id.* at 154.

52. *Id.* at 156.

53. *Id.* at 158.

54. Sources of information for the Shockley case are Shockley v. State, 218 Md. 491, 148 A.2d 371 (1959); W. BOWERS, supra note 1, at 448; and Sun (Baltimore), Apr. 11, 1959, at 22, col. 3, Apr. 9, 1958, at 38, col. 3, Apr. 8, 1958, at 10, col. 5, and Jan. 17, 1958, at 34, col. 1.

55. Sources of information for the Echols case are Echols v. State, 370 S.W.2d 892 (Tex. 1963); W. BOWERS, *supra* note 1, at 512; and Houston (Tex.) Post, May 7, 1964, sec. 5, at 16, col. 1, April 27, 1964, and April 7, 1964.

56. Echols v. State, 370 S.W.2d at 893.

57. Houston Post, May 7, 1964, sec. 5, at 16, col. 1.

58. *Id.*

59. *Id.*

60. Sources of information for the Rumbaugh case are Rumbaugh v. McCotter, 105 S.Ct. 3544 (1985); Rumbaugh v. Procunier, 753 F.2d 395 (5th Cir. 1985); Rumbaugh v. State, 629 S.W.2d 747 (Tex. Ct. Crim. App., 1982); Rumbaugh v. State, 589 S.W.2d 414 (Tex. Ct. Crim. App., 1979); D. STUBBEN, #555 DEATH ROW (1980); Cox, "Crime Rampage of the Trigger-Happy Texas Killer," True Detective, Jan. 1979, at 37; Brasfield, " 'I Had Wanted to Tell Charles Rumbaugh Goodbye,' " National Catholic Reporter, Nov. 8, 1985, at 12, col. 1; Drinan, "Too Young to Die, Even by Execution," National Catholic Reporter, Nov. 8, 1985, at 13, col. 4; National Catholic Reporter, Nov. 8, 1985, at 11, col. 4, at 12, col. 1, at 13, col. 1 (editorial), at 16, col. 1, and at 18, col. 2; N.Y. Times, Sept. 15, 1985, sec. E, at 6, col. 4 (editorial), Sept. 12, 1985, at 11, col. 4, Sept. 11, 1985, at 12, col. 6, Sept. 10, 1985, at 8, col. 1, and Sept. 5, 1985, at 12, col. 4; and Plain Dealer (Cleveland, Ohio), Sept. 12, 1985, sec. A, at 26, col. 1 (editorial).

61. D. STUBBEN, *supra* note 60, at 212.

62. *Id.* at 209.

63. N.Y. Times, Sept. 11, 1985, at 12, col. 6.

64. Cox, *supra* note 60, at 80.

65. *Id.*

66. Rumbaugh v. State, 589 S.W.2d at 419.

67. D. STUBBEN, *supra* note 60, at 215 (Letter written by Rumbaugh on Oct. 20, 1978).

68. N.Y. Times, Sept. 10, 1985, at 8, col. 1.

69. Rumbaugh v. Procunier, 753 F.2d at 397.

70. National Catholic Reporter, Nov. 8, 1985, at 16, col. 1 (Letter written by Rumbaugh on Jan. 10, 1984).

71. N.Y. Times, Sept. 10, 1985, at 8, col. 1.

72. Plain Dealer, *supra* note 60.

73. National Catholic Reporter, Nov. 8, 1985, at 16, col. 1.

74. Cox, *supra* note 60, at 80.

75. Plain Dealer, *supra* note 60.

76. National Catholic Reporter, Nov. 8, 1985, at 16, col. 1.

77. Sources of information for the Roach case are Roach v. Aiken, 106 S.Ct. 645 (1986); Roach v. South Carolina, 444 U.S. 1026 (1980); Roach v. Martin, 757 F.2d 1463 (4th Cir. 1985); In re Brooks, 267 S.E.2d 74 (S.Car. 1980); State v. Shaw, 255 S.E.2d 799 (S.Car. 1979); McCarthy, "A Last Talk with a Condemned Man," Washington Post, Jan. 13, 1986; A.B.A.J., March 1986, at 26, col. 1; Newsweek, Jan. 13, 1986, at 74, col. 2; Time, Jan. 20, 1986, at 22, col. 1; N.Y. Times, Jan. 11, 1986, at 7, col. 1, Jan. 10,

1986, at 8, col. 6, and Jan. 9, 1986, at 22, col. 1 (editorial); Plain Dealer (Cleveland), Jan. 11, 1986, sec. A, at 6, col. 1, and Jan. 10, 1986, sec. A, at 5, col. 1; and Statement of David Bruck concerning the Execution of Americans for Crimes Committed while under the Age of Eighteen (June 5, 1986) (Testimony before the Subcommittee on Criminal Justice, Committee on the Judiciary, U.S. House of Representatives, 99th Cong. 2d Sess.).

78. Roach v. Aiken, 106 S.Ct. at 647 (Marshall, J., dissenting).

79. McCarthy, *supra* note 77.

80. *Id.*

81. Time, *supra* note 77.

82. N.Y. Times, Jan. 11, 1986, at 7, col. 1.

83. Time, *supra* note 77.

84. N.Y. Times, *supra* note 82.

85. Statement of David Bruck, *supra* note 77.

86. Sources of information for the Pinkerton case are Pinkerton v. McCotter, 106 S.Ct. 400 (1985); Pinkerton v. McCotter, 106 S.Ct. 16 (1985); Pinkerton v. State, 660 S.W.2d 58 (Tex. Ct. Crim. App. 1983); Cox, "The Most Hideous Murder in Texas History," True Detective, Dec. 1981, at 30; and N.Y. Times, May 16, 1986, at 11, col. 1, May 15, 1986, at 11, col. 6, Nov. 26, 1985, at 8, col. 6, Aug. 16, 1985, at 8, col. 6, and Aug. 15, 1985, at 10, col. 6.

87. Cox, *supra* note 86.

88. N.Y. Times, May 16, 1986, at 11, col. 1.

89. *Id.*

90. *Id.*

7. ONE STATE'S EXPERIENCE

Information in this chapter is based largely on the author's article "Capital Punishment for Children in Ohio: 'They'd Never Send a Boy of Seventeen to the Chair in Ohio, Would They?' " 18 AKRON L. REV. 51 (1984).

1. W. BOWERS, LEGAL HOMICIDE 54 and 479–86 (1984), and NAACP LEGAL DEFENSE AND EDUCATIONAL FUND, INC., DEATH ROW, U.S.A. 4 (Aug. 1, 1986). These data begin with 1885, the start of state-imposed executions in Ohio, and not with 1803, the attainment of Ohio statehood.

2. Streib, "Death Penalty for Children: The American Experience with Capital Punishment for Crimes Committed while under Age Eighteen," 36 OKLA. L. REV. 613, 626 (1983); and chapter four, *supra.*

3. 2 LAWS OF OHIO 1–2 (1804–05).

4. 13 LAWS OF OHIO 86 (1815).

5. LANNING'S 1905 REVISED STATUTES OF 1880, sec. 1040 (enacted Apr. 23, 1898).

6. Clark v. State, 12 Ohio 483, 131 N.E. 706 (1843).

7. State v. Strong, 12 Ohio Dec. 698, 715 (Cuyahoga Common Pleas Court, 1902).

8. Juvenile Court Act, OHIO REV. CODE ANN. sec. 1639 et seq. (Page 1982).

9. See Akers v. State, 8 Ohio Abst. 106 (1929), and Gerak v. State, 22 Ohio App. 257, 153 N.E. 902 (1920).

10. OHIO REV. CODE ANN. sec. 2929.01 (Page 1975). This statute and the legislative process leading up to it are discussed in Comment, "Capital Punishment in Ohio: The Constitutionality of the Death Penalty Statute," 3 U. DAY. L. REV. 169 (1978); Comment, "The Constitutionality of Ohio's Death Penalty," 3 OHIO ST. L. REV. 617 (1977); and Comment, "Legislative Response to Furman v. Georgia—Ohio Restores the Death Penalty," 8 AKRON L. REV. 149 (1974).

11. Lockett v. Ohio, 438 U.S. 586 (1978).

12. Bell v. Ohio, 438 U.S. 637 (1978).

13. State v. Bell, 48 Ohio 2d 270, 358 N.E.2d 556 (1976).

14. Ohio Rev. Code Ann. sec. 2929.02 (Page 1982).

15. "If the offender . . . was not found at trial to have been eighteen years of age or older at the time of the offense, the court . . . shall not impose a sentence of death on the offender." Ohio Rev. Code Ann. sec. 2929.03(E) (Page 1982).

16. Benson, "Constitutionality of Ohio's New Death Penalty Statute," 14 Tol. L. Rev. 77, 89 (1982).

17. Telephone interview with State Sen. Richard Finan, Columbus, Ohio (May 26, 1983). These are Finan's recollections of discussions and considerations that occurred in committee before the bill was passed by the State Senate. Ohio has no written record of such legislative history.

18. NAACP Legal Defense and Educational Fund, Inc., Death Row, U.S.A. 17 (Oct. 1, 1986).

19. Sources of information for the Mann case are J. Artzner, The Black Minute (1981) (a detailed but somewhat fictionalized account of this triple hanging); Plain Dealer (Cleveland), Apr. 4, 1976, at 2, col. 1; and Cleveland Plain Dealer, June 26, 1880, at 1, col. 6, and June 24, 1880, at 1, col. 5.

20. Sources of information for the Ohr case are the same as those for Mann, *supra* note 19.

21. Sources of information for the Sammett case are the same as those for Mann, *supra* note 19.

22. Sources of information for the Leuth case are W. Bowers, *supra* note 1, at 480; H. Fogle, The Palace of Death 49–55 (1909); and Cleveland Plain Dealer, Aug. 29, 1890, at 1, col. 4, Dec. 28, 1889, at 8, col. 1, Dec. 27, 1889, at 4, col. 6, Dec. 25, 1889, at 6, col. 5, Dec. 24, 1889, at 6, col. 5, Dec. 20, 1889, at 6, col. 5, Dec. 19, 1889, at 6, col. 5, Dec. 17, 1889, at 6, col. 5, Dec. 15, 1889, at 8, col. 1, Dec. 13, 1889, at 6, col. 3, Dec. 12, 1889, at 6, col. 5, Dec. 11, 1889, at 6, col. 4, Dec. 10, 1889, at 6, col. 1, Dec. 3, 1889, at 6, col. 1, June 19, 1889, at 6, col. 3, June 16, 1889, at 5, col. 1, June 15, 1889, at 8, col. 1, June 12, 1889, at 6, col. 5, June 11, 1889, at 6, col. 5, and June 10, 1889, at 1, col. 2.

23. Cleveland Plain Dealer, Dec. 25, 1889, at 6, col. 5 (Statement by Leuth's defense attorney during closing argument to the jury).

24. H. Fogle, *supra* note 22, at 53.

25. Sources of information for the Taylor case are W. Bowers, *supra* note 1, at 480; H. Fogle, *supra* note 22, at 121–23; Cleveland Plain Dealer, July 26, 1895, at 1, col. 3; and Columbus Dispatch, Dec. 31, 1894, at 7, col. 3, Dec. 29, 1894, at 6, col. 1, Dec. 22, 1894, at 7, col. 4, and Dec. 21, 1894, at 7, col. 3.

26. Sources of information for the Haas case are W. Bowers, *supra* note 1, at 480; H. Fogle, *supra* note 22, at 135–42; Bean, "Old Thunderbolt: Farm Boy Was the First Victim of Ohio's Electric Chair," Plain Dealer (Cleveland), Mar. 8, 1981, at 25, col. 2; Cleveland Plain Dealer, Apr. 21, 1897, at 1, col. 3, and July 5, 1896, at 9, col. 3; Cleveland Press, Apr. 20, 1897, at 1, col. 6; and Enquirer (Cincinnati), Apr. 21, 1897, at 12, col. 1.

27. H. Fogle, *supra* note 22, at 135.

28. This phrase was part of the headline of an article written almost eighty-four years after the execution of Haas; Bean, *supra* note 26.

29. Sources of information for the Beard case are W. Bowers, *supra* note 1, at 481; Cleveland Plain Dealer, Dec. 14, 1914, at 13, col. 5, and, May 16, 1914, at 1, col. 2; and Portsmouth Daily Times, Dec. 4, 1914, at 1, col. 5.

30. Portsmouth Daily Times, *supra* note 29.

31. Sources of information for the Pupera case are W. Bowers, *supra* note 1, at 481; and Cleveland Plain Dealer, May 10, 1922, at 6, col. 2, May 20, 1921, at 1, col. 7, May 19, 1921, at 1, col. 6, May 18, 1921, at 1, col. 5, May 17, 1921, at 1, col. 3,

May 16, 1921, at 1, col. 2, May 8, 1921, at 1, col. 2, May 2, 1921, at 1, col. 1, Mar. 28, 1921, at 1, col. 6, Mar. 26, 1921, at 1, col. 1, Mar. 17, 1921, at 1, col. 8, and Jan. 1, 1921, at 1, col. 1.

32. Cleveland Plain Dealer, Mar. 26, 1921, at 1, col. 1

33. Sources of information for the Ross case are Ross v. State, 22 Ohio App. 304, 153 N.E. 865 (Ct. App. 1926); W. BOWERS, *supra* note 1, at 482; and Cleveland Plain Dealer, Nov. 26, 1926, at 1, col. 2, Nov. 25, 1926, at 1, col. 4, Nov. 17, 1926, at 18, col. 1, Sept. 10, 1926, at 1, col. 8, Sept. 9, 1926, at 5, col. 7, Sept. 2, 1926, at 3, col. 2, Aug. 29, 1926, at 2, col. 2, Aug. 28, 1926, at 1, col. 3, Aug. 26, 1926, at 1, col. 3, Aug. 24, 1926, at 5, col. 6, July 2, 1926, at 3, col. 2, June 3, 1926, at 6, col. 1, Jan. 20, 1926, at 5, col. 6, Jan. 15, 1926, at 1, col. 8, Jan. 10, 1926, sec. A, at 4, col. 4, Nov. 20, 1925, at 1, col. 1, and Nov. 6, 1925, at 1, col. 1.

34. Sources of information for the Hewitt case are W. BOWERS, *supra* note 1, at 482; and Cleveland Plain Dealer, Jan. 7, 1928, at 1, col. 1, Jan. 6, 1928, at 1, col. 7, Jan. 5, 1928, at 8, col. 3, July 7, 1927, at 3, col. 3, Apr. 27, 1927, at 1, col. 1, Apr. 21, 1927, at 4, col. 5, Apr. 16, 1927, at 3, col. 3, Apr. 14, 1927, at 7, col. 5, Apr. 7, 1927, at 2, col. 3, Apr. 5, 1927, at 2, col. 1, Feb. 18, 1927, at 3, col. 5, Feb. 17, 1927, at 3, col. 1, and Feb. 16, 1927, at 1, col. 3.

35. Sources of information for the Coverson case are Coverson v. State, 27 Ohio App. 166 (Ct. App. 1927); W. BOWERS, *supra* note 1, at 482; Cleveland Plain Dealer, Jan. 10, 128, at 1, col. 1; and Enquirer (Cincinnati), Jan. 10, 1928, at 22, col. 3.

36. Coverson v. State, 27 Ohio App. at 167.

37. Sources of information for the Coleman case are W. BOWERS, *supra* note 1, at 483; Cleveland Press, July 6, 1928, sec. 2, at 1, col. 5; and Portsmouth Daily Times, July 6, 1928, at 2, col. 1, July 5, 1928, at 2, col. 1, and Feb. 7, 1928, at 5, col. 1.

38. W. BOWERS, *supra* note 1, at 481–83.

39. Sources of information for the Akers case are Akers v. State, 8 Ohio Abs. 106 (1929); Juvenile Court Act, OHIO REV. CODE ANN. sec. 8–1639 et seq. (Throckmorton 1929); W. BOWERS, *supra* note 1, at 483; and Cleveland Plain Dealer, June 14, 1930, at 1, col. 7, Apr. 4, 1929, at 6, col. 3, Apr. 2, 1929, at 8, col. 5, Jan. 11, 1929, at 7, col. 1, Jan. 8, 1929, at 10, col. 1, Dec. 31, 1928, at 1, col. 4, Dec. 28, 1928, at 8, col. 2, and Dec. 27, 1928, at 1, col. 7.

40. Cleveland Plain Dealer, Jan. 8, 1929; at 10, col. 1.

41. *Id.*, Apr. 4, 1929, at 1, col. 3.

42. 'Sources of information for the Murphy case are W. BOWERS, *supra* note 1, at 483; Cleveland Plain Dealer, Aug. 15, 1933, at 2, col. 1; Cleveland Press, Aug. 15, 1933, at 10, col. 6; and Enquirer (Cincinnati), Aug. 15, 1933, at 1, col. 7, and July 15, 1933, at 20, col. 2.

43. Sources of information for the Young case are W. BOWERS, *supra* note 1, at 484; Cleveland Press, July 13, 1939, at 3, col. 3; and Enquirer (Cincinnati), July 13, 1939, at 10, col. 1.

44. Cleveland Press, *supra* note 43.

45. Sources of information for the Hand case are W. BOWERS, *supra* note 1, at 484; Cleveland Plain Dealer, Jan. 15, 1944, at 1 col. 4; and Greenville Daily Advocate, Jan. 15, 1944, at 1, col. 4.

46. Sources of information for the Hagert case are State v. Hagert, 58 N.E.2d 399 (Ohio Ct. App. 1944); State v. Hagert, 144 Ohio 316, 59 N.E.2d 764 (1944); W. BOWERS, *supra* note 1, at 485; and Cleveland Plain Dealer, Oct. 4, 1945, at 1, col. 3, Dec. 2, 1943, at 1, col. 1, Oct. 28, 1943, at 1, col. 1, Aug. 26, 1943, at 1, col. 2, Aug. 16, 1943, at 1, col. 8, Aug. 15, 1943, at 1, col. 5, and Aug. 14, 1943, at 1, col. 7.

47. Cleveland Plain Dealer, Aug. 14, 1943, at 1, col. 7, and at 3, col. 3.

48. Sources of information for the Frohner case are State v. Frohner, 150 Ohio 53 (1948); W. BOWERS, *supra* note 1, at 485; and Youngstown Vindicator, Aug. 21, 1948, at 1, col. 8, Aug. 19, 1948, at 1, col. 2, Feb. 29, 1947, at 1, col. 7, Feb. 25, 1947, at

1, col. 8, Jan. 18, 1947, at 1, col. 8, Jan. 17, 1947, at 1, col. 4, and Jan. 14, 1947, at 1, col. 6.

49. State v. Frohner, 150 Ohio at 69.

50. Sources of information for the Schreiber case are State v. Schreiber, 164 Ohio 389, 131 N.E.2d 396 (1955); W. BOWERS, *supra* note 1, at 486; Plain Dealer (Cleveland), Mar. 16, 1956, at 1, col. 3; and Toledo Blade, Mar. 16, 1956, at 1, col. 2, Mar. 15, 1956, at 1, col. 4, Jan. 12, 1955, at 1, col. 4, Jan. 10, 1955, at 1, col. 4, Aug. 20, 1954, at 1, col. 4, and Aug. 13, 1954, at 1, col. 4.

51. W. BOWERS, *supra* note 1, at 486.

52. Bell v. Ohio, 438 U.S. 637 (1978).

53. Furman V. Georgia, 408 U.S. 238 (1972).

54. See chapter three for more information about state laws.

55. *Id.*

8. JUVENILES' ATTITUDES
TOWARD IMPENDING EXECUTION

1. See chapter four for more information on these 281 executions.

2. For sources of information for the Ocuish case, see *supra* chapter five note 6.

3. For sources of information for the Guild case, see *supra* chapter five note 16.

4. For sources of information for the Stinney case, see *supra* chapter six note 21.

5. Columbia (S.C.) Record, June 16, 1944, at 1, col. 1.

6. Stout, "A Life for a Life, Even at Age 14," Sunday Record (Bergen/Pasaic/Hudson Counties, N.J.), Mar. 28, 1982, sec. E, at 1, col. 1.

7. For sources of information for the Lewis and Trudell cases, see *supra* chapter six note 40.

8. For sources of information for the Rumbaugh case, see *supra* chapter six note 60.

9. National Catholic Reporter, Nov. 8, 1985, at 16.

10. For sources of information for the Roach case, see *supra* chapter six note 77.

11. Roach v. Aiken, 106 S.Ct. 645, 647 (1986) (Marshall, J., dissenting).

12. Time, Jan. 20, 1986, at 22, col. 1.

13. For sources of information for the Nuana case, see *supra* chapter five note 28.

14. Paterson, "Did They Get the San Juan Killer?" Western Frontier 26 (March 1976).

15. For sources of information for the Coleman case, see *supra* chapter seven note 37.

16. *Supra* chapter six note 60.

17. D. STUBBEN, #555 DEATH ROW (1980), at 215.

18. National Catholic Reporter, Nov. 8, 1985, at 11–18.

19. *Id.* at 16.

20. *Supra* chapter five note 6.

21. JUVENILE OFFENDERS FOR A THOUSAND YEARS 323 (W. Sanders ed. 1970).

22. For sources of information for the Brad Beard case, see *supra* chapter five note 36.

23. For sources of information for the Oxnam case, see *supra* chapter five note 55.

24. Los Angeles Times, Mar. 4, 1916.

25. For sources of information about the Pupera case, see *supra* chapter seven note 31.

26. Cleveland Plain Dealer, Mar. 26, 1921, at 1, col. 1.

27. For sources of information for the Young case, see *supra* chapter seven note 43.

28. Cleveland Press, July 13, 1939, at 3, col. 3.

29. For sources of information for the Haight case, see *supra* chapter six note 16.

30. Letter from Thomas McDade to Watt Espy, University of Alabama (June 27, 1978).

31. *Supra* chapter six note 21.

32. Stout, *supra* note 6.

33. *Supra* chapter six note 77.

34. N.Y. Times, Jan. 11, 1986, at 7, col. 1.

35. McCarthy, "A Last Walk with a Condemned Man," Washington Post, Jan. 13, 1986.

36. For sources of information for the Dodd case, see *supra* chapter five note 22.

37. Parham, "David O. Dodd: The Nathan Hale of Arkansas," in Collection of Papers by the Arkansas Historical Association, Vol. II, 531 (J. Reynolds ed. 1908), first published in Benton (Ark.) Times Courier, Jan. 18, 1906.

38. For sources of information for the Deacons case, see *supra* chapter five note 34.

39. Galveston (Tex.) Daily News, July 11, 1888.

40. For sources of information for the Murphy case, see *supra* chapter seven note 42.

41. For sources of information for the Byers case, see *supra* chapter six note 48.

42. F. LIPSIG, MURDER—FAMILY STYLE 154 (1962).

43. *Id.* at 158.

44. *Supra* chapter six note 60.

45. Rumbaugh v. State, 589 S.W.2d 414, 419 (Tex. Crim. App. 1979).

46. Cox, "Crime Rampage of the Trigger-Happy Texas Killer," True Detective, Jan. 1979, at 37.

47. N.Y. Times, Sept. 12, 1985, sec. A, at 26, col. 1.

48. For sources of information for the Battin case, see *supra* chapter five note 2.

49. American Weekly Mercury (Philadelphia), Aug. 16–23, 1722, at 2, col. 2.

50. For sources of information for the Hernandez case, see *supra* chapter six note 1.

51. *Supra* chapter six note 21.

52. For sources of information for the Loveless case, see *supra* chapter six note 30.

53. Elko (Nev.) Daily Press, Sept. 29, 1944, at 1, col. 1.

54. For sources of information for the Echols case, see *supra* chapter six note 55.

55. Houston (Tex.) Post, May 7, 1964, sec. 5, at 16, col. 1.

56. *Supra* chapter six note 60.

57. N.Y. Times, Sept. 12, 1985, sec. A, at 26, col. 1.

58. *Supra* chapter six note 77.

59. N.Y. Times, Jan. 11, 1986, at 7, col. 1.

60. For sources of information for the Pinkerton case, see *supra* chapter six note 86.

61. N.Y. Times, May 16, 1986, at 11, col. 1.

62. *Id.*

63. *Id.*

64. *Supra* chapter five note 2.

65. American Weekly Mercury, *supra* note 49.

66. For sources of information for the Hanchett case, see *supra* chapter five note 40.

67. Times-Union (Jacksonville, Fla.), May 7, 1910, at 1, col. 1.

68. For sources of information for the Harley Beard case, see *supra* chapter seven note 29.

69. Portsmouth (Ohio) Daily Times, Dec. 4, 1914, at 1, col. 5.

70. For sources of information for the Whitfield case, see *supra* chapter six note 5.

71. Montgomery (Ala.) Advertiser, Aug. 19, 1938, at 1, col. 6.

72. For sources of information for the Francis case, see *supra* chapter six note 34.

73. Weekly Messenger (St. Martinsville, La.), May 10, 1946, at 1, col. 4.

74. *Id.*

75. *Supra* chapter six note 55.

76. Houston (Tex.) Post, *supra* note 55.

77. *Supra* chapter six note 77.

78. Statement of David Bruck, *supra* chapter six note 77.

9. JUVENILE DEATH SENTENCES IN THE 1980S

1. U.S. DEPARTMENT OF JUSTICE, CAPITAL PUNISHMENT 1984 16 (1986), and NAACP LEGAL DEFENSE AND EDUCATIONAL FUND, INC., DEATH ROW, U.S.A. (Dec. 20, 1981, through Oct. 1, 1986).

2. Sources of information for the Barrow case are Barrow v. State, 688 S.W.2d 860 (Tex. Crim. App. 1985), and information obtained from the files of the NAACP Legal Defense and Educational Fund, Inc., New York City, on Aug. 15, 1986. Information on all other cases discussed in this chapter also was obtained from the files of the NAACP Legal Defense and Educational Fund on that date.

3. Sources of information for the Cannon case are Cannon v. State, 691 S.W.2d 664 (Tex. Crim. App. 1985); Letter from Joseph J. Cannon to Victor L. Streib (Jan. 27, 1986); and the files of the NAACP Legal Defense and Educational Fund.

4. The source of information for the Carter case is the files of the NAACP Legal Defense and Educational Fund.

5. Sources of information for the Garrett case are Garrett v. State, 682 S.W.2d 301 (Tex. Crim. App. 1984), *cert. denied*, 105 S.Ct. 1876 (1985), and the files of the NAACP Legal Defense and Educational Fund.

6. Sources of information for the Johnson case are Johnson v. State, 303 Md. 487, 495 A.2d 1 (1985); Trimble v. State, 300 Md. 387, 478 A.2d 1143 (1984); Johnson v. State, 439 A.2d 542 (Md. 1982); Washington Post, Aug. 19, 1984, sec. A, at 1; and the files of the NAACP Legal Defense and Educational Fund.

7. Sources of information for the Lashley case are State v. Lashley, 667 S.W.2d 712 (Mo. 1984); Letter from Frederick Lashley to Victor L. Streib (July 9, 1986); and the files of the NAACP Legal Defense and Educational Fund.

8. Sources of information for the Legare case are Legare v. State, 250 Ga. 875, 302 S.E.2d 351 (1983); Legare v. State, 243 Ga. 744, 257 S.E.2d 247 (1979), *cert. denied*, 444 U.S. 984 (1979); and the files of the NAACP Legal Defense and Educational Fund.

9. The source of information for the Stanford case is the files of the NAACP Legal Defense and Educational Fund.

10. Sources of information for the Stokes case are State v. Stokes, 304 S.E.2d 184 (N.C. 1983), and the files of the NAACP Legal Defense and Educational Fund.

11. Sources of information for the Thompson case are Thompson v. State, 492 N.E.2d 264 (Ind. 1986), and the files of the NAACP Legal Defense and Educational Fund.

12. Sources of information for the Trimble case are Trimble v. State, 300 Md. 387, 478 A.2d 1143 (1984); N.Y. Times, Aug. 19, 1984, at 15, col. 5; Washington Post, Aug. 19, 1984, sec. A, at 1; Letter from James Trimble to Victor L. Streib (July 8, 1986); Letters from James Trimble to Denise Malasky, Cleveland State University (Apr. 22 and Apr. 9, 1985); and the files of the NAACP Legal Defense and Educational Fund.

13. Sources of information for the Bey case are Supplemental Letter Brief on Behalf of Defendant Appellant, State of New Jersey v. Marko Bey, Docket #22,230, Supreme Court of New Jersey (May 30, 1986); George, "Execution of Bey May Be Opposed," Woodbridge (N.J.) News Tribune, Dec. 19, 1983; and the files of the NAACP Legal Defense and Educational Fund.

14. Sources of information for the Cannaday case are Cannaday v. State, 455 So.2d 713 (Miss. 1984), and the files of the NAACP Legal Defense and Educational Fund.

15. Sources of information for the Harris case are Harris v. State, 642 S.W.2d 471

(Tex. Crim. App. 1982), and the files of the NAACP Legal Defense and Educational Fund.

16. Sources of information for the Harvey case are Harvey v. State, 682 P.2d 1384 (Nev. 1984), and the files of the NAACP Legal Defense and Educational Fund.

17. The source of information for the Hughes case is the files of the NAACP Legal Defense and Educational Fund.

18. *Supra* note 6.

19. Sources of information for the Lynn case are Lynn v. State, 477 So.2d 1388 (Ala. 1985); Ex Parte Lynn, 477 So.2d 1385 (Ala. 1985); Lynn v. State, 477 So.2d 1365 (Ala. Crim. App. 1984); and the files of the NAACP Legal Defense and Educational Fund.

20. Sources of information for the Mhoon case are Mhoon v. State, 464 So.2d 77 (Miss. 1985), and the files of the NAACP Legal Defense and Educational Fund.

21. *Supra* note 10.

22. Sources of information for the Aulisio case are Opinion of J. Walsh, Court of Common Pleas of Lackamanna County, Pa., Crim. Div., on Defendant's Motion in Arrest of Judgment and New Trial, Commonwealth v. Aulisio (May 8, 1984) (unpublished); Brief for Appellant (filed Feb. 25, 1986) and Brief for Appellee (filed June 23, 1986), Commonwealth v. Aulisio, Docket #105 of 1984, Eastern District, Supreme Court of Pennsylvania; Barcelo, "Hideous Case of the Shotgunned Babies," Official Detective, Dec. 1982, at 26; and the files of the NAACP Legal Defense and Educational Fund.

23. Sources of information for the Brown case are Letter from Attorney Adam Stein, Charlotte, N.C., to Victor L. Streib (July 18, 1986); Letter from Attorney Robert D. Jacobson, Lumberton, N.C., to Victor L. Streib (Nov. 9, 1984); and the files of the NAACP Legal Defense and Educational Fund.

24. *Supra* note 6.

25. *Supra* note 8.

26. Sources of information for the Patton case are Gelarden, "Youth Pleads Guilty in Slaying, Rape," Indianapolis Star, June 2, 1984, at 1, col. 2; McKinley, "2 Kill Man, Shoot, Rape Woman," Indianapolis Star, Oct. 23, 1983, sec. A, at 1, col. 1; McLayea, "2 Teens Charged with Murder in Park," Indianapolis Star, Oct. 28, 1983, at 1, col. 1; Pines, "Park Murder Suspects 'Highway Robbers,'" Indianapolis Star, Oct. 29, 1983, at 35, col. 3; Indianapolis Star, July 15, 1984, sec. C, at 1, col. 4, July 14, 1984, at 24, col. 1, and Oct. 24, 1983, at 21, col. 2; and Letter from Attorney Kit Keller to Victor L. Streib (Nov. 6, 1986).

27. Sources of information for the Thompson case are Olson, "Killer, 18, Sweats Out Death Row," Detroit News, June 2, 1985, at 1, col. 1, and the files of the NAACP Legal Defense and Educational Fund.

28. Sources of information for the Livingston case are Perry (Fl.) News Herald, Oct. 25, 1985; Letter and Data Sheet from Prof. Michael Radelet, University of Florida, to Victor L. Streib (Jan. 1986); and the files of the NAACP Legal Defense and Educational Fund.

29. Sources of information for the Morgan case are Morgan v. State, 453 So.2d 394 (Fla. 1984); Morgan v. State, 392 So.2d 1315 (Fla. 1981); Findings of Fact and Order, State of Florida v. James A. Morgan, Case #77–326CF, Nineteenth Judicial Circuit Court in and for Martin County, Fla. (June 7, 1985) (unpublished); and the files of the NAACP Legal Defense and Educational Fund.

30. Sources of information for the Ward case are Adams, "Spending Youth on Death Row," Dallas Morning News, Oct. 20, 1985, sec. A, at 1, col. 6; Garlington, "Ward Convicted Self, Juror Says," Sept. 21, 1985, "State Links Prints, Statement to Ward," Sept. 13, 1985, sec. A, at 8, col. 1, "Arguments Begin Today in Ward Trial," Sept. 12, 1985, "Death Penalty Foes Excluded from Jury," Sept. 11, 1985, at 1, col. 1, and "Ward Interview on Tape, Ruled Out," Sept. 10, 1985, Commercial Appeal (Memphis, Tenn.); Siegel, "How to Treat Youngsters Who Murder," Los Angeles Times, Nov. 3, 1985, at 1, col. 1; Kansas City Star, Sept. 20, 1985, sec. C, at 6, col. 1; N.Y. Times, Sept 22,

1985, at 14, col. 6; Portland (Me.) Evening Express, Dec. 17, 1985, at 11, col. 2; and the files of the NAACP Legal Defense and Educational Fund.

31. Sources of information for the Williams case are Philadelphia Inquirer, Mar. 18, 1987, sec. B., at 3, col. 1; Letter from Tanya Coke, NAACP Legal Defense and Educational Fund, Inc., to Victor L. Streib (May 5, 1987); and the files of the NAACP Legal Defense and Educational Fund.

32. Sources of information for the Comeaux case are Letter from Pat Koester, Georgia Clearinghouse on Jails and Prisons, Atlanta, to Victor L. Streib (April 1987); and the files of the NAACP Legal Defense and Educational Fund.

33. Sources of information for the Cooper case are O'Brien, "Girl, 16, Given Death Sentence for Gary Murder," Chicago Tribune, July 12, 1986, at 5; Thomas, "A Woman's Faith in Religion Stays Strong to the End," "Case Unique Because Death Penalty Sought for Girls," and "What Makes Teenagers Turn Violent?" Post-Tribune (Gary, Ind.), July 21, 1985, sec. C, at 1, col. 1; Reasoner, "I Hereby Sentence You. . . . ," CBS, 60 Minutes, Mar. 30, 1986, and Aug. 9, 1986; Wilkerson, "Indiana Case Kindles a Debate on Death Sentence for Juveniles," N.Y. Times, Nov. 2, 1986, at 11, col. 1; N.Y. Times, May 19, 1985; News-Standard (Kendallville, Ind.), July 16, 1986, at 6, col. 1; Plain Dealer (Cleveland), Nov. 4, 1985, sec. A., at 5, col. 1; and the files of the NAACP Legal Defense and Educational Fund.

34. Sources of information for the LeCroy case are Evening Times (Palm Beach, Fla), Mar. 11, 1986, and telephone and in-person conversations between James L. Eisenberg, attorney for LeCroy, and Victor L. Streib (Mar.-Oct. 1986).

35. Supra note 19.

36. Sources of information for the Sellers case are State's Bill of Particulars In Re: Punishment, State of Oklahoma v. Sean Richard Sellers (CRF–86–1231 and CRF–86–1232), District Court of Oklahoma County, Oklahoma (May 12, 1986); Reverse Certification Study, State of Oklahoma v. Sean Richard Sellers (CRF–86–1231 and CRF–86–1232) (May 7, 1986); Defendant's Motion to Dismiss, State of Oklahoma v. Sean Richard Sellers (CRF–86–1231 and CRF–86–1232) (April 14, 1986); Information, State of Oklahoma v. Sean Richard Sellers and Richard T. Howard III (CRF–86–1231) (Mar. 10, 1986); Information, State of Oklahoma v. Sean Richard Sellers (CRF–86–1232) (Mar. 10, 1986); Voluntary Statements Made by Richard Thomas Howard III to the Oklahoma City Police Department concerning Homicide of Robert Bowers and concerning Homicide of Paul Leon Bellafatto and Vonda M. Bellafatto (Mar. 6, 1986); Clay, "State's Youngest Killers Earn Seats on Death Row," Sunday Oklahoman (Oklahoma City), Oct. 5, 1986, sec. A, at 1, col. 2; Daily Oklahoman (Oklahoma City), May 13, 1986, at 1, col. 1, and Apr. 15, 1986, at 1, col. 3; and telephone conversations between Kindanne C. Jones, attorney for Sellers, and Victor L. Streib (May-Oct. 1986).

37. Sources of information for the Wilkins case are Hollan, "Youth, 17, Sentenced to Execution," Kansas City (Mo.) Times, June 28, 1986, at 1, col. 1; Kansas City Times, Oct. 4, 1986, sec. B, at 1, col. 3; N.Y. Times, June 29, 1986, at 19, col. 4; Letter from Dr. Harriet Frazier, Central Missouri State University, to Victor L. Streib (June 28, 1986); and the files of the NAACP Legal Defense and Educational Fund.

38. The source of information for the Williams case is the files for the NAACP Legal Defense and Educational Fund.

39. Supra note 2.

40. Supra notes 14, 16, and 20.

41. Supra note 11.

42. TEX. FAM. CODE ANN. sec. 54.02 (Vernon Supp. 1986) and TEX. PENAL CODE ANN. sec. 8.07(d) (Vernon Supp. 1986).

43. Supra note 1.

44. Sources of information for the Davis case are Ex Parte Davis, 408 So.2d 533 (Ala. 1982); Davis v. State, 408 So.2d 532 (Ala. Crim. App. 1981), vacated and remanded, 457 U.S. 1114 (1982); and the files of the NAACP Legal Defense and Educational Fund.

45. The source of information for the Jackson case is the files of the NAACP Legal Defense and Educational Fund.

46. *Supra* note 19.

47. *Supra* note 31.

48. *Supra* note 34.

49. *Supra* note 28.

50. Sources of information for the Magill case are Magill v. State, 428 So.2d 649 (Fla. 1983), *cert. denied,* 104 S.Ct. 1198 (1983); Magill v. State, 386 So.2d 1188 (Fla. 1980), *cert. denied,* 450 U.S. 927 (1981); Letter and Data Sheet from Prof. Michael Radelet, University of Florida, to Victor L. Streib (June 14, 1985); and the files of the NAACP Legal Defense and Educational Fund.

51. *Supra* note 30.

52. Sources of information for the Burger case are Burger v. Kemp, 753 F.2d 930 (11th Cir. 1985); Burger v. Zant, 513 F.Supp. 772 (S. D. Ga. 1981), *reversed,* 718 F.2d 979 (11th Cir. 1983); *reversed and remanded,* 104 S.Ct. 2652 (1984); Burger v. State, 245 Ga. 458, 265 S.E.2d 796 (1980), *cert. denied,* 448 U.S. 913 (1980); Burger v. State, 242 Ga. 28, 247 S.E.2d 834 (1978); and the files of the NAACP Legal Defense and Educational Fund.

53. Sources of information for the Buttrum case are Buttrum v. State, 249 Ga. 652, 293 S.E.2d 334 (1982), *cert. denied,* 459 U.S. 1156 (1983), and the files of the NAACP Legal Defense and Educational Fund.

54. Sources of information for the High case are High v. Kemp, 623 F.Supp. 316 (S. D. Ga. 1985); High v. Zant, 250 Ga. 693, 300 S.E.2d 654 (1983), *cert. denied,* 104 S.Ct. 2669 (1984); High v. State, 247 Ga. 289, 276 S.E.2d 5 (1981), *cert. denied,* 455 U.S. 927 (1982); State v. High, 145 Ga.Ap. 772, 244 S.E.2d 888 (1978); and the files of the NAACP Legal Defense and Educational Fund.

55. *Supra* note 8.

56. *Supra* note 38.

57. *Supra* note 33.

58. *Supra* note 26.

59. *Supra* note 11.

60. *Supra* note 9.

61. *Supra* note 32.

62. Sources of information for the Prejean case are Prejean v. Maggio, 765 F.2d 482 (5th Cir. 1985); Prejean v. Blackburn, 570 F.Supp. 985 (W. D. La. 1983), *aff'd,* 743 F.2d 1091 (5th Cir. 1984); State ex rel. Prejean v. Blackburn, 397 So.2d 517 (La. 1981); State v. Prejean, 379 So.2d 240 (La. 1979), *cert. denied,* 449 U.S. 891 (1980); and the files of the NAACP Legal Defense and Educational Fund.

63. *Supra* note 6.

64. *Supra* note 12.

65. Sources of information for the Jones case are Jones v. Thigpen, 555 F.Supp. 870 (S. D. Miss. 1983), *reversed,* 741 F.2d 805 (5th Cir. 1984), *vacated,* 106 S.Ct. 1172 (1986); Jones v. State, 381 So.2d 983 (Miss. 1980); *cert. denied,* 449 U.S. 1003 (1980); Jones v. State, 342 So.2d 735 (Miss. 1977); Letter from Sister Patricia Landreman, Holy Spirit Missionary Sisters, Holy Spirit Convent, Jackson, Miss., to Victor L. Streib (Sept. 13, 1985); and the files of the NAACP Legal Defense and Educational Fund.

66. Sources of information for the Tokman case are Tokman v. State, 475 So.2d 457 (Miss. 1985); Tokman v. State, 462 So.2d 687 (1984); Tokman v. State, 435 So.2d 664 (Miss. 1983), *cert. denied,* 104 S.Ct. 3547 (1984); and the files of the NAACP Legal Defense and Educational Fund.

67. *Supra* note 7.

68. *Supra* note 37.

69. *Supra* note 13.

70. *Supra* note 23.

71. *Supra* note 10.
72. *Supra* note 36.
73. *Supra* note 27.
74. *Supra* note 22.
75. *Supra* note 17.
76. *Supra* note 31.
77. *Supra* note 3.
78. *Supra* note 4.
79. *Supra* note 5.
80. Sources of information for the Graham case are Graham v. State, 671 S.W.2d 529 (Tex. Crim. App. 1984); Letters from Gary L. Graham to Victor L. Streib (July 24, June 16, and June 3, 1986); and the files of the NAACP Legal Defense and Educational Fund.
81. *Supra* note 15.
82. NAACP LEGAL DEFENSE AND EDUCATIONAL FUND, INC., DEATH ROW, U.S.A. 20–21 (Oct. 1, 1986).
83. *Id.* at 12.
84. *Id.* at 9–11.
85. *Id.* at 1.
86. *Id.*
87. *Supra* note 30.
88. *Supra* note 33.
89. *Supra* note 65.
90. *Supra* note 29.
91. *Supra* note 54.
92. High v. State, 247 Ga. 289, 296, 276 S.E.2d 5, 13 (1981).
93. *Id.*
94. *Id.*
95. *Supra* note 37.
96. Kansas City Times, *supra* note 37.
97. Charles Rumbaugh spent ten and one-half years on death row, Terry Roach eight years, and Jay Pinkerton five years. See chapter six for detailed descriptions of their cases.

10. PROGNOSIS FOR PROGRESS

1. May v. Anderson, 345 U.S. 528, 536 (1953).
2. F. ZIMRING, THE CHANGING LEGAL WORLD OF ADOLESCENCE (1982).
3. See Eddings v. Oklahoma, 455 U.S. 104, 115–16 (1982), and Haley v. Ohio, 332 U.S. 596, 599 (1948).
4. F. ZIMRING, *supra* note 2.
5. Trop v. Dulles, 356 U.S. 86, 101 (1958) (Warren, C.J., plurality opinion).
6. N.Y. Times, Jan. 7, 1962, at 81, col. 1.
7. See *supra* table 3–5 and accompanying text.
8. Ohio (1981), Nebraska (1982), Colorado (1985), Oregon (1985), and New Jersey (1986). See *supra* chapters two and three.
9. H. CANTRIL, PUBLIC OPINION: 1935–1946 94 (1951).
10. See "SCJP Poll Results: Don't Execute Juveniles," 13/1 Southern Coalition Report on Jails & Prisons 1 (Spring 1986); and Tuckel & Greenberg, Capital Punishment in Connecticut (May 1986) (Unpublished report prepared for the Archdiocese of Hartford by the Analysis Group, Inc., New Haven).
11. See *supra* table 2–2 and accompanying text.

12. U.S. Department of Justice, Capital Punishment 1984 6 (1986).
13. See *supra* tables 2–3 and 2–4 and accompanying text.
14. *Id.*
15. See *supra* table 2–1 and accompanying text.
16. *Id.*
17. *Id.*
18. See *supra* chapter nine.
19. *Supra* note 5.
20. 455 U.S. 104 (1982).
21. *Id.* at 128 (Burger, C.J., dissenting).
22. See, e.g., *supra* note 8.
23. Georgia Committee against the Death Penalty, " 'Juvenile and Death' Committee Meets," report, Oct.-Nov. 1986, vol. 1(4), at 1.
24. *Supra* notes 9 and 10.
25. See *supra* chapter three notes 57–65 and accompanying text.

BIBLIOGRAPHY

CASES

Akers v. State, 8 Ohio Abst. 106 (1929).
Barrow v. State, 688 S.W.2d 860 (Tex. Crim. App. 1985).
Bell v. Ohio, 438 U.S. 637 (1978).
Bellotti v. Baird, 443 U.S. 622 (1979).
Bracewell v. State, 401 So.2d 124 (Ala. Ct. App. 1980).
Breed v. Jones, 421 U.S. 519 (1975).
Burger v. Kemp, 753 F.2d 930 (11th Cir. 1985).
Burger v. State, 245 Ga. 458, 265 S.E.2d 796 (1980), *cert. denied,* 448 U.S. 913 (1980).
Burger v. State, 242 Ga. 28, 247 S.E.2d 834 (1978).
Burger v. Zant, 513 F.Supp. 772 (S. D. Ga. 1981), *reversed,* 718 F.2d 979 (11th Cir. 1983); *reversed and remanded,* 104 S.Ct. 2652 (1984).
Burnam v. Commonwealth, 289 Ky. 312, 158 S.W.2d 131 (Ky. Ct. App. 1941).
Burnam v. Commonwealth, 283 Ky. 361, 141 S.W.2d 282 (Ky. Ct. App. 1940).
Buttrum v. State, 249 Ga. 652, 293 S.E.2d 334 (1982), *cert. denied,* 459 U.S. 1156 (1983).
Cannaday v. State, 455 So.2d 713 (Miss. 1984), *cert. denied,* 105 S.Ct. 1209 (1985).
Cannon v. State, 691 S.W.2d 664 (Tex. Crim .App. 1985).
Chimel v. California, 395 U.S. 752 (1969).
Clark v. State, 12 Ohio 483, 131 N.E. 706 (1843).
Clay v. State, 196 So. 462 (Fla. 1940).
Coker v. Georgia, 433 U.S. 584 (1977).
Coleman v. State, 378 So.2d 640 (Miss. 1979).
Commonwealth v. Fisher, 213 Pa. 48, 62 A. 198 (1905).
Commonwealth v. Giacomazza, 42 N.E.2d 506 (Mass. 1942).
Commonwealth v. Green, 396 Pa. 137, 151 A.2d 241 (1959).
Coverson v. State, 27 Ohio App. 166 (Ct. App. 1927).
Davis v. State, 408 So.2d 532 (Ala. Crim. App. 1981), *vacated and remanded,* 457 U.S. 1114 (1982).
Echols v. State, 370 S.W.2d 892 (Tex. Crim. App. 1963).
Eddings v. Oklahoma, 455 U.S. 104 (1982).
Eddings v. Oklahoma, 455 U.S. 104 (1982), *cert. granted,* 450 U.S. 1040 (1981).
Enmund v. Florida, 458 U.S. 782 (1982).
Ex Parte Davis, 408 So.2d 533 (Ala. 1982).
Ex Parte Lynn, 477 So.2d 1385 (Ala. 1985).
Ex Parte Martinez, 66 Tex. Crim. 1, 145 S.W. 959 (1912).
Fare v. Michael C., 442 U.S. 707 (1979).
Ferguson v. Florida, 273 U.S. 663 (1927).
Ferguson v. State, 105 So. 840 (Fla. 1925).
Furman v. Georgia, 408 U.S. 238 (1972).
Garrett v. State, 682 S.W.2d 301 (Tex. Crim .App. 1984), *cert. denied,* 105 S.Ct. 1876 (1985).
Gerak v. State, 22 Ohio App. 257, 153 N.E. 902 (1920).
Gibson v. State, 53 Tex. Cr. R. 349, 110 S.W. 41 (1908).
Godfrey v. State, 31 Ala. 323 (1858).
Graham v. State, 671 S.W.2d 529 (Tex. Crim .App. 1984).
Gregg v. Georgia, 428 U.S. 153 (1976).

Haley v. Ohio, 332 U.S. 596 (1948).

Harris v. State, 642 S.W.2d 471 (Tex. Crim .App. 1982).

Harvey v. State, 682 P.2d 1384 (Nev. 1984).

Hasty v. State, 162 So. 910 (Fla. 1935).

Hernandez v. State, 32 P.2d 18 (1934).

High v. Kemp, 623 F.Supp. 316 (S. D. Ga. 1985).

High v. State, 247 Ga. 289, 276 S.E.2d 5 (1981), *cert. denied*, 455 U.S. 927 (1982).

High v. Zant, 250 Ga. 693, 300 S.E.2d 654 (1983), *cert. denied*, 104 S.Ct. 2669 (1984).

Ice v. Commonwealth, 667 S.W.2d 671 (Ky. 1984).

In re Brooks, 267 S.E.2d 74 (S.Car. 1980).

In re Gault, 387 U.S. 1 (1967).

In re Gladys, 1 Cal.3d 855, 464 P.2d 127, 83 Cal. Rptr. 671 (1970).

In re Lynette G., 54 Cal. App. 3d 1087, 126 Cal. Rptr. 898 (1976).

In re Winship, 397 U.S. 358 (1970).

Jackson v. Balkcom, 210 Ga. 412, 80 S.E.2d 319 (1954).

Johnson v. State, 303 Md. 487, 495 A.2d 1 (1985).

Johnson v. State, 439 A.2d 542 (Md. 1982).

Jones v. State, 381 So.2d 983 (Miss. 1980); *cert. denied*, 449 U.S. 1003 (1980).

Jones v. State, 342 So.2d 735 (Miss. 1977).

Jones v. Thigpen, 555 F.Supp. 870 (S. D. Miss. 1983), *reversed*, 741 F.2d 805 (5th Cir. 1984), *vacated*, 106 S.Ct. 1172 (1986).

Jurek v. Texas, 428 U.S. 262 (1976).

Jurek v. Texas, 522 S.W.2d 934 (Tex. Crim. App. 1975).

Kent v. United States, 383 U.S. 541 (1966).

Kirby v. Illinois, 406 U.S. 682 (1972).

Lassiter v. Department of Social Services, 452 U.S. 18 (1981).

Legare v. State, 250 Ga. 875, 302 S.E.2d 351 (1983).

Legare v. State, 243 Ga. 744, 257 S.E.2d 247 (1979), *cert. denied*, 444 U.S. 984 (1979).

Lewis v. State, 246 Ga. 101, 268 S.E.2d 915 (1980).

Lewis v. State, 28 So.2d 122 (Miss. 1946).

Lewis v. Mississippi and Trudell v. Mississippi, 331 U.S. 785 (1947).

Lockett v. Ohio, 438 U.S. 536 (1978).

Lynn v. State, 477 So.2d 1388 (Ala. 1985).

Lynn v. State, 477 So.2d 1365 (Ala. Crim. App. 1984).

Magill v. State, 428 So.2d 649 (Fla. 1983), *cert. denied*, 104 S.Ct. 198 (1983).

Magill v. State, 386 So.2d 1188 (Fla. 1980), *cert. denied*, 450 U.S. 927 (1981).

Martinez v. State, 232 U.S. 714 (1914).

May v. Anderson, 345 U.S. 528 (1953).

McClesky v. Kemp, 753 F.2d 877 (11th Cir. 1985).

McKeiver v. Pennsylvania, 403 U.S. 528 (1971).

Mhoon v. State, 464 So.2d 77 (Miss. 1985).

Miller v. Balkcom, 210 Ga. 415, 80 S.E.2d 321 (1954).

Morgan v. State, 453 So.2d 394 (Fla. 1984).

Morgan v. State, 392 So.2d 1315 (Fla. 1981).

Parham v. J.R., 442 U.S. 584 (1979).

People v. Byers, 309 N.Y. 908, 131 N.E.2d 580 (1955).

People v. Davis, 29 Cal.3d 814, 176 Cal. Rptr. 521, 633 P.2d 186 (1980).

People v. Deacons, 109 N.Y. 374, 16 N.E. 676 (1888).

People v. Ertel, 283 N.Y. 519, 29 N.E.2d 70 (1940).

People v. Guariglia, 279 N.Y. 707, 18 N.E.2d 324 (1938).

People v. Haight, 290 N.Y. 833, 50 N.E.2d 237 (1943).

People v. Hiemel, 49 A.D.2d 769, 372 N.Y.S.2d 730 (1975).

People v. Oxnam, 170 Cal. 211, 149 P. 165 (1915).

Pinkerton v. McCotter, 106 S.Ct. 400 (1985).

Pinkerton v. McCotter, 106 S.Ct. 16 (1985).
Pinkerton v. State, 660 S.W.2d 58 (Tex. Ct. Crim. App. 1983).
Prejean v. Blackburn, 570 F.Supp. 985 (W. D. La. 1983), aff'd, 743 F.2d 1091 (5th Cir. 1984).
Prejean v. Maggio, 765 F.2d 482 (5th Cir. 1985).
Pulley v. Harris, 465 U.S. 37 (1984).
Roach v. Aiken, 106 S.Ct. 645 (1986).
Roach v. Martin, 757 F.2d 1463 (4th Cir. 1985), cert. denied, 106 S.Ct. 645 (1986).
Roach v. South Carolina, 444 U.S. 1026 (1980).
Roberts v. Louisiana, 431 U.S. 633 (1977).
Robinson v. California, 370 U.S. 660 (1962).
Ross v. State, 22 Ohio App. 304, 153 N.E. 865 (Ct. App. 1926).
Rumbaugh v. McCotter, 105 S.Ct. 3544 (1985).
Rumbaugh v. Procunier, 753 F.2d 395 (5th Cir., 1985).
Rumbaugh v. State, 629 S.W.2d 747 (Tex. Ct. Crim. App. 1982).
Rumbaugh v. State, 589 S.W.2d 414 (Tex. Ct. Crim .App. 1979).
Santosky v. Kramer, 455 U.S. 745 (1982).
Schall v. Martin, 467 U.S. 253 (1984).
Shockley v. State, 218 Md. 491, 148 A.2d 371 (1959).
State v. Battle, 661 S.W.2d 487 (Mo. 1983)(en banc), cert. denied, 104 S.Ct. 2325 (1984).
State v. Bell, 48 Ohio 2d 270, 358 N.E.2d 556 (1976).
State v. Frohner, 150 Ohio 53 (1948).
State v. Guild, 10 N.J.L. Rep. 163 (1828).
State v. Hagert, 144 Ohio 316, 59 N.E.2d 764 (1944).
State v. Hagert, 58 N.E.2d 399 (Ohio Ct. App. 1944).
State v. High, 145 Ga.Ap. 772, 244 S.E.2d 888 (1978).
State v. Jenkins, 15 Ohio St. 3d 164, 473 N.E.2d 264 (1984).
State v. Lashley, 667 S.W.2d 712 (Mo. 1984).
State v. Leach, 425 So.2d 1232 (La. 1983).
State v. Leigh, 31 Ohio St. 2d 97, 285 N.E.2d 333 (Ohio 1972).
State v. Loveless, 150 P.2d 1015 (Nev. 1944).
State v. Loveless, 62 Nev. 17, 36 P.2d 236 (Nev. 1943).
State v. Maloney, 105 Ariz. 348, 464 P.2d 793 (1970), cert. denied, 400 U.S. 841 (1970).
State v. Maurer, 15 Ohio St. 3d 209, 473 N.E.2d 768 (1984).
State v. Perique, 439 So.2d 1060 (La. 1983).
State v. Prejean, 379 So.2d 240 (La. 1979), cert. denied, 449 U.S. 891 (1980).
State v. Schreiber, 164 Ohio 389, 131 N.E.2d 396 (1955).
State v. Shaw, 255 S.E.2d 799 (S.Car., 1979).
State v. Stewart, 197 Neb. 497, 250 N.W.2d 849 (1977).
State v. Stokes, 304 S.E.2d 184 (N.C. 1983).
State v. Strong, 12 Ohio Dec. 698 (Cuyahoga Common Pleas Court, 1902).
State v. Valencia, 132 Ariz. 248, 645 P.2d 239 (1982).
State v. Valencia, 124 Ariz. 139, 602 P.2d 807 (1979).
State v. Valencia, 121 Ariz. 191, 589 P.2d 434 (1979).
State ex rel. Prejean v. Blackburn, 397 So.2d 517 (La. 1981).
State ex rel. Francis v. Resweber, 212 La. 143, 31 So.2d 697 (1947).
Thompson v. State, 492 N.E.2d 264 (Ind. 1986).
Tokman v. State, 475 So.2d 457 (Miss. 1985).
Tokman v. State, 462 So.2d 687 (Miss. 1984).
Tokman v. State, 435 So.2d 664 (Miss. 1983), cert. denied. 104 S.Ct. 3574 (1984).
Trimble v. State, 300 Md. 387, 478 A.2d 1143 (Md. 1983), cert. denied, 105 S.Ct. 1231 (1985).
Trop v. Dulles, 356 U.S. 86 (1958).
Trudell v. State, 28 So.2d 124 (Miss. 1946).

United States v. Weedell, 567 F.2d 767 (8th Cir. 1977).
Vasil v. State, 374 So.2d 465 (Fla. 1979), *cert. denied*, 446 U.S. 967 (1980).
Whitfield v. State, 236 Ala. 312, 182 So. 42 (Ala. 1938).
Williams v. New York, 337 U.S. 241 (1949).
Woodson v. North Carolina, 428 U.S. 280 (1976).
Workman v. Commonwealth, 429 S.W.2d 374 (Ky. 1968).

STATUTES

ALA. CODE sec. 12–15–34(a) (1977).
ARIZ. REV. STAT. ANN. sec. 13–703(G)(5) (Supp. 1985).
ARK. STAT. ANN. sec. 41–617(12) (Supp. 1985).
CAL. PENAL CODE sec. 190.5 (West Supp. 1985).
COLO. REV. STAT. sec. 16–11–103(1)(a) (1985).
CONN. GEN. STAT. ANN. sec. 53a–46a(g)(1) (West Supp. 1985).
DEL. CODE ANN. tit. 11 sec. 4209(c) (Repl. 1979).
FLA. STAT. ANN. sec. 921.141(6)(g) (West Supp. 1984).
GA. CODE ANN. sec. 17–9–3 (1982).
IDAHO CODE sec. 16–1806A(1) (Supp. 1986).
ILL. ANN. STAT. ch. 38, sec. 9–1(B) (SMITH-HURD SUPP. 1985).
IND. CODE ANN. sec. 31–6–2–4(C) (BURNS SUPP. 1982).
KY. REV. STAT. ANN. sec. 208F.040 (1980) (repealed 1984).
KY. REV. STAT. ANN. sec. 208E.070(2) (Baldwin 1980).
LA. REV. STAT. ANN. sec. 13:1570(A)(5) (1983).
LANNING'S 1905 REVISED STATUTES OF 1880, sec. 1040 (enacted Apr. 23, 1898).
2 LAWS OF OHIO 1–2 (1804–05).
13 LAWS OF OHIO 86 (1815).
MD. CODE art. 27, sec. 413(g)(5) (Supp. 1985).
MISS. CODE ANN. sec. 43–21–151 (1985).
MO. ANN. STAT. sec. 211.071 (Vernon Supp. 1985).
MONT. CODE ANN. sec. 41–5–206(1)(a) (1985).
N.C. GEN. STAT. sec. 7A-608 (1986).
N.H. REV. STAT. ANN. sec. 630:5 (IX) (1986).
N.J. STAT. ANN. sec. 2C:11–3f (West 1986)(P.L. 1985, ch. 478, approved Jan. 17, 1986).
N.M. STAT. ANN. sec. 31–18–14 (A) (1979).
NEB. REV. STAT. sec. 28–105.01 (1984).
NEV. REV. STAT. sec. 176.025 (1979).
OHIO REV. CODE ANN. sec. 1639 *et seq.* (Page 1984) (Juvenile Court Act).
OHIO REV. CODE ANN. sec. 2929 (Page 1982).
OHIO REV. CODE ANN. sec. 2929.02(E) (Page 1984).
OHIO REV. CODE ANN. sec. 8–1639 *et seq.* (Throckmorton 1929) (Juvenile Court Act).
OKLA. STAT. ANN. tit. 21, sec. 701.01 (West 1983).
ORE. REV. STAT. sec. 161–615 (1985).
ORE. REV. STAT. sec. 161–620 (1985).
PA. CODE STAT. ANN, art. 42, sec. 9711 (e) (4) (1982).
S.C. CODE ANN. sec. 16–3–20(c)(b)(7) (1985).
S.D. CODIFIED LAWS ANN. 23A-27A-1 (Supp. 1984).
TENN. CODE ANN. sec. 37–1–134(1) (1984).
TEX. FAM. CODE ANN. sec. 54.02 (Vernon Supp. 1986).
TEX. PENAL CODE ANN. sec. 8.07(d) (Vernon Supp. 1985).
18 U.S.C.A. sec. 1111 (1969).
18 U.S.C.A. sec. 2031 (1969).

18 U.S.C.A. sec. 2113 (1969).
UTAH CODE ANN. sec. 78–3a-25(1) (Supp. 1985).
VA. CODE ANN. sec. 16.1–269(A) (1982).
WASH. REV. CODE sec. 10.95.070(7) (Supp. 1986).
WYO. STAT. sec. 6-2–102(j)(vii) (Repl. 1983).

OTHER GOVERNMENT DOCUMENTS

Brief for Appellant, Trimble v. State, 300 Md. 387, 478 A.2d 1143 (Md. 1984).
Brief for Appellant (filed Feb. 25, 1986) and Brief for Appellee (filed June 23, 1986), Commonwealth v. Aulisio, Docket # 105 of 1984, Eastern District, Supreme Court of Pennsylvania.
Commonwealth v. Eliza, Henry County, Ky. (Arraignment Entry in Transcript, Circuit Court Book No. 22, at 39, Sept. 5, 1867; Defense Motion for New Trial, Sept. 6, 1867; Indictment for Murder, Grand Jury of Henry County, Sept. 4, 1867; Order for Extra Jail Guards, Book No. 11, at 630, Feb. 5, 1868; Preliminary Hearing Transcript, Aug. 16, 1867; Sentencing Entry in Transcript, Book No. 22, Sept. 30, 1867; and Verdict Entry in Transcript, Book No. 22, Sept. 6, 1867).
Commonwealth v. Hartwell Seat's Clem (1787) (Deposition of Clem, taken by Col. David Mason, Coroner, and Report of Coroner's Inquisition, Apr. 14, 1787, at the Plantation of Hartwell Seat in Sussex County, Loose Court Papers of Sussex County, Va., 1754–1870; and Order Book, Court of Oyer and Terminer, Sussex County, Va., 1754–1801, at 46).
Court Record, Circuit Court, Fourth Judicial Circuit of Florida, in and for Duval County, Fla., Spring Term, 1938, State of Florida vs. Willie B. Clay, Nathaniel Walker, and Edward Powell (Indictment, Oct. 18, 1938; Arraignment, Nov. 8, 1938; Jury Charge, undated; Jury Verdict, Dec. 8, 1938; Denial of Defense Motion for New Trial, Jan. 13, 1939; and Sentence, Jan. 13, 1939).
Death Warrants for Willie B. Clay, Edward Powell, and Nathaniel Walker, signed by Gov. Holland on Dec. 17, 1941, executed by Prison Supt. Chapman on Dec. 29, 1941.
Death Warrant for Fortune Ferguson, signed on Apr. 13, 1927, and executed on Apr. 27, 1927.
Death Warrant for Irving Hanchett, signed by Gov. Gilchrist on Apr. 22, 1910, and executed by Sheriff Smith on May 6, 1910.
Death Warrant for Monroe Hasty, signed on Sept. 10, 1935, and executed on Sept. 16, 1935.
Electrocution Record of George Stinney, Jr., South Carolina Penitentiary (June 16, 1944).
FEDERAL BUREAU OF INVESTIGATION U. S. DEPARTMENT OF JUSTICE, UNIFORM CRIME REPORTS: CRIME IN THE UNITED STATES (1973–1983).
Findings of Fact and Order, State of Florida v. James A. Morgan, Case #77–326CF, Nineteenth Judicial Circuit Court in and for Martin County, Fla. (June 7, 1985) (unpublished).
Geneva Convention Relative to the Protection of Civilian Persons in Time of War, Aug. 12, 1949, 6 U.S.T. 3516, T.I.A.S. No. 3365, 75 U.N.T.S. 287.
International Covenant on Civil and Political Rights, *entered into force* Mar. 23, 1976, G.A. Res. 2200A, 21 U.N. GAOR, Supp. (No. 16) at 49, 52, U.N. Doc. A/6316 art. 6(5) (1967).
Mandate from the Supreme Court of Florida to the Judge of the Circuit Court for the Eighth Judicial Circuit (Nov. 23, 1925).

Opinion of J. Walsh, Court of Common Pleas of Lackamanna County, Pa., Crim. Div., on Defendant's Motion in Arrest of Judgment and New Trial, Commonwealth v. Aulisio (May 8, 1984) (unpublished).

II PLYMOUTH COLONY RECORDS (1742).

Report of the Committee on the Judiciary . . . to Accompany H.R. 6915, 25 Sept. 1980. S. REP. NO. 239, 99th Cong., 2d Sess. (1986).

State of Florida v. Monroe Hasty (Transcript of Record, Seventh Judicial Circuit Court in and for Volusia County, dated Nov. 4, 1934, and Indictment for Murder, July 18, 1934).

State of Oklahoma V. Sean Richard Sellers (CRF-86-1232), District Court of Oklahoma County, Okla. (Defendant's Motion to Dismiss, Apr. 14, 1986; Information, Mar. 10, 1986; Reverse Certification Study, May 7, 1986; and State's Bill of Particulars In Re: Punishment, May 12, 1986).

State of Oklahoma V. Sean Richard Sellers and Richard T. Howard III (CRF-86-1231), District Court of Oklahoma County, Okla. (Defendant's Motion to Dismiss, Apr. 14, 1986; Information, Mar. 10, 1986; Reverse Certification Study, May 7, 1986; and State's Bill of Particulars In Re: Punishment, May 12, 1986).

Supplemental Letter Brief on Behalf of Defendant Appellant, State of New Jersey v. Marko Bey, Docket #22,230, Supreme Court of New Jersey (May 30, 1986).

Transcript of Proceedings, Circuit Court of the Eighth Judicial Circuit of the State of Florida for Alachua County, State of Florida v. Fortune Ferguson, Jr. (Indictment, June 9, 1924; Arraignment, June 11, 1924; Order Appointing Defense Counsel, June 16, 1924; Verdict, June 16, 1924; Judgment and Sentence, June 16, 1924).

Transcript of Record of Proceedings in the Circuit Court of Volusia County, Fla., State v. Hanchett (Indictment, Apr. 6, 1910; Arraignment, Apr. 8, 1910; Trial Transcript, Apr. 8–9, 1910; Jury Charge, Apr. 9, 1910; Verdict, Apr. 11, 1910; Sentence, Apr. 11, 1910).

U.S. DEPARTMENT OF JUSTICE, CAPITAL PUNISHMENT 1984 (1986).

Voluntary Statements Made by Richard Thomas Howard III to the Oklahoma City Police Department concerning Homicide of Paul Leon Bellafatto and Vonda M. Bellafatto and concerning Homicide of Robert Bowers (Mar. 6, 1986).

BOOKS

AMNESTY INTERNATIONAL, THE DEATH PENALTY (1979).

W. ARNOLD, JUVENILES ON PAROLE: A SOCIOLOGICAL PERSPECTIVE (1970).

J. ARTZNER, THE BLACK MINUTE (1981).

H. BEDAU, THE CASE AGAINST THE DEATH PENALTY (1985) (published by and available from the American Civil Liberties Union, 132 W. 43rd St., New York, N.Y. 10036).

H. BEDAU, THE COURTS, THE CONSTITUTION, AND CAPITAL PUNISHMENT (1977).

H. BEDAU (ed.), THE DEATH PENALTY IN AMERICA (1964; 3d ed. 1982).

D. BESHAROV, JUVENILE JUSTICE PRACTICE (1974).

4 W. BLACKSTONE, COMMENTARIES ON THE LAW OF ENGLAND (1792).

J. BOLLES, GENEALOGY OF THE BOLLES FAMILY (1865).

W. BOWERS, LEGAL HOMOCIDE (1984).

W. BRADFORD, BRADFORD'S HISTORY OF PLYMOUTH PLANTATION, 1606–1646 (W. DAVIS ed. 1908).

H. CANTRIL, PUBLIC OPINION: 1935–1946 (1951).

Channing, "God Admonishing his People of their Duty, as Parents and Masters. A Sermon, Preached at New London, December 20th, 1786, Occasioned by the Execution of Hannah Ocuish, a Mulatto Girl, Aged 12 Years and 9 Months. For the Murder of Eunice Bolles, Aged 6 years and 6 Months." (1786) (Pamphlet published in New London, Conn., by T. Green).

F. CAULKINS, HISTORY OF NEW LONDON, CONNECTICUT (1895).

C. CORR & J. MCNEIL, ADOLESCENCE AND DEATH (1986).

P. CROMWELL, G. KILLINGER, R. SARRI & H. SOLOMON (eds.), INTRODUCTION TO JUVENILE DELINQUENCY (1978).

S. DAVIS, RIGHTS OF JUVENILES: THE JUVENILE JUSTICE SYSTEM (2d ed. 1985, release #6, June 1986).

A. DEUTSCH, OUR REJECTED CHILDREN (1950).

S. EHRMANN, FOR WHOM THE CHAIR WAITS (1957).

R. ELLIOT, AGENT OF DEATH (1940).

F. FAUST & P. BRANTINGHAM (eds.), JUVENILE JUSTICE PHILOSOPHY (1974).

H. FOGLE, THE PALACE OF DEATH (1909).

L. FORER, "NO ONE WILL LISSEN": HOW OUR LEGAL SYSTEM BRUTALIZES THE YOUTHFUL POOR (1970).

S. FOX, THE LAW OF JUVENILE COURTS IN A NUTSHELL (3d ed. 1984).

S. FOX, MODERN JUVENILE JUSTICE (1981).

1 M. HALE, PLEAS OF THE CROWN (1682).

D. HAMPARIAN, R. SCHUSTER, S. DINITZ & J. CONRAD, THE VIOLENT FEW (1978).

A. HUGHES, PECOS: A HISTORY OF THE PIONEER WEST (1978).

INTERNATIONAL RED CROSS HANDBOOK (12th ed. July 1983).

T. JOHNSON, INTRODUCTION TO THE JUVENILE JUSTICE SYSTEM (1975).

W. LAFAVE, ARREST: THE DECISION TO TAKE A SUSPECT INTO CUSTODY (1965).

W. LAFAVE & A. SCOTT, CRIMINAL LAW (2d ed. 1986).

J. LAURENCE, THE HISTORY OF CAPITAL PUNISHMENT (1960).

J. LEQUEAR, THE TRADITION OF HUNTERDON: A HISTORY OF THE COUNTY (1957).

F. LIPSIG, MURDER—FAMILY STYLE (1962).

F. MCCARTHY & J. CARR, JUVENILE LAW AND ITS PROCESSES (1980).

T. MCDADE, THE ANNALS OF MURDER (1961).

M. MELTSNER, CRUEL AND UNUSUAL: THE SUPREME COURT AND CAPITAL PUNISHMENT (1973).

R. MNOOKIN, CHILD, FAMILY AND STATE (1978).

P. MURPHY, OUR KINDLY PARENT—THE STATE: THE JUVENILE JUSTICE SYSTEM AND HOW IT WORKS (1974).

J. NASH, BLOOD LETTERS AND BAD MEN (1973).

J. NASH, MURDER, AMERICA (1980).

E. PEEL, THE NATURE OF ADOLESCENT JUDGMENT (1971).

A. PLATT, THE CHILD SAVERS (2d ed. 1972).

B. PRETTYMAN, JR., DEATH AND THE SUPREME COURT (1961).

D. RICHARDSON, PIG ISLAND WAR (1971).

M. RITTER, CHANGING YOUTH IN A CHANGING SOCIETY (1980).

W. SANDERS, ed., JUVENILE OFFENDERS FOR A THOUSAND YEARS (1970).

T. SELLIN, THE DEATH PENALTY (1982).

G. SHIRLEY, LAW WEST OF FORT SMITH 218 (1968).

L. SIEGEL & J. SENNA, JUVENILE DELINQUENCY (1981).

J. SNELL, HISTORY OF HUNTERDON AND SOMERSET COUNTIES, NEW JERSEY (1881).

W. STERLING, TRAILS AND TRIALS OF A TEXAS RANGER (1959).

V. STREIB, JUVENILE JUSTICE IN AMERICA (1978).

D. STUBBEN, #555 DEATH ROW (1980).

N. TEETERS & J. HEDBLOM, ". . . HANG BY THE NECK . . ." (1967).

R. TROJANOWICZ, JUVENILE DELINQUENCY: CONCEPTS AND CONTROLS (2d ed. 1978).

TWENTIETH CENTURY FUND TASK FORCE ON SENTENCING POLICY TOWARD YOUNG
    OFFENDERS, CONFRONTING YOUTH CRIME (1978).
B. WRIGHT, BURIALS AND DEATHS REPORTED IN THE COLUMBUS (GEORGIA) EN-
    QUIRER, 1832–1872 (1984).
F. ZIMRING, THE CHANGING LEGAL WORLD OF ADOLESCENCE (1982).

BOOK CHAPTERS

Kastenbaum, "Time and Death in Adolescence," in H. FIEFEL (ed.), THE MEANING
    OF DEATH 99 (1959).
Kohlberg, "Development of Moral Character and Moral Ideology," in HOFFMAN &
    HOFFMAN (eds.), REVIEW OF CHILD DEVELOPMENT RESEARCH 404–05 (1964).
Miller, "Adolescent Suicide: Etiology and Treatment," in S. FEINSTEIN, J. LOONEY, A.
    SCHWARTZBERG & A. SOROSKY (eds.), ASOLESCENT PSYCHIATRY 327 (1981).
Parham, "David O. Dodd: The Nathan Hale of Arkansas," in Collection of Papers by
    the Arkansas Historical Association, Vol. II, 531 (J. Reynolds ed. 1908), first pub-
    lished in Benton (Ark.) Times Courier, Jan. 18, 1906.
Paulsen, "The Delinquency, Neglect and Dependency Jurisdiction of the Juvenile
    Court," in M. ROSENHEIM (ed.), JUSTICE FOR THE CHILD 44 (1962).
Streib, "Juvenile Law," in R. JANOSIK (ed.), ENCYCLOPEDIA OF THE AMERICAN JUDICIAL
    SYSTEM (1987).

ARTICLES

"ABA Opposes Capital Punishment for Persons under 18," 69 A.B.A.J. 1925 (1983).
Adams, "Spending Youth on Death Row," Dallas Morning News, Oct. 20, 1985, sec.
    A, at 1, col. 6.
Bag, "A Tragic New Jersey Case," 24 N.J.L.J. 681 (Oct. 1901).
Barcelo, "Hideous Case of the Shotgunned Babies," Official Detective, Dec. 1982, at
    26.
Bean, "Old Thunderbolt: Farm Boy Was the First Victim of Ohio's Electric Chair,"
    Plain Dealer (Cleveland, Ohio), Mar. 8, 1981, at 25, col. 2.
Bedau, "Death Sentences in New Jersey: 1907–1960," 19 RUTGERS L. REV. 1 (1964).
Benson, "Constitutionality of Ohio's New Death Penalty Statute," 14 TOL. L. REV. 77
    (1982).
Brasfield, " 'I Had Wanted to Tell Charles Rumbaugh Goodbye,' " National Catholic
    Reporter, Nov. 8, 1985, at 12, col. 1.
Bruck, "Executing Juveniles for Crime," N.Y. Times, June 16, 1984, at 17, col. 1.
Bruck, "Executing Teen Killers Again," Washington Post, Sept. 15, 1985, sec. D, at 1,
    col. 1.
Burns, "Children on Death Row," ABC, World News Tonight, Apr. 15, 1985.
"Christian Virginia vs. Virginia Christian," NAACP, THE CRISIS: A RECORD OF THE
    DARKER RACES, Sept. 1912, Vol. 3(11), at 237.
Clay, "State's Youngest Killers Earn Seats on Death Row," Sunday Oklahoman (Okla-
    homa City), Oct. 5, 1986, sec. A, at 1, col. 2.
Comment, Capital Punishment in Ohio: The Constitutionality of the Death Penalty
    Statute," 3 U. DAY. L. REV. 169 (1978).
Comment, "The Constitutionality of Ohio's Death Penalty," 3 OHIO ST. L. REV. 617
    (1977).
Comment, "Legislative Response to Furman v. Georgia—Ohio Restores the Death
    Penalty," 8 AKRON L. REV. 149 (1974).

Cox, "The Most Hideous Murder in Texas History," True Detective, Dec. 1981, at 30.
Cox, "Crime Rampage of the Trigger-Happy Texas Killer," True Detective, Jan. 1979, at 37.
Drinan, "Too Young to Die, Even by Execution," National Catholic Reporter, Nov. 8, 1985, at 13, col. 4.
Erskine, "The Polls: Capital Punishment," 34 PUB. OPINION Q. 290 (1970).
Fox, "Philosophy and the Principles of Punishment in the Juvenile Court," 8 FAM. L. Q. 373 (1974).
Fox, "Juvenile Justice Reform: An Historical Perspective," 22 STAN. L. REV. 1187 (1970).
Fredlund, "Children and Death from the School Setting Viewpoint," 47 J. SCHOOL HEALTH 533 (1977).
Garlington, "Ward Convicted Self, Juror Says," Sept. 21, 1985; "State Links Prints, Statement to Ward," Sept. 13, 1985, sec. A, at 8, col. 1; "Arguments Begin Today in Ward Trial," Sept. 12, 1985; "Death Penalty Foes Excluded from Jury," Sept. 11, 1985, at 1, col. 1; and "Ward Interview on Tape, Ruled Out," Sept. 10, 1985, Commercial Appeal (Memphis, Tenn.).
Garlock, " 'Wayward' Children and the Law: The Genesis of the Status Offense Jurisdiction of the Juvenile Court," 13 GA. L. REV. 341 (1979).
Gelarden, "Youth Pleads Guilty in Slaying, Rape," Indianapolis Star, June 2, 1986, at 1, col. 2.
George, "Execution of Bey May Be Opposed," Woodbridge (N.J.) News Tribune, Dec. 19, 1983.
Georgia Committee against the Death Penalty, " 'Juveniles and Death' Committee Meets," REPORT, vol. 1(4), p. 1 (Oct.-Nov. 1986).
Greenberg, "Capital Punishment as a System," 91 YALE L.J. 908 (1982).
Hartman, " 'Unusual' Punishment: The Domestic Effects of International Norms Restricting the Application of the Death Penalty," 52 CIN. L. REV. 655 (1983).
Herberg, "Kanaka Joe," 48(4) Frontier Times 32 (June-July 1974).
Hill, "Can the Death Penalty Be Imposed on Juveniles: The Unanswered Question in Eddings v. Oklahoma" 20 CRIM. L. BUL. 5 (1984).
Hollan, "Youth, 17, Sentenced to Execution," Kansas City (Mo.) Times, June 28, 1986, at 1, col. 1.
Katz, "Child Neglect Laws in America," 9 FAM. L. Q. 1 (1975).
Knell, "Capital Punishment: Its Administration in Relation to Juvenile Offenders in the Nineteenth Century and Its Possible Administration in the Eighteenth," 5 BRIT. J. CRIMINOLOGY 198 (1965).
"Lawyers Strongly Favor the Death Penalty," 69 A.B.A.J. 1218 (Sept. 1983).
McCarthy, "A Last Talk with a Condemned Man," Washington Post, Jan. 13, 1986.
McKinley, "2 Kill Man, Shoot, Rape Woman," Indianapolis Star, Oct. 23, 1983, Sec. A, at 1, col. 1.
McLayea, "2 Teens Charged with Murder in Park," Indianapolis Star, Oct. 28, 1983, at 1, col. 1.
Mennel, "Origins of the Juvenile Court: Changing Perspectives on the Legal Rights of Juvenile Delinquents," 18 CRIME & DELINQ. 68 (1972).
Note, "Capital Punishment for Minors: An Eighth Amendment Analysis," 74 J. CRIM. LAW & CRIMINOLOGY 1471 (1983).
Note, "Eddings v. Oklahoma: A Stay of Execution for Juveniles?" 9 NEW ENGLAND J. CRIM. & CIV. CONFINEMENT 407 (1983).
Note, "Juvenile Offenders and the Electric Chair: Cruel and Unusual Punishment or Firm Discipline for the Hopelessly Delinquent?" 35 U. FLA. L. REV. 344 (1983).
O'Brien, "Girl, 16, Given Death Sentence for Gary Murder," Chicago Tribune, July 12, 1986, at 5.
Olson, "Killer, 18, Sweats Out Death Row," Detroit News, June 2, 1985, at 1, col. 1.
Paterson, "Did They Get the San Juan Killer?" Western Frontier 26 (Mar. 1976).

Patrick, "The Status of Capital Punishment: A World Perspective," 56 J. CRIM. L., CRIMINOLOGY & POLICE SCI. 397 (1965).

Pines, "Park Murder Suspects 'Highway Robbers,' " Indianapolis Star, Oct. 29, 1983, at 35, col. 3.

Reasoner, "I Hereby Sentence You . . . ," CBS, 60 Minutes, Mar. 30, 1986, and Aug. 9, 1986.

Reskin, "A Portrait of America's Law Students," 71 A.B.A.J. 43 (May 1985).

Reskin, "Majority of Lawyers Support Capital Punishment," 71 A.B.A.J. 44 (Apr. 1985).

Rest, Davidson & Robbins, "Age Trends in Judging Moral Issues: A Review of Cross-Sectional Studies of the Defining Issues Test," 49 CHILD DEVELOPMENT 263 (1978).

Sametz, "Revamping the Adolescent's Justice System to Serve the Needs of the Very Young Offender," 34 JUV. & FAM. CT. J. 21 (1983).

Schultz, "The Cycle of Juvenile Court History," 19 CRIME & DELINQ. 457 (1973).

"SCJP Poll Results: Don't Execute Juveniles," 13/1 Southern Coalition Report on Jails & Prisons 1 (Spring 1986).

Siegel, "How to Treat Youngsters Who Murder," Los Angeles Times, Nov. 3, 1985, at 1, col. 1.

Stout, "A Life for a Life, Even at Age 14," Sunday Record (Bergen/Passaic/Hudson Counties, N.J.) Mar. 28, 1982, sec. E, at 1, col. 1.

Streib, "The Eighth Amendment and Capital Punishment of Juveniles," 34 CLEVE. ST. L. REV. 363 (1986).

Streib, "Capital Punishment for Children in Ohio: 'They'd Never Send a Boy of Seventeen to the Chair in Ohio, Would They?' " 18 AKRON L. REV. 51 (1984).

Streib, "Executions under the Post-Furman Capital Punishment Statutes: The Halting Progression from 'Let's do it' to 'Hey, there ain't no point in pulling so tight,' " 15 RUTGERS L.J. 443 (1984).

Streib, "Death Penalty for Children: The American Experience with Capital Punishment for Crimes Committed while under Age Eighteen," 36 OKLA. L. REV. 613 (1983).

Streib, "The Juvenile Justice System and Children's Law: Should Juvenile Defense Attorneys Be Replaced with Children's Lawyers?" 31 JUV. & FAM. CT. J. 53 (1980).

Streib, "The Informal Juvenile Justice System: A Need for Procedural Fairness and Reduced Discretion," 10 J. MAR. J. PRAC. & PROC. 41 (1976).

Thomas, "A Woman's Faith in Religion Stays Strong to the End," "Case Unique Because Death Penalty Sought for Girls," and "What Makes Teenagers Turn Violent?" Post-Tribune (Gary, Ind.), July 21, 1985, sec. C, at 1, col. 1.

Vidmar & Ellsworth, "Public Opinion and the Death Penalty," 26 STAN. L. REV. 1245 (1974).

Vitello, "Constitutional Safeguards for Juvenile Transfer Procedure: The Ten Years since Kent v. United States," 26 DEPAUL L. REV. 23 (1976).

Wilkerson, "Indiana Case Kindles a Debate on Death Sentence for Juveniles," N.Y. Times, Nov. 2, 1986, at 11, col. 1.

NEWS STORIES

A.B.A.J., March 1986, at 26, col. 1.

Alabama Journal (Montgomery), Sept. 20, 1937, at 1, col. 4; Sept. 18, 1937, at 1, col. 6; and Sept. 17, 1937, at 1, col. 6.

American Weekly Mercury (Philadelphia), Aug 16–23, 1722, at 2, col. 2.

Birmingham (Ala.) News, Aug. 19, 1938, at 26, col. 4; Dec. 22, 1897; Dec. 18, 1897; Dec. 10, 1897; and Nov. 5, 1897.

Boston Globe, June 30, 1942, at 1, col. 4; June 29, 1942, at 20, col. 4; June 28, 1942, at 1, col. 3; June 25, 1942; June 23, 1942, at 14, col. 4; and Sept. 10, 1940, at 1, col. 2.

Catholic Action (Natchez, Miss.), July 31, 1947.

Clarion (Miss.) Ledger, Jan. 5, 1947.

Cleveland (Ohio) Plain Dealer, Oct. 4, 1945, at 1, col. 3; Jan. 15, 1944, at 1, col. 4; Dec. 2, 1943, at 1, col. 1; Oct. 28, 1943, at 1, col. 1; Aug. 26, 1943, at 1, col. 2; Aug. 16, 1943, at 1, col. 8; Aug. 15, 1943, at 1, col. 5; Aug 14, 1943, at 1, col. 7; Aug. 15, 1933, at 2, col. 1; June 14, 1930, at 1, col. 7; Apr. 4, 1929, at 6, col. 3; Apr. 2, 1929, at 8, col. 5; Jan. 11, 1929, at 7, col. 1; Jan.8, 1929, at 10, col. 1; Dec. 31, 1928, at 1, col. 4; Dec. 28, 1928, at 8, col. 2; Dec. 27, 1928, at 1, col. 7; Jan. 10, 1928, at 1, col. 1; Jan. 7, 1928, at 1, col. 1; Jan. 6, 1928, at 1, col. 7; Jan. 5, 1928, at 8, col. 3; July 7, 1927, at 3, col. 3; Apr. 27, 1927, at 1, col. 1; Apr. 21, 1927, at 4, col. 5; Apr. 16, 1927, at 3, col. 3; Apr. 14, 1927, at 7, col. 5; Apr. 7, 1927, at 2, col. 3; Apr. 5, 1927, at 2, col. 1; Feb. 18, 1927, at 3, col. 5; Feb. 17, 1927, at 3, col. 1; Feb. 16, 1927, at 1, col. 3; Jan. 10, 1927, at 1, col. 1; Nov. 26, 1926, at 1, col. 2; Nov. 25, 1926, at 1, col. 4; Nov. 17, 1926, at 18, col. 1; Sept. 10, 1926, at 1, col. 8; Sept. 9, 1926, at 5, col. 7; Sept. 2, 1926, at 3, col. 2; Aug. 29, 1926, at 2, col. 2; Aug. 28, 1926, at 1, col. 3; Aug. 26, 1926, at 1, col. 3; Aug. 24, 1926, at 5, col. 6; July 2, 1926, at 3, col. 2; June 3, 1926, at 6, col. 1; Jan. 20, 1926, at 5, col. 6; Jan. 15, 1926, at 1, col. 8; Jan. 10, 1926, sec. A, at 4, col. 4; Nov. 20, 1925, at 1, col. 1; Nov. 6, 1925, at 1, col. 1; May 10, 1922, at 6, col. 2; May 20, 1921, at 1, col. 7; May 19, 1921, at 1, col. 6; May 18, 1921, at 1, col. 5; May 17, 1921, at 1, col. 3; May 16, 1921, at 1, col. 2; May 8, 1921, at 1, col. 2; May 2, 1921, at 1, col. 1; Mar. 28, 1921, at 1, col. 6; Mar. 26, 1921, at 1, col. 1; Mar. 17, 1921, at 1, col. 8; Jan. 1, 1921, at 1, col. 1; Dec. 14, 1914, at 13, col. 5; May 16, 1914, at 1, col. 2; Apr. 21, 1897, at 1, col. 3; July 5, 1896, at 9, col. 3; July 26, 1895, at 1, col. 3; Aug. 29, 1890, at 1, col. 4; Dec. 28, 1889, at 8, col. 1; Dec. 27, 1889, at 4, col. 6; Dec. 25, 1889, at 6, col. 5; Dec. 24, 1889, at 6, col. 5; Dec. 20, 1889, at 6, col. 5; Dec. 19, 1889, at 6, col. 5; Dec. 17, 1889, at 6, col. 5; Dec. 15, 1889, at 8, col. 1; Dec. 13, 1889, at 6, col. 3; Dec. 12, 1889, at 6, col. 5; Dec. 11, 1889, at 6, col. 4; Dec. 10, 1889, at 6, col. 1; Dec. 3, 1889, at 6, col. 1; June 19, 1889, at 6, col. 3; June 16, 1889, at 5, col. 1; June 15, 1889, at 8, col. 1; June 12, 1889, at 6, col. 5; June 11, 1889, at 6, col. 5; June 10, 1889, at 1, col. 2; June 26, 1880, at 1, col. 6; and June 24, 1880, at 1, col. 5.

Cleveland (Ohio) Press, July 13, 1939, at 3, col. 3; Aug. 15, 1933, at 10, col. 6; July 6, 1928, sec. 2, at 1, col. 5; and Apr. 20, 1897, at 1, col. 6.

Columbia (S.C.) Record, June 16, 1944, at 1; June 15, 1944, at 1; June 13, 1944, at 1; and Mar. 30, 1944, at 1.

Columbus (Ohio) Dispatch, Dec. 31, 1894, at 7, col. 3; Dec. 29, 1894, at 6, col. 1; Dec. 22, 1894, at 7, col. 4; and Dec. 21, 1894, at 7, col. 3.

Columbus (Ga.) Enquirer, March 16, 1864.

Connecticut Gazette and Universal Intelligencer (New London), Oct. 20, 1786, at 2, col. 1; Oct. 13, 1786, at 3, col. 1; and July 28, 1786, at 3, col. 2.

Daily Arkansas Gazette (Little Rock), June 27, 1885, at 3, col. 1, and Mar. 29, 1885, at 1, col. 4.

Daily Oklahoman (Oklahoma City), May 13, 1986, at 1, col. 1, and Apr. 15, 1986, at 1, col. 3.

Elko (Nev.) Daily Press, Oct. 2, 1944, at 1, col. 3; Sept. 29, 1944, at 1, col. 1; Sept. 26, 1944, at 1, col. 5; Aug. 24, 1942, at 1, col. 8; Aug. 21, 1942, at 1, col. 8; and Aug. 20, 1942, at 1, col. 8.

Enquirer (Cincinnati), July 13, 1939, at 10, col. 1; Aug. 15, 1933, at 1, col. 7; July 15, 1933, at 20, col. 2; Jan 10, 1928, at 22, col. 3; and Apr. 21, 1897, at 12, col. 1.

Evening Times (Palm Beach, Fla.), Mar 11, 1986.

Florida Times-Union (Jacksonville), Dec. 30, 1941; Jan. 14, 1939; Dec. 9, 1938; and Aug. 8, 1938.

Galveston (Tex.) News, June 29, 1908, at 1, col. 7.

Galveston (Tex.) Daily News, July 11, 1888, and June 27, 1885.

Greenville (Ohio) Daily Advocate, Jan. 15, 1944, at 1, col. 4.

Houston (Tex.) Post, May 7, 1964, sec. 5, at 16, col. 1; April 27, 1964; and April 7, 1964.

Indianapolis (Ind.) Star, July 15, 1984, sec. C, at 1, col. 4; July 14, 1984, at 24, col. 1; and Oct. 24, 1983, at 21, col. 2.

Jackson (Miss.) Daily News, June 14, 1947; June 9, 1947; Jan. 15, 1947; Dec. 10, 1946.

Journal (Atlanta, Ga.), May 7, 1910, at 4, col. 5.

Kansas City (Mo.) Star, Sept. 20, 1985, sec. C, at 6, col. 1.

Kansas City (Mo.) Times, Oct. 4, 1986, sec. B, at 1, col. 3.

Katonah (N.Y.) Record, July 29, 1943; Nov. 19, 1942; and Sept. 17, 1942.

Lexington (Ky.) Herald, Mar. 27, 1942, at 1, col. 2; Mar. 26, 1942, at 1, col. 7; Jan. 26, 1941, at 1, col. 2; Nov. 13, 1940, at 12, col. 8; Nov. 22, 1939, at 2, col. 4; June 6, 1939, at 12, col. 8; May 16, 1939, at 14, col. 1; Apr. 23, 1939, at 1, col. 2; Apr. 21, 1939, at 1, col. 8; Apr. 14, 1939, at 20, col. 1; Apr. 8, 1939, at 3, col. 7; and Apr. 7, 1939, at 1, col. 1.

Los Angeles Daily Times, Mar. 4, 1916, and Mar. 3, 1916, at 9, col. 5.

Los Angeles Times, May 17, 1933, at 3, col. 6.

Louisville (Ky.) Daily Courier, Feb. 9, 1868, at 2, col. 3.

Manning (S.C.) Times, June 21, 1944, at 1, col. 5; Apr. 26, 1944, at 1, col. 5; Mar. 29, 1944, at 1; Mar. 27, 1944, at 1; and Mar. 25, 1944, at 1.

Milledgeville (Ga.) Union Recorder, June 17, 1954.

Mobile (Ala.) Daily Register, July 17, 1858.

Montgomery (Ala.) Advertiser, Aug. 19, 1938, at 1, col. 6.

National Catholic Reporter, Nov. 8, 1985, at 11, col. 4; at 12, col. 1, at 13, col. 1 (editorial); at 16, col. 1; and at 18, col. 2.

News & Courier (Charleston, S.C.), Dec. 31, 1984, sec, 4, at 2, col. 4; June 17, 1944, at 1, col. 4; June 17, 1944, at 4, col. 1 (editorial); June 16, 1944, at 1, col. 1; Mar. 30, 1944, at 2, col. 1; Mar. 28, 1944, at 5, col. 4; and Mar. 26, 1944, at 1, col. 2.

News-Standard (Kendallville, Ind.), July 16, 1986, at 6, col. 1.

Newsweek, Jan. 13, 1986, at 74, col. 2.

New York Times, Oct. 16, 1986, at 15, col. 1; June 29, 1986, at 19, col. 4; May 16, 1986, at 11, col. 1; May 15, 1986, at 11, col. 6; Jan. 11, 1986, at 7, col. 1; Jan. 10, 1986, at 8, col. 6; Jan. 9, 1986, at 22, col. 1 (editorial); Nov. 26, 1985, at 8, col. 6; Sept 22, 1985, at 14, col. 6; Sept. 15, 1985, sec. E, at 6, col. 4 (editorial); Sept. 12, 1985, at 11, col. 4; Sept. 11, 1985, at 12, col. 6; Sept. 10, 1985, at 8, col. 1; Sept. 5, 1985, at 12, col. 4; Aug. 16, 1985, at 8, col. 6; Aug. 15, 1985, at 10, col. 6; May 19, 1985; Feb. 7, 1985, at 13, col. 4; Aug. 19, 1984, at 15, col. 5; Jan. 16, 1983, at 5, col. 2; Jan. 7, 1962, at 81, col. 1; Jan. 13, 1956, at 7, col. 4; Jan. 27, 1939, at 42, col.1; Apr. 11, 1937, at 21, col. 1; and Feb. 14, 1868, at 6, col. 1.

North Westchester (N.Y.) Times, Nov. 19, 1942, at 1, col. 3; Nov.12, 1942, at 1, col. 3; Nov. 5, 1942, at 1, col. 1; Oct. 29, 1942, at 1, col. 6; Oct. 22, 1942, at 1, col. 2; and Sept. 24, 1942, at 1, col. 6.

Old West, Winter 1970, at 91.

Olympia (Wash.) Transcript, Mar. 14, 1874, at 2.

Perry (Fla.) News Herald, Oct. 25, 1985.

Philadelphia Inquirer, Mar. 18, 1987, sec. B, at 3, col 1.

Pittsburgh (Pa.) Courier, May 17, 1947.

Plain Dealer (Cleveland), Jan. 11, 1986, sec. A, at 6, col 1; Jan. 10, 1986, sec. A, at 5, col. 1; Nov. 4, 1985, sec. A., at 5, col. 1; Sept. 12, 1985, sec. A, at 26, col. 1 (editorial); Apr.4, 1976, at 2, col. 1; and Mar. 16, 1956, at 1, col. 3.

Portland (Me.) Evening Express, Dec. 17, 1985, at 11, col. 2.

Portsmouth (Ohio) Daily Times, July 6, 1928, at 2, col. 1; July 5, 1928, at 2, col. 1; Feb.7, 1928, at 5, col. 1; and Dec. 4, 1914, at 1, col. 5.

State (Columbia, S.C.), June 17, 1944, at 1, col. 2; June 14, 1944, at 2, col. 4; June 13, 1944, at 6, col. 3; June 12, 1944, at 2, col. 2; June 11, 1944, at 1, col. 6; June 10, 1944, at 1, col. 3; June 9, 1944, at 1, col. 1; June 8, 1944, at 11, col. 4; Mar. 30, 1944, at 1, col. 7; and Mar. 26, 1944, at 1, col. 4.

Sun (Baltimore), Apr. 9, 1958, at 38, col. 3; Apr. 8, 1958, at 10, col. 5; Jan. 17, 1958, at 34, col. 1; and Apr. 11, 1954, at 22, col. 3.

Time, Jan. 20, 1986, at 22, col. 1, and Feb. 2, 1968, at 64–65.

Times-Picayune (New Orleans), July 7, 1934, at 15, col. 4.

Times-Union (Jacksonville, Fla.), May 7, 1910, at 1, col. 1.

Toledo (Ohio) Blade, Mar. 16, 1956, at 1, col. 2; Mar. 15, 1956, at 1, col. 4; Jan. 12, 1955, at 1, col. 4; Jan. 10, 1955, at 1, col. 4; Aug. 20, 1954, at 1, col. 4; and Aug. 13, 1954, at 1, col. 4.

Tribune (Berkeley, Cal.), Jan 4, 1947, at 1, col. 1.

Union and Advertiser (Rochester, N.Y.), July 10, 1888.

Washington Post, Aug. 19, 1984, sec. A, at 1, and Nov. 8, 1983, sec A. at 18, col. 1.

Weekly Messenger (St. Martinsville, La.), May 9, 1947, at 1, col. 6; May 2, 1947, at 1, col. 1; Apr. 25, 1947; Apr. 18, 1947; Apr. 11, 1947; Jan. 17, 1947, at 1, col. 6; June 14, 1946, at 1, col. 6; May 10, 1946, at 1, col. 4; Sept. 14, 1945, at 1, col. 6; Aug. 10, 1945, at 1, col. 6; Nov. 17, 1944, at 6, col. 2; and Nov. 10, 1944, at 1, col. 3.

Woodville (Miss.) Republican, July 25, 1947, at 1, col. 6; June 6, 1947, at 1, col. 4; Mar. 21, 1947, at 1, col. 4; Jan. 17, 1947, at 1, col. 7; and Nov. 15, 1946, at 1, col. 6.

Youngstown (Ohio) Vindicator, Aug. 21, 1948, at 1, col. 8; Aug. 19, 1948, at 1, col. 2; Feb. 29, 1947, at 1, col. 7; Feb. 25, 1947, at 1, col. 8; Jan. 18, 1947, at 1, col. 8; Jan. 17, 1947, at 1, col. 4; and Jan. 14, 1947, at 1, col. 6.

LETTERS

Madge D. Barefield, Executive Secretary, Birmingham Historical Society, Birmingham, Ala., to Victor L. Streib (Aug. 3, 1985).

Dr. James C. Bonner, Milledgeville, Ga., to Watt Espy, University of Alabama (Jan. 3, 1977).

Joseph J. Cannon, Huntsville, Tex., to Victor L. Streib (Jan. 27, 1986).

Tanya Coke, NAACP Legal Defense and Educational Fund, Inc., to Victor L. Streib (May 5, 1987).

Helen Cubberly Ellerbe, Alachua County Historical Commission, Gainesville, Fla., to Victor L. Streib (Jan. 25, 1985, and Oct. 22, 1984).

Watt Espy, University of Alabama, to Victor L. Streib (Oct. 15, 1984).

Dr. Harriet Frazier, Central Missouri State University, to Victor L. Streib (June 28, 1986).

Gary L. Graham, Huntsville, Tex., to Victor L. Streib (July 24, June 16, and June 3, 1986).

Attorney Robert D. Jacobson, Lumberton, N.C., to Victor L. Streib (Nov. 9, 1984).

Attorney Kit Keller, Indianapolis, Ind., to Victor L. Streib (Nov. 6, 1986).

Pat Koester, Georgia Clearinghouse on Jails and Prisons, Atlanta, to Victor L. Streib (April 1987).

Sister Patricia Landreman, Holy Spirit Missionary Sisters, Holy Spirit Convent, Jackson, Miss., to Victor L. Streib (Sept. 13, 1985).

Frederick Lashley, Missouri Prison, to Victor L. Streib (July 9, 1986).

Thomas McDade to Watt Espy, University of Alabama (June 27, 1978).

Prof. Michael Radelet, University of Florida, to Victor L. Streib (Jan. 1986, with data sheet, and June 14, 1985, with data sheet).

Maurice S. Shelby, Historian, Jackson County Historical Society, Edna, Tex., to Watt Espy, University of Alabama (Apr. 25, 1975).

Attorney Adam Stein, Charlotte, N.C., to Victor L. Streib (July 18, 1986).

James Trimble, Maryland Prison, to Denise Malasky, Cleveland State University, Cleveland, Ohio (Apr. 22 and Apr. 9, 1985), and to Victor L. Streib (July 8, 1986).

Gary M. Williams, Clerk, Circuit Court of Sussex County, Va., to Watt Espy, University of Alabama (Oct. 11, 1984).

MISCELLANEOUS

Espy, 15,000 Confirmed Executions in America since Colonial Times: An Historical Data-Base (Oct. 30, 1986) (Paper presented at the Annual Meeting of the American Society of Criminology).

Frazier, Juvenile Executions: The Folly of the Inevitable (March 1985) (Paper presented at the Annual Meeting of the Academy of Criminal Justice Sciences) (available from the author, Prof. Harriet C. Frazier, Criminal Justice Adminstration Dept., Central Missouri State University, Warrensburg, Mo. 64093).

Gallup Report (Jan.-Feb. 1986), The Gallup Poll, Princeton, N.J.

Information obtained by Victor L. Streib from the files of the N.' ACP Legal Defense and Educational Fund, Inc., New York City, on Aug. 15, 1986.

Interview by Victor L. Streib with Elizabeth B. Knox, Secretary and Curator of the New London County Historical Society, in New London, Conn. (Aug. 15, 1985).

Model Penal Code sec. 210.6 commentary at 133 (Official Draft and Revised Comments 1980).

NAACP LEGAL DEFENSE AND EDUCATIONAL FUND, INC., DEATH ROW, U.S.A. (Dec. 20, 1981, through Oct. 1, 1986).

NATIONAL COMMISSION ON THE REFORM OF CRIMINAL LAW, FINAL DRAFT OF THE NEW FEDERAL CODE sec. 3603 (1971).

Recommendation and Report to the American Bar Association House of Delegates by the American Bar Association Section of Criminal Justice, August 1983.

Statement of David Bruck concerning the Execution of Americans for Crimes Committed while under the Age of Eighteen (June 5, 1986) (Testimony before the Subcommittee on Criminal Justice, Committee on the Judiciary, U.S. House of Representatives, 99th Cong., 2d Sess.).

Telephone and in-person conversations between James L. Eisenberg, attorney for Cleo LeCroy, and Victor L. Streib (Mar.-Oct. 1986).

Telephone conversations between Kindanne C. Jones, attorney for Sean Sellers, and Victor L. Streib (May-Oct. 1986).

Telephone interview by Victor L. Streib with State Senator Richard Finan, Columbus, Ohio (May 26, 1983).

Tuckel & Greenberg, Capital Punishment in Connecticut (May 1986) (Unpublished report prepared for the Archdiocese of Hartford by the Analysis Group, Inc., New Haven).

INDEX

Lawyers (attorneys), 6, 11–12, 14, 18–19; views on death penalties, 30, 33
Lethal injection: use in juvenile executions, 124–25, 129, 160
Leuth, Otto, 134–36, tables 150, 152, 153
Lewis, James, Jr., 114–15, 156
Lewis v. State, 47
Life imprisonment. *See* Imprisonment, life
Liquor (alcohol): right to purchase, 23, 26; underage consumption, 9
Lockett v. Ohio, 22, 131
Loneliness, feeling of: as attitude toward impending execution, 159
Louisiana, 9; death penalty statutes, 44, tables 44, 46; death sentences, 173, tables 29, 31–32, 169, 170, 172, 175, 178, 179; executions in, 57, 112–14, 196–97, tables 61, 63, 69
Loveless, Frank, 110–12, 161–62
Lynching, 55, 158; prevention of, 85, 86, 88, 89, 108, 114

McKeiver v. Pennsylvania, 6
Magill v. State, 49–50
Maine, 197, tables 42, 66
Mandatory death penalty statutes, 21
Mann, George E., 132–33, tables 150, 152, 153
Marshall, Thurgood, 35, 36, 37, 38, 115, 156–57
Martinez, Leon Cardenas, Jr., 90–92
Maryland, 48–49; death penalty statutes, tables 46; death sentences, tables 28, 31–32, 168, 170, 172, 175, 178, 179; executions in, 68, 118–19, 197, tables 59, 61, 63, 69
Massachusetts, table 42; executions in, 55, 60, 64, 73, 104–105, 197–98, tables 63, 66
Massachusetts Council for the Abolition of the Death Penalty, 105
Mass murder: execution for, 85–87
Maturity, 23–24, 212 n.34
Mental disabilities: use as defense, 135
Mental incapacity: use as defense, 100
Mental retardation, 35, 137, 140; death sentence in spite of, 92–93, 125–26, 181–82; role in attitude toward impending execution, 156–57, 159, 161, 163
Mexican-Americans: executions of, 68, 90–92, table 59
Mhoon, James, 169, 171, table 168
Michigan, 198, tables 42, 67
Miller, Herman Lee, 115–16
Minnesota, 198, tables 42, 63, 67
Mississippi, 49; death penalty statutes, 44, tables 44, 46; death sentences, 168, 171, 173, 181, tables 28, 31–32, 168, 170, 172, 175, 178, 179; executions in, 68, 114-i5, 198, tables 63, 69
Missouri: death penalty statutes, 42, tables 44, 46; death sentences, 173, 182, tables 28–29, 31–32, 168–69, 170, 172, 176, 178, 179; executions in, 64, 199, tables 59, 63, 67

Mitigating factors, 21–22, 125–26, 131; youthfulness as, 27, 29–30, 41, 45, 48–50, table 46
Model Penal Code: on juvenile death penalty, 30, 39
Monge, Luis, 25
Montana: death penalty statutes, 44, tables 44, 46; executions in, 199, tables 63, 70
Morgan, James A., 181–82, tables 169, 174
Murder, 27, 29, 36–37, 187; arrests for, 38, table 33; as child abuse, 18; criminal court jurisdiction over, 9, 13, 44; death sentences for, 130, 173, 180–82, table 174–77
Murder, executions for, 55, 58, 60, 62, 64, 68, tables 59, 65–67, 69, 70, 152, 153; in 18th century, 74–76; in 19th century, 76–84, 132–37; in 20th century, 85–93, 95–102, 104–15, 117–19, 122–29, 137–48
Murphy, James, 143–44
Murphy, Joseph, 143–44, 160, tables 150, 152, 153

National Association for the Advancement of Colored People (NAACP), 90, 109
National Commission on Reform of Criminal Law, 30
Nebraska, 26, 47, 199, table 67; death penalty statutes, tables 43, 46
Neglected children, 17–19
Nevada: death penalty statutes, 39, tables 43, 46; death sentences, 169, tables 28, 31, 168, 170, 177; executions in, 110-12, 199, tables 63, 70
New Hampshire, 200, table 66; death penalty statutes, 39, tables 43, 46
New Jersey, 26; death penalty statutes, tables 43, 46; death sentences, tables 28, 31–32, 168, 170, 172, 176, 178, 179; executions in, 64, 76–78, 200, tables 59, 63, 66
New Mexico: death penalty statutes, tables 43, 46; executions in, 200, tables 63, 70
New York, table 42; executions in, 64, 83–84, 99–100, 105–107, 116–18, 200–201, tables 63, 66
New York Times: on Rumbaugh case, 124
Nickerson, James, 104–105
Nineteenth century: executions in, 55, 76–85, 132–37, table 56
North Carolina, 9; death penalty statutes, 44, tables 44, 46; death sentences, 169, 171, 173, tables 28, 31–32, 168, 170, 172, 176, 178, 179; executions in, 64, 68, 201–202, tables 59, 61, 63, 69
North Dakota, 64, 212, tables 42, 67
Nuana, Joseph (Kanaka Joe), 81–82, 157

O'Connor (justice), 48
Ocuish, Hannah, 74–75, 156, 158, 159
Ohio, 21–22; death penalty statutes, 26, 130–31, 148–49, tables 43, 46; executions in, 64, 131–54, 202–203, tables 63, 67